INTERNATIONAL
TEXT AND CASES

—

EDITED BY JILL PRESTON

PITMAN
PUBLISHING

PITMAN PUBLISHING
128 Long Acre, London WC2E 9AN

A Division of Longman Group UK Limited

First published in Great Britain 1993

British Library Cataloguing-in-Publication Data
A catalogue record for this book is available from the British Library

ISBN 0 273 60148 2

Typeset by Mathematical Composition Setters Ltd, Salisbury, Wiltshire.
Printed in England by Clays Ltd, St Ives plc.

CONTENTS

CONTRIBUTORS

Dr Jill Preston is Head of the European Business R&D Centre, Anglia Business School, Anglia Polytechnic University, Cambridge.

Ron Allison is Director of International Business Programmes, Anglia Business School, Anglia Polytechnic University, Cambridge.

Erwin Blum is the Dean of the Business School, Landshut Fachhochschule, Germany.

Ross Catterall is Director of the Financial Markets Research and Consultancy Unit, Anglia Business School, Anglia Polytechnic University, Cambridge.

Dr Leigh Davison is a Senior Lecturer, Humberside Business School, Humberside University, Hull.

Dr John Flood is the University of Westminster/Vizards Reader in Law, School of Law, University of Westminster, London.

Sarah Gribbin is a Senior Lecturer at Humberside Business School, Humberside University, Hull.

Rudi Grunwald is an MBA student at Humberside Business School, Humberside University, Hull.

Alan Griffiths is Head of Economics in the Department of European Business Economics, Anglia Business School, Anglia Polytechnic University, Cambridge.

Dr Mike Hewins is a Principal Lecturer in the Total Quality Management R&D Centre, Anglia Business School, Anglia Polytechnic University, Cambridge.

Elizabeth Hill is a Senior Lecturer in the Department of European Business Economics, Anglia Business School, Anglia Polytechnic University, Cambridge.

Dr Theo Kiriazidis is a Research Assistant in the European Business R&D Centre, Anglia Business School, Anglia Polytechnic University, Cambridge.

Jonathan Knowles is a Principal Lecturer in the Department of Management, Anglia Business School, Anglia Polytechnic University, Cambridge.

John Macdonald is Customer Liaison Manager, Marconi Radar & Control Systems Ltd, Chelmsford.

Wolodymyr Maksymiw is a Senior Lecturer at Humberside Business School, Humberside University, Hull.

Alan Marchant is a Senior Lecturer at Humberside Business School, Humberside University, Hull.

Terry Mughan is Head of French, Anglia Polytechnic University, Cambridge.

Professor Toru Nakakita is Associate Professor of Economics, Toyo University, Tokyo, Japan.

Terry O'Sullivan is a Senior Lecturer at Trinity and All Saints College, University of Leeds, Leeds.

Stephen Regan is a Senior Lecturer at Anglia Business School, Anglia Polytechnic University, Chelmsford.

Margaret Robins is Managing Director of SEAB (UK consultants to NobelTech Systems AB), Billericay.

John Stittle is a Senior Lecturer at Anglia Business School, Anglia Polytechnic University, Chelmsford.

PREFACE

It is becoming increasingly important for management to be aware of the international dimension of business, even if they are not thinking of 'going overseas'; for international business is likely to affect their domestic market either directly or indirectly.

A study of international business focuses on the special issues facing companies and governments in dealing with activities that cross national boundaries. There is a whole range of factors which are driving management to give more attention to international issues; the speed of market change being a major item.

An important aim of the book is to identify for the reader some of the major issues involved in the internationalization of business activity. In addition, a range of themes has been identified so as to suggest ways in which organizations could take advantage of this situation. The cases illustrate how a selection of companies have responded to internationalization. To assist in the analysis of the case studies, the reader should keep in mind these issues and themes, as well as the more specific questions raised.

Jill Preston
European Business R&D Centre
Anglia Polytechnic University
Cambridge
November 1992

ACKNOWLEDGEMENTS

———

I should like to thank each of the authors who have contributed either a chapter and/or a case: Ron Allison, Erwin Blum, Ross Catterall, Leigh Davison, John Flood, Sarah Gribbin, Rudi Grunwald, Alan Griffiths, Mike Hewins, Liz Hill, Theo Kiriazidis, Jonathan Knowles, John Macdonald, 'Max' Maksymiw, Alan Marchant, Terry Mughan, Toru Nakakita, Terry O'Sullivan, Stephan Regan, Margaret Robins, and John Stittle.

I should also like to express my gratitude for the help and support given in the development of this book from the organizations studied:

Ruth Granville and David Oliver of Arthur Andersen & Co SC;
Frau Helga Raddatz, Head of Public Relations at BMW;
Terry Hogg, Production Control Director, and Keith Jones, Quality Assurance Director, at Nissan UK;
Mr P. Quaglia and Eugenio Alacevich of NH Geotech Ltd;
Chris Haskins and Alec Horsley of Northern Foods;
Roger Gugen of Typhoon International;
Scott Lichenstein of Hill Knowlton International, Belgium;
also, Eddie Eccleston of British Eagle Cycles Ltd, Roy Hatfield of Schwinn (UK) Ltd, Greg Oxenham of Fusion Cycles, Mark Pemberton of Liyanng (Europe) Industrial Ltd, and John Wood of Muddy Fox (UK) Ltd.

Many people from a wide range of organizations have contributed to this project and my thanks go to them all, but special mention must be made of Professor John Davies and my colleagues at the Anglia Business School for their support and encouragement in this venture. Finally, I should like to put on record my thanks to June Cheetham, Secretary at the European Business R&D Centre, for her enthusiasm and hard work.

CHAPTER ONE

INTRODUCTION

JILL PRESTON

No firm can ignore the international dimension. Even the most domestically orientated business is likely to find that it is operating in somebody else's international market.

Walter Wriston[1]

THE SCOPE OF INTERNATIONAL BUSINESS

International business is concerned with the special issues facing international companies and governments in dealing with activities that cross national boundaries. International business covers international trade in goods and services and international investment, as well as transactions in intangibles, such as cross-border data transmissions, technology transfer and trade marks. In addition, this activity involves the movement of people and it has created a special need for international management skills. Large corporations are major vehicles for internationalization but increasingly medium, and even smaller companies, especially in high-tech industries, are pursuing business at the international level.

In this book the terms 'multinational' and 'transnational' are interchangeable. A transnational or a multinational company is an organization that operates in a number of different countries simultaneously. It is normally defined as an enterprise which owns or controls production or service facilities outside the country in which its headquarters is based. Within each country the units of the organization retain a degree of distinctiveness. Between multinational companies there is much variety in the balance between autonomy and central control.

For the purposes of this book, a global company is an international organization in which the operational units are integrated across national boundaries; so that functions such as human resources management, marketing and R&D are grouped together, independently of national boundaries. In a global corporation the objectives of the overseas subsidiaries are integrated within the total corporate objectives with some inevitable loss of independence. In clarifying this point, Michael Porter makes the distinction between a self-contained series of national operations and a globally integrated network of production activities.[2] In practice most international companies

global ◄───► multinational

company   company

Figure 1.1
The global company/multinational company continuum

are found somewhere along a continuum running from global to multinational, as illustrated by Figure 1.1.

CHANGES IN THE INTERNATIONAL BUSINESS ENVIRONMENT

There are a whole range of factors which are driving management to give more attention to international issues; the speed of market change being a major item. The development of the European Community and other regional trading blocks is having a major impact on European companies, but it is also of significance to companies in other parts of the world. Free trade areas have also been established in North America and in the Far East.

The development of regional trading blocks has resulted in 'insiderization', whereby companies seek insurance against protectionism, for example, by the formation of joint ventures and other strategic alliances aimed at penetrating these new markets.

The liberalization of trade practices, deregulation and privatization were world-wide trends in the 1980s and that decade also saw a huge increase in investment across national frontiers, which included direct investment in plant and equipment as well as portfolio investments. Kenichi Ohmae refers to the interlinked economy of the Triad; Europe, the USA and Japan, plus the industrializing economies of Hong Kong, Singapore and Taiwan. The aim of many large corporations is to be large enough and efficient enough to compete in all the major markets of the world. In part, as a response to the free market revolution of the 1980s, a major restructuring of business has occurred.

The rapid developments in technology is another important issue in the internationalization of business activity. Communications, product cycles and the speed of financial transactions have all been influenced by technological developments. The 1980s saw major movements in the internationalization of production and markets as well as of competition.

ORGANIZATIONAL RESPONSES

A key organizational response to these developments has been the rapid increase of mergers and acquisitions at domestic and international level. Barrie Stevens identifies some of the motives behind this activity. These include:

- a shift in corporate strategy towards refocusing on core businesses and divesting peripheral activities, for example, in the chemicals industry;

- the need to achieve scale economies which narrow home markets no longer provide, for example, in telecommunications and consumer electronics, and to expand market share, preferably through adding 'ready-made' capacity;
- the need to establish or broaden a presence on foreign markets, be it to circumvent actual or potential barriers to trade or to ensure a diverse network of distribution or service outlets, for example, in banking;
- the need to share rapidly mounting research and development costs, or at least gain access to R&D and new techniques. [3]

The Ashridge Survey of international companies carried out in 1989–90 found that many companies are trying to modify their organizational forms to cope with the changing business environment. [4] For example, many companies in the survey were attempting to speed up the decision-making process by experimenting with task forces and project groups. In some international corporations, decentralizing is being achieved by focusing on specific markets. In other companies, the organizational focus is on the integration of world-wide businesses and acquisitions.

> *The nub of the problem is the balance that has to be struck between central authority and local autonomy. If the pendulum swings too close to the centre, the corporate outposts are left floundering between an inappropriate strategy and local realities; too far in the other direction and the centre may be dragged towards the strongest outposts with no capacity for radical moves when these become necessary.*
>
> Tom Lester[5]

In *Managing across borders* Christopher Bartlett and Sumantra Ghoshal suggest a very different approach to the issue of international organizational structures. [6] They argue that most companies have developed their operations around one of three strategies:

- a multinational strategy that enables a corporation to establish a strong local presence through responding to different national requirements. General Electric have pursued this approach;
- a global approach, which aims to achieve substantial cost advantages from centralized global scale operations. Matsushita have employed this strategy;
- development as international companies and exploiting parent company knowledge through world-wide diffusion and adaptation, for example, BMW.

Bartlett and Ghoshal argue that businesses can no longer afford to base their strategy on one approach. To cope with the complex environment, companies must have a multi-facet business strategy.

A GUIDE TO USING THE BOOK

The aim of the book is to identify for the reader some of the major issues in the internationalization of business activity. It is becoming increasingly important for management to be aware of this international dimension, even if they are not thinking of 'going overseas', for international business is likely to affect their domestic market. The case studies illustrate how a variety of companies are responding to the general trend of internationalization. In some instances the response is offensive in nature, in others it is mainly defensive.

In the choice of cases the aim has been to provide the reader with a variety of companies operating in different sectors, but we have not attempted to be representative in terms of all economic sectors. The cases are not intended to serve as a basis for illustration of either good or bad management practice, but a means to show how a variety of enterprises are responding to the increasing internationalization of business activity.

Most of the cases have been written in co-operation with, and have the approval of, senior management of the organization concerned. A number of themes run through the cases and these represent ways in which companies could respond to the increasing level of internationalization. Each case is followed by a series of questions that can be used as a basis for group activity or individual work.

THEMES

A major theme of the book is that business activity is becoming increasingly international and companies are responding to this situation in a number of ways. Within this overall theme, a range of issues have been identified within Parts 1 and 2 of the book, and it is within the context of the issues that the cases should be tackled. The case studies illustrate how a selection of companies have responded to the issue of internationalization. To assist in the analysis of the cases, the reader should keep in mind these issues or themes and the questions raised.

It has to be stated that when analysing an issue as broad as the internationalization of business activity, it is not possible for each of the case studies to deal with all of the themes identified. In addition, there is usually a range of items which, for a number of reasons, organizations are not willing to discuss. For example, pricing policy tends to come into this category. This is the reason why most of the case studies focus on a number of themes within the general area of internationalization, rather than dealing with the issues in a more holistic way. For example, some of the cases concentrate on the factors involved in international collaboration, others focus more on organizational and structural issues. The following gives some idea of the issues involved.

A. STRATEGIC ISSUES

- Is the organization a truly global or a transnational company?
- Why is the organization operating internationally?
- Is the company responding to the existence of regional trading blocs?
- Is the organization able to take advantage of the general global trend of deregulation and privatization?
- To what extent is the organizational structure centralized or decentralized?
- To what extent is the organization 'ethnocentric', 'polycentric' or 'geocentric'?
- What types of strategic alliances is the organization involved in and why?
- In what ways has technology had an impact on strategy?
- To what extent if any has the company been affected by political risks in the international market?
- What are the strengths and weaknesses of competitors?

- In what ways is the company responding to the competitive challenge?
- In what ways are cultural issues having an impact on strategy?
- In what ways are environmental issues impacting strategy?

B. OPERATIONAL ISSUES

(i) *Marketing*
What processes has the company used in the following areas?

- market research;
- market selection;
- market entry;
- product decisions and branding;
- pricing policies;
- promotional policies.

(ii) *International money management*

- In what currencies should reserves of cash be held?
- In what currencies should borrowings be made?
- Which tax régimes should be selected for the most favourable treatment of multinational companies' profits?
- How much hedging of foreign currency exposure is necessary?
- What accounting practices should be adopted, especially in relation to foreign exchange?

(iii) *Purchasing*

- What are the advantages of purchasing at the international level?
- What are the problems involved in purchasing at the international level?
- What are the specific advantages and disadvantages of purchasing from a single source?

(iv) *Production*

- What are the international dimensions of production?
- What are the costs and benefits of transnational production processes?
- Does transnational production require specialized forms of control including quality control?

(v) *Distribution*

- What methods are being used for distribution?
- How is the organization dealing with the issue of distribution?

(vi) *Research and development*

- What are the advantages of establishing international R&D teams?
- What are some of the problems likely to be encountered by international R&D teams?
- How is the organization tackling these problems?

(vii) *International human resources management*

- How effective is communication within the organization?
- How if at all is the organization internationalizing its personnel?
- How are staff selected and prepared for overseas assignments?
- What specific skills and qualities are required of international managers?
- In what ways is the organization addressing the issues of international industrial relations?

USING CASE STUDIES

The case study approach is a major feature of business and management education. A case study is normally a written description of an organization, but cases can be written about groups, institutions or nations. For example, a case study may include a general business situation or it may focus on a specific aspect of organizational activity. A case study details events and circumstances, including the historical context, external and internal environment, such as its organizational structure.

Cases may be long or short, fact or fiction. Organizations often require their identities to be disguised for fear of revealing information which may be useful to competitors. By its nature a case study is a partial and incomplete picture, being a simulation of the real world; business decisions have to be taken with incomplete information.

Analysis of each case should be based on the information given in the case itself, as well as on the issues identified in Parts 1 and 2 of the book. In addition, library research of other sources will be particularly valuable. The first two Parts of the book provide an environmental and organizational context for the studies and should be read before the individual cases are tackled. The purpose of a case analysis is to present, justify and defend recommended courses of action. This type of activity enables people to use problem-solving and decision-making skills in a simulated situation.

The cases in the book can be used for class discussion and/or written assignments; each study is followed by a number of questions. The questions can be used for individual work, although many more benefits are obtained if some group work is involved. For example, a situation where a student has to defend a decision before peers is very similar to the situation facing managers.

Case study work uses and develops a range of skills, as well as imparting knowledge about the organization concerned. It is assumed that readers will have some knowledge of economics and general business functions, although not necessarily from an international perspective. It is also assumed that readers will have some knowledge of writers on business strategy, such as H. Igor Asoff, R. Moss Kanter and M. E. Porter.

Skills used and developed in a case method include:

- *analytical skills*: problem identification, classifying, organizing and evaluating material; recognizing when vital information is missing;
- *application skills*: judging which techniques are appropriate and applying these techniques;

- *communication skills*: oral and written skills are usually required, group work normally encourages the development of presentational skills;
- *social skills*: group work involves listening, supporting, arguing;
- *creative skills*: cases require creative ideas as well as analytical skills.

Each of the cases should be viewed within the context of international business. For this reason it is essential that Parts 1 and 2 of the book are read before the cases are approached. The reader will find it helpful, when working on a specific case, to keep referring to the appropriate sections in Parts 1 and 2. The index is comprehensive and should help in this process.

The student should read the case through quickly to get a general overview of the study. Then the case should be read more slowly to look at the nature of the information given and how it may be used. A SWOT analysis, which involves identifying Strengths, Weaknesses, Opportunities and Threats facing an organization, may be useful to get a general picture.

A major aim of case study work is to enable students to acquire transferable skills. The ability to analyse one of the cases in this text should be seen as a starting-point for developing skills to analyse other case studies, as well as real life business situations. Equally, some of the questions will benefit from research from additional sources.

To take one example, the case study of 'NH Geotech: an international corporation's response to a contracting market'. This case includes the following discussion point: 'In the light of NH Geotech's rapidly changing business environment, evaluate the corporation's organization structure and processes?'.

This is a very broad-ranging question which is as much about the business environment as the organizational response. To analyse the changing environment, the reader would have to obtain some information about the declining market for agricultural machinery. Chapters 2, 3, and 4 provide some useful information on the nation state and international business, international trade and deregulation, respectively. But equally, research into the EC's common agricultural policy and the USA's agricultural policy, as well as changes in eastern Europe and the developing world, would be of great value. In addition, Chapter 7, which deals with environmental factors, and Chapter 8, which analyses cultural issues in business, would help the reader to get a broader picture of some of the issues involved.

In evaluating NH Geotech's organizational response, Chapter 12, which examines strategic issues, and Chapter 15, which examines some of the human resources aspects of international business, would both be useful. In addition, reference to a wider range of management sources would assist the reader to carry out a more comprehensive analysis.

THE STRUCTURE OF THE BOOK

PART 1   THE GLOBAL BUSINESS ENVIRONMENT

A major factor in the internationalization of business activity are the changes that have occurred in the global business environment. The nation state, its political system, laws and economic system and policies are a major part of this environment. Chapter 2 focuses on the nation state, as individual national governments both encourage international business and restrict this activity.

The third chapter examines the developments in international trade. A prominent feature of the world economy in the last decade of the 20th century is the growing interdependence of nations, although a fully interdependent global economy has as yet to be achieved. The emergence of regional trading blocks have also had a major impact on the international activities of companies.

Chapter 4 investigates the issue of deregulation and its implications for business. A reduction in the role of the state became a feature of many economies in the 1980s and this, in turn, has had the effect of encouraging business activity, especially transnational business. The fifth chapter examines another global phenomenon, privatization. Privatization was a significant part of the economic liberalization of the 1980s and early 1990s. It has been one of the most significant trends in many industrialized countries, as well as in an increasing number of developing nations. In most countries privatization has provided both domestic and foreign organizations with additional business opportunities.

Developments in technology are major driving forces in the globalization of business activity. In Chapter 6 Mike Hewins identifies technology as an agent of internationalization. He argues that technology promotes internationalization by providing new economies in innovation, manufacturing and service.

It was not until the end of the 1960s and early 1970s that there was any general concern for the environment. In Chapter 7 Ron Allison examines international business and environmental issues. It is clear that an increasing concern for the environment will result in additional costs for business, but it will also offer new opportunities to many types of company.

Business practitioners and theorists traditionally regard foreign cultures and languages as a significant constraint in international business. However, in Chapter 8 Terry Mughan questions this point of view and argues that companies from countries such as Germany, Japan and Sweden, who look upon cultural diversity as an advantage in business, are the ones succeeding in the international market-place.

The internationalization of business services has been both a driver and supporter of this general trend. In Chapter 9 Theo Kiriazidis and Stephen Regan examine the internationalization of financial services, including banking, insurance and accounting. In Chapter 10 John Flood looks at the issue of the globalization of legal services. He argues that we are beginning to see a convergence of professional business services, especially those of accounting and law, for professions can no longer rely on single service delivery: their clients demand a wider spectrum of service and this is widening the battle of which group is supposed to do what.

PART 2   THE ORGANIZATIONAL RESPONSE

Part 2 focuses on the organization. In Chapter 11 Ron Allison examines the multinational enterprise from a theoretical perspective.

In Chapter 12 Jonathan Knowles explores the idea of international business strategy. He questions some of the more traditional ways of examining strategy and deals with such issues as centralization versus decentralization. In addition, he provides some alternative views on international business strategy.

The internationalization of business activity involves the functions of business as well as corporate structures and strategy. To illustrate how the functions of business are affected and affect this process, three areas are examined: marketing, finance and human resources management.

In Chapter 13 Terry O'Sullivan examines some of the issues involved in marketing international goods and services. His argument is that the concepts and tools of marketing have a universality transcending national boundaries; whereas the social factors where individuals and groups act under a wide range of influences, both economic and non-economic, means that the marketing processes in different countries can differ considerably.

In Chapter 14 Ross Catterall and John Stittle examine some of the difficulties facing the corporate treasurer's department in a multinational company or a finance director in a smaller company. They examine the problems and risks presented by exchange rate fluctuations; transfer pricing; international taxation and the accounting treatment of international operations.

A major factor in the success of any organization is the best use of human resources and this is particularly true of an international company. Chapter 15 examines some of the ways in which human resources management is affected by the international-ization of business activity. Specific emphasis is given to communications, and staff mobility across national frontiers, including the skill requirements of international managers. The final section of the chapter looks briefly at some of the implications of internationalization on industrial relations.

PART 3 THE CASES

The case study section of the book contains examples from a range of organizations. A major focus of each of the studies is the response to the increasing level of internationalization of business activity.

1 Arthur Andersen & Co. SC: an international firm with a one-firm philosophy

The internationalization of business services is a vital element in the increasing level of business activity at the international level. This case shows how one of the 'big six' accounting firms is providing a range of services globally.

2 The year of the dragon: internationalization and corporate death: the case of the Midland Bank

In the second case Stephen Regan shows how a major element in the international-ization of business in the 1980s was the rapid development of a global market in finance. The 1980s was the decade of the 'mega' takeover. The case looks at how and why a new global superbank was created by the merger of two regional banks.

3 BMW: niche marketing in a global economy?

In their study of BMW, Ron Allison and Erwin Blum look at some of the technological developments taking place within this car-making organization. The case gives specific emphasis to environmental issues and how they are affecting BMW.

4 Nissan Motor Manufacturing (UK): a successful mixed marriage

The case of Nissan illustrates a number of the themes developed in the chapters on technology, the multinational enterprise and the environment. In his study

Ron Allison gives particular focus to Japanese production methods and working practices.

5 Global tyre war: Pirelli versus Continental

This case examines the competitive interaction within the tyre industry, emphasizing the importance that all major players give to the achievement of global scope in all aspects of their operations as a prerequisite for success. This has provoked a spate of transnational mergers since the late 1980s. In their case Leigh Davison, Alan Marchant and Rudi Grunwald, show how the protracted attempt by Pirelli to acquire Continental was affected by national business cultures and environments.

6 Marconi Radar Systems Ltd/NobelTech systems AB: international collaboration in the market for air traffic control systems

In their study of air traffic control systems, Elizabeth Hill, John Macdonald and Margaret Robins show how changes in the technological and political environment of companies can lead to collaboration rather than competition.

7 NH Geotech: an international corporation's response to a contracting market

This case shows how one international corporation within the Fiat Group has responded strategically to a major contraction in the European market for agricultural machinery. The case gives particular emphasis to NH Geotech's organizational structures, human resources management and product development.

8 Structure and strategy in a global environment: the case of the NEC Corporation

In their study of the NEC Corporation, Alan Griffiths and Toru Nakakita show how multinationals must be prepared to change their organizational design and strategies in an ever-increasing competitive environment. In addition, the case provides an insight into the important variables which determine competitiveness and it discusses briefly the general experiences which multinationals face when operating across international boundaries.

9 Philips: a Dutch electronics giant, a multinational or a global?

In his study of Philips, Mike Hewins shows how the company has altered its organizational structure to meet the new challenges of internationalization. The conflicts between local autonomy and central control are the specific issues addressed. In addition, the study shows how technology has informed both its strategy and the competitive environment within which it trades.

10 Northern Foods: a case of deinternationalization

In this case, Sarah Gribbins argues that although there are sound reasons for certain products and services to be standardized on a global basis, this approach is not appropriate for all products and services. The study shows how Northern Foods is concentrating on a national market and not actively looking to expand globally.

11 Changing corporate identity to succeed: the case of Typhoon International Ltd

By the end of the 1980s, Typhoon International was faced with a changing business environment and a major recession. This study shows how, in response to this situation, Typhoon changed its corporate identity and developed a radical new range of products.

12 The mountain bike: from Repack to Greenback

When it first went into commercial production in 1980, few had heard of the mountain bike. By 1991 the commercial development of the mountain bike concept had resulted in the globalization of the bicycle market with annual sales accounting for 80 per cent of the North American, Western European and developed Asian markets. In this study, Wolodymyr Maksymiw and Alan Marchant show how this concept has come to transform national bicycle markets across the world.

References

1 As quoted p. 13 in Buckley, P. J., and Brooke, M. Z., *International business studies: an overview*, (Oxford, Blackwell, 1992).
2 Porter, M., *Competitive strategy Techniques for analysing industries and competitors*, (New York, Free Press, 1980).
3 See p. 14 in Stevens, B., 'Prospects for privatization OECD countries', *National Westminster Bank Quarterly Review*, August 1992.
4 As quoted pp. 6/7 in Barham, K., and Oates, D., *The international manager*, (London, Ashridge/The Economist Books, 1991).
5 As quoted p. 24 in Barham, K., and Oates, D., ibid.
6 Bartlett, C., and Ghoshal, S., *Managing across borders*, (London, Hutchinson Business Books, 1989).

Bibliography

Ansoff, H. I., *Corporate planning*, (Harmondsworth, Penguin, 1975).
Barham, K., and Oates, D., *The international manager*, (London, Business Books/The Economist Books Ltd, 1991).
Bartlett, C., and Ghoshal, S., *Managing across borders*, (London, Hutchinson Business Books, 1989).
Buckley, P. J., *Studies in international business*, (New York, St Martin's Press, 1992).
Buckley, P. J., and Brooke, M. Z., *International business studies: an overview*, (Oxford, Blackwell, 1992).
Easton, G., *Learning from case studies*, (Hemel Hempstead, Prentice Hall, 1989).
Harvard Business School, *Going global: succeeding in world markets*, Harvard Business Review Paperback, 1991.
Hodgetts, R. M., and Luthans, F., *International management*, (New York, McGraw-Hill International, 1991).

Johnson, G., and Scholes, K., *Exploring corporate strategy*, 2nd edition, (Hemel Hempstead, Prentice Hall, 1988).

Kobrin, S. J., 'An empirical analysis of the determinants of global integration', *Strategic Management Journal*, Vol. 12, pp. 17–31, 1991.

McGrath, M. E., and Hoole, R. W., 'Manufacturing's new economies of scale', *Harvard Business Review*, May/June 1992, pp. 94–102.

Moss Kanter, R., *When giants learn to dance*, (Hemel Hempstead, Simon & Schuster, 1989).

Ohmae, K., *The borderless world – Power and strategy in the interlinked economy*, (London, Fontana, 1990).

Porter, M. E., *Competitive strategy*, (New York, Free Press, 1980).

Porter, M. E., *Competitive advantage*, (New York, Free Press, 1985).

Robock, S. H., and Simmonds, K., *International business and multinational enterprises*, 4th edition, (Boston, Irwin, 1989).

PART ONE

THE GLOBAL BUSINESS ENVIRONMENT

CHAPTER TWO

THE NATION STATE AND INTERNATIONAL BUSINESS

JILL PRESTON

INTRODUCTION

Developments in international trade are major factors in the increasing internationalization of business. However, it is clear that 'the golden age of globalization' has not yet arrived. National economies are increasingly interdependent, but global free trade is a long way from being achieved. Nation states encourage international trade, but at the same time different political and legal systems and various types of national economic policies have the effect of restricting international trade and therefore business activity.

An understanding of the various types of national business environments in which organizations function is crucially important to a more general understanding of the nature of international business.

THE POLITICAL ENVIRONMENT

Political environments; the systems, process and values vary considerably across the globe. This variety is partly due to historical and cultural issues. In Chapter 8 Terry Mughan examines some of the cultural issues involved in international business. The political environment of a host country affects international businesses in a number of ways and an understanding by business of this environment is important for effective operations.

Operating in any foreign country involves an element of political risk, but clearly the range of risks varies from one to another. Not surprisingly, most companies prefer to conduct business in countries with a stable political system and a friendly government. A political risk has been defined as:

> ... the likelihood that political forces will cause drastic changes in a country's business environment that affect the profit and other goals of a particular business enterprise. [1]

15

In some countries there is a major risk of conflict and violent change. Clearly, conducting business in a number of countries of eastern Europe and parts of the Middle East is a high-risk activity. Nationalism, guerrilla warfare, civil disturbance and terrorism often take an anti-industry bent, making companies and their employees potential targets; whereas in some countries, especially in the developing world, a coup d'état can result in drastic changes of government.

Less dramatic situations arise when governments change their policies towards foreign businesses, especially if this involves either expropriation or confiscation. A less extreme form of domestication is when a government aims to gain control over foreign investment. For example, it can ensure that a large share of a product is produced locally and that a high proportion of the profits is retained in the country. Changes in labour laws, patent protection and tax regulation can all be used for purposes of domestication.

Domestication can have important implications for international business; for example, if a company is forced to hire nationals as managers, poor co-operation and communication can result. Domestic content requirements can result in increased costs and lower quality products. However, it must be remembered that most states are very keen to obtain foreign investment and therefore governments are more likely to encourage foreign organizations than attempt to deter such activity.

The development of political risk assessment is a relatively new activity. A major aim of this process is to identify ways of minimizing political risk, such as by lobbying or direct negotiation with governmental authorities. For example, India prohibits international companies from expanding capacity beyond agreed limits without specific permission. The company Cheeseborough-Ponds was successful in obtaining expansion licenses, by promising to issue new equity exclusively to Indian investors. This was seen as part of an 'Indianization' policy.

Many organizations now offer services which track international risk situations. The case study of Arthur Andersen shows how one organization provides services in this area. Managers of international companies need to be aware of international political relations, agreements and treaties. Changes in relations can mean major new opportunities and sometimes threats to business. The case of Marconi/NobelTech Systems AB shows how political factors can have a major impact on international business activity.

NATIONAL ECONOMIC POLICIES AFFECTING TRADE

The liberalization of trade and investment has been recognized by most governments as a major source of welfare improvement. However, trade and investment liberalization can have a negative impact on specific industries or economies which cannot withstand foreign competition. While international trade and investment lead to overall economic benefits, these benefits are not distributed equally among countries. Governments may therefore intervene to protect the industries concerned and divert gains to the domestic economies.

Tariffs are one obvious restriction on international trade; world-wide, many tariffs were either removed or significantly reduced during the 1970s and 1980s. However, there were a number of disputes between trading nations, involving tariffs. For example, in 1992 Japan issued a complaint against duties imposed by the EC on imported audio cassette tapes; five Japanese companies (Sony, Hitachi Maxell, TDK, Fuji and Denon Columbia) initiated the complaint.

Non-tariff barriers (NTBs) contribute significantly to the fragmentation of markets. NTBs include voluntary export restraints; public procurement policies; health and safety regulations; subsidies on production and trade; and administrative and technical barriers. The effects of NTBs are difficult, and in some cases impossible, to quantify, therefore it is far more difficult to obtain agreements to lower NTBs than it is to reduce or remove tariffs. Part of the European single market programme is concerned with removing NTBs within the EC and the Uruguay Round of the General Agreement on Tariffs and Trade (GATT) had the item of NTBs on its agenda. Chapter 3 briefly examines the European single market programme and the GATT.

With a reduction in the level of tariffs, the relative importance of NTBs has grown and in recent years they attract most of the attention regarding trade policies. This section examines a number of NTBs.

VOLUNTARY EXPORT RESTRAINTS (VERs)

It is widely recognized that one of the principal dangers of protectionism is that it can lead to trade wars, in which each country retaliates against the tariffs that the other country is imposing by increasing its own tariffs. Retaliatory tariffs imposed by two countries on each other's imports lower the welfare benefits for both countries. A tariff war between two countries of equal size would lead to a loss of welfare for both countries equivalent to about 4 per cent of GNP.[2] This has led to an alternative method of restricting imports: Voluntary Export Restraints (VERs). VERs represent a physical limitation on the quantity of imports; they are either bilaterally negotiated between the importing and exporting countries or multilaterally negotiated among several countries.

The examples of VERs are numerous:

- The multifibre agreement involving over 40 countries and covering textiles and garments, set imports and export quotas and annual growth rates for the products concerned.
- In 1975 and 1985 the EC negotiated with South Africa and Japan VERs of carbon steel to the Community.
- In 1983 the USA negotiated with China a three-year agreement setting maximum export levels of textile products from China.

In 1986 the USA and Japan negotiated a six-year agreement establishing limits on Japanese car exports beginning in 1989. Under the agreement, individual Japanese producers were restricted in the number of cars they could export to the USA. The agreement had substantial effects on prices, sales and the types of Japanese cars exported to the USA. To maximize profits, Japanese car producers, such as Nissan and Honda, raised the price they charged for given models and shifted the mix of cars exported to the USA toward larger or more luxurious models. They also fitted more 'optional' extras in each car; in this way, the impact of the quota was reduced.

In 1990 an agreement was reached between Japan and the EC covering trade in semiconductors. The effects of the restraints on the prices, sales and types of products had not been estimated at the time of writing. However, since the responsibility of controlling the flow of the goods under the agreement is that of the foreign exporting countries and companies, these companies might sell the goods at the highest price possible, in order to offset the cost of the controls. Even if VERs are more attractive to the international community than tariffs, because they do not lead to trade wars, they can be costly to the importing country.

GOVERNMENT PROCUREMENT

In all countries, governments are important purchasers of goods and services, which cover activities ranging from health and defence to administration and education. Within the EC, it has been estimated that public procurement accounts for approximately 15 per cent of the goods and services produced. In theory at least, public contracts represent large markets for foreign companies. However, foreign producers often find themselves discriminated against by national authorities in favour of domestic producers. The case study of Typhoon International shows how business activity can be restricted by this type of discrimination. Part of the European single market programme is concerned with removing these barriers.

The procurement policies of many national governments are highly protectionist in intent. For example, in spite of the progress made towards the single market, many European countries implement public procurement policies to protect specific sectors, including telecommunication equipment, medical equipment, pharmaceutical products and railway equipment. To take another example, public procurement of computers in Japan has been used to support local manufacturers. Foreign companies had a 41 per cent share of the computers sold to the Japanese private sector by mid-1991, but only 10 per cent of the sales to the public sector.[3] In 1992 Japan made a promise to the USA that it would revise its procurement rules, but this will take years to have an effect.

HEALTH AND SAFETY REGULATIONS

National governments establish specific health and safety standards for a wide range of products; for example, food standards cover flavourings, colourings and other additives. In the case of drugs and proprietary medicines, standards are imposed to protect the public against physical harm. The existence of different health and safety regulations means that goods cannot be exported, or if they are exported they have to be adapted to meet the rules of each national market. This process can be very expensive for companies selling to a number of markets.

There are many examples where health and safety regulations are used, quite simply, to keep certain products out of a national market. For example, during the 1980s the UK used health and safety arguments to prevent French UHT milk from entering UK markets. The possibility of 'Newcastle Disease' was the line of argument for preventing French turkeys entering the UK market at this time. There was also the example where the EC argued that as US and Canadian animals had been treated with certain hormones, they constituted a health risk.

Different product standards can restrict market access and increase production cost by shortening production runs. These barriers result in significant distortions in the flow of international trade. The removal of this type of barrier is a major element of the European single market programme, as outlined in the next chapter.

To take another example of how different health and safety regulations can act as a barrier. In the mid 1980s European and American exporters of pharmaceutical products complained about the elaborate safety standards tests imposed by the

Japanese authorities. It was not uncommon for the process to take up to two years to complete, even if European and American exporters had previously achieved national approval.

Frequently, national governments deliberately set standards and regulations to allow national companies to develop competing goods and gain a competitive edge *vis-à-vis* foreign producers. For example, in many countries standards on electrical equipment act as a major restriction for exporters.

SUBSIDIES ON PRODUCTION AND TRADE

Subsidies affect the level of production and trade and distort international competition by giving some companies an artificial competitive advantage. A subsidy given to traders encourages domestic production and exports, and tends to discourage imports. Regional aids can have the same effects. However, this aid is provided as a general help to a disadvantaged region and is normally available to all actual or potential industries in the region concerned, not concentrated on an industry or a group of industries which may be exporters who are losing their competitive advantage.

The examples of subsidization are numerous. In the USA the Export-Import Bank facilitates the financing of the purchase of American exports. For example, it normally extends loans to foreign consumers at below the private market rates of interest. In EC countries the extent of financial support to industry is extensive. Table 2.1 shows the level of aids to manufacturing in EC countries. In Japan, the Ministry of International Trade and Industry (MITI), provides financial support to specific sectors, such as computers.

In the case of agriculture, the economic assistance to producers world-wide is enormous. For example, the agricultural support in Organization for Economic Cooperation and Development (OECD) countries amounted in 1991 to $117 billion and $34.7 billion in the USA.[2]

Table 2.1
Aids to manufacturing: average
1986–8 1987 prices

Country	ECU per worker
Italy	3,077
Greece	3,721
Ireland	2,551
Belgium	1,693
Netherlands	1,371
France	1,528
Luxembourg	1,812
UK	723
W Germany	1,134
Denmark	643
Spain	1,067
Portugal	701
EC12	1,439

The EC provides considerable levels of financial support to producers of agricultural products under the Common Agricultural Policy (CAP). For example, during the 1980s on average 62.3 per cent of the EC budget went on agricultural price support. The level of EC subsidies creates substantial problems for non-EC producers, many of whom cannot sell their products at a competitive price. The subsidization of production and especially trade often leads to serious disputes among the industrialized countries.

DUMPING

Dumping is a practice whereby foreign producers set a lower price in their export markets than in their domestic markets. Often the motive behind the practice of dumping is not simply profit maximization by increasing sales in the export markets. Foreign producers may establish a lower price in their export markets only temporarily, in an attempt to drive domestic competitors out of the market. This is referred to as 'predatory' dumping. Dumping is usually associated with export subsidies, whereby the price of goods exported is lower than the price of the same goods in the domestic market. Whatever the reason or practice of dumping, companies in the exporting countries are hit by the lower price of foreign goods.

Various international trade agreements have attempted to deal with the issue of dumping. For example, within the EC, European companies have recourse, under Community legislation, if they feel that other companies from either EC or non-EC countries are relying on dumping to increase their share in the market. Such companies may present their case to the national department as well as to the EC Commission which is responsible for implementing the European competition policy, as dumping is viewed as a breach of this policy.

In the USA, domestic companies can appeal to the US International Trade Commission (USITC) to obtain trade measures to protect them from the practice of dumping. In the 1980s the USITC initiated many investigations and anti-dumping duties were imposed against the imports from several countries, such as the imports of methyl alcohol from France, sugar from Belgium, tyres and tubes from Korea and perchlorethylene from Italy.

FISCAL DISTORTIONS

The free movement of goods throughout the world is hindered by the unequal application of internal tax systems. A purchase tax, for instance, applied at a higher rate to foreign goods obviously increases their price in relation to domestic goods.

In addition, governments have different tax systems. For example, in North America 'direct taxation', such as income tax is a major source of revenue whereas in other countries indirect taxes, such as value added tax, is more significant as a source of revenue. Indirect taxes tend to result in higher prices, while direct taxes affect prices only indirectly. Because of the difference in the impact of the two types of taxes on the price of final goods, national authorities can permit destination principle border tax adjustments. According to this principle, exports that are subject to indirect domestic taxes may have those taxes rebated. However, even under the destination principle considerable fiscal distortions may continue to exist. Frequently, it is not clear how much tax is incorporated in the price of the final product. If too much is rebated, the exporter gains an unfair competitive advantage, but if too little is rebated the exporter faces an unfair cost.

EXCHANGE RATE CHANGES AND UNCERTAINTY IN INTERNATIONAL TRADE

It is not surprising that unexpected changes in the foreign exchange rate create uncertainty and discourage the flow of international trade. When a company makes a contract to import goods, they normally settle the price in terms of the exporter's currency. If the price of foreign exchange rises between the date of entering the contract and the date when payment is due, the company's obligation will be greater in terms of the domestic currency. A similar problem is faced by exporters when the price of foreign exchange falls between the time of the contract of sale and the receipt of the sale's proceeds. The value of the receipts will be less than had initially been expected.

Producers and traders may insure themselves against the risks of exchange rate fluctuations through operations on the forward exchange market. This market allows producers and traders to buy a certain value in foreign currencies in the future at an agreed price. The financial markets can offer a wide range of services to traders to allow them to deal with the exchange rate uncertainty. However, these services involve considerable costs and these costs can be considered as a form of non-tariff barrier. Exchange rate changes can alter the strategies of multinational countries; for example, the revaluation of the Yen in 1985 led to a number of Japanese companies setting up production sites abroad.

The issue of foreign exchange rate fluctuations and international business are examined in more detail in Chapter 3 and also in Chapter 14.

ADMINISTRATIVE BARRIERS

The movement of goods across frontiers is also restricted by various administrative procedures and requirements. At national frontiers, national rules covering areas such as indirect taxation and the illegal importation of drugs are checked.

In many countries extensive documentation is required to move goods from one country to another. This tends to result in delays at border crossings, which in turn increases the cost of these goods and thereby acts as a barrier to trade. It is estimated that border controls add between 2 per cent and 10 per cent to the cost of goods as they move from one country to another. Chapter 3 shows how the EC and other trading groups are attempting to deal with this barrier.

RESTRICTIONS ON INTERNATIONAL INVESTMENT

International business is affected by measures which inhibit international trade, but it is also affected by measures which discriminate against foreign capital movements. It is not unusual for controls on capital flows to be stricter than those on the movement of goods. Transfers of capital is a highly sensitive economic and political issue, because of the adverse effect which a free flow of capital may have on a state's economy.

Capital movements are classified under foreign direct investment and portfolio investment. Foreign direct investment involves the acquisition of a lasting interest in an enterprise operating in an economy other than that of the investor. The purpose is to have some say in the management of the enterprise. All other forms of investment, such as the buying of stocks and shares, is classed as portfolio investment. Chapter 11 examines the issue of foreign direct investment and multinational enterprises.

RESTRICTIONS ON FOREIGN DIRECT INVESTMENT

Many countries prohibit the establishment of foreign companies in certain sectors. Some prohibitions are rather stringent, while other constraints are less drastic, although they still constitute hindrances. For example, foreign companies are not allowed to establish in the USA in such sectors as fresh water shipping and domestic radio communications. In addition, some states in the USA expressly prohibit the establishment of foreign banks and insurance companies. Foreign banks are excluded from many countries, including Australia, Iceland and Algeria. In Switzerland and in some provinces of Canada, certain specific classes of insurance, such as motor and fire, are operated by the state and foreign companies are not allowed to enter the national markets.

In Australia foreign acquisitions of existing companies, in which any individual foreign interest will acquire more than 15 per cent of total equity, require authorization by the national authorities. The authorization may be granted if the foreign companies produce evidence that their operations benefit the domestic economy.

Even in countries where there is no specific provision prohibiting the transfer of control of national companies to non-residents, foreign access to national markets may be restricted by national anti-trust and merger legislation.[4] This legislation usually applies equally, in principle, to both domestic and foreign companies. In practice, however, discriminatory treatment against foreign companies may arise in the actual application of such provisions; this happens in many European countries.

In addition, in many countries the establishment of foreign companies is often affected by the specific requirements attached to the granting of authorization. For example, in the USA, some states require deposits or financial guarantees from certain types of foreign companies. Other countries, and especially those which impose foreign exchange control, impose strict restrictions on the repatriation of profits. In the field of transport certain countries, such as Pakistan, Indonesia and Chile, specify the proportion of business which may be done by domestic and foreign companies respectively. Such constraints reduce the profitability of the foreign companies concerned and reduce the international flow of capital.

Another type of restriction on foreign direct investment may take the form of specifying the minimum amounts of certain factors of production, such as capital and local labour, that must be employed in the production process. In many cases host countries specify that foreign companies established domestically shall employ a minimum number or percentage of its management from the local labour market.

The main reason for this requirement is to ensure that some members of senior management have adequate knowledge of local laws and requirements. If there is an available supply of skilled local labour, then such requirements would have no effect on the output of the companies concerned. If, however, labour possessing the right experience and skills is not available domestically (which is often the case in many developing countries), the restriction that a certain number of persons from the local labour market must be employed limits the inflow of foreign direct investment. For example, as a general rule for a company domiciled in Switzerland the majority of the management must have Swiss nationality, while working permits for foreigners are subject to quotas.

Apart from the controls which attempt to regulate the inflows of direct foreign investment to particular countries, some national authorities, especially in the developing countries, try to regulate the outflow of foreign direct investment. In Brazil, Chile, Argentina, Turkey and Peru, annual limits are placed on direct capital outflows, restricting the total amount of investment abroad to a percentage of the amount invested at home. The same countries limit the total amount of short-term financial assets which can be held abroad by direct investors. The objective of these controls is to induce national firms to invest at home rather than abroad, thus contributing to the national economic development.

National restrictions on foreign direct investment clearly have a major impact on international business. However, the fourth chapter, which deals with the issue of deregulation, shows how during the 1980s many countries liberalized some of the restrictions on foreign direct investment.

RESTRICTIONS ON PORTFOLIO INVESTMENT

In a perfect market, capital will flow to areas where the returns are the highest. Capital would therefore flow out of low-return countries, which tend to include developing countries, having severe repercussions on economic performance. Thus it is necessary for these countries to guard against the adverse effects of capital exports by way of exchange control regulations. In fact, almost all developing countries impose foreign exchange control regulations which restrict their residents from transferring funds abroad.

Foreign exchange controls usually take the form of restraints on foreign borrowing and lending. In many cases the authorities place restrictions on the amount of funds which domestic residents may either lend to foreigners or borrow from abroad. For example, in Greece and Portugal, the outward transfer of capital originating from lending abroad by national residents requires prior authorization from the Central Bank, and it is not normally granted. Residents are also prohibited from borrowing from external banks. In the late 1980s the EC adopted legislation requiring Member States to allow free movements of capital. However, Greece and Portugal make extensive use of the protective clauses provided in the Treaty to maintain restrictions on capital movements which were, in principle, liberalized under EC law.

Foreign exchange controls also take the form of restriction on the issue of foreign securities on the national stock exchanges. These restrictions are intended to prevent domestic residents from acquiring foreign securities and to prevent capital outflows. Restrictions on the issue of foreign securities on the national stock exchange are usually imposed by developing countries concerned about the outflow of capital. A number of countries levy discriminatory taxes on the purchase of foreign securities. In Switzerland, for instance, a turnover tax is levied on the pursuit and sale of foreign securities which is twice that levied on domestic securities. Another example of foreign exchange controls is the restriction on the amount of foreign exchange which may be bought for the purpose of foreign travel.

The lack of currency convertibility can be the most important control on the flows of capital. Many developing countries, as well as countries of eastern Europe, suffer because their currencies lack international convertibility. The exchange rate régime in these countries is often marked by the co-existence of fixed official exchange rate for certain transactions and black market rates, which are substantially lower.

Up to this point, the links between government policies and international trade and investment have been viewed from within a static framework. However, government policies are normally subject to change. These policies are adopted and implemented as a response to specific and changing economic or social problems. For example, during the 1980s the national authorities in many countries decided, through deregulation, to reduce their intervention in specific sectors of the economy, such as transport and finance. At the same time the role of government in many countries has increased significantly in areas such as the environment and green issues. The changing nature of national government policies has far-reaching effects on the internationalization of business.

THE LEGAL ENVIRONMENT

A single international commercial system does not exist. Therefore the legal environment for international business consists of the laws and courts of individual nation states. Each nation state has its own set of courts and they differ in both philosophy and practice. Most legal systems are based on either the common law or the civil law system. In very general terms, the common law system has been adopted in most countries where the English have settled or governed; whereas in most continental European countries and many countries in Africa and Asia, civil legal systems prevail. Civil law systems embody their main rules of law in a legislative code and state officials interpret the code and develop rules for its implementation; whereas in a common law system the judiciary is the final interpreter and decision-maker and judicial decisions are guided by previous decisions, as opposed to a code. In Chapter 14, Ross Catterall and John Stittle show how different types of legal systems have a major impact on the finance function in an international business.

The only element of an international legal framework is the range of agreements, codes and treaties between certain states and these tend to apply only to selected areas of business. Multinational companies constantly face uncertainties as to which laws to apply; equally, many governments believe that multinational enterprises (MNE) flout national legislation. In addition, legal restraints affect the ability of multinationals to take over companies abroad as part of their international strategy.

The right to levy and collect taxes is a major element of the sovereignty of nation states. There is no universal law that specifies the tax jurisdiction of an individual country. Business activities which cross national borders are faced with both the problems and the opportunities from different taxation policies and overlapping national tax jurisdictions. For example, two states may claim the right to tax the same property or income.

Many governments have negotiated bilateral agreements and they provide credits for taxes paid abroad. For example, the USA has bilateral agreement with 40 countries in an attempt to provide relief from double taxation. Issues associated with different taxation systems are further developed in Chapter 14.

All nation states have the right to expropriate private property when the national welfare makes such a move desirable. The area of dispute can be the matter of compensation and how disputes should be settled. For example, in many developing countries foreign investors are frequently not willing to rely solely on local courts for the protection of foreign property. Many countries are keen to attract foreign investment and so they are aware that assurances are needed to encourage foreign investors.

During the 1980s and early 1990s there was a growing trend for international businesses to make use of international arbitration. It is becoming usual for mutually agreed arbitration clauses to be written into agreements between foreign investors and host nations. Similar clauses are usual in international commercial agreements between business partners, such as a distributorship or a sales contract. The main centres for major international arbitration are Geneva, London, New York, Paris and Stockholm.

Most countries protect intellectual property rights, such as patents, know-how and trade marks. To protect these rights, a company must file patent and registration applications in every country in which these property rights are to be used. This requirement is both expensive and time-consuming. The Uruguay round of the GATT has tried to obtain some agreement on this issue. And the European Patent Convention that was established in 1978 permits the office to issue a patent that is effective in the 11 participating countries.

The most important international legal issues facing business have developed from the growing number of agreements covering commercial matters. For example, through bilateral commercial treaties many governments seek to provide their nationals with the opportunity to carry out business in foreign countries on a non-discriminatory basis. However, it has to be added that many aspects of international business are not covered by these agreements.

A number of issues concerned with different national legal systems are discussed by John Flood in Chapter 10.

References

1 Robock, S. H., and Simmonds K., *International business and multinational enterprises*, 4th edition, (Boston, Irwin, 1989).
2 See p. 47 *IMF International Trade Special Report*, (Washington DC, IMF, 1990).
3 See 'Japan and international trade', *Financial Times*, 30 July 1992.
4 *OECD Trade in Services*, (Paris, 1990).

Bibliography

Bressand, A., 'Futures for economic integration', *International Affairs*, Vol. 66, No. 1, January 1990.
Chimni, B., *International commodity agreements: a legal study*, (London, Croom Helm, 1987).
Connolly, M., *International trade & money*, (London, Allen & Unwin, 1989).
Dixon, M., *International law*, (London, Blackstone Press, 1990).
Gill, S., *The global political economy*, (New York, Harvester).
Hodgson, J., *International economic relations*, (New Jersey, Prentice Hall, 1987).
OECD Tax expenditure – a review of the issues and country practices, (Paris, 1984).

Rogers, J., *Global risk assessment: issues, concepts and applications*, (California, Riverside, 1987).
Strange, S., 'Firms and world politics', *International Affairs*, Vol. 68, No. 1, January 1991.
Wallace, R., *International Law*, (London, Sweet & Maxwell, 1987).
Yoffie, D., *Power & protection*, (New York, Columbia University Press, 1989).

CHAPTER THREE

INTERNATIONAL TRADE

JILL PRESTON

INTRODUCTION

It was suggested in the first chapter that there are several factors within the business environment that are encouraging economic activity to become increasingly global. This chapter briefly examines developments in international trade, and how these developments are having an impact on business. It is important for business to be aware of major issues in international trade.

DEVELOPMENTS IN INTERNATIONAL TRADE

A major feature of the world economy is the growing interdependence between nations. Between 1965–80 international trade had been a major driving-force behind world expansion. This was due in part to the post-Second World War multinational trading system and the commencement of financial deregulation. The significance of deregulation in the international business environment is examined in Chapters 4 and 9. The level of international business had increased dramatically in the 1980s, but this pace had slowed down quite markedly by the early 1990s. For example, in 1991 world trade grew by only 1.5 per cent, the smallest rise since 1985. The stagnation that afflicted the world economy in the early 1990s had a major impact on international activity. The issue of political and economic barriers to international business was examined in the last chapter.

A fully interdependent world economy, where markets for goods and services are unified and there is no discrimination against foreigners, has not been achieved. For example, in most countries private direct investment is a long way from being treated on a fully non-discriminatory basis and in most parts of the world international migration is controlled. In addition, by the early 1990s it was obvious that nationalism was emerging as a potential threat to a globalized economy. Figure 3.1 illustrates the developments in world trade.

I should like to thank Alan Griffiths of Anglia Business School for his comments on the draft of this chapter.

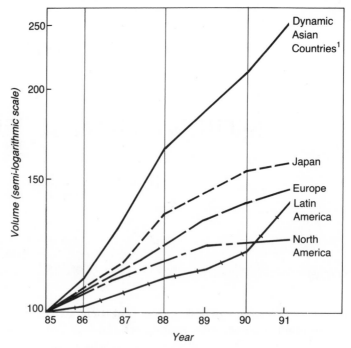

1 Dynamic Asian Countries = Hong Kong, Indonesia, Malaysia,
   Singapore, South Korea, Taiwan and Thailand.

Figure 3.1
Import volume by selected groups of countries (1985 = 100)
Source: Adapted from IMF.

For most economists the ideal state of affairs is a system of free trade, where there
are no man-made obstacles to the trade. It is argued that free trade allows individuals
to exploit their comparative advantage, and therefore to specialize in what they do
best. The idea of comparative advantage suggests that mutually advantageous trade
can occur even when one trading partner has an absolute advantage in producing all
the products being traded. Thus protectionism by either individual countries or
blocks of countries is regarded as being less efficient.

From the 1960s the rise in the volume and impact of world trade has led to what
Kenichi Ohmae refers to as the interlinked economy of the Triad: Europe, the USA
and Japan, plus the developing economies of Hong Kong, Singapore and Taiwan.[1]
Some of these interlinkages first emerged during the world oil crisis of the mid-1970s.
Suddenly a number of countries and companies that had thought themselves largely
isolated from international occurrences were rudely awoken. The recession of the
early 1990s again illustrates the extent of global interlinkages.

World trade has also brought about a global re-orientation of production. It is not
so very long ago when it would have been unthinkable for a motor car to be partly
produced in a number of countries, assembled in others and then sold elsewhere. Yet
consistent with the theory of comparative advantage, this type of production and
distribution is occurring with increased frequency. The case studies of Nissan, NH
Geotech, the NEC Corporation, Philips, and the Mountain Bike illustrate the idea of
global production.

THE GENERAL AGREEMENT ON TARIFFS AND TRADE (GATT)

By the end of the Second World War, many policymakers in the Western World, particularly in Britain, Canada and the USA, wished to push the global economy away from the economic depression and protectionism of the inter-war years and to create a new world economic order, based on new international institutions. For example, at that time the International Monetary Fund was established to try to solve short-term international liquidity problems, by lending short-term to countries which had balance of payment problems. In addition, the International Bank for Reconstruction and Development was established to deal with long-term capital flows. In 1947 tariff negotiations were held in Geneva and this resulted in the signing of the General Agreement on Tariffs and Trade (GATT).

The GATT is a binding agreement between 108 governments which together account for 90 per cent of world trade. Its main purpose is to encourage trade liberalization by reducing barriers such as quotas and import duties. The GATT does not directly affect individual companies, but it does affect them indirectly by providing some predictability in the international environment. The fundamental principles of the GATT are liberalism, non-discrimination and upholding the international rule of law.

GATT operates in three ways:

- It provides a set of rules governing trade behaviour.
- It acts as a forum for negotiations to liberalize trade.
- It is a court in which governments settle their differences.

Since 1947 the GATT has developed into a permanent organization with a secretariat and a director general. The task of the organization is to monitor the implementation of its own rules and to encourage further liberalization, providing a framework and a forum for trade negotiation.

The GATT is multilateral in character in that it encompasses the trade relations between all members, either directly or indirectly, at the same time. The most important feature of the GATT system is the 'rule of non-discrimination'. This rule requires that any 'advantage, favour, privilege or immunity' granted to a GATT member must immediately and unconditionally be made available to all other members. As members are still free to set different tariffs for different products, it is possible to favour some countries' products against others. In addition, GATT's rules permit the existence of customs unions and free trade areas which, by their nature, discriminate against non-members. The GATT rules try to ensure that a customs union promotes trade among members rather than being a device to discriminate against non-members.

By 1980 three major rounds of negotiations under the GATT had been completed: the Dillon Round 1960–62; the Kennedy Round 1964–67 and the Tokyo Round 1973–79. These negotiations reduced the level of tariffs among developed economies to very low levels. However, tariff reductions for goods coming from developing countries were not so generous and as the level of tariff protection was reduced, the importance of non-tariff barriers to trade such as quotas and government procurement legislation becomes more apparent.

In 1986 a new round of trade liberalization negotiations was launched, the Uruguay Round. This Round aims to reduce some of the trade restrictions which had crept in by the 1980s; for example, standards or technical barriers to trade were on the agenda.

In addition, it aims to bring within the GATT framework agriculture, and textiles and clothing, which accounted for 10.1 and 5.3 per cent of total world trade in 1990, respectively. Business services such as banking, insurance and advertising, as well as intellectual property rights, for example, patents and trade marks, have also been subject to negotiation.

In some respects, these negotiations took place in a more difficult environment than was the case in previous rounds. The diversity of interests and the complex agenda made the Uruguay Round of trade negotiations particularly demanding. For example, by the early 1990s the USA was running a large and unsustainable trade deficit. Many developing countries were in the position of having to achieve, and then maintain and increase their trade surpluses, if they were to have any chance of servicing their external debts.

Developing countries tend to be antagonistic to the aims of developed countries for liberalizing trade in services, agricultural products and technology transfer. The former see these initiatives as leading to domination by foreign financial and media companies and higher prices for imported foods, as well as higher prices for products with patents. The main interest of developing countries lies in regaining the market access that they lost during the 1980s as a result of the protectionist measures implemented by developed countries.

Yet in spite of this difficult environment, 108 governments were involved in the Round and at least 45 countries, including many developing countries, have liberalized their trade policies since 1986. However, the EC, the USA and Japan, which together account for over 50 per cent of world exports, have shown only limited commitment. For example, President Bush's sales trip to Japan in January 1992 would suggest a wish for bilateralism and managed trade, as opposed to a multilateral trading system and liberalism.

If the Round succeeds, it will provide a secure foundation for the extension of the trading system into such new areas as global competition and the environment. In addition, it will underpin the global market economy, as well as help to stabilize global political relations. The world recession of the early 1990s desperately required the boost that an agreement was likely to bring. Writing in the *Financial Times* on 20 January 1992, Martin Wolf stated that the choice is 'between the rule of the jungle and the rule of international law'.

At the time of writing, in November 1992, the Uruguay Round of negotiations had broken down once more, although the Round was due to be implemented in January 1993. In addition, there was a real fear that a trade war between EC countries and the USA would result. If this happens, then it could easily sink the Uruguay Round and cause extensive damage to the GATT itself. The impact on international business activity would be critical, for it has been estimated that a Uruguay-round agreement would give an annual boost to world trade of something in the region of $200 billion. If general agreement is not reached, international trade will be an increasingly risky activity. For individual companies involved, these negotiations are important, for the expansion of international trade activities is normally a long-term investment; a high degree of uncertainty makes this a particularly risky business.

DEVELOPING COUNTRIES AND WORLD TRADE

The economies of industrialized nations have become increasingly interdependent through global products and global trade. However, approximately 20 per cent of the world's population, viz. Africa and Latin America, has been adversely affected by internationalization, especially international trade. For example, Latin America lost 1 per cent of its world market share during the 1980s to a level of 4 per cent, whereas Africa's share fell by more than half, from 4.8 per cent in 1980 to 2.2 per cent in 1988. This decline may appear a little surprising, as both regions have a wide range of natural resources and are well situated with regard to large markets. For example, the existence of the Lomé Convention, an agreement signed in 1974 between the EC and 66 African and Latin American countries, gives the latter preferential treatment in the European market.

To take one or two examples, Mexico has large copper, oil and iron reserves and shares a border with the USA; its market share is about 5 per cent. In contrast, Japan, which is nearly 6,000 miles away from the USA, has few natural resources and supplies something in the region of 20 per cent of all American imports. The lack of capital resources and basic infrastructure, as well as inadequate skill levels, have resulted in low levels of growth in African and Latin American countries.

In addition, this low level of growth has not been helped by the failure to remove barriers to trade. Whereas developed countries made it easier to trade among themselves; tariffs among industrialized nations fell from 40 per cent in 1947 to roughly 5 per cent by 1990. Countries in Africa and Latin America tried to protect their own industries from international competition. This issue is further examined in Chapters 4 and 5.

During this period many countries of Africa and Latin America implemented import substitution policies and priced their own exports out of the market. This had the effect of stopping the growth of new, internationally competitive businesses. For example, in Venezuela the import substitution strategy adopted in 1983 included multiple exchange rates: an official rate, a rate for debt payment, a rate for 'essential' exports, and a free market rate. Importers had to apply for foreign exchange at one of the official rates, wait for a period of up to two months to obtain one-third of the authorized foreign exchange, and then submit another request for the balance, once the merchandise had arrived. This did not make for business efficiency, nor did it help business confidence.

In the area of tariffs, Venezuela had 41 *ad valorem* rates ranging from 0 per cent to 135 per cent, with an average tariff of 37 per cent. In addition, the Venezuelan government supplemented its tariffs with a wide range of import restrictions. In general, the government prohibited the importation of goods if domestic producers had sufficient capacity to supply the domestic market. Initially, these kinds of protectionist policies resulted in quick industrialization. For example, during the 1960s and 1970s, Central American countries performed well, although many of the companies that grew under protectionism were inefficient and unable to export.

In many African and Latin American countries, economic growth was also stunted by 'statism', the idea that state officials can successfully manage businesses. For example, the Morogoro shoe factory cost Tanzania $500,000 per year to keep open. Morogoro has yet to attain more than 4 per cent capacity utilization or to realize a profit.

In addition, many countries of Africa and Latin America mishandled the oil shocks of the 1970s – regardless of whether they were oil importers or oil exporters. Oil importing countries borrowed extravagantly to maintain their high standards of living in spite of their diminishing purchasing power. Oil exporting countries borrowed extravagantly to improve *their* standards of living, with the expectation of indefinitely rising future oil earnings.

By the mid-1980s as the after-effects of the shock of the oil crisis were beginning to bite, one Latin American or African government after another decided that import substitution and protectionism could not result in efficiency and economic growth. The experience of the rapidly advancing Asian countries suggested that liberalization and privatization were both more efficient and effective than protectionism and statism.

The 1980s saw a major shift to export-orientated growth strategies in many of these countries. In Latin America a host of countries initiated liberalization policies, for example, Chile, Mexico, Brazil and Argentina. In Africa the moves have been slower, but Ghana, Malawi and Zambia are among the pioneers of the movement in that continent. Chapter 4 deals with deregulation and its impact on international business.

There is a real danger that companies in the developed countries of Europe, the Pacific rim and the USA will ignore the changes that are happening in Africa and Latin America and thereby miss out on significant opportunities based on the regions' abundant natural resources and low labour costs. To take one or two examples of the new direction of trade that is opening up: since 1985, Mexico has reduced the coverage of import licenses, reduced import tariffs to a maximum of 20 per cent and joined the GATT. In 1970 Mauritius was a single-crop economy, dependent almost entirely on sugar; by 1990, having adopted an export-led economic strategy, it had become one of Africa's most successful examples of export-led growth.

TRADE AND EXCHANGE RATES

The exchange rate is simply the price of one currency in terms of another; for example, £1 may be exchanged for $1.60. The exchange rate is important because, to a great extent, it determines the price at which goods and services are traded internationally. When one company trades with an organization in another country, it is usual to agree which currency will be used. Whichever currency is used, one or both parties will need to transfer to or from its national currency. The foreign exchange market provides the mechanism for these currency transactions. The foreign exchange market is a world-wide network of institutions, mainly working for commercial banks and linked by rapid means of communications. It is highly competitive, with prices adjusting rapidly to demand and supply influences. The most important economic factors influencing exchange rates are relative inflation and interest rates.

Any organization with international dealings must have contact with a foreign exchange market. Smaller companies do not enter the market themselves; they will normally deal through a local bank. Frequently, national governments intervene in the market to affect currency values.

If there is an interlude between a transaction and payment, there is a risk that the exchange values of the currencies may fluctuate. From the early 1970s the system of floating exchange rates became widespread; the value of individual currencies was determined by market forces. In effect, countries had to accept the exchange rate given to them by the market. Short-term exchange rates are determined by the demand for, and the supply of, currencies and capital flows, rather than by trade in goods and services. This can result in the overvaluation or the undervaluation of a currency.

Almost all foreign exchange trading takes place among a small number of currencies: the US dollar, the British pound sterling, the German Mark, the Japanese yen, and the Swiss franc. The size of the market is enormous and trading volume has grown dramatically over recent years. For example, the volume of exchange trading in the world's three leading markets of London, New York and Tokyo totalled $188 billion daily in March 1986. In global terms, there is continuous trading as the markets overlap each other and the centre of trading shifts from one country to another, following the sun. The study of Arthur Andersen shows how one organization assists its clients in responding to continuous trading.

The foreign exchange system allows companies to buy and sell currencies, 'spot' for immediate delivery or 'forward' for delivery at a future date. An 'option' gives the holder the 'right' to buy or sell currency in the future at a perspective price, whereas the 'futures' contract entails an 'obligation' to buy or sell. Relatively small transaction sizes are allowed, but they do provide the smaller company with an opportunity to hedge exchange rate risks.

The theory of purchasing power parity (PPP) states that the prices of tradable goods will tend to equalize across countries. The currency of the country with higher rates of inflation will tend to depreciate to compensate for the loss in purchasing power. For example, if the UK is experiencing a higher rate of inflation than the USA, the PPP theory predicts that the pound sterling will decrease in value relative to the US dollar in order to keep purchasing power equal in the two currencies.

However, this implies an exchange rate flexibility that leads to uncertainty and restricts international business. The International Monetary Fund (IMF) was established in the 1950s to promote international monetary co-operation and reduce exchange rate flexibility. The IMF has an organization like a credit union: each member country has a quota which determines the member's voting weight, the amount of its expected contribution to the IMF under normal circumstances and how much the member can withdraw when the need arises. Any member country may borrow from the Fund to finance its balance of payments deficit. As a result, the country concerned will be able to offset any payment imbalances without resorting to exchange rate depreciation and trade restrictions.

The IMF provides only short-term financial support and no member should be a permanent borrower. This means that at the end of the day a member may use restrictive trade practices or/and exchange rate depreciations to correct balance of payments disequilibrium. The IMF has been criticized by many developing countries for lacking adequate financial resources and the political will to reduce their payments imbalances. In Chapter 14 Ross Catterall and John Stittle examine the implications of fluctuations in exchange rates from the perspective of the company.

THE DEVELOPMENT OF REGIONAL TRADING BLOCKS

One feature of the world economy is the development of regional trading blocks such as the EC, although this organization is, of course, much more than just a trading block. The development of the EC and its success in generating trade between its members has encouraged the emergence of other regional trading blocks. These blocks are viewed by some observers as a step towards the fully interdependent global economy. Other observers suggest that the reverse will happen, where free trade is increased within the blocks but protectionism is increased between them. It

Table 3.1
Inter-regional world trade

Reporting areas	Direction of trade in 1990 (1975 figures in parentheses)[1] Percentage share in reporting areas' total trade[2]				
	European Community	EFTA	NAFTA	Eastern Asia	Rest of the World
European Community	59.2 (51.4)	10.0 (9.4)	8.4 (8.7)	7.3 (3.6)	15.1 (26.9)
EFTA	59.4 (51.7)	13.3 (17.0)	7.9 (7.0)	7.7 (3.9)	11.8 (20.4)
NAFTA	18.3 (18.6)	2.8 (2.5)	37.6 (26.2)	26.7 (15.6)	14.6 (27.1)
Eastern Asia	16.0 (12.0)	2.6 (1.9)	26.9 (24.8)	37.6 (28.0)	16.8 (33.3)

[1] The prospective North American Free Trade Area (NAFTA) comprises Canada, Mexico and the United States, Eastern Asia includes the ASEAN countries (except Brunei) China, Hong Kong, Japan, South Korea and Taiwan. There are no data on direct Taiwanese trade with China and Mexico.
[2] Total trade equals the sum of merchandise exports and imports[3] 1975–90.

Source: Adapted from IMF Directory of Trade Statistics.

is true that European countries do three-quarters of their trade with one another. But the countries of the Americas and of Asia send more than half of their exports outside their respective regions as Table 3.1 shows. Almost 40 per cent of all world trade is inter-regional.

In addition to the development of the EC, including the establishment of the European Economic Area (EEA) with EFTA countries, new free trade zones are emerging in North and South America. The six members of the Association of South-East Asian Nations (ASEAN) have agreed to establish an ASEAN free trade area by the first decade of the new century. This development is a product of ASEAN fears that they will be excluded from the benefits of global free trade and foreign direct investment. They suspect that developed countries are more concerned with safeguarding their regional trading interests than with a multilateral trading system. The study of the NEC corporation shows how one organization is using the ASEAN free trade area.

THE EUROPEAN COMMUNITY

One of the major aims of the EC is the development of an integrated market with the barriers to trade and mobility removed. The EC has not only had a major impact on its own members, but also on the trading patterns of the wider world. A special feature of the EC is its ability to legislate; it can propose laws which, once adopted, become binding on the Member States.

The EC has a number of general aims; these include:

● upholding peace in Europe by integrating national economies;
● increasing prosperity by developing a common market;
● pooling the energies of member states for technological and industrial development;
● easing the inequalities between peoples and regions;

- assisting people of the third world;
- developing an effective means of resolving political disputes.

One of the major aims of the Treaty of Rome was to develop a Europe without frontiers. This was also a major theme of the White Paper 'Completing the internal market', which was agreed in 1985. The object was to implement a series of measures by the end of 1992 which would, in effect, achieve a market free of practically all restraints to trade – the single market programme; a major objective being to enable European business to compete more effectively with American and Japanese companies, especially in high technology industries.

The White Paper identifies three types of barriers to trade:

- physical barriers, for example, custom posts and immigration controls;
- technical barriers, for example, different product regulations and standards in different member states;
- fiscal barriers, for example, various approaches to indirect taxes.

It is generally accepted that these barriers, which resulted in a fragmented Community, have been costly to business and expensive for consumers.

At the time of writing it appeared that by the end of 1992 much, but not all, of the single market legislative programme would be in place.

An issue closely associated with the single market programme is the establishment of an economic and monetary union (EMU). Under EMU a European Central Bank would set interest rates and regulate exchange rates for all EC member states; a common currency would also be involved.

The idea of EMU is not new, for as long ago as 1970 the Werner Report set out a three-stage process for greater economic and monetary integration; but the process never really got off the ground. However, in 1979 the European Monetary System (EMS) was launched to create a zone of monetary stability in Europe, by attempting to move towards stable exchange rates within the EC. It was hoped that the EMS might become part of a step-by-step approach to complete monetary union within the EC.

The EMS operates through a mutually linked web of currency exchange rates; all participating currencies have values expressed against all other currencies and against the European Currency Unit (ECU). The ECU is used mainly for accounting purposes; it is a basket of currencies and the share of a particular member state is determined by its Gross Domestic Product. The Exchange Rate Mechanism (ERM) keeps most EC currencies tied to each other within fixed exchange rates. The currencies move as block against other world currencies, such as the dollar and the yen. EC member governments must adjust their interest rates at a level that will keep their currency at its ERM rate. For example, if a currency is falling on the money markets, a government must make it more attractive by raising interest rates. In the autumn of 1992 there were major fluctuations in the value of currencies and the UK left the ERM in October.

In December 1991 a crucial agreement was reached in Maastricht which, if ratified, would amend the original Treaty of Rome. The Maastricht Agreement brought the ideal of European integration closer to reality. The participants agreed to a political union, as well as economic and monetary union.

Under the provisions for economic and monetary union, a European Central Bank could be operating by January 1997 and Europe could have a single currency by

January 1999. The UK was granted an opt-out clause, which gave it no obligation to move towards a single currency. The new Treaty signed at Maastricht required ratification in all member states.

If EMU were achieved, currency volatility would be removed to make overseas investment decisions without the need to worry about currency risk. The second major advantage of an EMU is the costs saved in transactions; exchanging one EC currency into another involves costs which would not, of course, apply with a single currency. However, it has been argued that EMU would result in the loss of monetary sovereignty; elected parliaments would no longer have control over their national currency. Yet in reality, with the dominance of the Bundesbank, much monetary sovereignty has already been lost; for example, the interest rates of all EC countries are greatly influenced by the decisions of the Bundesbank.

At the time of writing, doubts were emerging about the reality of political and economic and monetary union; a referendum in Denmark rejected the Maastricht Agreement and in France the Agreement was accepted by a very small majority. In addition, a number of states most notably the UK, were concerned that European law was going beyond that required to uphold the free flow of people, goods and services.

The EC has a variety of agreements with other countries. There are, for example, association agreements with countries such as Turkey and Hungary and Poland which are likely to result in eventual membership. There are also Trade Agreements with a number of countries of SE Asia and Latin America. The Lomé Convention with 66 African, Caribbean and Pacific (ACP) countries gives members special trade status and, in addition, a European Development Fund has been established to provide grants and loans for capital projects. There are also co-operation agreements with other regional associations such as the Association of SE Asian Nations, as well as with individual countries, such as Israel.

THE NORTH AMERICA FREE TRADE AGREEMENT (NAFTA)

In August 1992 the governments of Canada, Mexico and the USA signed the North America Free Trade Agreement (NAFTA). This Agreement established a free trade market of 350 m people and a gross national product of $6,000 bn. This makes the zone very similar in size to the EC in terms of population and in the size of the economy. Table 3.2 gives some details about the three countries involved. The Agreement covers such areas as tariffs, rules of origins and insurance and telecommunications, as well as customs regulations, industrial standards, intellectual property rights and food safety regulations. There are also specific trade agreements for cars, sugar and textiles. For example, in the motor industry, vehicles will have to have between 50–70 per cent local content in order to avoid tariffs and Mexico will drop most tariffs on US imports to zero.

For the rest of the world, especially Asia, the NAFTA may give some cause for concern, as the US purchases and corporate investments are transferred from their economies to Mexico. Figure 3.2 illustrates the projected effects of NAFTA.

Many people hold the view that a regional trade agreement is second best to global trade liberalization. For example, in a wider negotiating forum such as GATT, Mexico can join with other developing countries to maximize negotiating leverage on industrial powers like the USA, Japan and the EC, whilst alone and heavily dependent on the USA, its negotiating clout is limited.

Table 3.2
The Three NAFTA countries

	US	Canada	Mexico
GDP per capita, 1988 (US$)	19,678	18,747	2,116
Population, mid-1988 (million)	246.33	25.95	82.73
Employment (million), 1988	118.0	12.4	7.4
% in services	69.6	69.8	31.3
% in agriculture	3.0	4.9	33.1
Industrial production as % of GDP, 1987	30	35	34
Capital goods as % of industrial production, 1987	35	25	14
Labour compensation per employee (wages plus fringes), 1988 (US$)	13.92	13.58	1.57
Per capita public expenditure on education (US$)	1,126	1,171	59
Productivity, GDP/employee, 1988 (US$)	42,161	39,733	7,935
Gross domestic investment as % of GDP, 1986–88	17.3	20.9	19.1
Expenditure on R&D as % of GDP, 1988	2.7	1.3	0.5

Source: Institute for International Economics.

David Dodwell argues that the USA will also stand to lose if regionalism undermines the multilateral trading system.[2] More than 55 per cent of US exports in 1990, totalling $393 billion, went to Europe or Asia, while less than 8 per cent went to Mexico. The wider trading interests of the USA would suggest that the NAFTA ought to complement multilateral trade reforms rather than be seen as an alternative.

THE ASSOCIATION OF SOUTH-EAST ASIAN NATIONS (ASEAN)

The creation of economic groupings of industrialized countries such as the EC focus on trade liberalization. The integration of developing countries such as ASEAN rely heavily on measures to promote and regulate investment in new, regionally based industries.

Singapore, Thailand, Malaysia, the Philippines and Indonesia have joined together to form the ASEAN. These countries are attempting to influence the pattern of industrial development. For example, an ASEAN Finance Corporation has been established to encourage new industrial investment by providing equity capital and low-cost funds for start-up initiatives. The Corporation also encourages the development of joint ventures with foreign companies and investment from outside the area, especially from Japan.

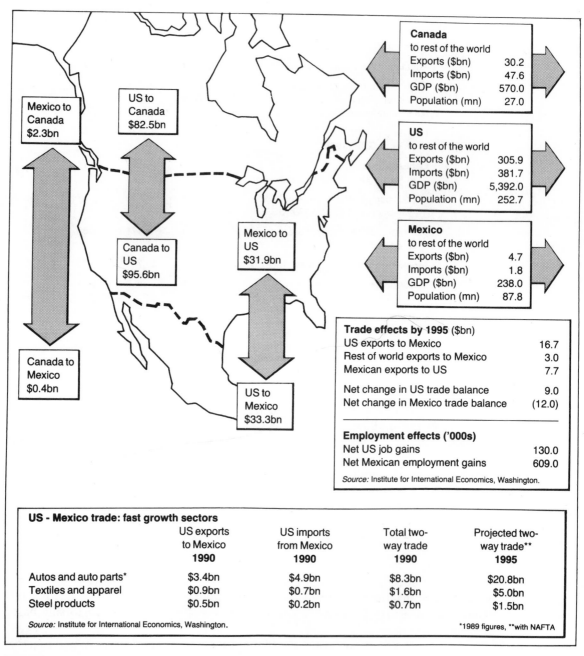

Figure 3.2
Projected effects of NAFTA
Source: *Financial Times*, 13 August 1992.

References

1 Ohmae, K., *The borderless world*, (London, Fontana, 1991).
2 See the *Financial Times*, 9 June 1992.

Bibliography

Bhagwati, J., *International trade*, (Massachusetts, MIT Press, 1987).
Greenway, D., *Current issues in international trade*, (London, Macmillan, 1987).
Griffiths, A., (Editor) *European Survey*, (Harlow, Longman, 1992).
Helleiner, G., *Trade policy, internalization and development*, (London, Clarendon Press, 1992).
Helleiner, G., *Intra-firm trade and the developing countries*, (London, Macmillan, 1985).
Helpman, E., *Trade policy and market structure*, (Massachusetts, MIT Press, 1989).

CHAPTER FOUR

DEREGULATION AS A PROMOTER OF INTERNATIONAL BUSINESS

JILL PRESTON

INTRODUCTION

A reduction in the role of the state became a feature of many economies in the 1980s and this, in turn, had the effect of encouraging business at the international level. Until the 1970s, Keynesian interventionism in the economy enjoyed wide political support from both right and left wing parties across the Western World.

Regulation of the private sector of the economy by government has existed for centuries. It is considered essential, for instance, that there should be some regulation of the financial system to protect the public from the insolvency of financial institutions and maintain the public confidence in the system. But by the 1970s it was argued that government regulation in many countries went far beyond the needs of the public interest. These regulations were in some instances highly restrictive; for example, regulation of specific product features, such as price, had the effect of limiting competition. Furthermore, differences in national regulatory systems resulted in major barriers to market access. A company wishing to expand internationally had to comply with different and often restrictive national regulatory systems.

The economic crisis of the 1970s and early 1980s raised doubts in the minds of many about the adequacy of state interventionist policies. And from the 1970s there has been a strong preference among economists and most governments of the Western World, as well as an increasing number of developing countries, to return to the principles of the free market and to reduce the level of government intervention. Deregulation is an expression of this move.

From the mid 1970s there has been a steady increase in the number of countries implementing deregulatory policies. This had the effect of reducing the differences that existed between national regulatory systems, which in turn has become a strong incentive for the internationalization of markets.

DEREGULATION IN THE USA

The USA was the starting-point for the move towards deregulation in the 1970s and the 1980s. In 1975 the US authorities abolished fixed rates for US securities brokers and introduced the Securities Amendments Acts, which provided for the development of interlinked competitive securities markets. This was followed by deregulation of the transport sector.

In 1976 the Railroad Revitalization and Reform Act increased the rate setting freedom for railways. In 1978 the Air Deregulation Act introduced progressive, and eventually total, deregulation of entry, rates and operations in the air transport industry; and in 1979 the International Air Transport Act provided for maximum reliance on competitive market forces in international airline agreements. As a result of this legislation, an agreement was reached in 1982 between the USA and a number of European countries, on the introduction of zones of rate freedom on North Atlantic air routes.

In 1980 banking was deregulated in the USA, following the Depository Institutions and Monetary Control Act. This enabled the elimination of controls on deposit interest rates and the easing of restrictions on the permitted range of lending activities.

Deregulatory measures were also introduced in the telecommunications sector. Until the 1980s, the private telephone system was operating under a strict regulatory régime which restricted both efficiency and competition in the market; 1980 saw the liberalization of long distance services. For many years American Telephone and Telegraph (ATT) was the only supplier of international voice communication in the USA, and only ITT and Western Union International were able to offer international and data transfer services. However, with the liberalization of these services, Sprint and Graphnet entered the market.

ATT was the only supplier of terminal equipment, but with liberalization in the early 1980s competition was introduced and new equipment companies were developed. By the middle of the decade private telephone users were able to purchase their own equipment, such as microwave facilities and fibre optics systems, from companies such as Philips, as well as from ATT.

The general deregulatory initiative was reinforced under the Reagan administration when new measures were adopted in the field of anti-trust policies. Concentrated industries were viewed in a more positive light as a result of their exploitation of scale economies and their ability to compete internationally.

DEREGULATION IN THE UK

The experiments carried out in the USA attracted world-wide attention. During the 1980s, with the advent of Thatcherism, it was the UK that made the most pronounced changes towards a free market economy, including the deregulation of a number of service sectors, most notably finance and transport.

In the financial services sector, it was the decline of London as an international finance centre which was a major factor behind deregulation. By this time all the major financial markets had become more global in character, which had left the traditional financial market in London less than competitive. The trading of UK shares by large companies was taking place in financial centres other than London, and £ billions-worth of portfolio investment was leaving the UK.

In 1986 in response to this situation, the UK authorities launched the 'big bang' – a major deregulation effort which transformed the whole nature of UK financial markets. The 'big bang' brought considerable changes in every segment of the financial sector. Access to particular markets was eased and foreign firms were allowed a 100 per cent ownership of member firms, as opposed to the former ceiling of 29.9 per cent. As a result, a considerable number of foreign financial firms, especially from the USA but also from continental Europe and Japan, acquired member firms within the UK Stock Exchange. Moreover, the competitive rates for listing and trading of securities after the 'big bang' increased the attractiveness of London as a world-wide financial centre. Increasingly, continental European banks and other financial institutions made London their home for capital market operations.

The 'big bang' was the first step toward deregulation in Europe. London had not only made itself a centre for financial trading within Europe, but it had also become the route through which institutional funds from Japan and the USA flowed into Europe.

In the UK the transport sector was subject to deregulation legislation; for example, the Transport Act 1980 removed the regulation of express coaches and buses. In the air transport industry controls over entry, fares and operation were eased and the Civil Aviation Authority authorized more than one airline to provide a particular service. The gradual process of deregulation covered not only national, but also international, rules. For example, the UK relaxed the rules concerning traffic between countries and liberalization treaties were signed with Germany in 1984, the Netherlands in 1984, Luxemburg in 1985, Belgium in 1985 and Ireland in 1988; these significantly deregulated air services between the respective countries.

Deregulation was also introduced into other sectors of the UK economy, such as energy and telecommunications. In these sectors nationalized industries were stripped of their statutory monopolies to allow for more competition. Until 1981 British Telecom operated as a monopolistic supplier for the whole UK telecommunication sector. In 1981, with the passing of the Telecommunication Act, British Telecom's monopoly came to an end. From 1983, Mercury was allowed to provide international services and by the end of the decade, most telecommunication services nationally. In addition, Cable and Wireless, the owners of Mercury, were allowed to build a transatlantic, fibre-optics cable in order to increase international competitiveness. At this time, the British authorities also liberalized the controls on prices of international calls, pay-phone calls, telex and mobile radio services. The aim of these measures was to enable new entrants to be able to compete on fairer terms with British Telecom.

DEREGULATION IN FRANCE

During the 1980s the focus for deregulatory polices moved from the UK to continental Europe, especially France. Until the 1980s one of the most significant structural features of the French economy was the high degree of central government involvement and control. This was reflected in the state's planning and regulatory functions, as well as the degree of nationalization; and until the 1980s, France had one of the most regulated financial systems.

The capital market in France was fragmented: the banks were not allowed to trade in securities and the system was dominated by government debt. In addition, investment banks were not allowed to take deposits from the public, and commercial banks were not encouraged to take shareholdings in industry, nor could they participate in the French Stock Exchange. At the same time, commissions and price movement in the financial sector were controlled by the state. As early as 1989, it was obvious that competition from British financial firms was adversely affecting the profits of French organizations. For example, the French Stock Market was losing a large share of trade in financial products to London.

In an attempt to regain the initiative, the French authorities implemented a major programme of reform which was designed to remove unnecessary controls and to improve efficiency. In view of the competition from London, New York and Frankfurt, the French authorities were particularly concerned that the strict, national, regulatory régime was threatening the position of Paris as a major financial centre.

The liberalization of the financial system in France was further encouraged by the removal of foreign exchange controls in 1989. In the mid 1980s a new Banking Act introduced competition into the banking system, as it removed many of the restrictions on the banks. For example, banks and other financial institutions were allowed to participate in the Stock Exchange, while the level of charges was left to market forces. At the same time a computerized system for continuous trading was introduced, which enabled continuous dealing with automated clearing. After the reforms had been implemented, the French and British financial markets operated under similar regulatory frameworks.

By 1989 two-thirds of France's 60 stock exchange firms had opened up to participants from other financial institutions; a quarter of these were foreign companies. By the early 1990s all the big French banks were present on the Stock Exchange, as were foreign firms, such as James Capel, National Westminster, and Warburg.

The reforms in the financial sector were implemented quickly. However, in the other sectors very little has been achieved as many of the proposed reforms were blocked by local political factors.

DEREGULATION IN ITALY AND SPAIN

The trend towards deregulation in both Italy and Spain included the liberalization of capital outflows, the reduction of entry barriers into the national financial market and the complete liberalization of legal constraints which separated deposit business and securities business.

THE EUROPEAN COMMUNITY

At the European level, attitudes within the EC have been greatly influenced by the economic state of Europe, in relation to the USA, Japan, and the new industrial powers of the Pacific rim. The EC aimed to liberalize and integrate the service sectors, thus encouraging competition and the free mobility of goods, services and capital, the overriding objective being to improve the competitiveness of European firms in the global market-place.

In the early 1980s the EC Commission was concerned about the lack of progress towards a single market. A major reason for this lack of progress was the feeling that freedom of establishment and freedom to provide services across borders could not safely be granted, without first carrying out a complete harmonization of individual national laws and regulations.

The EC Commission's White Paper, 'Completing the internal market', shifted the emphasis away from the harmonization of regulatory systems towards the principle of 'home country control' and the 'mutual recognition' by EC Member States of each other's systems. One result of this change in approach was that the authorities of the strictly regulated states, such as Germany, have had to ease their regulatory régimes. If this had not happened, domestic firms in Germany would inevitably have faced very stiff competition from more flexible operators.

The liberalization of capital movements is a major element of European deregulation and is closely linked to the freedom of providing financial services. The elimination of all restrictions on capital flows allows financial intermediaries the freedom to offer services throughout the EC.

A major step towards capital movement liberalization took place in 1988, when the Community adopted legislation requiring Member States to liberalize capital movements before the end of 1992. At the time of writing, only Portugal and Greece imposed controls on the movements of capital.

In the financial field, the most fundamental piece of EC legislation is the Second Banking Coordination Directive adopted in 1989 for implementation in 1993. This Directive provides that any banking organization established in one Member State would be allowed to open branches in all the others; its operation being governed by the supervisory authorities of the country where the head office is situated. This legislation was passed to overcome the barriers imposed by host country supervisory authorities, which included the type of services that banks can offer.

In the area of transportation, the White Paper envisaged that the EC should move to a more liberalized régime in areas such as entry and tariff control; the aim being to bring to this sector the same benefits and opportunities of a single market, which consumers of manufacturing products enjoyed. In this context a series of measures was adopted, and by the end of 1992 some progress had been made in the field of fare controls and access to routes for Member States' transport undertakings.

In the field of telecommunications, the EC's Commission is attempting to integrate the telecommunication sectors of the 12 Member States. The aim is to the provision of telecommunication services and of technical equipment liberalize both within and between Member States. However, the attitude of the majority of EC Member States, which still consider telecommunications as a natural monopoly, has restricted progress in this sector.

Partly as a result of these deregulation policies, Japan's foreign direct investment (FDI) increased in the financial and manufacturing sectors in both the EC and USA. For example, in 1981 the EC accounted for 8.9 per cent of Japanese FDI, but by 1990 this had grown to 18.7 per cent. Clearly, this form of investment increases the integration of the world economy. The case study of Nissan illustrates this point.

JAPAN

Liberalization also gained momentum in Japan, especially in the financial and telecommunications sectors. For example, in the late 1980s the Japanese authorities approved the entrance of any type of financial institution into wholesale banking.

Controls such as interest rates and commissions were also liberalized at this time. In addition, the restrictions on the entry and establishment of foreign banks in Japan were eased. At the same time, foreign securities firms without a branch in Japan were allowed to do dealing and broking business with any resident in Japan.

By the late 1980s more than 80 foreign banks were operating in Japan, with assets of around ¥17,000 billion as compared to ¥7 billion in the late 1970s. In addition, as a result of deregulation, the penetration of the Japanese market by foreign firms increased not only in terms of FDI, but also in trade.

In 1985 the Japanese Government adopted new laws to liberalize controls on its tightly regulated telecommunications sector. Until 1985 Japanese telecommunications were monopolized by Nippon Telephone and Telegraph (NTT), while international telecommunications were controlled by Kokusai, Denshin & Denwa (KDD). The new legislation introduced competition and allowed new organizations, including foreign companies, to enter the market. This sector was not completely deregulated, as approval in the form of licensing from the national authorities was still required.

Since 1985 a number of Japanese, as well as foreign, companies have become active as telecommunication suppliers in competition with NTT and KDD. In 1989 a group of international companies, including Cable and Wireless, and the American Nynex and Pacific Telesis, was granted a licence to offer a world-wide service network.

DEVELOPING COUNTRIES

We saw in an earlier chapter that by the 1970s, developing countries were liberalizing their trade régimes. At the same time many were also attempting to increase the role of market forces in their domestic economy and reduce the level of state intervention. The authorities in these countries changed the regulatory framework adopting outward-orientated policies, improving the business climate and encouraging foreign investment. The aim of these reforms was to increase competition and encourage greater efficiency.

Previously the authorities favoured a controlled economic system, since it allowed them to exercise control over resource allocation according to their political objectives. The access by foreign institutions to the domestic market was restricted, because there was some fear in allowing certain domestic industries to be controlled by foreigners.

However, external developments made it difficult to maintain a tightly regulated system, while the effects of economic isolation were having harmful effects for many developing countries. For example, restrictions on the free flow of funds had reduced the availability of financial resources and thus increased the cost of credit to the private sector. As a result of this, the authorities of many developing countries, especially in Taiwan and Latin America, implemented a wide range of reforms, especially in the financial sectors. Such policies included the reduction of interest rates and credit controls, as well as the easing of restrictions on international capital mobility.

The regulatory reform was not only concerned with the freer functioning of the domestic market, but also with the reduction of barriers to the entry of foreign firms. One of the main objectives of allowing the entry of these organizations, many of whom had superior technology at their disposal, was to encourage greater competition, in the hope of improving productivity within the home banks. For example, in 1990, foreign banks were given greater entry opportunities in Taiwan;

prior to that date foreign banks were not permitted to provide consumer loans. Partly as a result of these reforms, Citibank opened three new branches in Taiwan and introduced new products, including lending to individuals.

The new laws also provided for the entry of foreign securities companies and financial institutions into the securities business, as well as the foreign ownership of domestic securities companies. The same laws allowed securities companies to engage separately or concurrently in any combination of the three business areas: underwriting, dealing and brokerage. Up to 1990 securities companies could engage in, and obtain a securities licence for, only one of these three business areas.

As a result of deregulation, many companies in developing countries looked beyond their own financial markets to raise funds. The new regulatory framework permitted them to diversify their funding base by issuing securities abroad. Clearly, these developments have increased the level of integration in the global economy.

The financial reforms undertaken in developing countries were different in terms of both the types of measure and the speed of implementation. For example, in Korea and Taiwan, these reforms were sustained over a long period; whereas in other countries, for example, Chile and Argentina, the reforms were abandoned. Where reforms were abandoned, it was often the case that the beneficial effects did not emerge clearly or quickly. For example, in Chile domestic interest rates failed to move downwards as expected. This was due in part to the nature of the domestic financial sector and its uncompetitive structure.

Unstable domestic conditions were another reason for the eventual failure of reforms in some developing countries. Fiscal problems led to capital outflow, which in turn resulted in an increase in gross external debt. In other cases, government departments failed to prevent their financial institutions from funding risky enterprises. This resulted in many insolvencies.

CONCLUSIONS

The reduced role of the state has been a major factor in the integration of the global economy. To take the example of bank lending: Table 4.1 shows that the amount of international bank lending, that is cross-border lending plus domestic lending dominated in foreign currency, was $7.5 trillion as opposed to only $324 millions in 1980. In terms of the OECD GDP, this lending has risen from 4 per cent to 44 per cent.

Securities transactions have also increased substantially in many countries. Table 4.2 reveals that in 1970 the USA's securities transactions with foreigners as a percentage of the country's GDP was only 3 per cent. In 1980 the figure was 9 per cent and in 1990 it had grown to 93 per cent. The respective figures for Japan are 2 per cent, 7 per cent and 119 per cent and for Germany, 3 per cent, 8 per cent and 58 per cent.

Liberalization has had a major impact on the international organization of banks. The elimination of operational constraints and the freedom for residents to hold accounts abroad have provided new opportunities for branches of domestic banks active in the international markets. On the other hand, there has been an increasing trend for financial institutions to enter foreign markets in order to develop local domestic business, thus increasing the competitive pressures on indigenous institutions.

Table 4.1
Stock of international bank lending

	1980	1990
in absolute terms	$32.4 million	$7.5 trillion
as % of OECD GDP	4	44

Source: Adapted from the Bank of International Settlements.

Table 4.2
Securities transactions* with foreigners as % of GDP

	1970	1980	1990
US	3	9	93
W Germany	3	8	58
Japan	2	7	119

* Gross sales and purchases of bonds and equities involving a resident and a non-resident.

Source: Adapted from the Bank of International Settlements.

Bibliography

Dooley, M., 'Financial Liberalization in Developing Countries', *Finance and Development*, September 1989.

'Liberalizing Capital Movements', *The OECD Observer*, June 1992.

Majone, G., *Deregulation or Reregulation*, (London, Pinter, 1990).

Melitz, J., 'Financial Deregulation', *European Economic Review*, January 1991.

Swann, D., 'Deregulation and its Problems', *Journal of Common Market Studies*, June 1989.

'World Economy', *The Economist*, 19 September 1992.

Yoshinari, K., 'Assessing the International Capital Markets', *Finance and Development*, September 1991.

CHAPTER FIVE

———

PRIVATIZATION – A GLOBAL PHENOMENON

JILL PRESTON

INTRODUCTION

Privatization has been a major element of the economic liberalization of the 1980s and early 1990s. It has been one of the most significant economic trends in many industrialized nations, as well as in an increasing number of developing countries. The underlying idea behind privatization is that increased efficiency is gained by increasing the role of market forces. Many state-run organizations have been sold to the private sector. In most countries, privatization has provided both domestic and foreign organizations with additional business opportunities. Thus this trend has encouraged the internationalization of business activity.

Until the 1980s nationalized industries were viewed by many states as an appropriate way to protect national production; ensure the availability of supply; and support a range of social policies. In many countries the state-owned sector accounted for more than 20 per cent of GDP.

During the 1980s state ownership went out of fashion in favour of economic liberalism; some argued that national enterprises were too vulnerable to the political interference of government, whilst at the same time operating under a bureaucratic strait-jacket. In many states, especially developing countries, state-owned enterprises operated at substantial deficit and were responsible for as much as 50 per cent of all domestic debt.

The arguments for privatization include the following points:

- The private sector provides greater incentives for efficiency.
- By reducing government involvement in decision making privatization provides a good way of giving management the independence to develop appropriate business strategies.
- Private producers are more responsive to the needs of consumers and are able to offer a wider range of goods and services.

Budgetary problems had encouraged a number of governments to consider privatization as a means of raising finance without increasing taxation.

PRIVATIZATION IN THE WESTERN WORLD

Many European countries have implemented privatization policies. For example, in the 1980s and early 1990s, the sale of public enterprises was a major part of the UK Government's policy to 'roll back the frontiers of the state'. During the 1980s the numbers employed in the state sector was reduced from just over 9 per cent to well under 5 per cent of the workforce. The aim was to raise capital, promote competition and reduce government involvement in the decision-making process.

In the first part of the 1980s, privatized companies such as British Aerospace, Britoil, Cable and Wireless and Amersham International were each operating in a competitive industry. After 1984, the privatization programme accelerated dramatically and included a considerable number of former state monopolies, such as British Telecom, British Petroleum, and British Gas, and the state-owned part of the water industry. The newly privatized companies were allowed to borrow freely from the capital market, without the restrictions imposed on the public sector. This policy offered a range of opportunities to foreign as well as domestic companies. A number of these privatized corporations lost no time in seeking a presence in international markets through systematic acquisitions abroad. For example, British Telecom acquired the US data communications group Tymnet.

In France many state-owned assets were sold to private investors, including the two investment banking groups, Suez and Paridas, and Société Général. But in both France and Italy the more ambitious privatization programmes were blocked by local political considerations.

Since 1988 Spain has sold $535 million worth of state-controlled companies; for example, in September 1990 a 60 per cent stake in ENASA, the state-controlled truck maker was sold to Fiat. In Portugal, Central de Cervegas, a state-owned drinks company, was sold. The state electricity and oil-and-gas producers were also among the candidates for full or partial privatization.

In the late 1980s the German Government announced the sale of shares in Lufthansa, the national airline and Deutsche Telecom, the state-owned telecoms corporation. However, the German Government holds the majority of shares in both of these organizations. On privatization VIAG, the German aluminium, energy and chemicals group, purchased interests in the Netherlands, Spain and the USA. In Germany privatization was seen as a means of reducing the public sector borrowing requirement in the light of the increasing costs of German reunification, rather than as a policy to improve economic performance by increasing competition.

In the former East Germany privatization is a major objective. In 1990 the Trenhadanstalt, the public agency responsible for privatization, arranged the sale of more than 300 companies worth $1.3 billion. In 1992 the agency had over 5000 enterprises looking for buyers.

In the USA the sale of state-owned enterprises began in the late 1980s. The Federal Government owns very few companies; these include the Amtrack railway, the US air traffic control network and some electric power systems. It is the state governments in the USA which own a wide range of enterprises, especially in the area of infrastructure, such as airports, roads and bridges. Many state governments adopted programmes of privatization. This provided a range of opportunities for international financial institutions, corporate investors and consultancy firms with expertise in privatization programmes. In addition, the private sector in the USA was encouraged to finance the construction of new facilities such as toll roads.

European financial and consultancy firms such as SG Warburg, the British merchant bank, have provided both finance and advice on privatization.

ASIA

Countries in Asia, including Hong Kong, Indonesia, Singapore, South Korea and Taiwan, are turning control of many government assets to the private sector. For example, Taiwan has partly privatized the three state-owned banks: Chang Hua, First Commercial, and Hua Nan.

DEVELOPING COUNTRIES

In many developing countries such as Argentina, Chile, India, Mexico, and Turkey, privatization programmes are being implemented. For example, in Argentina the government has sold its major telecommunication monopoly, the national airline and a petrochemical company.

In developing countries, privatization has tended to result from external pressures from international aid agencies, the World Bank and the International Monetary Fund, rather than from an ideological belief that the state's role in the economy should be reduced. These organizations view privatization as one way of reducing the public sector debt.

However, in most developing countries only a small proportion of state-owned assets have been privatized. This is due to the limited development of capital markets and the shortage of domestic capital. At the same time, the offering of ownership rights to foreign investors is often ruled out on protectionist grounds; there is the feeling that a strategic industry should not be controlled from abroad.

EASTERN EUROPE

Since 1989 an increasing number of countries in eastern Europe have begun to establish a free market economy, or at least to incorporate free market elements into their own economic systems. Privatization is a major part of these reforms and is seen as a pre-condition for the development of a market economy. In Poland and Hungary the state-owned sector represents two-thirds of the economy, and in other countries as much as 90 per cent. The aim is to encourage new investors at home and abroad, as well as encouraging new corporate initiatives.

The economic reforms have created opportunities in the form of joint ventures between foreign and domestic partners, but there are major difficulties in realizing these opportunities. In a report by Paul Reynolds and Peter Young, it is clear that the hopes that privatization would be achieved by the early 1990s have turned out be 'wildly optimistic'.[1] Reynolds and Young argue that at the present rate it will take Poland, Czechoslovakia and Hungary an average of 28 years to privatize only half of the state companies. It also has to be stated that the opportunities for international business activity will be drastically reduced if political stability is in question. The case study of Arthur Andersen shows how one organization is taking advantage of the business opportunities resulting from these reforms.

Eastern Europe has become a major element in the struggle by European and US car makers to reduce their costs and to increase market share in their global struggle with the Japanese producers. For example, Fiat, Ford, General Motors and Volkswagen have made substantial investments in new assembly plants and component factories in the former East Germany, Czechoslovakia, Hungary and Poland. The Rover Group is involved in a joint venture with the Bulgarian defence ministry to assemble cars as well as Land Rovers and pick-up trucks, at former military factories. Low wage costs of around 10 per cent of German levels for assembly line workers were a major attraction.

In Poland the Law on the Privatization of State-owned Enterprises of 1990 set the foundations for broadly based privatization. The first five large-scale state-owned enterprises were privatized in 1990 with sale of their shares to the public. Foreigners were able to acquire up to 10 per cent of the equity of a Polish company; larger participations required prior approval of the Bureau for Foreign Investments.

The objective of this large-scale programme is the privatization of 8,000 state-controlled companies. A small scale privatization programme was launched in 1990 to divest to private investors the lease of small- and medium-size companies still in the state's hands. The Polish approach to mass privatization is based on the belief that it can attract western-trained managers by a fee and an incentive scheme.[2]

However, there are concerns about the unfamiliarity of these managers with the Polish-type socio-economic conditions. The economic reforms have involved other areas such as pricing which, with the exceptions of areas such as housing and energy, is almost free of state intervention. Controls on foreign direct investment have also been liberalized and it is possible to establish wholly foreign-owned companies. However, because of the difficult foreign exchange situation, profit transfers are still restricted.

In Hungary the Assets Bureau established in 1990 was given the task of implementing the government's privatization policy. By 1992 about 30,000 out of the 55,000 state-controlled small- and medium-size companies had been sold by auction. The Assets Bureau is also inviting international bids for the purchase of larger companies. Foreign access to the Hungarian market, through equity participation in domestic companies, has been liberalized. The national authorities do not impose controls on the maximum degree of non-resident participation in the capital stock of a Hungarian company, or on the repatriation of profits. Furthermore, the extensive de-control of prices, the liberalization of foreign trade and the gradual introduction of convertibility of the domestic currency have made the country fairly attractive to foreign investors as well as accelerating the integration of Hungary into the global economy. It has been estimated that of all the joint ventures undertaken by the end of 1992 in eastern European states, about one third are located in Hungary. This point is illustrated by Table 5.1 overleaf.

In Bulgaria the national law was amended in 1990 to include the general right of private ownership of the means of production. The national authorities privatized about 10,000 small companies, such as retailers, restaurants and other service companies, out of the total 35,000 to 40,000 companies of this type. At the time of writing, the government was hoping to privatize half of its state-owned industrial sector by the end of 1994. Foreigners and Bulgarian residents were granted equal opportunities to acquire shares. In addition, the government has introduced legislation to allow the operation of wholly owned foreign companies in Bulgaria.

Table 5.1
Joint ventures with selected
Eastern European countries in
1991

Hungary	5,000
Poland	3,000
Czechoslovakia	1,700
Former Soviet Union	2,600

Source: Adapted from the Austrian
Economics Ministry

However, the implementation of price reform proved to be very difficult and in many cases, the reduction of state subsidies triggered drastic price increases.

In Russia the privatization programme is particularly complex. In the first stage, vouchers giving the bearer the right to purchase company shares are to be distributed to every member of the public through 40,000 branches of savings banks across the country. Between 5000 and 7000 enterprises, representing about 70 per cent of Russia's productive capacity, are completing privatization plans. In theory, foreigners are in most cases as free as Russians to purchase shares. In practice, it seemed likely in 1992 that few foreign buyers would be involved until an ownership and control pattern had emerged.

In most countries of eastern Europe, national authorities still impose some restrictions on foreign access to the domestic market through majority equity participation in domestic companies. Most of these countries are wary that the openness of the domestic market must not extend to a point that the control of the domestic economic system passes to foreign investors. However, foreign minority participation in domestic firms is seen as a means of acquiring the sophisticated managerial capacity, expertise and technology which major multinational groups possess. The acquisition of these factors is seen as means by which domestic companies can produce new products and increase their capacity to export.

Most of the countries in eastern Europe have established or are in the process of establishing, a new legislative framework for the banking and financial systems. The aim is that all the old and newly founded banks enter the market fully responsible for their operations; for example, in the way that they allocate scarce resources to the most productive uses.

Financial institutions in eastern Europe are facing considerable difficulty in adapting to this competition-oriented environment. They suffer from a lack of know-how and technological infrastructure, and accounting and auditing practices are still far from adequate. Both the old and newly founded banks have a limited capital base, one factor being that the capital markets are underdeveloped. The banks are having particular difficulties in sourcing the substantial capital increases that are necessary. The commercial banks that have evolved out of formerly state-owned banks, are also faced with the problem of outstanding loans to companies, which resulted from the past imposed planning targets. A considerable proportion of these loans cannot be collected, as many of the companies in question are in a very weak financial position.

Only Hungary seems to have a relatively advanced banking system, with a comparatively large number of commercial banks, specialized banks and a few investment banks. Banks operating as joint ventures with foreign partners play an important role in the Hungarian market. This country is trying to foster the inflow of foreign capital by improving the conditions imposed on foreign banks entering the national market. Western banks, primarily from Europe, have already founded a large number of joint venture banks in Hungary.

The serious shortage of capital and the challenges of privatization make the establishment of an efficient stock and bond market an urgent requirement in east European countries. The first securities exchange in eastern Europe was opened in Budapest in June 1990. Many companies were listed for official trading, including the Postbank Corp, the Konzum Ltd department store, the Muszi Ltd service company and the Duna holding, an asset management company. The opening of the Hungarian exchange coincided with the start of trading in Hungarian issues on the exchange in Vienna.

A stock exchange was also opened in Warsaw in 1991 and the banks, such as Bank Gdanski, Bank Slaski and Bank Wielkopolski, began issuing and selling stock in the first five state-owned enterprises that had been privatized. Foreign investors are allowed to buy and sell stock in this market.

The existence of effective stock and bond markets are of crucial importance for companies and the state to cover their financial needs without having to create money, a move which leads to accelerated inflation and undermining confidence in the currency. However, the nominal values of shares are relatively high, scaring away domestic investors.

Generally speaking, privatization, the liberalization of controls on foreign investment and free external trade are assisting in the integration of eastern European countries into the international market. However, the economic adjustment problems are great. The move from central control to a market economy is particularly difficult where there are few entrepreneurial skills.

CONCLUSIONS

The trend towards economic liberalization in general and privatization in particular has had a major impact on business activity. The shift in ownership or control from public to private hands should lead to further increased competition and cost reductions. However, in many east European states and developing countries the problems involved in developing a market economy are likely to reduce these benefits considerably in the short to medium term.

References

1 Reynolds, Paul, and Young, Peter, *Eastern Promise*, Adam Smith Institute, October 1992.
2 *Commission of the EC Economic Survey for Europe 1991–2*, New York, 1992.

Bibliography

Corbo, Vittorio, *Reforming central and eastern European economies – initial results and challenges*, The World Bank, 1991.
Deutsche Bank Special Reports on eastern Europe, 1989, 1990 and 1991.

Goodwin, J., 'Does privatization serve the public interest?', *Harvard Business Review*, November/December 1991.

'Privatization in eastern Europe' IMF, July 1990.

Jenson, M., 'The eclipse of the public corporation', *Harvard Business Review*, September/October 1989.

Stevens, B., 'Prospects for privatization in OECD countries', *National Westminster Bank Quarterly Review*, August 1992.

Vernon R., *The promise of privatization*, New York, 1991.

Vickers, J., 'Economic perspectives on privatization', *Journal of economic perspectives*, Spring 1991.

CHAPTER SIX

TECHNOLOGY AS AN AGENT OF INTERNATIONALIZATION

MIKE HEWINS

The liberalization of trade and the process of deregulation are two trends within the global business environment which are having a crucial impact on the development of international business. Within the framework of these trends technology promotes internationalization by providing new economies in manufacturing and service, based on global scale operations. It is a vehicle that delivers goods and services at ever lower costs. It can often reduce production costs by more than the cost increases imposed by transient local factors, such as labour rates or currency fluctuations. Matsushita, between 1985 and 1987, reduced the cost of its video recorders by 20 per cent, despite a 46 per cent appreciation in the yen, for example. Many other Japanese industries have been outstandingly successful in using this aspect of technology to achieve global growth, reducing prices in world markets to levels lower than their competitors could profitably sustain.

However, technology goes much further. It encourages more extensive internationalization by offering a vision of new markets which can exist meaningfully only in an international setting. Satellite communication and air travel, unknown until new technologies arrived, are two such examples which have become multi-billion pound businesses. In this context, technology behaves not just as the vehicle for lower costs, but also sets a target to develop an entirely new business or international trade. It offers the option to make markets which have no existence in a purely national setting. Organizations with a strategy for growth through international trade can target such markets through technology's new products. Technology is only one of four elements of innovation, however: without a co-operative blend of technology, marketing, logistics and finance, innovation would rapidly grind to a halt. Before developing the role of technology further, we should pause to consider what is meant by technology.

WHAT IS TECHNOLOGY?

Perhaps the simplest definition is, 'the practical application of science, new or old, to meet a need or solve a problem'. A simple illustration is applying salt to roads in winter: this application of science, lowering the freezing point of water by adding salt to it, is the simplest and earliest form of what is now called 'de-icing technology'. The technology has grown beyond the simple spreading of salt to include highly sophisticated systems which keep airport runways open, prevent ice building up on aircraft wings, and remove frost from car windscreens.

Most modern technology is really a combination of several others. The de-icer used on car windscreens combines two, aerosol and chemical technologies; supersonic flight combines scores of technologies, including special metals, upper atmosphere engines, wing shapes and others. It is this innovative combination, supported by finance, marketing and logistics, that allows technology to be both the vehicle and target for internationalization. The OECD Frascati Manual brings these various elements together and talks about 'technological innovation' as:

> ... *the transformation of an idea into a new or improved saleable product or operational process in industry and commerce or into a new approach to a social service. It thus consists of all those scientific, technological, commercial and financial steps necessary for the successful development and marketing of new or improved manufactured products, the commercial use of new or improved processes and equipment or the introduction of a new approach to a social service.*[1]

This broader definition is more useful than the earlier one because it emphasizes the imaginative combining of technology, science, commerce and finance. It stresses the idea of saleable products and services, that is those capable of growth and profit. Technology can result in reduced prices and the promotion of growth, but there are many instances where this has not yet happened. Supersonic passenger flight is just one of many such cases where, even after some 20 years, the return on assets employed clearly signalled failure in conventional financial terms, because growth had not occurred. In general, however, technology is successful for company profit and growth; just how successful?

THE VALUE OF TECHNOLOGY

An analysis across several companies by Collier *et al.*, linking historic spending on innovation with current revenue, revealed a strong relationship to gross margins which increased by circa 50 per cent, with quite modest increases in the funding of technology via R&D spending.[2] This is summarised in Figure 6.1. More significantly, this relationship points to the long-term loss of growth if technology funding is reduced. Within global markets, a more dramatic proof of the growth achievable from technology is afforded by the UK pharmaceutical industry. These global companies have achieved a profit growth of 22 per cent average compound annual rate over 1984 to 1989;[3] Figure 6.2 shows Glaxo with 32 per cent growth.

This growth is not due to technology alone, but most pharmaceutical companies attribute a large proportion of their success to it. It is not confined to pharmaceuticals. Within an entirely different sector of manufacturing, Komatsu increased its share of the world market for earth-moving equipment from 11.3 per cent in 1976 to 25 per cent in 1984, spending on average some £240 million per year on engineering and innovation. The Philips' case study gives a detailed picture of the value of technology

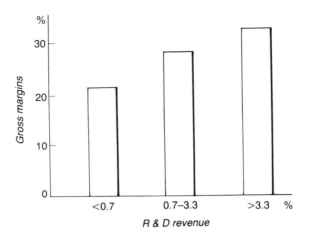

Figure 6.1
Gross margins rising with increasing R & D spending

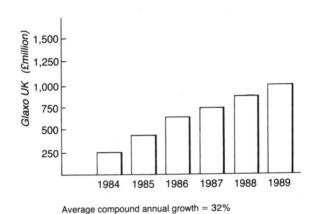

Average compound annual growth = 32%

Figure 6.2
Profit growth in Glaxo UK

to another industry, consumer electronics. Continued funding of this technology is predicted by some to make it Europe's largest manufacturing industry by the year 2000. The case studies of the NEC Corporation, Nissan and NH Geotech show how a wide variety of companies are using technology to obtain competitive advantage.

The value of technology is easy to see within manufacturing industries, but it is not confined to them. The OECD Frascati Manual links technology with services to customers.[1] Banking and airlines are two international service industries which have invested heavily in technology and shown great innovation in its use. The case study of the Midland Bank illustrates this point. To take another example, credit transactions for American Express are authorized in any country in the world by electronically interrogating a single data base held in mid-Western USA.

Given such a strong picture of profitable growth by using technology within international organizations, which aspects of technology have most significance for international trade? The Frascati definition identifies two, new products and new processes; and there is a third, Information Technology, not identified. We will briefly examine these three in turn.

NEW PRODUCTS AND SERVICES

The opening paragraphs of this chapter singled out products that have no significant markets in a national sense, but depend on internationalization; for example, satellite communications and modern air travel. Their importance and numbers will grow rapidly in the 1990s and beyond. The development of new products and services is without doubt the most obvious example of technology's international influence. The case of Marconi/NobelTech illustrates this point.

Even products with truly national markets are internationally manufactured, internationally distributed and internationally marketed. White goods, TVs and personal computers, for instance, are made and distributed on a global scale. NEC's products are developed on a global scale and a similar point can be made about the agricultural machinery made by NH Geotech, as illustrated in the appropriate case. This internationalization is a direct response to recovering the investment costs of development and production. These costs are very large for any high technology product, whether it has international or national markets. Not only are the costs high, but the time-spans available for their recovery are continuously reducing as product life shortens. Only a global market offers the necessary scale for rapid investment recovery. By offering ever improved versions of goods and services, it is technology which drives product life-times down. It is the vehicle for designing and engineering at an ever increasing rate. The mountain bike case study shows how technology has been used to develop ever improved versions of this product, as well as driving product life-time down.

Figure 6.3 illustrates this point for the consumer electronics industry, where in ten years model life has shortened by 40 per cent and models have proliferated twelvefold amongst major Japanese producers.

Similar pictures are emerging in services and any other industries where the pace of technological innovation and the demands of an affluent market combine to give more features and facilities per unit of price. For instance, US automotive manufacturers produce a new model every 10 years, but their Japanese competitors now produce one every four years;[4] a point discussed in the Nissan case. Development and marketing capital investments must be recovered within a shorter life-cycle. The problem is compounded by the ever increasing investment needed to provide more features at lower unit cost. Figure 6.4 shows, again for the electronics industry, an ever accelerating rise in development costs for integrated circuit chips (IC) with a fortyfold increase in investment cost over a 12-year period.

Telecommunications systems show a similar picture for public telephone networks. These cost some £100 million in the 1970s, rising to some £600 million by the 1980s, as system life-times fell from about 14 years to about 10 years.

The extent to which this will continue in the 1990s is currently the subject of debate, some arguing that consumers are saturated with new products. There seems little reason to believe that this will happen, however, and all companies in the global

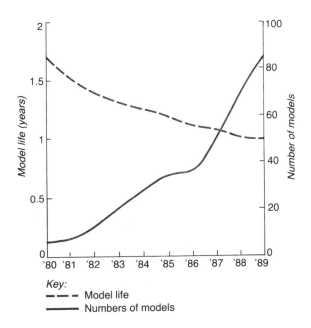

Figure 6.3
Product proliferation

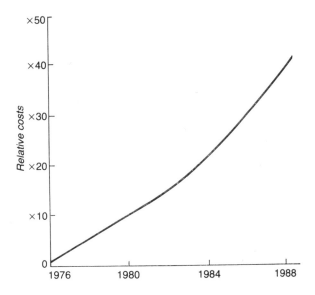

Figure 6.4
Rising investment costs

market-place are planning and investing on the assumption of continued expansion of consumer demand. These issues are explored more fully in the Philips' case study, particularly under the heading, 'The competitive environment'.

The extremely high investments required for developing new technologies and new markets, such as high-definition TV or mobile telephone systems, call for them to be funded by joint ventures or strategic alliances. By way of example, a project to develop a new electronic memory chip was reported by Philips to require a £735 million investment in 1987. It was jointly funded by Philips, Siemens and the governments of Holland and Germany.

Such investments cannot be funded by individual companies and various types of strategic alliances have been set up in consequence. Large companies may agree to jointly fund a specific project or to form a separate, but jointly owned, company to develop a new market. Alternatively, equity purchase or cross-licensing of technology may be used to limit the down side to the investment risk. A joint venture in effect extends the resources available to partners by bringing in the complementary expertise of others, additional capital or new marketing expertise. Siemens, for instance, has separate joint ventures with Nixdorf and Fujitsu to develop different sectors of its IT business. The former strengthens its systems whilst the latter strengthens its mainframe and supercomputers.[5]

Future joint ventures in the aircraft industry could involve ten or more companies in interlinked ventures. *R & D Magazine* has reported discussions on second-generation, supersonic commercial aircraft involving Aerospatiale, BAe, Deutsche Airbus, McDonnell Douglas, Boeing, Pratt and Whitney, GE, Rolls Royce, Snecma (France) and Italian and Japanese companies.[6] The issue of the very high investment required for developing new technologies, and the need to share these costs by collaboration, is discussed in the study of Marconi /NobelTech Systems AB case.

Strategic alliances in applications will be found increasingly frequently in the 1990s, driven by the need to bring expertise of the end-use of systems alongside their design and marketing. These points are explored further in a number of the cases; for example, the Global tyre war, NH Geotech, Marconi/NobelTech Systems AB, NEC and Philips. Increasingly, consumers are demanding greater compatibility between products and services from different vendors. In international markets, competing manufacturers must now agree world-wide standards, as well as joint funding. For example, consumers expect to exchange money between different banks and countries, information between different computers or pictures between competing TV systems; a point made in the study of Midland Bank. The Centre Commun d'Etude de Télédifusion et Télécommunications (CCETT) is working to define picture and broadcast standards for high definition TV.[5] British and French Railways are co-operating on standards for track clearance to support Channel Tunnel rail traffic. The future seems firmly committed to a global-scale operation in which technological innovation provides a target for new products, as well as a vehicle for producing them.

NEW OPERATIONAL PROCESSES

The development of new processes is another area where technology is playing a crucial role in internationalization. These are needed to reduce operating costs where an organization's strategy is to dominate globally their competitors, or where competitors attack home or developing markets. Manufacturing and service industries need economies in scale to support the price reductions and reliable deliveries which win shares in mass markets, other things being equal.

The classical Product Life Cycle Model, as described and later modified by Vernon, puts much emphasis on market forces as the prime mover of the later stages of the model.[7] Others, such as Freeman, have stressed the part played by technology in these later stages, when the technological understanding gained throughout the earlier stages of the life cycle can be applied with advantage.[8] This use of the frequently neglected learning curve, augmented by newly available technology, when appropriate, offers the opportunity to introduce new facilities into products along with more efficient production processes. The latter can bring about spectacular reductions in costs and indeed technology is the only vehicle that offers scope to continuously reduce prices across a broad spectrum of goods and materials.

When the Yen appreciated against other currencies in the late 1970s and mid-1980s, video recorders, for example, fell in price by 20 per cent at point of sale whilst the Yen appreciated by 46 per cent against the dollar. Technology was used to reduce prices by increasing process yields, reducing parts counts and reducing the build-time. At the same time, product facilities were enhanced.

Lower prices and new products are not the only competitive weapons which technology offers for use in the market place. The quality of the product or service delivered has become a highly significant feature of global competition, following the almost legendary Japanese improvements to the quality of television sets in the 1970s. Technology is being used increasingly to improve quality, through the design and manufacturing processes, and this trend can be expected to continue throughout the 1990s.

The study of Typhoon International Ltd shows how the application of advanced technology is being used to improve the quality of wetsuits, as well as survival and protective suits. IBM talks of technology making '100 per cent product quality a practical, achievable, sustainable objective' as new technologies 'reduce errors, rework and scrap'.[9] Nichols claims:

> ... it is not unusual for there to be over one million separate documents to support a major product [and explains how Digital have used CAD (computer aided design) to manage and update their large engineering data base.][10]

The concept of technology as a vehicle for new processes leads on to technology transfer. Contrary to the impression given by many, this is not a new phenomenon of the 1980s. Information has always been transferred between research, development and production in technology-based companies. Originally, the transfer paths were short and in company, but they lengthened without comment as the companies became international. What is new is transfer of information by companies using electronic data systems. According to IBM:

> data must be usable across all parts of the organization that are in different locations, or between a company and its sub-contractors. This is critical where different parts of product design are developed in different parts of the enterprise. Data transfer provides simple, consistent (and) transparent communication of anything from drawings to administrative information.[11]

Lister-Petter, part of the Hawker Siddeley group, transferred engine production and design information between three UK sites, saving 20–25 per cent of component costs and recovering the £750,000 costs in 1.9 years.[11] On a world-wide scale, CAD/CAM designs can be passed electronically around the world to design, supplier and manufacturing centres located in, say, the UK, California and Taiwan. This allows centres to integrate their special expertise and minimize problems. Automotive industries use this to achieve world-wide integrated manufacture. General Motors and Ford assemble cars in England or Mexico, for example, but use components made in manufacturing plants in Brazil, Spain, Germany and elsewhere. These are shipped and brought together for final assembly.

Technology transfer is not restricted to logistical operations within the same company. The US Department of Energy is reported by *R & D Magazine* to have increased its royalty income by nearly 9 per cent in 1992 to £1 million from licences offered to industry and universities.[15] Co-markership and technology transfer, where sub-assembly or even complete product assembly is carried out on behalf of another company, can offer improvements in quality, cost and delivery by concentrating production into larger units. Processes are transferred to the co-maker or sometimes sold to another company in cross-licensing agreements. Philips and Matsushita, who jointly manufacture the digital compact cassettes, have offered licences on the process to other companies.[16] All of these developments in technology transfer depend on Information Technology (IT) and this is discussed in the next section.

INFORMATION TECHNOLOGY

According to Toffler, we have entered a third wave of human history centred on information:

> *information is exploding in our midst, showering us with . . . images and drastically changing the way in which each of us perceives and acts upon our own . . . world.*[12]

It is the arrival of the information society, based on the technologies of computing and software, which will have the most impact on internationalization. More specifically, it is the way we will access and use the information available, rather than the technologies themselves, that will shape internationalization.

Europe, the world's largest single market after 1992, will become a major proving ground for the use of information. Mobile telephone services, computer-integrated manufacturing, design, process control and order scheduling, financial information and transactions (movement of funds and credit), business information and entertainment, are all set to become pan-European and each a major business – according to the IT industry.[5]

Major alliances have been formed, for example between Groupe Bull and IBM and between SGS-Thomson and GEC Plessey. R & D joint ventures are being nurtured by the EC's framework programmes, the latest of which is worth ECU 86 billion annually for five years. Information exchange protocols, like those for high-definition television, are being promoted by the EC – unfortunately causing significant delays to development.[13] Another concept in standards, Open Systems, allows IT hardware from one manufacturer to work with that of another and freely exchange information from networked computers, mobile telephones and other sources. It is now agreed that this exchange actually increases the size of the IT market, compensating for the freedom of customers to switch from one manufacturer to another. European governments in the mid 1980s forced the pace by insisting that public sector contracts should be based on Open Systems. The world market in IT service is set to grow from less than £110 billion in 1990 to £390 billion by 2000.[13]

Today as much as half of all corporate information is held on personal computers (PCs) according to Toshiba Information Systems (UK). These PCs, even the portable ones, are being linked together by networks, the workhorse of the IT industry, making them an integral part of corporate strategy. Interactive control of business through up-to-date, on-line information available on the desk top is the new strategic business weapon that IT has given companies. Technologies to support this, such as electronic data interchange (EDI), carry data in paperless, standard form between companies and third parties such as suppliers.

Groupware, a new software tool for management communication, shares routes and adds value to information. It directly supports interactive business management and is used by companies such as Chase Manhattan Bank, General Motors and Amadeus, a European travel services company. The scale of corporate business available in integrated IT strategies such as these can be judged from the International Computer Group. This computer services company, formed a joint venture between Computacentre, Random and Compunet in 1989 and, specializing in corporate IT systems across Europe, had a £1.1 billion turnover by 1991.[14]

In addition to these benefits, IT can transfer product and process technology from one country to another when conditions become uncongenial. It already transfers designs, specifications, process control and orders to specialized supply centres in other parts of the world, encouraging suppliers, for instance, to become co-designers of the product itself. The coupling of telecommunications with image processing, text and business data will allow business functions to be separated around the world, rather than centralized within one country.

In the consumer field, banks and retailers are developing electronic point-of-sale cash transactions; a fact illustrated by the study of the Credit Bank. Such transactions are no more difficult within the UK than across Europe or the world and this should lead to increased co-operation and mergers within these industries. As briefly mentioned in the Philips' case study, education services and home entertainments will grow into new businesses via IT. The developments within IT and its impact on internationalization are only limited by the imagination of the users and their suppliers.

THE FUTURE

In terms of time-scale the development of IT and electronics will, during the latter part of the 1990s at least, continue along the lines already established. These, however, are just two of four interrelated technologies, which Toffler has identified as the backbone of future businesses.[12] Of the others, genetic engineering is already creating new industries and may change the direction of many international businesses by the end of the 1990s. Research and development is investigating products as diverse as food stuffs that give high yields under drought conditions, and the growing of human transplant organs in host animals. The former product is much closer to commercial realization than the latter, but many new products will be developed within this spectrum before the 21st century opens. The fourth technology, marine exploitation, has yet to demonstrate its importance.

All these technologies cross national boundaries and need greater investments than anything else to date. Strategic priorities of organizations will therefore determine how quickly they affect international trade. A high priority must lead to the formation of large and powerful strategic alliances, which will demand even greater deregulation and liberalization of world trade as a means of recovering their investments. It seems likely that the immediate future will see large groupings of former competitors working together to build global markets, often based on IT. By the beginning of the 21st century, genetic engineering may replace IT as the major technical force in international trade.

References

1 OECD, *Frascati Manual*.
2 Collier, D. W., Mong, J., and Conlin, J., 'How Effective is Technological Innovation?' *Res. Management*, September-October 1984, pp. 11–16.
3 DTI, *Innovation Plans Handbook*, Central Office of Information, HMSO, 1991.
4 Washington, J. A., 'Japanese Cars Drive Rings Round Detroit', *Sunday Times World News*, 12 January 1992, p. 13.
5 Nakamoto, M., 'The Barriers Are Falling', *Financial Times Survey*, 17 March 1992, p. III. 1.
6 'High Speed Plane Requires Global Alliance', *R & D Magazine*, December 1991, p. 50.
7 Vernon, R., 'The Product Cycle Hypothesis in a New International Environment', *Oxford Bulletin of Economics & Statistics*, Vol. 41, November 1979.
8 Freeman, C., *Economics of Industrial Innovation*, 1st edition, (London, Pinter, 1974).
9 *Computer Integrated Manufacturing: the IBM experience*, Findlay Publications for IBM UK, 1987, p. 54.
10 Nichols, K., 'Digital Competes Through Design', *Engineering Computers*, May 1990, pp. 21–25.
11 *Computer Integrated Manufacturing: the IBM experience*, ibid., pp. 32 & 76–77.
12 Toffler, A., *The Third Wave*, (London, Wm. Collins Sons & Co.Ltd, 1980).
13 Taylor, P. 'Shrieks Over Eureka', *Financial Times Survey*, 17 March 1992, pp. 3 & 5.
14 Computacentre, *Annual Reports and Accounts*, 1991.
15 'Upward Trend Shown In National Labs' Ability To Transfer Technology', *R & D Magazine*, May 1992, p. 17.
16 'Makers Begin DCC Licensing', *J Electronics Industry*, January 1992, p. 11.

CHAPTER SEVEN

ENVIRONMENTAL ISSUES AND INTERNATIONAL BUSINESS

RON ALLISON

INTRODUCTION

It was not until the late 1960s and early 1970s that there was any noticeable generalized interest in the environment. It is not surprising that the Treaty of Rome, for example, did not include any provision for a joint EC policy on controlling pollution. There were isolated acts of concern that led to legislation; for instance, in the early 1950s the UK passed the Clean Air Act, which controlled domestic coal fires, but this did not give rise to a more general concern with air pollution. At this time there was little interest in the environment in the USA, and the same was true for Japan, the USSR and eastern Europe.

The beginning of significant generalized concern about the environment can be traced back to the early 1970s. In 1972 the Club of Rome published some research from the Massachusetts Institute of Technology, 'The Limits To Growth'. The conclusion of this work was forbidding:

> *If the present growth trends in world population, industrialization, pollution, food production, and resource depletion continue unchanged, the limits to growth on this planet will be reached some time within the next hundred years.*[1]

Not long afterwards Paul Ehrlich's *The Population Bomb* was published.[2] One of the predictions in the book was that a quarter of the world's population would starve to death between 1973 and 1983. Self-evidently, this has not happened, although there have been serious localized famines in Africa.

The problems discussed in 'The Limits to Growth' (for example, the exhaustion of raw materials, atmospheric pollution, the population explosion, the build-up of toxic wastes, and land erosion) occasioned much comment at the time.[1] But the world's birth rate began to rise more slowly in the 1970s and the imminent exhaustion of raw materials predicted in the Club of Rome report did not occur. One of the reasons for the latter was that rising prices encouraged new sources of supply. One example is that the quadrupling of oil prices in 1973–74 made it profitable to tap the oil reserves in the North Sea and extend the search for further reserves.

For a time, anxiety about the environment was placed on a back burner, but by the 1980s it became a world-wide phenomenon. In 1990, the British Prime Minister Margaret Thatcher, an ardent free marketeer, said:

> *No generation has a freehold on this earth. All we have is a life tenancy –*
> *with a full repairing lease.*

A speaker at an Organization for Economic Development and Cooperation (OECD) conference in 1990 stated that:

> *. . .one can track the evolution of environmental concern over the last twenty*
> *years by watching it move from the back page of major newspapers to the front*
> *page, and now to the financial page.*

The 1990s have been identified by politicians and journalists as the decade of the environment. The threats to the environment are many, including global warming, ozone depletion, urban smog and drinking water contamination. The other side of the coin is that these threats offer significant opportunities to companies possessing foresight and vision.

One manifestation of this concern is the labelling of consumer products as, for example, 'CFC free', 'biodegradable', and 'ozone friendly'. Behind this change is the so-called 'green' consumer. In 1985 in the USA, only 0.5 per cent of all new products were green products. By 1990 this had risen to 9.2 per cent. In a 1990 nationwide poll in Canada, 80 per cent of the respondents stated that they were willing to pay up to 10 per cent more for environmentally less harmful products.

Environmental labelling is world-wide. By the end of 1992, the OECD estimates that 22 of the 24 OECD countries could have products with environmental labels on sale. There is an EC proposal for a Community-wide environmental labelling programme. Common to all labelling programmes within the EC is a committee which determines, or suggests to a government ministry, which products should be eligible for labelling. Manufacturers can voluntarily submit products for consideration and, where successful, pay a fee for the use of the label.

ENVIRONMENTAL ISSUES AND BUSINESS

Environmental concern is of great significance to business. What has been and what will be its impact on products, production methods, costs, profits and location decisions? Peter Wallenberg, the President of the International Chamber of Commerce, said in a speech in 1991 that:

> *the withering away of the Marxist challenge to the free enterprise system*
> *leaves the environmental challenge as the most fundamental one that*
> *businessmen all over the world are going to face in the foreseeable future.*

The policy instruments that governments are using to achieve environmental objectives have changed noticeably over the last 20 years. At the beginning of the

1970s 'command and control' measures were largely relied on. However, the increasing costs of pollution control and the increasing complexity of regulatory régimes, coupled with the failure of these measures to bring about more than minimum technology innovation, led to a search for other policy tools.

Not surprisingly, in view of the market-oriented thinking of most OECD countries in the late 1970s and 1980s, the market was looked to for salvation. Measures adopted included environmental charges and taxes, deposit-refund schemes and the use of tradeable emission permits. As the 1990s unfold, a battery of methods are being used. Long-term performance standards and targets are being set with the use of command and control regulations, and the most cost-effective routes are being found with the aid of market instruments.

A parallel change has been the adoption of more comprehensive approaches, which have replaced the control of one pollutant at a time. The problem of the latter approach is that it tended to move pollution rather than eliminate it. For instance, if the control of a solid waste was achieved by its incineration, the toxic material then became airborne. Then again, regulating the use of one chemical often gave rise to a hazardous replacement. The use of broader approaches has coined slogans such as 'multi-media management', 'integrated pollution prevention and control' and 'cradle-to-grave management'.

The first EC environmental programme was approved in November 1973 to cover the period 1973–78. There have been subsequent programmes and the fourth programme, lasting six years, ended in 1992. By 1990 around 160 pieces of environmental legislation had been passed although Member States, with the possible exception of Denmark, do not have a good record of enforcement. The Single European Act 1986 gave environmental policy something of a fillip by stating not only that there was a need for more environmental legislation, but that future laws should meet three key objectives: firstly that the quality of the environment should be protected, preserved, and improved; secondly, that natural resources should be carefully and rationally used; and finally, that human health should be protected.

ECONOMICS AND POLLUTION

Economists have been writing about pollution for many years. Many textbooks include a section on externalities and often pollution is the example used to illustrate this concept. Pollution is an example of a problem which cannot be controlled by the operation of free markets left to their own devices.

Standard economic theory states that an individual will undertake some course of action up to the point where the marginal benefit associated with it is equal to its marginal cost. In the same way, a competitive company will produce and supply goods up to the point where the marginal cost of the last unit supplied is equal to the marginal revenue of the last unit supplied. In reaching this production decision, though, the company is only taking into account its private costs, such as wages, raw materials, and transport. In many cases, however, the organization may be imposing additional costs on the community, for instance pollution of the atmosphere by smoke or the discharge of poisons into rivers. In other words, there is a divergence of private costs and social costs. This may be illustrated diagrammatically.

In Figure 7.1 the supply curve of the competitive company is equal to its marginal cost curve. The demand curve is given by D and then the optimum output is Q_0

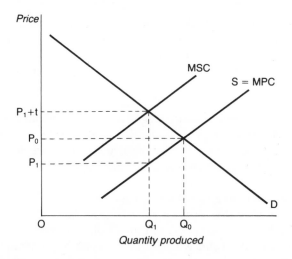

Figure 7.1
Social and private costs of pollution

where MC = MR. The market price of this quantity of output is P_0. From society's point of view, this is not an optimal output as the costs of the pollutant have not been taken into consideration by the organization. If the costs of the pollutant are taken into account, then the sum of the marginal costs is given by MSC, the optimal output is Q_1 and the price $P_1 + t$.

From Figure 7.1 it may be seen that if pollution is caused by the production of the goods, the price of the product is too low and the output too high. It also emphasizes that the cost of controlling pollution is not zero. The disadvantage of this approach is that it doesn't show explicitly what happens to pollution or whether pollution can be controlled other than by reducing output of the goods which caused the pollution. For these reasons, the approach used in Figure 7.2 may be useful. PC shows the total

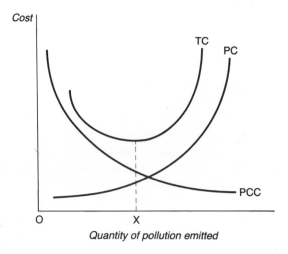

Figure 7.2
Pollution cost and control

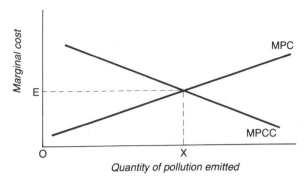

Figure 7.3
Marginal cost of reducing pollution by 1 unit

social cost of each level of discharge of a pollutant, at a given level of output. Clearly, the greater the amount of pollution emitted, the higher is the level of costs incurred by society. The curve PCC shows the costs of controlling pollution at each level of discharge of pollution. This curve is downward sloping because the less industry cuts down on pollution, the smaller are the costs in so doing.

The curve TC is a vertical summation of PC and PCC and shows the total cost of pollution control at each level of discharge of pollution. From society's point of view, the industry should reduce the discharge of pollution to the point where the sum of the two costs is minimized and thus the optimal amount of pollution is at output X. Figure 7.2 also shows that usually the optimal amount of pollution is not zero, a solution that is unpalatable to many people with strong environmental views.

The same conclusion may also be demonstrated using another technique from the economist's toolkit – marginal analysis. In Figure 7.3 the curve MPC shows the marginal cost of an extra unit of pollution, at each level of discharge of pollution. The curve MPCC shows the marginal cost of reducing the discharge of pollution by one unit. The socially optimal level of pollution is where the two curves cut one another. Here, the cost of an extra unit of pollution is just equal to the cost of reducing it by one unit. In the absence of government action, the industry will not cut back its pollution level to OX, because it does not take into account all the social costs of its pollution.

CONTROLLING POLLUTION IN PRACTICE

There are two basic ways of controlling the polluting activities of business and each has implications for the organization concerned. The first is to use quantitative regulations, the so-called 'command and control' approach. This approach has a number of advantages: governments know what they are asking for, consumers know what the outcomes should be, and companies know what they should be achieving. Economists of a market persuasion do not like this approach; they believe that it is not as cost-effective as using the price mechanism.

The regulatory approach often has an uneven effect on the polluters, with some facing high costs and others low costs. For instance, suppose a country passes a regulation that bans the use of petrol containing lead. Motorists owning older cars will need to pay for their cars to be converted to run on this type of petrol. Owners of modern cars will face zero costs, as these cars were designed to run on both lead-free petrol and petrol containing lead.

Regulations can also act as a disincentive to meet more than minimum standards. There is no reason for a company to discharge less than the maximum level of pollutants permitted under the regulations, as once this has been achieved the company is within the law. In the same way, there is no incentive for organizations to search for new technology that will bring pollution down below the permitted maximum. A related disadvantage is that regulation means in practice that it will also specify the technology. Another disadvantage is that regulations are often tougher for potential new entrants to an industry than for existing companies, as existing companies could be given temporary subsidies or time to phase-in measures.

The second approach is to use the price mechanism, usually by placing a tax or levy on polluting activities. To give one example, pollution taxes have not been common in EC member countries. Effluent charges for water pollution were used with considerable success in the Ruhr area in Germany. A tax differential between leaded and unleaded petrol in a number of EC countries has undoubtedly been influential in persuading consumers to switch in significant numbers to the more environmentally friendly lead-free petrol. In Finland charges are levied on non-returnable containers and in Sweden on batteries containing cadmium or mercury. In Japan, Germany, and Switzerland, noisy aircraft are charged higher landing fees than quiet ones.

The effect of a pollution tax is illustrated in Figure 7.1. If the government imposes a tax on the company of t – equal to the cost to society of the nuisance caused by the polluting activity – then the optimum level of production is achieved. Diagrammatically, the supply curve has been moved vertically upwards by the amount of the tax.

The effect of a pollution tax may also be shown in Figure 7.3. Suppose the government charged organizations in the industry a tax equal to OE; in other words, the marginal cost of an additional unit of pollution is OE. Then the level of pollution discharge will be reduced to OX. To see why, imagine the level of discharge was greater than OX before the tax. After the tax of OE is imposed it is profitable to reduce pollution as long as the marginal cost of reducing pollution is less than the extra cost (OE) of another unit of pollution. Inspection of Figure 7.3 shows that this is the case for all units of pollution greater than OX. Thus profits will be maximized at a pollution level of OX.

One of the arguments used against quantitative restrictions is that governments do not possess enough information to establish accurately the optimal amount of pollution discharge. But, as Marin and others have argued, the information needs required to set a tax that brings about the optimal amount of pollution are just as demanding as the information required to achieve this goal by regulation.[3] If governments and regulatory agencies possessed perfect information, then the tax or levy would impose on polluters an amount equal to the external costs of their polluting activities. It would then be up to the polluters to decide for themselves, rather than it being decided for them by the regulatory approach, how to meet these charges. For example they could install new equipment or modify existing technology.

In practice, governments have tended to use charges in combination with regulations, rather than as a direct alternative. This point is illustrated in a study by the OECD 'The Application of Economic Instruments For Environmental Protection'.[4]

The study further shows that charges are used as a revenue-earning device to pay for the costs of regulatory measures, and are normally not high enough to significantly affect company behaviour.

The market mechanism and the regulatory approach can be combined in a manner which gains the approval of economists. This is the system of tradeable permits. In essence, the system is quite simple: companies are given permits to discharge a certain level of pollution and these permits can be traded. This method allows the government to set the total amount of pollution considered desirable at the time, and allows the level to be reduced over time. It provides companies with some freedom of action. Clean companies can profit by selling their permits to dirty companies. Dirty companies can decide whether it is cheaper to install new equipment or processes, or to buy permits from their competitors.

Despite these advantages the approach has not yet gained wide currency and results have tended to be less than might have been anticipated. One successful experiment, which is cited in the literature, was that carried out by the American Environmental Protection Agency (EPA). Oil refineries in the USA were given two years to cut down on the amount of lead in petrol. They were given tradeable quotas of lead which enabled them to phase-in the reduction at their own pace. Upon analysis, there are three features that led to the success of the scheme: the goals were clear and had widespread public support; there were a relatively small number of firms in the industry (half of which traded permits); and the amount of lead in petrol could easily be monitored.

The EPA has attempted to reduce air pollution by tradeable permits since 1974, but success has been limited. One reason has been litigation by environmentalists and the reason for such opposition is not hard to understand. Imagine you live in the shadow of a factory which is pouring out vast clouds of smoke. It is of small or zero consolation to hear that the firm has been a keen participator in the tradeable permit scheme, that average pollution in the whole country has been greatly reduced, and that the experiment is featuring in economics textbooks as a glowing tribute to the efficiency of using the market to reduce pollution, if you cannot use the vegetables from your own garden, your house is unsaleable, your children have chronic bronchitis and your partner is threatening to leave you because of the nuisance.

Despite the varied success of tradeable permits to date, it is likely that they will play an important role in the future in pollution control programmes. In 1989 a scheme was announced in the USA to use marketable permits to cut sulphur-dioxide emissions by electricity generating companies, and their use is being considered by the EPA to phase-out the production of chlorofluorocarbons (CFC gases).

A specific example of the use of the price mechanism to limit polluting activities is the so-called 'carbon tax'. This tax would be levied on the carbon content of fossil fuels and would cut down the amount of carbon dioxide being released into the atmosphere. Unlike many of the other environmental tax proposals, it would be relatively simple to tax coal, gas and oil on the basis of their carbon content.

A general principle used by the OECD and the EC is the 'polluter pays principle' (PPP). This should not be confused with the taxation approach advocated by many economists. Basically, it is an agreement that companies should be responsible for any costs incurred by anti-pollution measures rather than those costs being subsidized by governments. As long as the polluters bear the cost of achieving polluting abatement measures, the PPP is satisfied. In effect, the PPP is a way of making companies 'internalize the externality'.

COMPANY LEVEL STRATEGIES

More and more companies world-wide have come to realize that environmental issues are important and must be taken into account in the determination of corporate strategy. BMW and VW, who are swiftly developing the concept of the recyclable car, are two examples. The case studies of BMW and Nissan illustrate this point. There are several reasons for being pro-active here. Consumer pressure is potentially powerful; by exercising their 'money votes', consumers can materially affect the sales and profitability of the firm. National and international legislation is another powerful guiding factor. In some cases, companies have realized that environmentally friendly processes and products are actually cost-effective, particularly when a long-run perspective is adopted. Finally, there is the more philosophical area of business ethics. In considering environmental factors, there are several points for companies to think about.

- To what extent is the company meeting existing environmental legislative requirements and how is it placed if, as is increasingly likely in the future, the legislation becomes tougher?
- To what extent are employees at all levels committed to environmental improvement as a goal of the company and how can this commitment be increased?
- What is the position of the organization's competitors, both actual and potential, with relation to the environment?
- How can the company's environmental performance become a competitive advantage?
- Are there financial and other constraints to improving the company's environmental performance? If so, how can these be remedied?
- Are there new or modified products that the organization could produce which are more favourable to the environment?
- Does the company possess the information and skills to evaluate the environmental impact of its products and processes, both existing and proposed?

It is the answers to questions such as these that enable organizations to evolve a strategic plan that takes the environment properly into account. In incorporating environmental issues into its strategic thinking, it is fundamental that the company knows how well or badly it is currently performing in relation to the environment. One method of dealing with this issue is environmental auditing.

ENVIRONMENTAL AUDITING

Environmental audits are common in business in the USA and their subsidiaries abroad and are becoming increasingly common in European-owned companies. Cook (1991) defined an environmental audit as:

> *an independent, systematic, periodic, documented and objective evaluation of how well organizations, management and equipment are performing, with the aim of helping the company management to safeguard the environment by facilitating management and control of environmental practices and assessing compliance with company policies which include meeting regulatory requirements.*[5]

In the USA, the US Environmental Protection Agency has played an important role since the early 1980s in promoting environmental audits and has published policy guidelines. The 1986 Superfund Amendment and Reauthorization Act (SARA) was a powerful stimulus to auditing. Title III of this Act (the Emergency Planning and Community Right-to-Know provision) requires all companies to report all the pollutants they emitted.

In the EC the Commission only became actively involved in the preparation of a directive on environmental auditing in the early 1990s, although they have been taking place in individual member countries prior to this.

The technique has been used by large firms in the Netherlands since the mid-1980s. The CBI in the UK has published a set of environmental auditing guidelines. In Norway there is a requirement for factories to use an internal environmental control system under the supervision of a government agency, although environmental auditing itself is not legally required. However, some organizations carry out environmental audits on a voluntary basis.

LEVEL PLAYING FIELDS

Environmental standards differ greatly around the world. As a generalization, they tend to be high in wealthy, developed countries and low in developing countries. For example, in many poorer countries water is of a low quality, there are high levels of lead in the air in cities, sewage is untreated, and primitive coal-fired boiler technology results in soot and dust. Within this generalization, there are also considerable differences. For instance, in the EC standards are higher in countries such as Germany and the Netherlands than in the Southern European Member States. These differences raise an important question, the answer to which is of great importance to international trade and individual companies: the question is, to what extent should countries be free to pursue different environmental standards? Differing standards could be viewed as providing the opportunity to protect companies in countries where they are high, or providing an unfair cost advantage to companies in countries where they are low.

Increasingly, environmental policies are affecting trade flows. An interesting and important dichotomy has arisen: trade officials are concerned with trying to remove encumbrances to trade, whereas environment officials are increasingly arguing for the use of trade-policy instruments to help achieve the objectives of environmental policy. Environmental regulations can act as non-tariff barriers and charges and taxes can alter the competitiveness of companies.

If international trade is considered to be beneficial, environmental policies should not unduly distort trade in fulfilling their objectives. Often, though, it is difficult to separate out environmental concerns from protectionism. Recent examples include rules on the amounts of contaminants allowed in food products, minimum sizes for certain fish, and recyclable drink containers. One way to cut down on the number of these disputes is to increase the level of international co-operation and policy convergence. Here the work of organizations such as the OECD is important.

The General Agreement on Tariffs and Trade (GATT), is mainly concerned with freeing world trade and a basic principle is that of non-discrimination. GATT was drafted in 1948 and, understandably, had few references to the environment. An important environmental aspect arises from the principle of non-discrimination: it is permissible under GATT regulations for countries to tax or regulate imports and exports, as long as it does the same to its own products, but it is very difficult to impose rules on processes used in other countries. This then raises the possibility that companies producing in countries where the cost of complying with demanding environmental standards is high will move production to countries with lax environmental standards. This has happened in certain industries including steel, chemicals, and pulp and paper, where European, Japanese and North American firms have moved some productive capacity to South America and Africa.

There are also problems within the EC. A basic principle of the internal market is that each member country's standards are recognized by others; but in 1988 the European Court ruled that Denmark could require that all drinks sold in Denmark must be in returnable bottles. This ruling clearly breached this basic principle. As far as processes are concerned within the EC, there is a levelling-up doctrine that tries to prevent countries with dirty processes gaining an advantage over those with more demanding standards.

An example is the Large Combustion Plant directive of 1988. The effect was to require coal-fired power stations to reduce the emission of gases that contributed to acid rain. The directive appeared to come about as a result of pressure by German companies, which argued that the fitting of this expensive equipment by German generating firms, as a result of a law passed in Germany in 1983, would drive up their power costs and leave them with a competitive disadvantage.

So far it might appear that companies in countries with high environmental standards might be at a disadvantage compared with producers located in countries where standards are low. Michael Porter argues that regulations may actually help the development of new technology and reduce the costs of meeting advanced standards.[6] His argument is essentially a leadership and 'catching up' one. He cites the case of Germany and Japan, where strict regulations have allowed businesses located there to gain a dominate share in pollution control devices in world markets, as other countries raise their standards.

THE COMPANY AND THE ENVIRONMENT

The concept of sustainable growth or development has come to prominence in recent years. 'Our Common Future', sometimes known as the Bruntland Report, is the report of a commission headed by the Norwegian prime minister and was published in 1987. The report defined sustainable development as 'development that meets the needs of the present without compromising the ability of future generations to meet their own needs'.[7]

The clear implication is that growth will be sustainable only if it is environmentally sound, and that there should be a long-run time perspective.

Individual organizations which take this approach need to ask themselves three basic questions.

- What type of products should we be producing, what should they be made of, and how should they be packaged?
- What should be our policy on open disclosure of pollution and health information?
- How can we reduce pollution and waste at source, i.e. how can we eliminate pollutants during the production process rather than capture them at the end of the operations?

PRODUCT CHOICE

A well-known example of a company making significant changes to a product is the decision by McDonalds to change the packaging of its hamburgers. In 1990 the clamshell plastic boxes were abandoned in favour of paper wrappings. A considerable irony was involved here: the reason for the change was mainly that McDonald's customers did not like the styrene packaging as they thought it environmentally unfriendly. This was in contradiction to the results of an intensive research campaign by the firm that showed that styrene was more recyclable than paper. The company changed because of potential pressure from their customers.

Support for McDonald's own findings came from an article in *Scientist* by Martin Hocking.[8] He showed that styrene is less harmful to the environment if all relevant costs such as forest clear-cutting, the energy requirements of paper manufacture, and the difficulties of recycling heat-preserving wrapping paper are taken into account. Scientifically rigorous methods of assessing the environmental impact of products are now emerging.

DISCLOSURE

It is arguable that a policy of maximum disclosure would have prevented the 1984 Bhopal disaster in India. In the two years prior to the disaster, Union Carbide, the American owner of the plant, had denied reports of faults in the plant. If there had been full disclosure, the leak might have been prevented or emergency defensive measures might have been established.

One of the reasons why, in the past, organizations have resisted open disclosure is that it might help competitors. Another is that it might trigger off action by environmental pressure groups. One effect of the passing of SARA in the USA is that firms have seen the benefits of disclosure. SARA does not establish any legal limits in emissions, but it does require all emissions to be publicly reported. So far there have not been many instances of pressure groups using the information against firms.

The greatest impact of SARA has been within businesses themselves. The Tufts research group looked at eight companies which included Dow Chemical, Intel, Occidental Chemical, and Vista Chemical. Amongst the findings was that merely by gathering the information required by the Act, mutual technical assistance was promoted within the company, as was the transfer of good practices from division to division and increased (beneficial) contact with customers and suppliers.

The impact of SARA on the Dow company is particularly noteworthy. Until 1984, when it was required to report its major emissions to a Congressional subcommittee, it had never actually calculated its polluting activities. Executives were staggered to find that over 4.5 million kgs of dangerous chemicals were being released into the environment. The short-run reaction was to spend large sums of money on equipment such as scrubbers, filters and incinerators. Even so, millions of kgs of chemicals were still being released. This in turn triggered off further investigations and further large reductions in emissions resulted. Savings of hundreds of thousands of dollars have been established as a result of all these measures.

POLLUTION PREVENTION

In the 'new' approach to quality control, pioneered by Japanese car makers, quality is designed into the product by designing manufacturing processes in which variations are reduced to a minimum, rather than by an inspection for defects at the end of the line. This approach is used in Nissan and reference is made to this point in the Nissan case. Similarly, companies which take a long-term view of the environment design processes in which harmful emissions have been designed out of conversion processes, rather than by capturing them at the end of the process. This latter method is often called the end-of-the-pipe approach. One example of the design approach is the switch to water-based paints by Volvo and BMW.

Both end-of-the-pipe measures and the design approach have costs, often substantial. In many cases it is difficult to prove that the latter may ultimately cost less than the former, but if the analogy with quality control is valid then this will be the case in many industries.

Electricity produced from coal-fired generating stations is an interesting example of the issues involved. The burning of coal in conventional, pulverized coal boilers, that have dominated the past 30 years, is a major source of sulphur dioxide and nitrogen oxide emissions. These emissions can be cut by the installation of expensive flue gas scrubbers. An alternative is to use two new technologies. Fluidized-bed combustion enables up to 95 per cent of the sulphur to be removed from the furnace directly, without the need for scrubbers, and more than 50 per cent of the nitrogen oxides. When coal gasification is added to this process, further improvements are obtained.

There are nevertheless some disadvantages. The cost of the new plants is greater than the conventional plant and they are complicated to maintain. It is only when the fluidized-bed process is combined with the degasification process that energy per unit of input is equal to, or greater than, that from a conventional plant.

BUSINESS OPPORTUNITIES

Some managers view the concern for the environment and associated legislation in an adversarial light. By way of contrast, other managers believe that environmentalism offers opportunities rather than threats and punishments.

The OECD has estimated that the global market for goods and services for pollution abatement in 1992 is $200 billion. End-of-pipe equipment makes up 75 cent of the total and environment-related services accounts for the remainder. The figure excludes 'clean technologies', as it is very difficult to place a value on these. The market is growing steadily at an estimated annual average rate of nearly 6 per cent and by the year 2000 it will be worth $300 billion. The importance of the environmental service sector is expected to increase as the demand for end-of-pipe systems decreases, and the demand for clean technologies conversely increases. Firms in OECD countries have 85–90 per cent of the world market for environmental equipment and services. Thus significant business opportunities are being created as concern for the well-being of the environment grows.

The environment industry is very wide-ranging. OECD estimates indicate that there are 30,000 companies in North America, 20,000 companies in Europe and 9,000 companies in Japan, employing in total 1.7 million people, involved in the environment business. For historical reasons, some countries dominate particular aspects of environmental clean-up. German companies are prominent in equipment that treats water effluents because there has been stringent water pollution legislation in Germany for many years. In the same way Japanese legislation requiring flue gases to be desulphurized gave Japanese organizations producing this technology a head start. Similarly, Dutch companies specializing in cleaning contaminated soil, together with US firms, have a lead in dealing with hazardous wastes.

There is a strong international dimension to the environment industry. Germany sells about 40 per cent of its environmental production outside the country. Japan and the USA are also important in international trade in these products. Although a considerable amount of equipment is directly imported and exported, the licensing of technology is important, too. There is increasing globalization in the industry by the large multinationals, as the pace of international acquisitions and joint ventures quickens.

CONCLUSIONS

This chapter has outlined some of the issues and challenges related to business and environmental pollution. Concern for the environment is not new, but it will undoubtedly become even more pronounced than it is now in the early 1990s as we move closer and closer to the 21st century. A majority of economists favour using the market mechanism to cut down the amount of pollution by charges of various kinds. This approach shows clearly that the socially optimal amount of pollution is greater than zero and that controlling pollution is not cost-free. The Earth Summit at Rio de Janeiro in 1992 gave a powerful impetus to environmental protection measures. Many companies, particularly in Europe, North America and Japan, are taking a pro-active attitude, viewing likely future legislation and increasing consumer concern and pressure as business opportunities rather than threats.

References

1 Meadows, D., *The limits to growth*, Pontomac Associates, 1972.
2 Erlich, P., *The population bomb*, (London, Ballantine Books, 1976).
3 Marin, A., 'Environmental policy', *Economics of the EC* (Ed. El-Agraa), 3rd edition, (London, Philip Allan, 1990).
4 OECD, *The application of economic instruments for environmental protection*, Paris, 1989.
5 Cook, S., 'Environmental audits: theory and practice', *European Environment* 1.1.
6 Porter, M., 'Competition in global industries', *Harvard Business Review*, 1986.
7 World Commission on environment and development, *Our common future* (Oxford, OUP, 1987).
8 Hocking, M, 'Paper versus polystyrene: a complex choice', *Scientist*, Vol. 251, 1 February 1991.

Bibliography

Victor, P., *Economics of Pollution*, (London, Macmillan, 1972).

CHAPTER EIGHT

CULTURE AS AN ASSET IN INTERNATIONAL BUSINESS

TERRY MUGHAN

INTRODUCTION

Theorists and practitioners of international business have traditionally regarded foreign cultures and languages as among the most significant constraints on companies venturing into, or developing their activities in, foreign markets. Foreign languages are regarded as a 'problem' that companies have to contend with, implying that no single, simple solution to it exists. Anecdotes abound about culture in business and most of them reinforce the message of the nuisance-value of unfamiliar languages and behaviour. How unreasonable it is of the Italians to like their chocolates packaged in large, decorated cardboard boxes, when we happen to package them in densely packed tins. The Spaniards will insist on taking long lunch-hours when we, the British, like a working lunch.

In a field of activity such as business and management, which, by its very nature, constantly searches for new ideas, solutions and products, this attitude is surprisingly negative. Other variables in the business equation, such as decision-making, leadership or excellence, can be equally elusive, but efforts are made to understand and master them so that they can be addressed by business techniques and skills. Yet the traditional view of most managers and academics, particularly the British and American, has been that culture and language are different and cannot be managed effectively.

A NEW VIEW OF CULTURE IN BUSINESS

This rather negative approach to the most basic of business considerations – for culture surely lies at the heart of consumer taste and behaviour – has been gradually overtaken in the last 30 years by a much more positive one preferred by, amongst others, the Scandinavians and the Japanese. These and other countries, which were forced to reconstruct totally after the Second World War, set about doing so without the complacency which came from having economic superpower status and approached international business with an open mind. Many saw, more quickly than their Anglo-Saxon competitors, a link between giving international customers what they want and the ability and readiness to listen and modify.

An open and receptive attitude towards other cultures, tailored to the needs and the character of the organization, is described by Percy Barnevik, Chief Executive Officer of Asea Brown Boveri (ABB), a global company with its headquarters in Zurich but roots across Europe and activities world-wide.[1]

> *Global managers have exceptionally open minds. They respect how different countries do things, and they have the imagination to appreciate why they do them that way. But they are also incisive; they push the limits of culture. Global managers don't passively accept it when someone says, 'You can't do that in Italy or Spain because of the unions.'*

Barnevik goes on to describe the responsibility of the organization in shaping global managers. Multi-country, mixed nationality experience, international business teams and mixed, international recruitment are just some of the methods his company uses to enhance cross-border communication. Yet sensitivity to national needs is not diminished by this global push.

> *We can't have managers who are 'un-French' managing in France because 95 per cent of them are dealing every day with French customers, French colleagues, French suppliers.*

This conscious effort to create a company and managers who do not baulk at the emergence of a cultural obstacle may reflect the Swedish origins of Asea and the requirement for managers to learn to operate in other languages and cultures if the company was to expand. The result is a large, modern company, well placed to 'think global, act local', by eschewing the arrogance of universalists who claim that consumers in Bologna are no different from consumers in Birmingham. Of course, as Barnevik stated, this may imply less than total deference to local customs, but a sensitive and respectful process of compromise and adaptation. Thus Japanese companies setting up subsidiaries in the United Kingdom diluted and adapted some of their treasured working methods. They adopted others in order to obtain the commitment of the British workforce and invested in some costly training methods, such as secondments to Japan for British workers.

The keystone for such compromise must be an understanding of the indigenous culture. Only when this is secured can the nature and extent of adaptation be gauged. When Volkswagen bought SEAT and attempted to transfer German methods without a full understanding of the Catalan workforce, they were met by resistance and intransigence, which surprised them and turned out to be unnecessarily costly. Adjustments to the strategy included the recruitment of a more mixed nationality management and less confrontational methods, which seem to be bearing some fruit. The cases of the global tyre war and Northern Foods show how different national cultures can have a major impact on business.

The learning process was a lot more difficult for the Atlantic partners, whose business methods rested on advantages which accrued to them for reasons in some respects unconnected with product and service quality. As we approach the end of the 20th century, British and American companies are having to compete in markets without the protection previously afforded to them by governments keen to expand economically and culturally, as well as militarily. Thus, British and American international companies today, unlike their predecessors of the late 19th and mid 20th centuries, cannot rely on foreign policy to smooth the way for them when it comes to encountering overseas administrative and economic systems.

Each company wishing to establish itself in a foreign market in the 1990s has to study and understand the environment in direct competition with international competitors, without the advantage of an infrastructure and consumers who are favourably predisposed to the English language or British and American products. Companies and countries which grew up in the post-war period having to go alone are more likely to realize the importance of local knowledge and responsiveness in international dealings, and to develop methods and strategies for achieving these. The speed at which the lessons learnt in this field have found their way back into the English-speaking community is ironically constrained by the preference of British and American academics and theoreticians to be confined in their reading habits to . . . the English language!

THE ROLE OF CULTURE IN BUSINESS

So if culture is a more complex component in international business than the usual anecdotes would have us believe, what role does it play and can it be a positive one? Let us this time choose an anecdote which proves that it can. A manager in a Swedish pharmaceutical firm described what happened when a multicultural team was put together.

> *Product design was traditionally carried out at our Stockholm headquarters. Once, by accident or design, we brought in an international team to discuss the design of a new allergy product. Due to extreme differences of opinion on what constitutes good medical practice, the team designed the new product with maximum flexibility to suit the major demands of each country. Later, we discovered this flexibility to be of great advantage in developing and marketing internationally competitive products.*[2]

The pro-active gesture of composing a group of people from different cultures produced a highly profitable outcome for international dealings. At the root of this achievement was the respect for different perceptions, traditions, needs and solutions. Regarding cultural difference as a challenge rather than a problem may mean a little more investment of time and funds, but it is more likely to produce internationally workable teams, systems and products. This general approach, albeit with variances in each case, has helped Japanese, Germans and Scandinavians adapt successfully to international markets. It has, incidentally, also helped cultivate the deep awareness of quality and consumer-friendliness which characterizes the products of these successful countries, and pervades business thinking and aspirations in general today. The study of NH Geotech shows how that organization has used cultural diversity to its advantage.

So if international companies are to tackle the challenge of culture and language, where do they start? Let us look in more detail at the areas of business activity which need to be culture-responsive. Steven Globerman discussed this issue in 1986.

> *Cultural differences do not as a rule prohibit doing business internationally, although they often oblige management to modify the way business is done from region to region. While modifications may be required, to a greater or lesser extent, in virtually all of the international firm's activities, the particular areas that seem to be affected by cultural differences are the marketing and personnel relations functions.*[3]

This rather begrudging acknowledgement of the challenge is not uncharacteristic of American academics, who have been more inclined to universalistic theories of management. These theories hold that all organizations and markets are ultimately the same and what works in one country will work in all others. None the less it points in the right direction and its implications are clear: managing and communicating with a culturally different or varied workforce requires new methods and techniques. Success in this first objective is needed so that the company may understand consumers whose behaviour and tastes are different from that of the home country.

HUMAN RESOURCES AND CULTURAL DIVERSITY

More and more attention is being paid to the maximizing of organizational performance through improved communications between, and within, companies. As a company extends its orbit of operations to encompass other countries and cultures, it should not make the mistake of thinking that other organizations and the individuals within them necessarily behave in ways which resemble its own.

Human resources policies, which apply to the internal and external operations of a company active in just one country, are based on legislation, strategies and markets of a single national character. Such policies inevitably presuppose behaviour, problems and responses which can be anticipated and implemented with considerable certainty. Interpretation of the national environment is facilitated by the use of a common language and the sharing of a relatively uniform educational background and professional training. Within this framework, there is a natural tendency to make assumptions about communication in the organization, which then take on an unconscious or unspoken character. These shared assumptions encompass matters of both an organizational and interpersonal nature, and whilst it is generally acknowledged that every individual has to 'learn the ropes' and that this may take anything from a few weeks to several months, most organizations expect considerable skills of the individual in this respect.

In Britain, for instance, one might be forgiven in the first month for bypassing a particular administrative procedure or even for usurping the responsibility of a colleague or superior. More often than not, the remedy for such transgressions will even be informal, consisting of a quiet word in the ear. Most such rules or codes are unwritten and stem from highly developed communicative skills of an implicit, unspoken or unwritten nature, amongst a relatively homogeneous national group. This is not to say that we all immediately understand each other, but we do develop the antennae needed to realize that we have made a gaffe or offended somebody, even though it has not been spelt out to us.

On the other hand, even within an homogeneous group things go wrong when communication is not as good as it should be and is not effectively corrected. The kinds of misunderstandings involved here are not just of an interpersonal, social nature. Many are serious enough in efficiency, cost and image terms to prompt the company to develop systems, train staff and publish missions and statements which promote guiding values. The most successful modern organizations are those which share a set of commonly understood aims and values, and which minimize the scope for misunderstanding and inefficiency.

If poor communication can be a problem in monolingual, culturally homogeneous content, then the scope for breakdown is at least twofold when it comes to expanding into foreign markets. Even a company which functions and communicates effectively will find that it is exposed to an organization and individuals with different assumptions, values, reflexes, systems and methods and will have to learn to interpret them through a different language. 'Learning the ropes' becomes a task for the whole organization. Differences in accounting methods, in attitudes to punctuality and authority, and in perceptions of the very nature of business itself are just some of the problems that can arise here, and if they are not challenged pro-actively they can easily degenerate into almost xenophobic mistrust. The business consequences of this state can be dire, as one nationality systematically absolves itself of responsibility for errors or misunderstandings by blaming the other. All the progress made in improving monolingual communication evaporates as staff slip back into the bad habits of the past.

International operations should build on existing good practice by widening the social and communicative competence of the organization. This will involve several steps. One of the first and most important ones should be to learn to appreciate the impression your organization gives to the foreigner, to understand your strengths and weaknesses *as they perceive them*. An important principle is at stake here: if culture is a problem, then it is usually your own which is as much to blame as that of foreigners. What you regard as normal and proper may appear illogical or wasteful to a German. If he says so, your response should not be to flare up, but to explain why you find it normal and proper. He probably needs you to do this rather than take offence. This process of reciprocal education should cover all key areas of interaction between the company and the individuals within it. Areas of interaction susceptible to variance across cultures are:

- organizational codes, rules, systems, procedures;
- human relations, status, hierarchy, degrees of formality;
- decision-making, expert versus committee, vertical versus lateral methods.

Thus a British businessman is accustomed to approaching tasks on a pragmatic level. He is not excessively hindered by prescribed procedures or by conferring with a number of colleagues whom he addresses on first-name terms in order to negotiate a solution amongst them which is ultimately the property of the organization, and not one individual. This approach contrasts sharply with what might happen in a French organization where the manager would be delegated the task by a superior, whom he addresses by his surname, would confer formally with designated managers and would ultimately be expected to explain and justify his rationale for reaching a given decision. The potential for inefficiency and misunderstanding between such French and British individuals and organizations who are brought into contact with each other is great. The matter is compounded when both go into the relationship unprepared and ready to blame the other. What can be done to avoid this scenario?

- self-analysis;

- cultural training;
- a wider recruitment policy.

SELF-ANALYSIS

As already intimated, the instinctive response of people from most cultures, when misunderstanding takes place, is to blame the other partner. For the British, the Germans are inflexible and to the Germans, the British lack method and rigour. In reality, both parties will reject such a simplistic characterization. Yet if they were systematically to assess the effect their approach has on the other party they would have to admit that there is some foundation for it. Subsequent 'businesslike' action would be to analyse where and how a particular approach meets with a positive or a negative result, and consciously to adjust it. This is no more than the application of basic sales technique and can be honed and perfected according to the customer. If it works with the Germans to be direct and detailed, then it should be done. If, on the other hand, the Americans prefer a more informal, less long-winded approach, then that should be adopted.

CULTURAL TRAINING

So limited and controlled has been interaction between different business and management cultures that in most countries it does not form part of the educational process that most managers undergo. Nowadays the growing likelihood is that personnel from all levels will sooner or later come into regular and meaningful contact with counterparts from other countries. The culture shock and alienation which can ensue is costly for any company and minimizing it must be a priority. Training methods exist which prepare people to adapt and to see beyond the initial unproductive experience how it can be improved upon. The best incentive to get on with people from other cultures must be the certainty that your career development depends on it.

RECRUITMENT

National educational patterns, and restrictions on professional mobility, have largely limited international career choice to movement within subsidiaries of multinational companies. The mobility that has occurred has been minimal by the standards of what will take place, for example, in the single European market. It has been confined to the best qualified managers, the most adventurous or those employed on special projects requiring a large, short-term influx of expertise.

Direct recruitment in the international labour market presents the quickest route to internationalization of the organization and its culture. Notwithstanding uncertainty about the status of foreign qualifications, which will cause some reluctance to take risks, the opportunity to capture technically competent personnel also able to form a cultural bridge between subsidiaries, companies and individuals will be of great appeal.

A staging post on the way to this destination is the use of foreign students to fill work placement vacancies. This represents a valuable learning opportunity for the pro-active company wishing to benefit from the complementary technical insight of professional trainees from Germany, France or elsewhere, and to conduct initial cultural analysis of itself and the foreign guest. The theme of culture and human resource management is further developed in Chapter 15.

MARKETING AND CULTURAL DIVERSITY

Product modification in international marketing is not a new concept. Governments impose regulations on all kinds of technical areas for purposes ranging from health and safety to protectionism. This is one factor which, in the long term, contributes to the curious mishmash of expectations and 'taste' on the part of consumers, which businesses ignore at their peril. The fact that German consumers expect electrical appliances to come fitted with a plug may have been conditioned by such regulations, but has gradually become a quality expectation and a signal which has to be respected. Similarly, their preference for German beer over any other was conditioned by the Purity Law, but is now inseparably linked with a subjective conviction that their product is simply superior to other beers. Market opportunities have to emphasize distinctiveness and quality rather than compete on the same terrain; Guinness is a good example.

This is not to say that any market niche in the increasingly competitive international market-place is sacred. Deregulation is even opening up the German beer market wider than the Germans themselves would like. Companies attempting to penetrate and develop such a market clearly need to be able to read and interpret consumer and competitor behaviour on the ground, in order to adjust their own strategy. Such demands clearly argue in favour of the possession of loyal, multilingual and indigenous personnel, who are able to process data and read qualitative aspects of market research. Now that the Germans will be able to buy 'impure' foreign beers, will they experiment and, if so, at what price, and can product loyalty be developed?

This process of broad and deep adaptation to foreign markets puts great demands on any international company. The whole world and not just one country must be regarded as its market-place and resources must be deployed to ensure that individual cultures within that market-place are understood and respected. Respect for different languages, tastes, behaviour and decisions is essential, if you wish to ensure that the product picked up off the shelf is yours and not your competitor's. In Chapter 13 Terry O'Sullivan develops further the theme of culture and international marketing.

SUMMARY AND CONCLUSION

This chapter has considered culture as a constraint on international business and has suggested that the traditional view of this – that people from other cultures who do not know how to use or recognize the value of your products are being awkward – is now defunct. The greatest cultural constraint starts with you and it is the expectation that people from other cultures will understand and even defer to yours, while you make little attempt to understand theirs. This approach has characterized the British and American business communities more than most others in recent history and there is increasing evidence that it is contributing to a growing lack of competitiveness on their part. In order that culture and language may not be a constraint on international business, and indeed that they may be an asset, a company which is, or aims to be, internationally active should adopt a positive policy of adaptation. This policy comprises four key points.

ADAPTATION OF THE SELF

All of the following points presuppose the willingness of the organization and its personnel to put to one side prejudgements and principles, and to be aware that they, too, have an impact on others, sometimes a negative one. Even if your company or country is successful, associated stereotypical behaviour, such as aggression, arrogance, discourtesy and aloofness, will in many contexts fail to endear or impress. The cultural imperialism associated with earlier models of international business cannot prevail in a world where the customer is king. Similarly, the expectation that native speakers of English need make no allowance for, or gesture towards, those with no command of the language is now dangerous. The language of business is the language of the customer and anthropology has taught us that the best route to the understanding of a foreign culture is through its language.

ADAPTATION TO HOST GOVERNMENTS

Awareness of relevant laws, regulations, ethics and the general business environment are essential. In spite of deregulation, every company needs to ensure that its practices and products are acceptable to the target community. Cultural competence required here will be of a formal kind involving links with government agencies, banks etc., and demanding knowledge of the local business environment.

ADAPTATION TO COLLABORATORS

Whether the method used is an agent, partner, distributor or a subsidiary, the business methods of the indigenous culture will differ from those you take for granted. Cultural competence here will be of a more informal nature. Frequent personal contact with agents, partners and the like will demand extensive language skills and background knowledge if you are to be able to trust your judgement and theirs. This exposure is clearly at its greatest when a full subsidiary employing members of the indigenous population is set up. Every assumption must be tested here. It would, for example, be easy – yet wrong – to think that attitudes to women in business are the same all over Europe. Female British managers have reported encountering greater condescension, or even hostility, in Germany than they are accustomed to in Britain. Similarly, young British finance executives have found that their European equivalents are usually older than they are and reluctant to put the age difference to one side.

ADAPTATION TO CONSUMER AND CLIENTS

Products and services need to be tailored to the demands of foreign markets. In a sophisticated international economy, anything other than short-term presence in the market demands respect and attention to the tastes and subtlety of that market. Companies must be prepared, and able, to listen and observe. Reading of market research data and keeping abreast of consumption patterns and trends involve both formal and informal communication skills of the highest order. Every organization should have at least one person at its disposal who is able to interpret primary data and relay it to colleagues. This capacity ultimately entails a detailed knowledge of the people, language and culture of the country.

The accelerating internationalization of business activity is forcing more and ever smaller companies to venture into unknown foreign markets. In doing so, those companies have to confront many practical, concrete problems of a logistical or operational nature and there might be a tendency to dismiss or postpone consideration of the less immediate one of culture. This temptation should be resisted. The experience of many companies, large and small, in what is an increasingly competitive environment, has been that market proximity and close relations with partners, clients and other agencies are essential. Most of these attributes are dependent on good, cross-cultural communication and can be achieved by adding an international dimension to management, marketing, human relations, recruitment and training. The result of this will be a fuller understanding and the ability to adapt to different markets and consumers. When seen in this way, culture ceases to be a constraint and becomes a basic business technique.

References

1 *Harvard Business Review*, March/April 1991, pp. 91–105.
2 Allport, G. W., *The nature of prejudice*, (Reading, Mass, Addison Wesley, 1954) p. 281.
3 Globerman, Stephen, *Fundamentals of international business management*, (Englewood Cliffs, New Jersey, Prentice Hall, 1986).

Bibliography

Adler, N., *International dimensions of organizational behaviour*, (Kent, PWS, 1991).
Hall, E. and M., *Understanding cultural differences – France, Germany and the USA*, (Intercultural Press, 1990).
Terpstra, V., and David, K., *The cultural environment of international business*, (Cincinnati Ohio, Southwestern Publishing, 1985).
Tung, R. L., *The new expatriate – managing human resources abroad*, (Cambridge, Mass, Allinger/Harper & Row, 1988).

CHAPTER NINE

THE GLOBALIZATION OF FINANCIAL SERVICES

THEO KIRIAZIDIS AND STEPHEN REGAN

INTRODUCTION

In the 1980s and early 1990s, the global expansion of financial institutions contributed significantly to the internationalization of overall business activity. These institutions provide a range of services that are essential for this activity.

Initially, financial institutions expanded internationally to provide financial services to companies operating abroad so as to meet their demand for capital in the foreign markets. These institutions acquired considerable international business experience, which they were able to offer to customers who were expanding, or wishing to expand, abroad.

The gradual move towards a single financial market in Europe is having a major impact on the globalization of these services. The single financial market, completed on 1 January 1993, is designed to enable corporate and private individuals to be free to move funds around the EC without hindrance. In essence, the financial services market will open up on three fronts:

- freedom of capital movement;
- the right to sell financial services throughout the EC;
- the right for financial organizations to establish themselves in any EC Member State.

This chapter briefly examines the banking, insurance and accounting sectors, and identifies ways in which these services have helped and can assist their corporate customers to expand into foreign markets.

The authors would like to thank Ross Catterall of Anglia Business School for his most helpful comments and suggestions during the writing of this chapter.

BANKING

Quite simply, banks operate in foreign markets in anticipation of making greater profits in these markets than can be obtained from alternative forms of expansion.

The theory of direct foreign investment suggests that any multinational enterprise, including banks, possesses some specific assets, such as expertise, technology or special know-how, which can be exploited in foreign markets. This theory helps to explain why organizations do not concentrate all their production functions in one country and export to foreign markets.

Given the established technology, financial products can be transferred to new locations at little cost. As a result, multinational banks have developed financial products such as project evaluation, arranging mergers and acquisitions, and corporate financing, that can be transferred to other markets. These products enable multinational banks to gain a competitive edge over domestic organizations. For example, Citibank has a substantial amount of corporate banking business in many markets outside the USA. Products are designed, produced and marketed globally. Table 9.1 lists the world's ten largest banks in 1991.

Certain banking services can be provided on a trade basis from a foreign location. The introduction of micro-electronic technology and telecommunications equipment enables services to be supplied without the need of physical proximity between the user and the provider.

However, the availability of a comparative advantage in terms of expertise, technology and special know-how does not in itself explain the growth in multinational banking. The banks could exploit their advantage by producing services domestically and exporting to foreign markets. In fact, financial services can be provided on either an 'establishment' basis, through branches and acquisitions, or a 'services' basis, through the provision of services from the country of origin.

In the financial services industry, proximity is a significant factor, for the relationship between banks and their customers is particularly important. Only through physical establishment can a foreign financial organization compete effectively with local banks, since individuals are notoriously reluctant to do business with a bank which lacks a domestic location. This point explains why most

Table 9.1
The world's ten largest banks in 1991

Rank	Bank	Shareholders' equity $m	Total assets $m	Net profits $m
1	Sumitomo	15,217.33	406,107.00	1,024.78
2	Dai-Ichi Kangyo	13,599.58	425,509.25	649.54
3	Fugi	13,257.15	396,450.92	710.03
4	Sanwa	13,019.83	400,740.67	801.64
5	UBS	12,858.07	138,911.94	897.09
6	Mitsubishi	12,010.69	380,439.89	724.50
7	Barclays	11,676.91	263,708.84	529.41
8	Sakura	11,550.57	405,953.71	609.96
9	Deutsche	11,230.44	298,158.53	912.43
10	Companie Financière	11,067.17	199,727.41	211.78

Source: Adapted from Euromoney June 1992.

international expansion in banking has taken place through the establishment of local branches, mergers and/or acquisitions. Case 2, a study of the Midland Bank illustrates this point.

In most countries financial organizations are subject to more stringent controls than is normal with the suppliers of other goods and services. This is because the financial services sector plays a crucial role in the development of other sectors. National authorities may also attempt to influence the allocation of resources in the economy. For example, financial institutions may be urged to provide finance for certain economic sectors on favourable terms.

National governments also have some control over the financial system as part of their financial and economic policy. For example, the conduct of monetary policy involves restrictions on the activity of financial institutions, notably banks. Furthermore, in the financial sector, where large sums of money are involved, there is a danger of fraud and other malpractices, while if a financial organization defaults for any reason, the financial consequences for the consumer would be very serious. For all these reasons, most governments intervene in the financial services sector to ensure that financial institutions are able to honour their commitments.

The actual extent of government intervention and control differs from country to country. Several financial organizations have transferred part of their interests abroad in order to escape the more stringent financial regulations at home. For example, despite substantial deregulation in the USA, as identified in Chapter 4, American banks are still subject to stricter controls than many of their rivals in other markets. As a result, many American banks prefer to conduct their business from London.

BANKING SERVICES

The major factor promoting multinational banking has been the growth of multinational trading companies. For example, the growth of US investment abroad in the late 1960s and 1970s induced US banks to follow their customers abroad. In turn, 'cross-hauling' by Japanese companies into the American and European markets has been accompanied by the 'cross-hauling' of Japanese banks into US and European financial markets.

The initial aim of the pioneering national banks established abroad was to provide financial services to national companies operating in foreign markets and to meet their demand for capital in these markets. At a later stage, banks were able to provide more sophisticated financial products, such as economic intelligence and advice to companies expanding, or wishing to expand, abroad.

An international bank, by definition, will normally enjoy a presence in the main financial centres of the world and have a commitment to deliver a wide range of services to corporate customers in any location. The aim of an international bank is to ensure that, wherever in the world their corporate customers need to transact business, they will have access to appropriate services.

EXPORT AND IMPORT ADVICE

Each of the big banks has an international department, which is able to provide a range of information to both exporters and importers. The international departments are in contact with bank branches, subsidiaries and partner banks abroad. Thus many banks can introduce clients to agents, as well as provide information on national trading terms and conditions. For instance, the export of some goods, such as live animals and military equipment, is restricted and export licences may be required. In some cases, the national authorities may demand a certificate of origin to confirm that the goods come from a particular country. In other cases, countries impose foreign exchange controls that restrict the transfer of funds out of the countries concerned. As a result, the national authorities need to ensure that the transfer of funds from international trade takes place according to their rules.

FINANCE AND INTERNATIONAL TRADE

Some of the most important problems in international trade relate to the risk of non-payment and the provision of finance. In fact, there are considerable problems in collecting debts in the export trade. Exports have often to be sold on extended credit and the terms have to be better then those offered by competitors. Furthermore, it is not as easy to persuade an overseas customer to settle his debt as it is a customer in the home country. As a result of these problems, most international banks provide special finance and information facilities, although for many organizations these services can be expensive.

FINANCE FOR INTERNATIONAL TRADE

Banks are usually prepared to grant advances in the form of overdraft facilities to exporters, when they are handling the shipping documents. In most cases, the shipping document is an acceptable security for the advance.

Banks are also willing to buy bills of exchange. In this case, the exporters are credited with the amount, less charges, and the bank collects the proceeds of the bill when it becomes payable. Here companies engaging in international trade may receive payment almost immediately.

The major international banks offer factoring services and many have special schemes tailored to meet the needs of companies in international trade. Broadly speaking, factoring involves providing finance against the trade debtors of businesses. When companies sell goods to other companies, they have to allow a certain period of time, depending on the contract, for the receipt of the payments. Until then valuable cash is tied up, thereby restricting the growth of the business and representing a potential barrier to international trade. Banks, however, may opt to offer an immediate amount of money against these debtors. Finance can be provided by purchasing debtors and making an immediate payment, which is usually restricted to a certain percentage of the debt due.

SALES ACCOUNTING

The banks may also take responsibility for all aspects of sales accounting within the business, such as maintaining the sales ledger, sending out regular statements of account and collecting payments as they become due. In addition, the banks can guarantee the payment on approved sales to customers. In this case the payment is made, even if the customers are unable to pay. Obviously, factoring services serve to relieve the management of the business from the time and the expense of running a sales ledger, but the downside is that bank charges for this facility can be expensive.

SERVICES FOR IMPORTERS

Importers usually find their suppliers require a guarantee of their ability to pay. International banks can provide such guarantees, facilitating the transactions and enabling the suppliers to obtain finance on the best possible terms. This can prove a useful negotiating point when discussing price. It is also particularly useful where the limit of credit with the exporter has been reached.

However, the provision of such guarantees implies a considerable cost for companies operating, or wishing to operate, at the international level. This may represent a prohibitive barrier to the international expansion of some enterprises, especially small- and medium-size ones which lack adequate financial resources.

GENERAL ECONOMIC AND FINANCIAL ADVICE

Successful international trading demands a great deal of research and planning. International banks can provide a wide range of specialist information; for example, they prepare economic and political reports, in order to inform their customers about the political and economic background of specific countries where they wish to operate. In addition, these banks can prepare status reports on specific companies for clients. These ensure that traders wishing to enter into a foreign contract can ascertain whether the targeted foreign companies are likely to be able to honour their contractual obligations. These status enquiries are one of the most useful financial products offered by banks to international business.

BALANCE REPORTING

Balance reporting is another core service which the global banks offer to corporate customers, through the provision of an electronic window into their bank accounts. Through this window, corporate treasurers are able to check on balances and transactions. For example, changes in a company's currency exposure and credit balance are reflected in its accounts held at the bank, as each transaction is recorded on a running basis.

Most international banks have supported the provision of a wide range of services to customers, often with a 24-hour dealing service. This invaluable facility enables customers in a number of countries to dial a global telephone number and to be switched to whichever global services centre is open for business.

THE BANKS AND EXCHANGE RATE FLUCTUATIONS

International banks provide various services to protect corporate assets from exchange rate fluctuations. In fact, changes in the exchange rates affect the value of the payment and represent an important risk and barrier to international trade. Where payments for traded goods are made in a foreign currency, there is a danger that exchange rate fluctuations, occurring between the date of the signing of the contract and the date of payments, may reduce a participating company's profits or even turn whole transactions into losses.

Banks can remove the exchange rate risk and uncertainty by offering their corporate customers forward foreign exchange contracts. According to these contracts, the banks agree to buy the foreign currency from the exporter at the date of payment of a fixed, predetermined exchange rate. In this case the bank's customers will know how much they will receive, irrespective of the exchange rate fluctuations in the interim. The banks can cover their own positions by matching the various deals.

The implications of exchange rate fluctuations is developed further in Chapter 14 and the case studies of BMW and NEC show how two international companies have responded to these changes.

INSURANCE

International trade and investment require not only help by way of finance and banking facilities, but also through insurance services. Since the start of international trading the need for insurance cover related to goods and their means of transport.

During the 19th and early part of the 20th centuries, there was a growth of insurance companies in the UK, to cope with the increasing losses associated with trade and other operations abroad. When trading companies established premises abroad, they insured them in the same market which they used for their UK risks: London. Japan has also become a major provider of international insurance cover, and similarly Germany developed a strong insurance industry to support its manufacturing industry in its expansion abroad. Today the large and powerful German insurance companies, Allianz and Munich Re, can provide insurance cover in the whole of Europe, North and South America and the Middle East, through their extensive network of branches and agencies.

Originally, domestic foreign departments were established to underwrite foreign business. Where a policy holder or potential policy holder had risks outside the country of origin, it was this department which would consider the aspects of the policy. This method of work obviated the need and expense of running a network of agencies or branches overseas. However, some local presence was required in order to survey risks, issue policies and settle claims.

As the volume of business increased, there was a need for a local presence in foreign markets, through agencies or branches. Many insurance companies expanded through branches abroad to handle the increasing volume of business in foreign markets. In addition, some insurance companies have also acquired majority or minority interests in local organizations to obtain a share in a foreign market. Table 9.2 lists the world's ten largest insurance companies.

MARINE INSURANCE

The importance of marine insurance in international trade is obvious. Traders and shipowners would be reluctant to allow their investments to be hazarded in marine ventures without the protection of insurance, as a vessel can represent an outlay in excess of £40 million. Marine insurance plays a major role in compensating for the financial results of sea disasters. In addition, one has to consider the immense potentialities of any liabilities arising from its use. Every marine insurance contract includes collision, fire, theft and stranding. War risk may also be insured on special terms.

Table 9.2
The world's ten largest insurance companies

Rank	Company	Assets $m	Capital $m	Net income $m
1	Prudential	140,931	13,669	867
2	Nippon	122,658	5,451	5,028
3	Metropolitan	88,140	4,322	201
4	Dai-Ichi	83,698	3,988	3,483
5	Aetna	72,574	7,069	931
6	Sumitomo	69,436	3,013	2,729
7	Equitable	59,929	1,748	57
8	Cigma	53,495	6,400	728
9	Travelers	50,165	5,132	374
10	Prudential Corporation	49,177	14,660	324

Source: Adapted from Global Finance Ranking 1989.

The main types of marine insurance cover available differ according to the period for which the insurance operates.

- *Time policy* – is for a pre-determined period of time.
- *Voyage policy* – operative from the port of departure to destination, irrespective of the time element.
- *Mixed policy* – covers a combination of time and voyage insurance.
- *Floating policy* – refers to a type of cargo insurance which is effected for a relatively large lump sum insured. The policy holder makes a declaration as to the precise amount involved with individual shipments. These declarations are set against the floating policy, reducing the total shipment insured by that amount, until the cargo is exhausted. This type of policy obviously avoids the issue of separate policies for every shipment.

Banks, and other institutions which finance commercial transactions abroad, normally require that the venture is covered by marine insurance. For example, marine insurance policy is considered to be one of the 'documents of title' that must be produced before banks will discount the bills of exchange through which much foreign trading is financed. The insurance policy is lodged with the bank as security against the money advanced.

Re-insurance is a type of risk-spreading which has become ever more important, as the increasing size of risks and technological developments have caused insurers to run to re-insurance as additional protection. Many multinational, non-insurance companies establish their own insurance companies to handle their insurance business in full or in part in the host countries. These companies need to rely on re-insurance protection for their large risks and exposures, because the ability to meet large-scale risks usually demands resources that are not available in one country. The growth in re-insurance has in turn helped to expand the activities of multinational companies in foreign markets.

CREDIT INSURANCE

One of the most important financial problems in engaging in international trade is the risk of non-payment. International insurance companies are able to offer their customers credit insurance to eliminate this risk and uncertainty in international trade.

Credit insurance is designed to offer cover against future uncertainty associated with the potential inability of customers to pay for goods delivered or services rendered, due to their insolvency. In this type of insurance the characteristic of the policies, such as the premium, together with policy conditions, depends very much on subjective judgements of the likelihood of insolvency and the amount which it is reasonable for a company to put at risk on a buyer. Most credit insurers control their risk by setting credit limits on individual buyers. If any insurer believes that the figure he is asked to cover is too high for the buyer's resources, he may only agree a lower figure.

ACCOUNTING

Accounting firms followed the same pattern of internationalization developed in the banking and insurance sectors; in the main they were encouraged to go abroad by multinational clients. The increasing business activity at the international level has created a considerable demand for cross-border accounting services. The case study of Arthur Andersen illustrates how one firm of international accountants provides a world-wide range of services.

Many of the international accounting firms, such as Arthur Andersen, Coopers and Lybrand, and Price Waterhouse, expanded first in the developed North American and European markets and later in Latin America, Asia, the Pacific rim, Africa and the Middle East, following the same pattern of development as their main clients.

A number of the large accounting firms merged in order to provide a global network of services to clients. For example, in the late 1980s Peat Marwick Mitchell and Klynveld Main Geordder merged. The international accounting firms have themselves become very large organizations. In 1985 Deloitte, Haskins and Sells (now part of Deloitte Touche Tohmatsu) estimated that the firm was employing almost 1,400 full-time people world-wide just to audit General Motors.[2] Table 9.3 gives a league table of accounting firms world-wide in 1991.

Table 9.3
League table of accountancy firms world-wide 1991 (*September 1991 position, adjusted for mergers to reflect current operating strengths*).

		Fees US $bn	Staff Numbers
1	KPMG	6.0	76,200
2	Ernst & Young	5.4	66,800
3	Coopers & Lybrand	5.0	67,800
4	Arthur Andersen	4.95	59,800
5	DRT	4.5	56,000
6	Price Waterhouse	3.6	49,500

Source: Adapted from *International Accounting Bulletin*, January 1992.

The creation of large international accounting firms with an international network of agencies was not only prompted by the demands of multinational corporations. The need to become well known and establish a strong reputation in national and international markets was also an important factor. In all areas of financial services, including accounting, reputation is a crucial element. By their nature, financial services are more difficult than other goods and services to test at the time of sale and they are taken largely on trust. As a result, clients prefer to do business with firms which already have sound names and reputations in the market.

The international expansion of accounting firms has been a difficult exercise. There are significant restrictions in many countries on the range of services that international accounting firms are allowed to offer. For example, in many European countries, the certification of accounts and the preparation of accounts are two types of services that should be kept separate. The latter is undertaken mainly by bookkeepers, who usually keep books and prepare tax returns for mainly small- and medium-size enterprises. The certification of accounts, on the other hand, involves the conduct of independent audits of large corporations, as required by law. The international accounting firms undertake both these activities.

A number of European countries require all state-owned companies to use national accounting firms. In addition, some European countries put pressure on private enterprises who depend on a wide variety of concessions, such as tax incentives, to deal with indigenous accounting companies. These types of administrative practices have to some extent restricted the international operations of accounting firms. Table 9.4 gives a list of the top accounting firms in Europe. Many of the major accounting firms have been able to overcome a number of these obstacles by acquiring or merging with local accounting firms. For example, Price Waterhouse in its European operation merged with Befec M in France, Revisuisse in Switzerland and Seiet Peterson in Denmark, thereby obtaining a significant size and capability in these markets. A further example of this tactic was the acquisition of Stora in Sweden by Touche Ross, which allowed the latter to expand in the Scandinavian market.

To some extent, the globalization of accounting firms has been restricted by the international immobility of labour and the lack of expertise in many countries, such

Table 9.4
Table of accountancy firms in Europe
(*September 1991 position, adjusted for mergers to reflect current operating strenghts*).

		Fees US $bn	Staff Numbers
1	KPMG[1]	3.08	35,520
2	Coopers & Lybrand	2.6	30,300
3	Ernst & Young	2.09	24,800
4	Arthur Andersen	1.85	19,486
5	DRT	1.46	17,525
6	Price Waterhouse	1.22	15,123

[1] KPMG includes $200m bookkeeping practice (1600 staff) in France.

Source: Adapted from *International Accounting Bulletin* April 1992.

as eastern Europe and developing regions. Clearly, the production of accounting services is a labour-intensive activity, requiring a well-educated labour force, including a wide range of professional expertise in financial and other technical subjects. To deal with this problem, many international accounting firms have implemented a systematic recruitment and training policy. One of their first tasks is to recruit the best national people available in local markets and then to train them to international standards. The case study of Arthur Andersen shows how that organization is providing special training courses for personnel in eastern European countries.

Accounting methods and practices do vary in different countries, which can represent a barrier to the internationalization of business: this is a truism, even within the EC. For example, in Japan and many continental European countries, there is a tradition which allows companies to set aside a part of their profits in a good year to offset losses in a bad year. This profit forms part of the hidden reserves and this type of creative accountancy is permissible because of the low degree of disclosure of information required in these countries.

By contrast, in the US and UK, this low level of disclosure is considered harmful. In both of these countries accounts which are used as indicators of a company's performance are drawn up, mainly with the intention of attracting potential investors. Consequently, they tend to overestimate earnings. On the other hand, Japanese and most continental European accounts are more directly linked to distributability of profit and taxation requirements and therefore tend to understate earnings.

Because of the widely different uses for accounts, accounting practices differ markedly and it is therefore imperative for companies operating in foreign markets to know how to treat particular items (such as reserves and provisions) in their accounting statements. The need for accountants with expertise and experience in these different systems is obvious.

Financial reporting practices are influenced by the nature of the legal system.[4] Some countries, such as Germany, have a legal system which relies upon a considerable amount of statute law, allowing very little flexibility. This obviously influences company law, which accordingly prescribes a large number of detailed rules on how financial statements should be published. In such countries the valuation of the particular assets of companies, for example, involves as little flexibility and judgement as possible. Flexibility and judgement would make it difficult for auditors to determine whether the law was implemented.

However, in other countries – such as the UK, US, Ireland the Netherlands and Australia – the legal system is based on a limited amount of statute law and legal requirements give accounting firms far greater flexibility. In such countries valuation methods rely on fair values rather then book values, and companies revalue their assets to reflect current prices.

Usually, financial institutions, before extending loans to industrial companies, require that the latter should have their books audited. International accounting firms offer a financial audit which companies need in advance of capital funding. Those accounting firms with a good reputation and standing in the market-place may enhance their clients' trusts and enable them to raise new capital at a favourable interest rate. For example, Mitchell, a French company, managed to attract a long term loan at an interest rate of almost two percentage points lower, after having its books audited by Ernst and Whinney.

On the negative side, the use of sophisticated accounting services implies considerable costs for the companies involved and may represent a prohibitive barrier to the internationalization of business. This is particularly true for small- and medium-size firms which do not possess adequate financial resources.

Most international firms of accountants have taken advantage of a close working relationship with their clients to develop and deliver a range of services, mainly in the field of management and tax consultancy. A company's accountant has unique access to his client's books, and so develops an understanding of their needs and is in a very good position to suggest additional services.

The late 1980s and early 1990s have seen a continued expansion of management and tax consultancy services offered by international accounting firms. For example, Price Waterhouse combined auditing work for the Spanish electricity industry with human resources consultancy, advice on corporate restructuring, financial management and Information Technology. The same firm audited Smith Kline (a US company) and Beecham (a UK company) and later provided advice on the merger of these two companies. General Electric (USA) and Tungstarn (Hungary) employed Ernst and Whinney (now part of Ernst Young International), for international tax planning and assistance in their merger.

CONCLUSION

Financial services have played a major role in the development of international business. In the area of business services, including financial services, the nature of the firm–client relationship has had a major impact on the pattern of internationalization. As international trade and investment has expanded, financial institutions have expanded in tandem to serve their corporate customers. Through the provision of sophisticated financial services, these institutions have facilitated the international operations of corporations.

References

1 Lewis, M., *Domestic and international banking*, (London, Philip Allan, 1989).
2 Thierry, M., *International trade in business services*, New York.
3 Samuels, J., *International accounting*, (London, Croom Helm, 1985).
4 Archer, S., 'Financial reporting', (Ed. Hopwood) *International pressure for accounting change*, (London, 1989).

Bibliography

Briggs, D., *Credit insurance*, (New York, Woodhead Faulker, 1988).
Choi, F., *Handbook of international accounting*, (New York, Wiley, 1991).
Davies, A., *Banking operations*, (London, The Chartered Institute of Bankers, 1991).
Farag, S., 'Accounting in the 1990s: An international perspective', *The International Journal of Accounting*, Vol. 26, No. 4, 1991.
Howells, P., *Financial markets and institutions*, (London, Longman, 1990).
Lewis, R., *Advanced financial accounting*, (London, Pitman, 1991).
Lipscombe, G., *Economics and the Banks' role in the economy*, (London, The Chartered Institute of Bankers, 1991).
Smith, T., *Accounting for growth*, (London, Century, 1992).

CHAPTER TEN

THE GLOBALIZATION OF BUSINESS LEGAL SERVICES

JOHN FLOOD

INTRODUCTION

It was stated in Chapter 1 that the internationalization of business services, including finance and legal services, has contributed to the increased level of business activity at the international level. This chapter looks specifically at how the globalization of business legal services has contributed to this process.

By the early part of the 1990s, mega-law, mega-banking and mega-accounting, operating within complex corporate and partnership structures that span the world, had become the norm. The 'mega' prefix refers to the large-scale organizations that deliver services to the corporate world. Commerce and finance demand global services because time and space are no longer limits for them; they have become mere epiphenomena to be tackled in the same way as any other problem. For example, in dealing with foreign exchange markets, businesses and governments cannot be solely concerned with the London markets, because the Tokyo markets open six hours earlier than London and the New York markets remain open for five hours after London's close. Therefore expert knowledge has to be on hand to solve these problems, rapidly and efficiently.[1] The case study of Arthur Andersen shows how one firm of international accountants is responding to this opportunity.

The 'gentlemen's club' atmosphere of professional services has evaporated in the 'new world order' resulting from the effects of 'big bang' – the technical change in the Stock Exchange rules of 1986 that led to huge changes in the securities and banking industries in the UK. Stephen Regan's case study of the Midland Bank shows how one bank has responded to this new environment. Morality now follows the bottom line and external regulation has taken over from self-regulation.[2]

The new world order of professional services is fluid and all one can do in describing it is to capture moments, but this is the essential nature of the corporate professional game. The partner of one of the largest English law firms remarked that by the year 2000 he expected that there would be about 12 major players in the international legal market. The intense competition we see in the professional marketplace in the 1980s and 1990s is to give way to quasi-monopolistic forms of supply. In some areas it is already occurring; for example, in the world of banking the Hong Kong and Shanghai Bank's takeover of Midland Bank illustrates this point.[3] In the field of international accounting, the Big Eight have become the Big Six through mergers.[4] However, the law business is constrained from realizing the same expectations as those found in banking and accountancy, because of law's cultural specificity and the limits of partnership as an organizing mode.

THE LARGE LAW FIRM AND THE CRAFT OF LAW

The international business arena is dominated by large law firms based primarily in the United States and the UK. Large American law firms normally contain between 400 and 2,000 lawyers. English firms, although smaller, are still large, with around 150 to 1,000 lawyers on staff. Legal firms are essentially simple organizations composed of two layers: associates and partners.[5] The former are employees who aspire, after a probation of about eight years, to become the owners of the firm, the partners who share the profits. Becoming a partner is a competitive process; and with firms taking on up to approximately a hundred new graduates each year, only a handful can expect to win this prize.

Other countries are just beginning to develop the large law firm, notably the Netherlands, Germany and France. One feature which explains the differential rates of growth is the difference between the Anglo-American common law and the Continental civil law models. In his work on the sociology of law, Max Weber argued that modern capitalism required a formally rational system of law, one that was intrinsically coherent and constantly refined by jurists, as the civil code system aspires to be.[6] The Dutch Civil Code of 1992 is such an exemplar: it replaced the Code of 1838 after revision was begun in 1947.[7]

Common law is a substantively rational system in that it receives inputs from outside, for example, in the form of policy statements. In addition, it is dependent on its practitioners rather than jurists for its development.[8] The result of this craft domination of the making and interpretation of law in Anglo-American cultures is that it is very responsive to the exigencies of business life. A large proportion of the law has to be made up piecemeal from particular fact situations rather than drawn from established codes of law, as is the case in continental Europe. For example, there is a type of security transaction called a 'floating charge', which is a claim on a class of assets, such as a stock of cars, that from time to time will change. This type of transaction was invented by contractual agreement, but would have been impossible to create under most civil code systems without legislation.[9] In a world where international business transactions are weakly regulated by norms, flexibility and an inclination to take risks are essential if business is to function efficiently. An increasing number of Continental law firms are sending their new recruits to American and English law schools to acquire the business skills not taught in their own.

THE WORK OF INTERNATIONALIZATION

The work of large law firms is concentrated on corporate clients, and it is the demands of clients that have led these firms to internationalize their practices. The problem for many law firms is how this should be accomplished. The cultural specificity of law has acted as a brake on internationalizing tendencies. Accounting principles vary from country to country and this is also true of the law. The idea of jurisdiction is central to the exercise of law. Although jurisdiction-bound with respect to, say, auditing,[10] accounting firms have been more successful at diversifying their services into areas such as management consulting; a point illustrated by the Arthur Andersen case study.

Law firms have focused on three routes to international practice: in part, this is due to the claims of jurisdiction and in part to the orthodox view of their development, compared with accounting firms. Firstly, law firms can practice their own domestic law in other jurisdictions, so US firms can export US law. Secondly, they can practice both their own domestic law and the local law of their overseas offices. And thirdly, they can create forms of law and practice not tied to any particular state; for example, *lex mercatoria* (merchant law), which is a kind of international customary law practised by business.

The first route emphasizes domestic law as a competitor, with rival systems of law. In 1989 the City of London Law Society wrote:

> *The advantages of English law as a 'product' enables solicitors to contribute to this country's balance of payments some 250,000,000 per annum in invisible exports.*[11]

A senior partner of a large UK law firm was adamant that his firm was an 'English firm with overseas offices. We practice English law.' The idea here is that the firm's role is to capture foreign clients for UK law. For example, much of Japanese securities work is carried out under UK law.[12] In another case concerning the Eurodollar market a London law firm was

> *... instructed by a Luxembourg bank which had put together a syndicate to lend to a Portuguese company, where the draft documents were originally expressed to be governed by Luxembourg law, only for the bank to find that the international lending syndicate insisted on English law.*[13]

Many lawyers argue that to establish offices overseas and not to practice the local law is a waste of resources and a squandering of potentially rich markets. However – and this is the second route – sometimes the necessity of using local law is forced upon lawyers. One London partner has argued the point that, in order to put together a complex cross-border merger, he had to become conversant with local laws. Frequently, joint-venture agreements between, say, an English company and a Chinese state agency to produce diesel engines in China will, at the agency's insistence, be drafted according to Chinese law, and if disputed will be dealt with within the Chinese jurisdiction.

The third route is the most interesting, because in many respects it frees lawyers from the ties of jurisdiction. One area in which this has occurred is international arbitration, which often involves parties from different countries agreeing to handle their disputes with substantive laws and procedures devised by non-governmental agencies, such as the International Chamber of Commerce or the Stockholm Chamber of Commerce. One of the arbitrators in the IBM-Fujitsu arbitration, which resolved a seven-year dispute, commented:

> *Arbitration is a creature of the parties, necessarily created by contractual agreement. It can be enormously flexible – with the agreement of both sides – in developing procedures that are efficient and responsive.*[14]

Another area, which is not directly legal in the usual sense, is lobbying. Since the late 1980s Brussels has become the centre of European law-making for business. Consequently, many US, UK and other European law firms have established offices there. One of their primary tasks is to monitor and influence the developments of directives and regulations. This involves lobbying various EC institutions, especially the Commission. One partner in a large UK law firm maintained that 75 per cent of his time was spent lobbying; and it is an activity where competition between lawyers is rife. As one lawyer commented:

> *This is a field where lawyers from many countries compete to offer a similar service. Essential qualities are knowledge of general Community law, good languages, and an imaginative approach.*[15]

THE ORGANIZATION AND STRUCTURE OF MEGA-FIRMS

Banks and many accounting firms take corporate form; they have a pyramidical, hierarchical structure with well-defined lines of authority. Moreover, corporate structures often limit their exposure to risk by limiting liability. Lawyers still practice in partnerships, which are essentially flat structures with two levels: partners and associates, with all their attendant hazards of unlimited liability and undercapitalization. However, one of the notable features of professional partnerships in the 1980s is their decline as a lifelong commitment to an organization. Firms will dissolve and reassemble partnerships if they need to remove partners or departments.

However, internationalization has created pressures towards alternative forms of organization. The two main forms are multinational partnerships (MNPs) and multidisciplinary practices (MDPs). Both exist in weak and strong forms. US and UK law firms have formed 'strategic alliances' with firms in other countries which are close to being full mergers in MNPs. The dramatic phrase 'strategic alliance' was coined when a large Los Angeles law firm, O'Melveny & Myers, associated – without actually merging – with the London law firm, Macfarlanes. The senior partner of the American firm, Warren Christopher, had worked in the US State Department where such language was the norm.

MDPs exist in countries such as Germany, where accountants and notaries practice in the same firms. The Big Six accounting firms have huge legal departments that are, in some cases, as big as large law firms. In both cases lawyers lament over what they see as the dilution of the special culture of their individual firms. Thus it is unclear how far they will go towards full-blown MNPs and MDPs. Indeed, one fear of lawyers is that the large accounting firms would happily take over a law firm, if permitted.

CONCLUSIONS

We began with the idea of mega-professional organizations becoming the norm in the modern age, especially in the new world order. What we are beginning to see is a convergence of professional services, especially those of accounting and law, which are still intensely competitive with and within each other.

Professions can no longer rely on single service delivery; their clients demand a wider spectrum of services and of course it is in this widening that battles over which group is supposed to do what take place. Two examples illustrate this point. As European Community law increases its presence in commercial life, lobbying the EC Commission for changes in proposed legislation grows more urgent, for example, the merger regulations. Here there is a three-way struggle between US and UK law firms and accounting firms to be the main conduit between business and the Commission. In 1989 the 'Velvet Revolution' in eastern Europe paved the way for a massive restructuring of centrally planned economies to free market régimes. These changes required the privatization of many state industries. Not only did privatization laws have to be drafted, but the mechanics of the operation had to be designed. Again, we see the same kind of three-way battle as before, with many professional advisers using this kind of work as a 'loss leader' for more future lucrative business in the emerging economies.

Much of this competition is friendly in that, whatever the outcome, these groups have to work together, given current jurisdictional constraints. As long as lawyers are able to deliver expert knowledge which is only partially available from other professions, they will continue to be central players in the international market-place.

References

1 Neate, F., *The Developing Global Securities Market*, (London, International Bar Association, 1987).
2 Burrough, B., and Helyar, J., *Barbarians at the Gate: The Fall of RJR*, (New York, Nabisco Arrow Books, 1990).
   And Stewart, J., *Den of Thieves*, (New York, Simon & Schuster, 1991).
3 Smith, R. C., *The Global Bankers*, (New York, Plume, 1989).
4 Stevens, M., *The Big Six: The Selling Out of America's Top Accounting Firms*, (New York, Simon & Schuster, 1991).
5 Flood, J., 'Megalaw in the UK: Professionalism or Corporatism? A Preliminary Report', *Indiana Law Journal* 64, 1989, pp. 569–592.
   And Heinz, J., and Laumann, E., *Chicago Lawyers: The Social Structure of the Bar*, (New York and Chicago, Russell Sage Foundation & American Bar Foundation, 1982).
6 Weber, M., *Economy and Society: An Outline of Interpretive Sociology* (Eds. Roth, G., and Wittich, C.), (Berkeley, CA, University of California Press, 1978).
7 Whincup, M., 'The New Dutch Civil Code', *New Law Journal*, 4 September 1992: p. 1208.
8 Hermann, A., 'The Need for Scholarship and Specialization', *Law v. Business: Business Law Articles from the Financial Times 1983–1988*, (London, Butterworths, 1989).
   And Glendon, Mary Ann, Gordon, Michael W., and Osakwe, Christopher, *Comparative Legal Traditions*, (St. Paul, MN, West Publishing Co., 1985).
9 McCormick, R., *La Pratique Anglo-Americaine*, (London, Freshfields, 1991).

10 Weetman, Pauline, Adams, Carol, and Gray, Sidney, *Issues in International Accounting Harmonization: The Significance of UK/US Accounting Differences and Implications for the IASC's Comparability Project*, (London, ACCA, 1992).

11 *The Work and Organization of the Legal Profession: A Response to the Government's Green Paper*, City of London Law Society, 1989.

12 Flood, J., 'Conquering the World: Multinational Legal Practice and the Production of Law' in *Social Change and the Solicitors Profession* (Ed. E. Skordaki), (Oxford, OUP, 1993).

13 *Memorandum of Evidence by the Court and the Professional Business Committee to the Royal Commission on Legal Serivces*, (City of London Solicitors' Company, 1977).

14 Hellyer, C., 'Beyond Litigation', *Stanford Lawyer*, Spring/Summer 1989, pp. 5–8, 43–5.

15 'Highly Recommended, Solicitors Working in EC Competition Law Elect Their Key Competitor', *Legal Business Magazine*, December 1990, pp. 57–9.

PART TWO

THE ORGANIZATIONAL RESPONSE

CHAPTER ELEVEN

———

THE MULTINATIONAL ENTERPRISE: SOME THEORETICAL ISSUES

RON ALLISON

INTRODUCTION

The multinational enterprise (MNE) is the major institution through which international production occurs, although a body of specific theory concerning the MNE is only three decades old. In this time-span, which is relatively short in terms of much economic theory, a substantial body of literature has already accumulated. At first sight it might appear strange that there is no definition of either the MNE, or the multinational corporation (MNC) which has universal currency.

In 1973 a United Nations publication, *Multinational Corporations in World Development*, defined the MNC as 'enterprises which own or control production or service facilities outside the country in which they are based'.[1] Caves views a MNE as a firm that controls and manages plants located in at least two countries.[2] Other economists, for instance Hood and Young, prefer a rather broader definition that includes all income-generating assets,[3] such as a sales subsidiary. Another school of thought (for example, Vernon) prefers a stricter definition which requires the firm to operate in more than two countries.[4]

Common to all definitions are the concepts of ownership and control, but these two concepts raise problems and difficulties as well. Normally, direct investment in another company means that at least 25 per cent of the share capital is owned by the parent company. However, it is possible for a larger percentage of shares to be owned by a parent company without effective control being exercised, and effective control could occur with a shareholding of less than 25 per cent of the total.

Control is the essence of the multinational and this could be established, not by shareholding, but in other ways; for instance, by the provision of advanced technology or management skills. Thus the relationship between ownership and control may be more diffuse than at first thought.

Another difficulty is that the theory of multinational enterprises draws upon three main sources of well established theory: the theory of the firm; international finance;

and international trade theory. Further, as a study of the literature suggests, it has not been easy to integrate these bodies of theory. In summary then, it is not so strange after all that there is a lack of consensus amongst economists regarding the theory of the MNE. Bearing this in mind, it appears that there is broad agreement that the important elements of multinationals are that they operate in several countries, they have control over decision-making in companies in which they have an interest, and that there are transfers of resources such as technology and entrepreneurship. If so, the definition by Hood and Young is a useful starting point:

> ... *a MNE is a corporation which owns, in whole or in part, controls and manages income-generating assets in more than one country. In doing so it engages in international production, namely across boundaries financed by foreign direct investment.*[5]

AN OVERVIEW OF MNE THEORY

S. H. Hymer, an American economist, is generally credited with having pioneered the modern theory of the MNE.[6] His doctoral dissertation was presented in 1960, but it was not published until 1976. By this time a number of other economists had independently produced work of some similarity.

Much of the early work sprang from an attempt to explain the wave of US direct investment in Western Europe after the end of the Second World War. A great deal of investment took place in the late 1950s and early 1960s. At first this was not only welcomed, but encouraged, by the European governments concerned, who competed actively with one another to attract US firms by offering tax concessions and other inducements. Later, though, there was some concern about the growing impact of this investment on their economies.

There were two main questions which the early writers asked and attempted to answer.

- Why did the companies undertaking this foreign direct investment (FDI) in Europe do so, rather than building plants in the USA?
- How could the US companies compete with the European companies, given that producing abroad was more costly?

At one level the answer to the first question is that the formation of two large trading blocks in Europe, the European Community (EC) and the European Free Trade Association (EFTA), provided both a threat and an opportunity to American companies. The threat was the formation of tariff barriers against imports from countries that were not members. The opportunity was the large markets within these blocks, and the associated scale economies arising from high levels of production.

To the European governments the existing neoclassical economics suggested that the benefits of FDI – such as new manufacturing techniques, the provision of physical and financial capital, more and better social overhead capital, and increased employment – simply had to be weighed against the disadvantages. The main disadvantage was the impact on the balance of payments of profit transfer back to the host country. Overall, the benefits appeared to far outweigh the costs.

Hymer's approach centred on monopolistic aspects of ownership and location. An observable fact was that US investment in Europe after the Second World War had changed from portfolio to direct. An obvious difference between the two forms of investment is the control that the latter allows. Hymer argued that the two forms of investment are not substitutes for each other. According to him, direct investment takes place only when a company has a major advantage over its competitors and can gain a particular advantage from co-ordinating its actions on an international basis. Advantages include factors such as access to capital; access to modern technology; and information-gathering skills. Control enables the economic rent associated with these advantages to be fully exploited. These advantages are greater than the increased costs associated with setting up in a foreign business environment.

An associated question considered by Hymer was why did US companies not licence their technology to indigenous organizations? Licensing appears to yield the benefits of transferring technology abroad, without the costs involved in setting up abroad. His answer revolved around the point that the market for knowledge is not perfectly competitive.

Hymer has been criticized by other writers for not distinguishing between two types of market imperfection. The first is associated with market structure, the concentration of buyer and selling power. The second is associated with transaction costs, such as defining property rights and negotiating, monitoring and enforcing contracts.

Much of the literature that has tried to resolve this point is complex. But a useful, and approachable, summary is provided by Mark Casson. He suggests the following answer to the question, 'Why are plants in different countries commonly owned and controlled?':

> ... because the transaction costs incurred in intermediate products markets can be reduced by internalising these markets within the firm.[7]

FOREIGN DIRECT INVESTMENT

Multinationals achieve managerial control over their assets abroad through foreign direct investment. The capital flows involved in FDI are smaller than portfolio investment flows, but the theory of FDI has engaged the attention of many researchers and writers because it is central to understanding the activities of MNEs.

In 1977 the IMF defined foreign direct investment as,

> ... investment that is made to acquire a lasting interest in an enterprise operating in an economy other than that of the investor, the purpose being to have an effective voice in the management of the enterprise.[8]

All other forms of investment, such as the buying of stocks and shares, is classed as portfolio investment. At this point it might be noted that it is not always easy in practice, to distinguish between the two. The Organization for Economic Cooperation and Development (OECD) expanded this definition in 1982 by suggesting that a firm has a controlling interest in the management of a foreign firm if it holds at least 10 per cent of the voting stock, unless it can be shown in individual cases that control is ensured at a lower level, or that the investment is essentially of a portfolio nature, regardless of the percentage ownership.

FDI can take many different forms. In the past, FDI in agriculture, mines and quarries has been very important. Post-1945 the main thrust has been in manufacturing and marketing. The latest development is investment in service-based activities such as banking, insurance and tourism. For instance, by the end of the 1980s, FDI in services by OECD countries represented more than 40 per cent of total FDI outflows, compared with 25 per cent a decade earlier.

The motivations for FDI tend to be very diverse and many reasons can be listed and discussed. One approach is to group the reasons under a number of sub-headings. For instance, four broad determinants of marketing factors, barriers to trade, cost factors and investment climate can be used. Another approach is to classify by the type of company or goals of the company. Thus for natural resource seekers, for example oil and mining organizations, the main reason is the security and other benefits which follow from owning and controlling natural resources that are unobtainable or scarce in the home country.

Market protectors, sometimes unwillingly, resort to FDI in an endeavour to protect their market share abroad which has been established through exports. The market may have become eroded, or seen to be in danger of being eroded, by increasing transport costs or a failure to provide a satisfactory level of service to the customer. These are natural barriers to exporting and they may be reinforced by artificial barriers arising from protectionism.

Information seekers invest overseas to establish 'listening posts'. By controlling their operations in sophisticated and competitive foreign markets they obtain valuable knowledge and experience. As the name implies, cost and efficiency investors produce overseas because it is more efficient and less costly to do so.

Regardless of the approach adopted to look at the type of FDI and the reasons for it, the diversity is readily apparent. It may involve vertical or horizontal integration and/or geographical diversification. It is undertaken by a huge variety of different types of company, spanning the whole spectrum from basic mineral extraction to highly sophisticated service activities. The enabling vehicle is also varied, for example, mergers, takeovers, joint ventures, shareholding in existing companies, and greenfield developments. This makes it difficult to develop a comprehensive general theory of FDI. As Casson points out, none of the theories which claim to be general theories are general theories.[9]

A detailed discussion of these theories is outside the scope of this book, but it might be useful to outline one of them. Recent theories are based on a market-imperfections paradigm, where MNEs are viewed as oligopolists deriving specific ownership advantages from controlling assets not readily available to their competitors. Usually, these assets are of an intangible nature, for example, copyrights, knowledge, and trade marks, and provide a means of achieving product differentiation that competitors are unable to replicate, because of the protected nature of the assets.

Oligopolists with ownership-specific advantages do not themselves account for FDI. In the eclectic model, two additional elements, internalization and location specific advantages, are incorporated to explain FDI. Companies possessing ownership-specific advantages undertake FDI because of the benefits of locating operations within foreign markets. Usually, cost-related factors are important; for instance, cheap local labour may be available, or the high transport costs of exports may be avoided. In other cases, it may not be costs but revenue related factors, such as the avoidance of artificial barriers to exports or the ability to serve customers better from a local production base.

The final element concerns the advantages of internalizing economic transactions within the company, rather than utilizing external markets. It is argued that MNEs find this advantageous because of market imperfections, which cause high transaction costs for companies using external markets.

The internalization framework explains why companies engage in FDI, rather than in arrangements such as licensing, when exporting is difficult. With licensing, there are associated transaction problems, including the costs of identifying, negotiating with, and controlling potential licensees. There is also an interesting application of the concept of a public good. Knowledge is a public good and this complicates pricing. Thus external market transactions may be undesirable and firms will then internalize across national barriers through FDI. Successful internalization is possible because of the ownership-specific advantages possessed by the company which are projected by FDI. The conclusion is that despite the inherent problems of operating abroad, MNEs can still enjoy comparative advantage over local companies, even though these organizations enjoy substantial advantages just from being local.

MARKET-BASED AND FACTOR-BASED FDI

Thomsen and Nicolaides have developed an interesting taxonomy of FDI. It was developed to analyse direct investment into the EC but it appears to offer wider possibilities as well. Their starting-point is the observation that two general conditions are needed for FDI to occur, each of which is a necessary, but not sufficient, condition. The first is that there must be a reason for wanting to conduct some operations abroad and the second is that there must be some enabling factor which allows the company to do so. Their taxonomy is presented in Table 11.1.

Table 11.1
A taxonomy of FDI

Type	Advantage sought	Enabling factor
Market-based FDI		
1 Greenfield	Proximity to clients	Firm-specific assets
2 Greenfield	Reduction in transaction	Firm-specific costs
3 Cross-border M&As	Access to distribution networks	Access to finance or technological advantage
4 Cross-border M&A or Greenfield	Sales to home country	Affiliation with those MNEs firms in home country
Factor-based FDI		
5 Cross-border mergers	Diversification of risk	Dissimilar activities and acquisitions
6 Cross-border M&As	Firm-level economies of scale	Similar or complementary activities
7 Cross-border M&As	Access to technology	Cheap source of finance
8 Acquisitions	Splitting up conglomerates	Access to finance or managerial skill
9 Greenfield	Availability of resources	Access to finance or managerial skill

Source: Based on table in Thomsen, S., & Nicolaides, P., *Foreign Direct Investment: 1992 and Global Markets*. RIIA 1990.

They point out that where goods are homogeneous and price is the main competing factor, FDI will only occur if the company possesses some technological advantage that reduces costs, thus allowing it to compete with local businesses. This, for instance, explained the comparative lack of FDI in the steel industry world-wide, although the interesting exception was Japanese FDI in US steel making. Here the Japanese did possess cost-saving advantages in technology and had preferential access to Japanese car companies in the USA.

Where goods are differentiated and competition is not mainly on price, there are greater opportunities for FDI, as production costs are not as important. Typically, these types of goods require expenditure on R&D, which acts as an entry barrier. By investing abroad a monopoly position is maintained, especially where there is greenfield investment.

Much FDI stems from a factor basis. Low wages have accounted for investment in developing countries and the southern Members of the EC. Some factor-based FDI occurs in order to acquire technology which is not available at home. As long ago as 1982, Caves pointed out that Japanese firms began to invest in the USA after American firms stopped licensing their technology in Japan[2].

THE MNE AND DEVELOPING COUNTRIES

As Table 11.3 (see p. 115) illustrates, developing countries have been increasingly involved in the internationalization of business. The operations of MNEs in developing countries have been a topic of controversy for many years. Although there are shades of grey, there tend to be two widely different perspectives. One camp sees multinationals as important engines of development, with generally beneficial effects on the host country. The opposing school of thought, the Dependency Theorists, views them as agents of repression and exploitation.

Critics of the activities of MNEs emphasize their role in exploiting raw materials and cheap labour in the host countries. They claim that the capital intensive technology typically used by these organizations drives out indigenous, labour-intensive production methods and, in doing so, destroys the jobs of local workers. Moreover, one large modern plant produces the output of many traditional plants and so unemployment tends to be large-scale. This aspect is exacerbated by the destruction of native entrepreneurs.

Another criticism is the bribery and corruption that, it is alleged, often accompanies the operation of MNEs in poorer countries. Another aspect that concerns the local population is the interference of these companies in political matters. The example often quoted is the part the US giant ITT supposedly played in deposing a democratically elected, but left wing, president of Chile, *Señor* Allende. Allende was opposed to foreign investment in his country and was seen by ITT as a serious threat to their activities.

Some countries have tried to moderate the control MNEs exercise over their economies by wholly or partly nationalizing the firms. However, the critics believe that this has only limited success, as the MNEs still control the international marketing of the output, the technology and production know-how. Further, the government-owned company may have to continue to rely on expatriate managers. Thus the degree of control the host country government has over the company may be much less than it intended.

The practice of transfer pricing, which enables artificially low profits to be declared, is another criticism levelled at MNEs. The level of profits is important, as taxation yield is reduced if profits are low. Further, it is common for host country governments to have an agreement with the multinationals that they will receive royalties and these are often based on profits.

Another aspect of profits is their repatriation back to the home country. This has a dual disadvantageous effect. Firstly, it takes revenue away from the local economy and this effect is greater than the amount of the profit repatriation, because of its effect on the regional multiplier. Secondly, it can affect the terms of trade. If exchange rates are fixed, then domestic investment is reduced via changes in the money supply and the resulting upward pressures on interest rates. If there is a régime of flexible exchange rates, then it is likely that the domestic currency will depreciate.

As well as causing an outflow of capital, multinational operation may result in increased payments for imports. One example is the hotels built in the Caribbean by multinational chains. These chains have been unable to find, or unwilling to use, local suppliers and scarce foreign exchange has been used to import the necessary supplies.

The turnover of some multinationals is larger than the GNP of the host country. For instance, the sales of General Motors in 1986 was over $100 billion. The economic power that huge corporations wield may interfere in the planning decisions of host governments. Important decisions affecting the economy are made by the MNEs and often the government has little or no control over these decisions.

Supporters of the activities of multinationals in developing countries stress the associated benefits to the host country of the capital, modern technology, and improvements to the infrastructure. Broadly speaking, they are viewed as facilitating growth and development.

One aspect often stressed is the inward capital flows associated with a multinational establishing operations in a host country. Many developing countries have relatively low sources of domestic capital and/or have difficulty in finding development capital in world markets. Proponents of the MNE emphasize the long-term favourable impact of FDI on the balance of payments, rather than the drain caused by profit repatriation. Once the enterprise has become established, there will be export earnings and some of its production will replace consumption formerly met from imports. Export earnings are seen as important by some host nations. Brazil is one country that has made these a precondition for permission for multinational operation.

Technology transfer is seen as an important benefit. Technology transfer has several dimensions; an obvious one is the introduction of new plant and equipment to the host country. Associated with this are the skills and techniques required to operate the machinery. Managerial skills, which are necessary to operate the plant efficiently, are vital; they are of particular importance in service industries. In the long term, it is important that a managerial class is developed from indigenous personnel, so that the performance of the enterprise is not dependent on expatriate managers.

In the case of employment creation, supporters of the advantages of MNE operation emphasize job creation arising from new plants, rather than job losses from the displacement of local production. In many cases, there may not be significant employment losses, because the output is goods and/or services which did not exist before and which have no close substitutes. An indirect advantage is the fact that usually wages and salaries paid by multinationals are higher than those paid by local companies. However, critics argue that this might attract workers and managers from local companies who cannot afford the level of these payments, and thus their ability to compete with the foreign firm is further weakened. The operations of the MNE may create a new or larger pool of skilled workers and managers and this could beneficially overflow into local companies

Moran is a staunch advocate of the MNE in developing countries and he answers some of the criticisms that are outlined above.[10] He argues that over time LDCs acquire skills in bargaining with, and controlling, MNEs as well as developing the technical and managerial skills required to run the industry. In the copper industry, Chile increased its share of profits over time and he postulated that this came from:

> ... *moving up a learning curve of negotiating, operating and supervisory skills ... that lead from monitoring industry behaviour to replicating complicated corporate functions.*

His evidence shows that Chile increased the share of profits it received from multinational copper companies and that an indigenous class of middle managers and engineers arose, who performed most of the day-to-day operations. He also argued that multinational copper companies did not displace the old-established local businesses. Rather, they breathed fresh life into an industry that was unable to exploit profitably the lower quality ores left over from the earlier ventures which had concentrated on mining the high quality veins.

More controversially, perhaps, he argued that the ruling right wing political élite gradually moved away from being 'uncritical supporters' of the copper multinationals and adopted a more nationalistic attitude. The culmination of this was the nationalization of the firms and an increase in taxes.

THE IMPORTANCE OF FOREIGN DIRECT INVESTMENT

Until comparatively recently, foreign direct investment received inadequate attention. For example, until 1974 there was no comprehensive list available of foreign companies investing in the USA. Further, it was not known which organizations were foreign-owned. Given the sophistication of information gathering in the USA, it seems likely that even less information was available at the time of FDI in other countries. Data gathering has improved since then, and the OECD and the International Monetary Fund (IMF) have both made considerable efforts.

Some idea of the scale of FDI world-wide is provided in Tables 11.2 and 11.3. Table 11.2 shows the importance of the USA, both as an investor in other countries and as a host country for FDI. Not shown in the table is the fact that both Japan and the UK have overtaken the USA as the most important investing countries and that, by way of contrast, the UK has been overtaken by the USA as the chief recipient of FDI.

The high rate of growth of outward FDI by Japan is readily apparent from Table 11.3. One of the reasons for the large increase in productive capacity by Japanese companies in other countries was the trade tensions caused by the huge growth in exports from Japan in the 1970s and 1980s. What the table does not show is the sevenfold increase in Japanese FDI in the UK between 1986 and 1990. One of the reasons for this growth was the pioneering efforts in deregulation and privatization in the UK in the early 1980s, which created a favourable climate for FDI; a point which

Table 11.2
USA-related FDI

USA-based firms in foreign countries	1960	1970	1980	1984
Manufacturing	11.0 (35)	31.0 (41)	89.0 (42)	93.0 (40)
Petroleum	10.8 (34)	19.8 (26)	47.0 (22)	63.3 (27)
Other	10.0 (31)	24.7 (33)	77.5 (35)	77.0 (33)
Total	31.8	75.5	213.5	233.3
Foreign-based firms in the USA	*1960*	*1970*	*1980*	*1984*
Manufacturing	2.6 (38)	6.1 (46)	24.1 (37)	50.7 (32)
Petroleum	1.2 (17)	3.0 (23)	12.3 (19)	25.0 (16)
Other	3.1 (45)	4.2 (32)	29.1 (44)	83.9 (53)
Total	6.9	13.3	65.5	159.6

Notes: 1 Figures in billions of US dollars based on book values.
2 Figures in brackets are percentages of total.

Source: Adapted from table in 'Multinationals are Mushrooming', Raymond Vernon, *Challenge*, May/June 1986.

Table 11.3
Stock of foreign direct investment in selected countries

Country	Assets				Liabilities			
	1975	1980	1985	1989	1975	1980	1985	1989
USA	124	215	230	373	28	83	185	401
Japan	17	20	44	154	3	3	5	9
Germany	15	31	43	104	19	25	23	40
France	–	14	28	73	–	17	37	61
Italy	3	7	18	47	9	9	19	51
UK	38	79	107	224	24	63	63	138
Canada	10	23	39	64	40	60	62	103
Netherlands	20	42	50	63	20	11	15	30
Australia	1	5	7	27	9	25	27	57
Total	228	436	566	1129	152	296	436	890

Note: Figures in $ billion.

Source: Adapted from OECD *Economic Outlook*, December 1991.

is examined in more detail in Chapters 4 and 5. The UK was also regarded as a good base for manufacturing production, particularly in cars, for exports to other EC countries. During the late 1980s, Japanese investment in the USA also grew rapidly.

GLOBAL TRENDS IN FDI

In the 1950s and 1960s, investment by multinationals was generally welcomed by the governments of EC and other countries. By the 1970s, the simple approach to evaluating the possible benefits of FDI had largely disappeared, serious doubts were expressed about its net advantages and the climate for this activity was made more difficult. The pendulum swung in the opposite direction in the 1980s as there was a world-wide movement towards deregulation and liberalization.

FDI was seen as promoting employment opportunities and helping national savings, as well as introducing new technologies and attitudes. In addition, it was thought that there would be a demonstration effect on existing domestic competitors, causing them to adopt the best practices of the incomers. This appears to have happened in the car industry in the UK, where the establishment of several major Japanese companies has provided a considerable stimulus to older established companies.

At the same time, the world economy was becoming increasingly international in operation and new markets were opening up. New technologies, particularly those associated with Information Technology and its application to production and management, were gaining in importance. This issue is discussed in Chapter 6. There were major reforms to financial services, exchange controls were loosened and in many cases abandoned, and financial markets were more closely integrated. Most OECD countries now allow subsidiaries of foreign banks, insurance companies and brokerage houses to be established. A further impetus to liberalization will occur in 1993, when the measures in the creation of a single market in the EC have to be applied. This will be reinforced by the creation of the European Economic Area and the free trade area between Canada, Mexico and the USA.

The increase in Japanese investment in other countries has been mentioned in the preceding section. A large amount has taken place in the USA and southern hemisphere countries, such as Malaysia and Thailand, but there has been a considerable amount of FDI in the EC also. In total, it is still small in comparison with that of the USA, but it is growing rapidly and this trend is likely to continue. By the early 1990s, there were more than 500 Japanese companies producing in the community with a further 28 in EFTA countries, employing 82,000 workers in total.

According to figures from the Japanese Ministry of Finance, the stock of Japanese FDI between 1951 and 1989 in Europe was ECU 7.88 billion. Manufacturing accounted for only 17.67 per cent of this total, whereas finance and insurance accounted for 47.27 per cent. Commerce and real estate totalled 20.18 per cent.

Table 11.4 provides another view of trends in foreign direct investment over the last 16 years from that shown in Table 11.3, and allowing for the partly estimated nature of the data, some noticeable changes occurred between 1990 and 1991. In 1991 the volume of FDI by multinational corporations in industrial countries fell by 22.5 per cent, whereas it rose by 27.6 per cent in developing countries. In absolute terms, the total amount of FDI in industrialized countries was still two and a half times as great as that in developing countries.

FDI by Japanese companies fell considerably, particularly in the USA. According to the 'Bank For International Settlements' report in 1991, which was the source for the table in the *Financial Times*, this was partly due to the general weakness of the US economy, and partly because the returns on capital by Japanese companies in the USA had been less than expected.[11] In percentage terms, FDI in eastern Europe increased sharply, although it is still very low in absolute value. Press comment suggests that eastern Europe will be attractive to Japanese companies in the future, as wage rates are relatively low. Also, there is a large pool of skilled labour and much of this will be investment diverted from the UK.

The world-wide movement towards deregulation is the subject of a separate chapter in this book. This is an important reason for the increase in FDI in Latin America. FDI

Table 11.4
The global pattern of foreign direct investment

	1975–79	*1980–84*	*1985–89*	*1990–1991*	
Outflows					
Industrialized countries	34.7	41.0	128.4	209.5	165.5
USA	15.9	9.6	22.8	33.4	29.5
Japan	2.1	4.3	23.8	48.0	30.7
EC	14.2	20.9	59.4	97.5	80.5
Developing countries	0.6	1.4	6.5	12.9	11.8
Asia	0.3	0.8	5.6	11.2	10.3
Latin America	0.1	0.2	0.4	1.1	1.0
Total	**35.3**	**42.4**	**134.9**	**222.4**	**177.3**
Inflows					
Industralized countries	19.9	36.2	98.1	148.7	115.2
USA	6.1	18.6	48.2	37.2	22.2
Japan	0.1	0.3	0.1	1.8	1.4
EC	11.4	14.2	38.4	85.9	67.7
Developing countries	7.0	16.4	19.5	30.9	42.7
Asia	1.9	4.7	10.8	19.9	25.7
Eastern Europe	0.0	0.1	0.1	0.5	2.3
Latin America	3.6	5.4	5.7	7.8	12.0
Total	**26.9**	**52.6**	**117.6**	**179.6**	**157.9**

Notes: 1 Total inflows and outflows do not balance because of official reporting errors.
2 Figures for 1991 are partly estimates.
3 Figures in $ billion, annual averages.

Source: Adapted from the *Financial Times* 30 July 1992.

rose steadily, if slowly, between 1975 and 1989, but the table shows it has increased much more rapidly since then. According to the BIS, this was largely due to liberalized trade policies and a greater openness to foreign investment, coupled with more stable macro-economic policies.

The remarkable increase in FDI by Japanese companies is easily observable. Also easily observable is the tiny amount of FDI into Japan. For a number of reasons (outside the scope of this chapter), Japan is thought not to welcome FDI inside its borders. This perception could be important if the EC develops a common policy on inward FDI and it is based on reciprocity.

CONCLUSION

This chapter has dealt with some aspects of the phenomenon of the multinational enterprise: organizations that are a major vehicle for the internationalization of business. Strategic decision-making in multinational corporations is globally oriented and has a global impact. The increasing impact of the MNE and the globalization of business may be inferred from the data in Tables 11.2, 11.3 and 11.4. The scale of FDI is explicit in these tables. It seems reasonable to assume, writing in the second half of 1992, that the importance of the MNEs and their associated world-wide investment activities will continue, as the 1990s unfold, given the continuing liberalization of the world economy and the opportunities presented by the dramatic changes in the former USSR, eastern Europe, and South Africa. Further, the Chinese market is huge and offers enormous opportunities; will China be able to, or want to, hold back the tide which appears to be flowing so strongly in this direction?

References

1 *Multinational corporations in world development*, United Nations, 1973.
2 Caves, R., *Multinational enterprise and economic analysis*, (Cambridge, CUP, 1982).
3 Hood, N., and Young, S., *The economics of the multinational enterprise*, (London, Longman, 1979).
4 Vernon, R., *Sovereignty at bay*, (New York, Basic Books, 1972).
5 Hood and Young, op. cit. p. 41.
6 Hymer, S., 'The international operation of national firms' (doctoral dissertation) (Massachusetts, MIT, 1961).
7 Casson, M., in Clarke, R., and McGuiness, T., *The economics of the firm*, (Oxford, Blackwell, 1987).
8 *The balance of payments manual*, IMF, 1977
9 Casson, op. cit.
10 Moran T., *Multinational corporations and the politics of dependence: copper in Chile*, (New Jersey, Princeton, 1977).
11 *Annual Report*, 1991, Bank for International Settlement.

Bibliography

Casson, M., *The Growth of International Business*, (London, Allen and Unwin, 1983).
Caves, R., *Multinational Enterprise and Economic Analysis*, (Cambridge, CUP, 1982).
Clarke, R., and McGuiness, T., *The Economics of the Firm*, (Oxford, Blackwell, 1987).
Houde, M-F., 'Foreign Direct Investment', *OECD Observer*, No. 176, June/July, 1992.
Thomsen, S., 'Inward Investment in the European Community', *Panorama of EC Industry 1991–1992*, Commission of the European Communities, 1991.
Thomsen, S., and Nicolaides, P., *Foreign Direct Investment: 1992 and Global Markets*, The Royal Institute of International Affairs, 1990.

CHAPTER TWELVE

EXPLORING THE IDEA OF INTERNATIONAL BUSINESS STRATEGY

JONATHAN KNOWLES

INTRODUCTION

The literal meaning of the word 'strategy' is 'the art of the general', deriving from the Ancient Greek word for 'general' *strategos*. Prior to Napoleon's times, the word had a military connotation, implying that the strategy was part-process and part-outcome, that it involved reconnaissance or environmental analysis, internal appraisal, a consideration of alternative ways forward, so as to secure a preferred state of affairs. As the assessment of risk was involved, it was an activity normally seen as a key responsibility of the higher echelons of a hierarchy.

Thus strategy entails the proper and effective marriage of organizational resources and capabilities and environmental opportunities. The effectiveness of this marriage is based on the belief that the organizational resources and capabilities can be effectively organized and that environmental opportunities can be identified and seized upon. This, in turn, presupposes that a useful paradigm or model of the enormously complex and changing international business environment is possible. Later in this chapter these two assumptions are explored and discussed.

This idea of strategy must be investigated before its strengths and weakness can be discussed.

THEORETICAL APPROACHES TO STRATEGY

Two main parallel approaches to strategy formulation have attracted wide support from both researchers and practitioners. Both started life in the mid-1960s and have been refined extensively in the light of political, economic, social and technical changes. The increased rate of environmental change to which businesses have been subjected since the mid-1980s are discussed later in this chapter, when the conventional approach to strategic planning is reviewed.

E. LEARNED

The first of these approaches was developed at Harvard by Learned *et al.*[1] This approach stresses the top management standpoint, it acknowledges the increasing involvement of specialists and middle managers and the modification of the previously profit-growth centred direction of companies. Central to this approach was the belief that an organization is only capable of sustaining competitive advantage over the medium and long terms if managers can overcome their inability to think strategically. Managers should be encouraged to forget that it is senior management's sole responsibility to formulate strategy. The emphasis was one of greater ownership of strategic responsibility.

H. I. ANSOFF

In his increased concern for strategic capability, as opposed to short-term profitability, Ansoff broadened this into four major stages in the formulation of a corporate strategy:

- formulation of long-term corporate objectives;
- identification of possible target markets;
- definition of environmental constraints (external and internal to the organization);
- allocation of corporate resources via a strategic plan.[2]

Ansoff saw the first stage in developing a strategy as the formulation of organizational objectives. These should be realistic, be capable of refinement, contain both quantitative and qualitative elements, and carefully thought through with regard to the issue of implementation. These objectives are long-term and need to be reassessed in the light of corporate performances and changing environmental circumstances. The term 'long-term' will vary from company to company, and environment to environment. For example, for a small, multiple retail chain, long-term may be 5 years, but for a large oil company it might be 20 years.

MICHAEL PORTER

From the late 1980s, it was suggested by a number of theorists that objectives should capitalize on the core competencies of the organization, so that organizational objectives would be informed by their particular strengths rather than by the environment. Selection of objectives should be influenced by the product/service capability of the organization, accessibility of the markets, and their significance, the level of technology and the competition expected. This approach was formalized and rendered much clearer diagrammatically by Michael Porter's five forces model, see Figure 12.1

Porter's model provides practitioners with a means of highlighting the competitive forces at work in the environment, thereby providing management with a basis for strategic evaluation. He argues that competition in an industry is rooted in its underlying economics and competitive forces and goes well beyond the established competitors in a particular industry.

According to this approach, the first stage is to identify the needs of the target market(s) and then a strategic plan for meeting these needs can be developed, in the light of corporate objectives. The cases of the NEC corporation and Nissan illustrate some of these points.

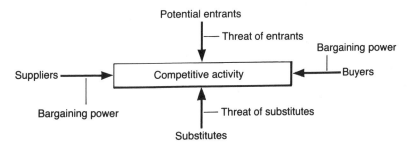

Figure 12.1
Michael Porter's five forces model

Source: Adapted from M. E. Porter *Competitive Strategy*, Free Press, 1980.

Environmental analysis might normally be the next stage. Because the assumption is made that the environment is capable of being analysed and exploited, the superior partner in the company environment marriage is the company. This may have been the case up to the late 1980s, but since then most corporate plans are geared to survival rather than supremacy over a chosen environment.

The steps taken during the environmental analysis by those responsible for formulating strategy are:

● audit environmental influences;
● assess the nature of the environment;
● identify key environmental forces through structural analysis
● identify competitive position;
● identify key opportunities and threats.

STRATEGIC POSITION

Environmental constraints can affect many different parts of organizations and their influence is extremely complex. Some influences may be direct and dramatic; for example, changes in the price of oil. Others may be subtle yet significant, such as changing managerial attitudes toward employee-empowered work groups.

The final stage is planning for the deployment of corporate resources in such a manner as to enable the business organization to attain its planned strategic stance, as described by its corporate objective in the target markets. This stage involves the formulation and implementation of specific policies, for functions such as production, human resource management, marketing, finance and R&D. This should represent a co-ordinated effort by the organization to pursue, maintain or improve its relative position in its chosen market segments.

The marks of an excellent strategy are normally considered to be:

● bias for action;
● encouragement of autonomy and entrepreneurial action;
● development of a clear value system throughout entire organization;
● simple organization design and administration systems;
● strong limited central control, together with an appropriate degree of decentralization.

121

The implementation of a corporate plan requires the involvement and commitment of management at all levels and therefore differs according to the type of organization, its size, objectives, external operating environment and internal culture. These issues take on a significant dimension when considering companies that operate internationally.

This said, the holistic nature of corporate planning becomes apparent. The success of a corporate plan is heavily dependent on the appropriateness of the links between organizational structure, management style and corporate plan. One of the main causes of strategic failure is the lack of resources directed at implementation issues; implementation is often an afterthought. Implementation becomes an increasingly contentious issue when an international corporate strategy is considered. For example, decisions have to be made about which functions should be centralized and which decentralized, an issue which is discussed later in the chapter.

Researchers and practitioners have supported the general idea that the business environment can be observed, understood and responded to, using the appropriate tools and techniques. However, this idea of strategic intent had become flawed by the end of the 1980s, due to the increased difficulty in predicting environmental changes, including international and global markets. These changes include:

- the speed at which technology improves and technological knowledge increases;
- increased environmental complexity;
- internationalization of data as a business commodity;
- fragmentation of markets;
- convergent life-styles;
- loss of economies of scale caused by fragmentation of markets;
- the harmonization of European markets;
- the opening up of eastern Europe;
- shifts in balance of economic power to Pacific rim countries;
- the internationalization of consumer taste;
- the compression of the different stages of product development;
- the wider adoption of flexible manufacturing systems by international companies;
- the greening of international business;
- the shortening of product life cycles.

This list is not exhaustive and in no order of significance. These types of issues make the preparation and successful implementation of a corporate plan increasingly difficult. Added to this, organizations may fall into two strategic traps' in their efforts to deal with the environmental complexity.

Trap 1: The tendency to consolidate and 'stick with the knitting' and become a leaner fitter organization.

The tendency to oversimplify suggests that an organization is minimizing environmental and other effects rather than managing it.

Trap 2: Devise increasingly complex organization structures in order to manage the environmental complexity.

In this case, if the organization has little experience in refining the structure/ strategy/style relationship, then in sizing up, the chances of creating and maintaining competitive advantage are minimal.

In both cases, the opportunities for capitalizing on core competencies are reduced. It is difficult to clarify the confusion surrounding what is effective and ineffective practice in international corporate planning.

THE MATRIX APPROACH

Increasingly, a matrix-style organization structure has been adopted as a solution to the need to draw upon core competencies. A matrix organization is a flexible structure often used in situations which require a mix of people with different skills and experience to be focused on a particular task, or an unusual project that crosses existing departmental boundaries in an organization. The case study of NH Geotech shows how one international corporation is using this style of management. The people involved in this kind of task force will continue to report officially to line management, but for their day-to-day work they will be responsible to the project leader. This solution can result in a number of problems. For example:

- dual reporting;
- the proliferation of information channels;
- the proliferation of committees;
- the loss of accountability especially in an international context.

To take one example, in 1989/90 the hospitality industry was characterized by a period of intense divestment and acquisition. The rationale for this was the expressed need to consolidate, to support and develop successful brands, and the desire to compete in developing international markets. This illustrates Trap 1.

CORPORATE STRATEGY – SOME CONCLUSIONS

Are international planners incapable of managing the increasing complexity brought about by the internationalization of business? Evidence is emerging which suggests that managers are tending not to concentrate on issues of strategy and structure, but on details of managing people and processes. In this scenario, senior management is concerned with exploring individual capabilities and motivating the entire organization to respond in co-operative fashion to a very complicated and dynamic environment. This, however, is not workable. Competitive strategy will not evolve as the organization structure is unlikely at any one time to be appropriate.

What then emerges from this is that 'the outside looking in' paradigm, on the lines of Ansoff and Porter, might not serve corporate planners. More likely, 'the inside looking out' paradigm, which recognizes the futility of trying to manage the complexity of the environment, is more valuable in attempting to deal with environmental complexity. This second paradigm suggests a more dynamic model of opportunity, in which the organization plays a genuine role in creating opportunities. However, many texts in developing the 'outside looking in' paradigm give insufficient weight to the issues of implementation.

Clearly, a corporate plan is not competitive unless it is implementable. Implementation in theory and practice is often seen as an adjunct to the two steps preceding it mentioned earlier. This may be because new strategies offer potential benefits, whereas implementation involves risk and change. Ideally, implementation strategies should seek to maximize benefits and minimize risks.

NIGEL PIERCY AND NEIL MORGAN

There are other reasons for strategic failure that should be examined as they throw light on issues of international strategy implementation. Nigel Piercy and Neil Morgan, of Cardiff Business School, suggest that the commonest reasons for strategic failure are as follows.

- *Separation of planning from management*, i.e. staff and line responsibilities are separated so that plans are imposed. Although participation is costly, time-consuming and causes top management stress, Piercy and Morgan suggest that this is the price that organizations should be prepared to pay.
- *Hopeless optimism*, i.e. corporate objectives are often far removed from reality. Their research suggests that many strategic plans are so far removed from reality that it is probably just as well they never get implemented.
- *Implementation difficulties are recognized too late*. Substantial management time is consumed, research done, management is 'sold' and only then are the barriers to implementation recognized as the costs of change are comprehended.
- *Denial of implementation problems*. Piercy and Morgan's evidence suggests that the most significant barriers are covert and become more covert and problematic when driven underground by macho top-management posturing. An assumption is often held by top management that commitment of people at all levels is achieved by simply telling them about their innovative and exciting plan. Genuine commitment is gained through genuine participation in decision-making, education, and internal communication.
- *Implementation is bolted on at the end*. Piercy and Morgan suggest that many of the causes for strategic failure are, in fact, made worse because implementation is seen as just tidying up the loose ends when the real work has been done.
- *The barriers to implementation are not analysed*. Peircy and Morgan suggest that when implementation difficulties are raised, the senior management team often over-reach and drop the plan before the failure sticks to them. Often the barriers turned out to be personalities or stereotypical reasons for not introducing change. Some examples of this type have been well documented; an example is Clive Sinclair, who in the 1970s and 1980s ran into a succession of problems in managing resources. (*Management Today*, March 1981).

HENRI FAYOL

Henri Fayol provided a very useful definition of a manager's group of responsibilities: 'to plan, organize, motivate, and control'. This working definition is still helpful today, as these responsibilities are central to the creation of a corporate plan, but in practice is less useful with corporate planning implementation. Western management practice tends to emphasize and reward input rather than output. Perhaps it is for this reason that this received wisdom, outlined by Ansoff and others, surrounding corporate planning activities has survived for so long. If the output of corporate planning activity had been reviewed with the same rigour as the input, and subject to the same level of intellectual detail, then it is indeed possible that Ansoff's major contribution may not have been central to strategic thinking and practice for so long.

A strong thread emerging from this discussion is the rise in the significance of core competencies in grasping strategic competitive advantage. By adopting this line of discussion, the inference may be drawn that support for the 'inside looking out' model by researchers and practitioners is gaining support over the 'outside looking in' model. If this is the case, then there are difficulties ahead for those organizations operating across national boundaries, as core competencies are notoriously difficult to access when a company has become decentralized as a result of operating internationally. The issue of accessing core competencies in order to secure international competitive distance is a very contentious issue, and subject to considerable debate.

INTERNATIONAL STRATEGY – CENTRALIZATION V. DECENTRALIZATION

The most useful way of examining the issue of decentralization is to qualify the type of decentralization as either operational or strategic.

Centralization is normally considered to be the policy and process of trying to run everything in an organization from one central point. The issue of central concern to those responsible for organizing the corporate planning effort of an international or global company is which activities should be centralized and which should be decentralized. The resolution of this difficulty is made worse when one is reminded of the unpredictability of change. The only certainty is that, given the apparent shrinking of the globe in business terms, the question is not whether we consider decentralizing in order to cope with the trend of internationalization, but rather what should be decentralized? The benefits and costs of any solution to this problem are difficult to evaluate. Many international businesses have juggled with centralized/decentralized issues. This point is illustrated in the studies of the following organizations: NH Geotech; the NEC Corporation, and Philips.

The issue is not one where an observer is able to say, 'Ah yes, that is a centralized organization and that is a decentralized organization'. What is more appropriate is the appreciation that an organization moves on a continuum, viz Figure 12.2.

In Figure 12.2 incremental moves are made to and fro along this continuum in response to significant environmental influences. At point A, it is possible that an organization can suffer loss of control as a result of having a highly hierarchical organization structure, together with the likely attendant management style and strategy. Alternatively, at point B, too much decentralization may lead to co-ordination inadequacy between operating units dispersed internationally. The resolution of this issue is very complex.

The move towards greater decentralization would appear to be the main trend. The broad rationale for this would seem to be that an organization which is centralized in terms of the core management functions is likely to be more insensitive to environmental influences than one which is more decentralized. The co-ordination is managed by endeavouring to centralize the control of organizational values.

There is a tendency for some organizations to pingpong in a limited fashion between points A & B, subscribing to the view that the benefits of moving the other

Figure 12.2
The centralization/decentralization continuum

way along the continuum are greater than those currently being experienced. Balance between the two extremes is the issue that corporate planners need to address, as the point on the continuum will have a strong bearing on the other two S's – strategy and management style. The position on the continuum will strongly influence the efficiency in which core competencies are utilized, and therefore how efficient the value adding process is and how quickly adjustments can be made in environmental influences. The significance of the position on the continuum extends beyond having a bearing on how the structure/strategy style relationship develops. In addition, the position will have a bearing on how different functions are organized and the relative power they can draw upon to influence the strategic planning process.

The pattern that appears to be emerging is for organizations to adopt the notion of co-ordinated decentralization, i.e. a balance is struck – a point made in the NH Geotech and NEC Corporation cases. A widely held view, popular with both practitioners and researchers, is that those activities that have a direct input to the creation of strategy and the implementation of strategy should be centralized. Those issues that are operational in nature should be decentralized. The strongest means of control should normally be centralized, for example, finance and the control of organizational values. This is clearly a generalization and there will be many exceptions to it; for example, Ford Motor Company is normally associated with a high degree of centralization and General Motors with decentralization.

As a result of organizations pursuing the notion of co-ordinated decentralization, many functions have had to adjust their contribution to the achievement of strategic aims; for example, marketing. The majority of marketing texts concentrate on large manufacturing organizations manufacturing fast-moving consumer goods (FMCGs). In practice, most marketing effort and expenditure falls within the definition of business-to-business marketing. The increased internationalization of business has meant that the role of the business-to-business marketer is undergoing some fundamental changes.

Firstly, there is a clear trend towards business organizations organizing themselves into autonomous, decentralized operating units. This, in turn, means that a new breed of manager is required, i.e. managers who are able to operate in an environment not disciplined by constraints of large hierarchy organization designs. This change in managers is not likely to happen quickly. Indeed, one of the more obvious problems experienced by companies, when they begin to decentralize in order to satisfy geographically fragmented markets, is the difficulty of co-ordinating the efforts of managers operating in diverse local markets over a large geographical area.

Apart from this, another trend that has emerged as a result of the growth in the internationalization of business is the increased difficulty being experienced in identifying and maintaining competitive advantage and unique selling proposition (USP). In the eyes of the consumer, many types of products or service are having shorter and shorter life cycles as other, different products or services come along to replace it. In response to this, reference is being made to elements of the marketing mix not normally draw upon to make a large contribution to the identification and maintenance of competitive advantages.

THE EXAMPLE OF BUSINESS-TO-BUSINESS MARKETING

Distribution has long been regarded as the Cinderella of the so-called marketing mix, those other elements being price, promotion and product. However, the rise in significance of distribution as a source of competitive advantage, as the traditional sources dry up, is evidenced by the trend towards a rise in the number of intermediate marketing organizations (IMOs). An IMO is an organization which facilitates marketing, in particular the distribution of goods between two successive stages of processing.

Allied to the growth in IMOs is the increase in influence which information technology can have on international strategy. Chapter 6 considers the broad issue of technology as an agent of internationalization. It is clear that data is becoming the most significant business commodity in a shrinking world. Timely and accurate data is an increasingly essential input to the value-adding process when product life-cycles are becoming shorter, product development processes are becoming compressed and markets are becoming increasingly fragmented.

In response to the increased environmental complexity and unpredictability, the buyer-and-seller relationship within the business-to-business context is undergoing a fundamental change. This relationship, which is characterized by the buyer and seller enjoying equal status, is developing by way of increased co-operation in order to deal with increased environmental complexity and to sustain competitive distance. This reinforces the view given earlier that the traditional sources of competitive advantage are drying up. The pursuit of enhanced quality is requiring that greater integration occurs between those elements of international strategy which address marketing via communication strategy and a merchandizing strategy. This, though, does not ally happily with the observation made earlier that a strong trend towards decentralization is occurring. To resolve this dilemma or set up opposing forces, a compromise must be made that offsets the cost and benefits of setting both sides of the *'equation'*. This is the new challenge to strategic planners in the 1990s and beyond.

INTERNATIONAL BUSINESS STRATEGY – SOME ALTERNATIVE VIEWS

For a number of reasons, corporate planners may be accused of applying planning tools and techniques in an inappropriate fashion. This view is offered as a consequence of conventional corporate planning tools and techniques letting corporate planners down.

Earlier in this chapter, a varied list of environmental trends was offered as a major source of environmental change, for example, the compression of product life cycles and the internationalization of tastes. These dynamic changes will manifest themselves increasingly in what might be termed open-ended change situations which are difficult to predict.

The proposition is that grand designs or strategies fall apart in open-ended change situations, i.e. those most likely to be found in an international context, and conventional strategic management is not a suitable form of control in those conditions. Indeed, in circumstances not characterized by open-ended change, conventional strategic planning methods and the paradigm that supported them are prone to failure, for the sort of reasons contributed by Piercy and Morgan.

Ralph Stacey suggests that we cannot forecast and apply analytical procedures when the problems and opportunities are ill-structured and accompanied by inadequate, possibly suspect, information.[6] Unless this is acknowledged by senior managers, then they run the danger of applying established tools and techniques to sets of circumstances that have changed a great deal from those existing when the tools and techniques evolved. In other words, managers may become 'skilled incompetents'. The signs of this incompetence might include the holding of fixed, long-term objectives, mission statements, or a long-term plan developed by simple deterministic analytical techniques, such as Porter's environmental model. The presumption that the past can safely inform the future is still held by many who should know better. In other words, senior managers are guilty of focusing on contained change and they seek clarity on where they are going and how they are going to get there. Strategic fit is sought, a coherence and a fit of the company's capabilities to its chosen markets, which means that innovative potential and new direction will rarely be considered.

The view that international strategy should not be pre-determined, but rather should emerge opportunistically in the form of strongly backed, opportunistic issue responses or experiments that extend the boundaries of the business while adjusting cultural values and control systems, is more likely to gain support in light of recent trends, if managers are able to perceive them in a deliberate and rational manner. Probably the best example is Sony: Sony have in relatively small ways shaped customer requirements for new products. Their approach is dynamic and not static, as the conventional approach might infer. This suggests that strategies are consequences of opportunistic experimental behaviour, not determinants. The NEC Corporation case deals with some of these issues.

Traditionally, organization structures and management roles, control systems, management selection procedures, etc. are designed to fit strategies. The strategy under this paradigm provides the framework within which individual disturbances, tactics or single issues are then handled.

The turbulence of the 1990s and beyond in the international arena would suggest that the old view, the 'outside looking in' model, has little practical value in enabling organizations to identify and seize competitive distance internationally. Stacey's view is more likely to be helpful in enabling planners to break away from the conventional approach in the development of an appropriate organizational culture – one that supports the right mixture of management style, organization, structure and flexible strategy, able to detect change and develop and progress issues in an opportunistic fashion. Strategies under this alternative, perhaps radical, view do not determine structures, systems and culture; they are determined by them. If this turns out to be the norm, then a whole new generation of views and contributions to the debate of strategic planning will emerge to inform planning practice in the international context in the 1990s, and beyond.

References

1 Learned, E., Christenson, C. R., Andrews, I. C. R., and Guth, L. D., *1965 Business Policy*, (Boston, Irwin, 1965).
2 Ansoff, H. I., *Corporate Strategy* (Harmondsworth, Penguin, 1969).
3 Porter M. E., *Competitive Advantages: Creating and Sustaining Superior Performance*, (New York, Free Press, 1985).
4 Piercy, Nigel, and Morgan, Neil, *Sunday Times*, 21 October 1990.
5 Stacey, R., *Dynamic Strategy Management for the 1990s*, (London, Kogan Page, 1991).
6 Stacey, R., *Managing Chaos: Dynamic Business Strategies in an Unpredictable World*, (London, Kogan Page, 1992).

Bibliography

Channon, D. F., *Multinational strategic planning*, (London, Macmillan, 1979).

Davidson, W. H., *Global strategic management*, (Chichester, Wiley, 1982).

Doz, Y., *Strategic management in multinational companies*, (Oxford, Pergamon, 1984).

Greenly, G. E. *Strategic management* (Hemel Hempstead, Prentice Hall, 1989).

Going global: succeeding in world markets, (Boston, Harvard Business Review Paperback, 1991).

Newbold, G. D., *et al.*, *Going international: the experience of smaller companies overseas*, 2nd edition, (Associated Business Press).

Robock, S. H., and Simmonds, K., *International business and multinational enterprises*, 4th edition (Boston, Irwin, 1989).

CHAPTER THIRTEEN

INTERNATIONAL MARKETING

TERRY O'SULLIVAN

INTRODUCTION

The aim of this chapter is to look at some of the issues involved in marketing international goods and services, as opposed to marketing in a purely domestic market. It is argued that the concepts and tools of marketing have a universality transcending national boundaries; whereas the social factors, whereby individuals and groups act under a wide range of influences both economic and non-economic, mean that the marketing process in different countries can vary considerably.

Marketing is all about creating and keeping customers. Using the tools of product, price, promotion and distribution, the marketing organization moulds its offering to the needs and wants of the customer in a way that guarantees lasting mutual benefits: for the consumer – satisfaction and quality, for the organization – long-term sustainability and growth.

Traditional marketing wisdom developed earlier this century from the experience of the packaged goods industries. Their kind of thinking has now been successfully applied to services and non-profit enterprises such as health, education and the arts. In this chapter we will concentrate on marketing consumer goods and services in an international environment.

The marketing approach is thriving all around us for one very good reason: it works. But applying it successfully to situations where the customer whom you are trying to create and keep lives in a foreign country is still an area fraught with difficulty. This is true at a time when addressing the needs of the customer on an international scale has never been more important.

Almost a third of all investment in the industrial world produces goods for export.[1] This emphasis on international business has been accompanied by the formation of trade agreements between groups of countries on the one hand, and the growth of multinational corporations on the other. Certain types of industry, such as cars and electronics, have no choice but to market internationally because of the enormous cost of research and development, as identified in Chapter 6. Other companies, faced with market saturation in their domestic environments, have gone international in search of expansion and growth. But whatever the motivation, the difference between marketing in a domestic context and marketing internationally

Table 13.1
Domestic v. international marketing

Domestic marketing	*International marketing*
Single language	Multilingual/multicultural
Relatively homogeneous market	Fragmented and diverse market
Data available and usually accurate	Data collection is a formidable task
Relatively stable business environment	Some environments are highly unstable
Single currency	Currencies differing in value
Business 'rules of the game' understood	Rules diverse and unclear.

must be recognized. Table 13.1 summarizes some of the main differences between international and domestic marketing.

In general terms, international marketing differs from domestic marketing in the following respects:

- places greater emphasis on environmental analysis;
- makes more complex demands on internal planning and control disciplines;
- requires a larger repertoire of skills such as languages, law, treasury, etc;
- necessitates a greater diversity of manufacturing decisions, covering what to make and where to make it;
- increases the importance of sound legal and financial systems;
- demands higher risk investment, and higher cost of market entry;
- creates a greater range of debt-collection problems and ways of paying for goods;
- introduces a different balance of 'competition' and 'co-operation';
- offers less marketing experience and expertise upon which to draw.

THE INTERNATIONAL ENVIRONMENT

Marketing depends on a number of variables. Four of them are within the organization's direct control: product, price, promotion and place. But everything else is outside the organization's control. These 'external' factors need to be planned round so that the bad effects of negative factors can be minimized and the positive factors can be fully exploited.

'Environmental analysis' is usually the first step in this process – a structured look at the context in which the organization is operating. A useful technique is 'STEP' factor analysis; working through the four areas of social, technological, economic, and political aspects. Important as it is in domestic marketing, this process comes into its own in international marketing, where the environment is very often a major unknown.

SOCIAL/CULTURAL ENVIRONMENT

'Culture' is a particular set of learned behaviours that unite a community or country in a particular way of life. Covering language, education, taboos, religion, life-style and taste, it is one of the main stumbling blocks to international marketing success. In Chapter 8 Terry Mughan addresses some of these issues.

TECHNOLOGICAL ENVIRONMENT

No consumer is an island. Consumption patterns are interrelated through technology. To take a crude example, microwaveable-meals are unlikely to sell well in a country where microwave ovens, and the electricity to operate them, are not widely available.

Technology affects other aspects of the marketing mix. It determines the nature and scope of promotional activity, in the shape of the availability and sophistication of advertising media. Access to customers through distribution channels is constrained by the technology available. In Chapter 6 Mike Hewins examines a number of these issues in more depth.

ECONOMIC ENVIRONMENT

Market potential is governed by the number of likely customers and their level of wealth, as well as by the strength and nature of competition. However, both the world economy and the wealth of individual nations are subject to dynamic fluctuations. The swift progress made by countries such as Taiwan, Singapore and Hong Kong to becoming independent high-tech manufacturers, has created a sudden cluster of highly discriminating and status-conscious consumers.[2]

Statistics such as per capita income can conceal enormous disparities between rich and poor. Gross national product (GNP) can be a more useful indicator, especially for the potential for industrial goods and products.

POLITICAL/LEGAL ENVIRONMENT

It was stated in Chapter 2 that political factors, as well as legal and economic, have a major impact on business, including international business. Political changes can be very expensive for an international company. The results can vary from expropriation, the confiscation of all assets; to the imposition of currency controls and tariffs. On the other hand, governmental attitudes to incoming business can be very positive. The trade-off here is employment opportunities in exchange for cheap facilities and fiscal concessions.

Laws covering product standards, labelling, packaging, price (through taxation and duty) and advertising or data protection restrictions, can impinge on every area of marketing activity. Major companies spend a great deal of time and money lobbying legislators accordingly.

All these environmental factors are linked in their effect on marketing. The international marketing company needs to be committed to fastidious, long-range planning, coupled with great tactical sensitivity, in order to be able to survive the minefield of the international environment.

WHY GO INTERNATIONAL?

Many companies appear to have fallen almost by accident into international marketing. The Coca-Cola Company, responsible for one of the very few indisputably 'global' brands in fast-moving consumer goods, has based its success on the acceptance which the product found as part of the 'Americanizing' influence of GIs posted abroad during the Second World War.

Other companies are faced with static or shrinking total markets on the domestic front. Rather than slug it out in a bitter war of attrition with competitors for very small returns, they look to open up new sources of profit overseas.

A third reason for internationalizing is that you simply have no choice. The R & D costs of a new car or computer mean that in order to ensure pay-back on investment in a reasonable time-scale, international market segments are the only ones large enough to offer enough consumers.

MARKET RESEARCH

By listening to the customer in a planned and systematic way, research reduces risk, leading to better marketing decisions. In both domestic and international contexts, it has to be undertaken in the right way for the right reasons. For the international marketer, the task is made more difficult by the unfamiliarity of the environment in which the research takes place.

Research falls into two main categories: 'primary' and 'secondary'. Primary research is conducted direct by the company or by an independent agency. It is 'primary' in that this is the first time the information has been gathered. It may be a one-off examination of a particular issue, such as testing a recipe change in a product. This is known as *ad hoc* research. Or it may be 'continuous', where a situation is examined over a period of time in order to spot trends. The case of Typhoon International shows how that company commissioned some market research before changing its corporate identity and radically changing its product line.

Secondary or 'desk' research uses published sources of information, such as censuses, reports and directories. It is far less expensive than primary research, but there is obviously less flexibility as to the questions it can answer. Secondary sources are often inconsistent in the way they define categories of products and groups of customers. The information frequently needs reworking in order to make it comparable.

In some international markets, systematic research towards secondary material may be in its infancy, preventing meaningful trends from being visible. In other markets, research may be absent altogether, or interrupted for long periods by political upheaval. Response rates to all sorts of research may be distorted by local considerations: literacy levels, cultural and social protocols. Research companies are increasingly organizing themselves into international groupings in order to cope with this.

Other sources of market intelligence include statutory bodies, such as national trade associations, and chambers of commerce and their equivalent in the host country. Personal visits to gather information and attend trade events are essential in order to dispel illusions about the market and competitors. Finally, international marketing tends to use a large number of intermediaries. Their value as a source of marketing information should never be underestimated.

MARKET SELECTION

The first step in selecting a market to enter is the fundamental process of market segmentation. Identifying the precise range of consumers to be targeted with an offering enables a company to differentiate itself from competitors in a way which is relevant to its customers' needs.

In order to be viable, a market segment must contain a sufficiently large number of consumers with similar needs and wants. Furthermore, the chosen segment needs to be:

- accessible, so that the customers can be reached with promotion and distribution;
- measurable, so that evaluation and control of the marketing programme is possible;
- actionable – the company's scale and resources must be appropriate.

Traditionally, geography has been one of the bases used for segmenting markets. The other ways of describing segments are: demographics, quantifiable facts such as age and sex; psychographics, plotting the aspirations of consumers; and behavioural, focusing on how consumers use the product or service on offer. International marketers often pursue segments which cross geographical frontiers, but are united by life-style and behaviour.

Segmentation, and the targeting that follows it, take place against a background of market dynamics which sees certain areas in the world growing in attraction, while others decline. An area which currently commands new concentration of interest is the 'Pacific rim .

While this type of growth swells the overall size of a market, new entrants to the fray may swiftly create a maelstrom of competition. Market selection needs to take into account the nature of existing and potential competition, and the peculiar benefits of the company's offering to its prospective customers.

MARKET ENTRY DECISIONS

Deciding how to enter a foreign market is a fundamental strategic step. Entry methods vary from the low-risk, but low-return, 'indirect' entry, to the more lucrative, but hazardous, 'direct' entry. The most economically binding choice is to manufacture the product in the foreign market itself. The scale and experience of a company will obviously play an important part in the trade-off between risk and return.

INDIRECT METHODS

There are three main varieties. Each features the exporting company's goods being sold by others in the export market.

- *Domestic purchasing* This is simply the sourcing by a foreign buying organization of a company's product for sale in the foreign market, 'Import' record shops are a good example.

- *Export management companies* Here a manufacturer 'buys in' the services of a specialist company to manage the whole process of exporting.
- *Piggybacking* When an existing exporter allows another manufacturer access to its distribution network in exchange for a financial consideration, the resulting relationship is called 'piggybacking'. Obviously, the two businesses must be complementary rather than competitive.

DIRECT EXPORTING

This involves the direct intervention of a company in a foreign market; choosing agents or distributors, and directly servicing their efforts, as it would in the domestic market. This approach has greater cost implications than indirect methods, but the level of control and potential profit is much higher.

FOREIGN MANUFACTURE

In many instances, because of legislation to protect host country economies, the only route to a market is to abandon the idea of export in favour of manufacturing in the host country itself. This can take the form of assembling products which arrive completely knocked down (CKD) in order to escape import controls. An alternative is to contract the services of a manufacturing company exclusively to make the product. Licensing is a similar process, popular with brewers and soft-drinks manufacturers. Here, however, the exclusive manufacturer also has responsibility for marketing the product.

More capital-intensive foreign manufacturing options include joint ventures, where companies share expertise, capital, and risk, and wholly-owned manufacturing facilities, which are easier to manage but enormously risky in the event of political or economic instability.

Whatever the initial choice of market entry method, this fundamental relationship with the market needs to be kept under constant review.

PRODUCTION DECISIONS

Product is the fundamental element of the marketing mix in international marketing, as well as in domestic marketing. However, in international markets the economies of standardizing the offering across as many markets as possible need to be balanced by a sense of what the customer in each market actually wants. Ideally, all manufacturers would wish to emulate the 'one product suits all' approach of truly international companies, like Coca-Cola or McDonalds. Yet environmental conditions may force a product to be 'adapted' rather than offered as standard. The mountain bike case study shows that the vast majority of mountain bikes made available in the UK are sourced from just two Japanese companies.

Products and services, like their users, have life cycles. A product will go through four stages: introduction, growth, maturity and decline. Profit levels vary throughout the life cycle, peaking during the growth phase. Moving into new markets with an established product can give it a new lease of life. The Western market for typewriters, for example, is in decline since the advent of word-processors; but they are still highly relevant to the needs of many developing countries. Thus a product in decline at home can find pockets of growth abroad.

New product development (NPD) keeps a company in touch with the evolving wants and needs of its customers. Certain international markets are known as 'lead' markets, because of their higher-than average proportion of consumers who respond well to innovation. A presence in such markets can give a company access to ideas and technology that keep it abreast of the competition. Home-entertainments and electronics manufacturers need to be active in the Japanese market, for example, so that they can spot trends early enough to plan for Western markets (which tend to be at an earlier stage of development).

Established international marketing companies need to manipulate the combinations of their products in each market in order to strike the best balance between investment and profit. Portfolio management, as this is called, draws on a number of forms. While they are all useful as models, they are easy to misapply. Their focus is usually short-term, and so they may make companies impatient for returns. A premature withdrawal from a market can be disastrously permanent, if it leads to the unchallenged development of a competitor.

INTERNATIONAL BRANDING

When Nestlé paid five times the book value for Rowntree Mackintosh in 1987, it was recognizing the enormous international potential of the company's brands. As the number of international brands available to consumers proliferates, it is the tried and trusted mega-brands which will win out. International branding is, therefore, a hot issue.

There are, however, very few truly international brands. A brand is that part of a product that can be communicated, through 'utterable' branding (the name of the brand, as in 'Persil') and 'unutterable' branding (the design logo, be it a particular typeface or symbol). Because of the difficulty presented by language, 'unutterable' branding tends to play a dominant part in international marketing.

In the 1980s Shell redesigned its logo, dropping the word 'Shell' altogether. As a result, it now has an instantly recognizable, and translatable, international brand. There are, on the other hand, plenty of examples of the failure of brand names to work across cultures. Sometimes this is because of language; Vauxhall's 'Nova' would, literally, not work in Spain, where '*no va*' means 'doesn't go'. Sometimes it is just an accident of history, as in Australia, where 'Durex' denotes a brand of adhesive tape.

Branding is grounded in product performance and quality, but adds personality to the 'naked' product. However, because of the highly subjective nature of brand communication, what works in one country (or even a group of countries) does not always find universal acceptance.

Aspirational brands, such as European 'designer labels' are enormously popular in newly industrialized countries as badges of prosperity. Branding has an international aspect, in that the country of origin carries certain connotations: German efficiency, British sang-froid, French style, Japanese ingenuity are all reflected in the international image of company products. Both the Typhoon International and the Mountain Bike case studies illustrate the importance of branding in international marketing.

PRICING DECISIONS

All pricing decisions are governed by competition, production costs and company objectives; but international pricing decisions need also to take into account local taxation, exchange rates, the difficulties of invoicing and payment, and company policy in each market.

LOCAL TAXATION

The effects of tariffs and purchase tax may make imported goods expensive, compared with host-country alternatives. The company either takes a cut in margin to remain competitive, or changes its relationship with the host country in the longer term.

EXCHANGE RATES

The fluctuating relative values of international currencies can alter profit levels overnight. A long-term perspective is necessary.

INVOICING AND PAYMENT

Countertrade, which introduces barter-like elements into payment, is increasingly popular. It has fiscal advantages, and helps trade with countries where hard currency is in short supply. Designing methods of invoicing and payment which are proof against all the vagaries of international trade has proved impossible, in spite of progress towards the standardization of documentation. It is therefore prudent to allow for a level of irrecoverable debt when setting price levels.

POLICY MARKET-BY-MARKET

A company may have different pricing policies in different national markets. 'Dumping', disposing of a surplus of goods in a market at very low prices, is unpopular with host-country competition because of its destabilizing effect. On the other hand, existing players in a market can deter new entrants by lowering prices.

PROMOTION DECISIONS

This is an area where cultural differences make for some interesting problems, along with technological and politico-legal considerations.

When Procter and Gamble launched their shampoo 'Wash and Go' in post-glasnost Poland, the television advertising formula which had worked wonders elsewhere in the world fell flat.[3] The locker-room ambience recognized by Western viewers as sophisticated and healthy, reminded Polish consumers of the factory changing-room. The creative execution was hastily altered to replace lockers with a well-known Polish sporting heroine. This appeal to patriotic pride has gone a long way to rehabilitating the brand in Poland, but the first strategy badly dented its early sales curve. The dangers of cultural dissonance in promotion can be reduced by using local agencies and extensive research.

Technological considerations affect the choice of promotional media in foreign markets. It is no use extending your press advertising policies to a market where print technology is not competent to execute them. As media empires grow through diversification and vertical integration, this is becoming less of a problem.

Sometimes the choice of promotional vehicle in a new foreign market may bear little resemblance to what is usual on the domestic front. Many companies have their first significant experience of the sales promotion techniques of exhibitions when representing themselves at international trade fairs. Such exhibitions provide not only the opportunity of informing a new market about one's product or service, but also an invaluable source of first-hand market intelligence.

Regulation provides another potential problem. We have seen the impact of cultural differences on 'Wash and Go', but legal differences could prevent an ad like that from being screened at all in a country like Saudi Arabia, because of the fact that it features women in a state of undress. For those companies who can implement a unified promotional policy world-wide, the synergy benefits can be considerable; but even 'global' advertisers need to make the distinction between homogeneity of approach at a strategic level and flexibility of execution in local markets.

INTERNATIONAL DISTRIBUTION AND LOGISTICS

Distribution makes a company's offering accessible to the maximum number of consumers at the minimum cost. The temptation for the international marketer is to concentrate on those elements of the chain nearest the manufacturer, rather than nearest the customer. This is neglecting to give 'logistics' (working back from the customer to the manufacturer) as much importance as 'distribution' (working from the manufacturer to the consumer).

Distribution channels between nations are chosen with a number of considerations in mind: product characteristics, economy and ease of management are all part of the equation. Channels within nations are more difficult to influence: the company needs to adapt its practices to those of the local environment. Shopping patterns familiar to Western packaged goods manufacturers, dominated by the motor car and large supermarket, are alien to many less developed countries where consumers shop on a daily basis. This leads to enormous numbers of retail outlets in a country like India, with goods passing through a lengthy chain of wholesalers first. Using local agents and brokers familiar with the system is a way of managing this complexity in the medium term. Their careful recruitment, support and review, is a large part of the workload of most export marketing managers.

INTERNATIONAL MARKETING PLANNING

Planning is the continual matching of a company's capabilities to the opportunities presented by its environment. It involves establishing the aims of the organization, the systematic examination of its external and internal environments, and the determination of a plan of action to carry out the aims. Companies below a certain size can get by without formal planning, but in a competitive environment their growth will depend on replacing short-term forecasting with a more deliberate and analytical approach.

International organizations have a particular problem eliciting full participation in, and compliance with the planning process. This is often due to estrangement between the centre of the organization and its various outposts. Different companies have different planning cultures, but a successful common theme balances centrally determined overall strategy with local flexibility as to its tactical implementation.

There remain some major obstacles to international marketing planning, however. Sketchy international market intelligence limits the quality of much of the information input and there is a shortage of reliable theory. Marketing itself is a relatively young science. International marketing theory is in its infancy as a result. Much of the literature reflects American experience, which is not always the most appropriate model. Another drawback is that many of the models used in planning have been developed from very particular domestic marketing situations. The temptation to apply them too literally may have a distorting effect.

Strategic planning uses theoretical models, such as the Boston Consulting Group's matrix, which assume the possibility of isolating strategic business units and predicting their likely response to investment and marketing effort. Defining a strategic business unit is a complex process – it can be a single product, a group of products, or of markets. The permutations available in the international market-place are even more complex. So the use of such theories needs to be tempered with caution.

Michael Porter has developed a theory specifically applied to the nature of international competition, which has proved enormously influential in the 1980s and beyond.[4] He argues that companies operating in an international environment can gain 'competitive advantage' by concentrating on their 'value chain', the various stages in their production and marketing processes, and performing these stages better than their rivals. A key factor here is the geographical location of each stage in the chain.

Porter's thinking is reminiscent of the very first theorist of international trade, the classical Scots economist David Ricardo (1772–1825). Ricardo developed a theory of 'comparative advantage', in which he expounded the benefits of trade between nations on the grounds of utility. It is easier, he argued, to make good wine in Portugal; so, rather than trying to make indifferent wine in Britain, it makes better sense to import. In return, the importing country can export what it has 'comparative advantage' in. Thus inefficiencies are eliminated and greater wealth is available to all.

Attractive though it is, Ricardo's theory does not take into account the conditions of international turbulence in which multinational companies plan and operate. Taiwan, for example, is now a player in the aerospace industry whose success is beginning to threaten American jobs. Even ten years ago, this would have been hard to envisage.

Another influential theory of international trade which affects international marketing planning is the idea of 'life cycle'. Advanced in the 1960s by the American theorists Vernon and Wells, this traced a process whereby a country starts exporting a particular sort of product, which prompts production in the export market, resulting in competition in the export market. The final phase involves competition in its own domestic market from imports.[5] The Japanese car industry is often pointed to as a prime example of this. In broad terms, the theory is an attractive one; but with life cycles of products and markets becoming ever shorter, its reliability as a planning aid is questionable. Nevertheless, planning pays. It keeps the organization focused on its basic purpose – no mean feat in the shifting international environment – and helps determine roles and responsibilities.

CONCLUSIONS

Major companies will find themselves becoming increasingly international as we near the end of the 20th century. Marketing attitudes will move from 'ethnocentric', seeing foreign operations as secondary to domestic ones, to 'geocentric', in which the world itself is the market. International marketing will come into its own as the primary, integrating, business principle of the 21st century.

References

1 Gilligan, C., and Hird, M., *International Marketing Strategy and Management*, (London, Routledge, 1989) p. 12
2 'The Miracle Workers' in *Business Matters*, (BBC2, 1 October 1992).
3 *Europe Express*, (Channel 4, 16 August 1992).
4 Porter, M. E., *The Competitive Advantage of Nations*, (London, Macmillan, 1990).
5 Wells, L. T., 'A Product Lifecycle for International Trade', in Thorelli, H., and Becker, H., *International Marketing Strategy* (New York, Pergamon, 1980).

Bibliography

Gilligan, C., and Hird, M., *International Marketing Strategy and Management*, (London, Routledge, 1989).
Paliwoda, S. J., *International Marketing* 2nd edition (London, Heinemann, 1992).
Terpstra, V., and Sarathy, R., *International Marketing* 5th edition (Orlando, The Dryden Press, 1991).
Walsh, L. S., *International Marketing* (London, Pitman, 1981).

Note: Newspapers and magazines are an excellent source of information, especially the *Economist*, the *European*, the *Financial Times* and the *Guardian*.

CHAPTER FOURTEEN

INTERNATIONAL FINANCIAL MANAGEMENT

ROSS CATTERALL AND JOHN STITTLE

INTRODUCTION

This chapter examines some of the chief difficulties facing the corporate treasurers' department in a multinational company (MNC), or a finance director in a smaller company, when they consider further expansion into overseas markets. In particular, it examines the problems and risks presented by exchange rate fluctuations in planning the management of remittances, working capital and liquidity, as well as longer-term investment flows. Strategies to minimize these risks are discussed, and then other factors influencing the 'internationalization' of the company's activities are examined. Especially important are issues relating to transfer pricing, international taxation and the accounting treatment of international operations.

Chapter 3 showed that since the 1960s, there has been a gradual reduction of tariff barriers and the removal of quotas on imports under the various rounds of the GATT. More recently, Europe's progress towards a single market has enormously increased the liberalization of trade between EC countries. In general terms, international trade and specialization in the production of manufactured goods has increased markedly in the last 40 years. In services such as banking, insurance, shipping and tourism, as well as in manufacturing, the market has become one for international enterprises.

The process of internationalization of business does not, of course, apply only to the sales side of enterprises. In manufacturing it also applies to the production side, where large quantities of raw materials, capital equipment and semi-finished goods are purchased abroad. This creates additional challenges for the international business. It must forecast future input costs and the gains or losses of holding raw material stocks, as changes in exchange rates alter these costs in terms of domestic currency. Input costs may fluctuate for other reasons than just changing exchange rates. Prices in world markets will be affected by perceived or actual world gluts or shortages, and these price fluctuations may be offset, or exacerbated, by changes in the external value of the currency on which the international company bases its financial accounts.

Despite the problems associated with expanding overseas, internationalization is not only the preserve of the MNCs. Recent research by international accountants Deloitte Touche Tohmatsu, focusing on almost 400 companies in 20 countries below the MNC level, has shown that they have extensive international operations. Of these 'middle market companies', typically with sales less than US$ 100 million and mostly without a stockmarket listing, 49 per cent had established manufacturing operations abroad while 86 per cent sold abroad. The most common reasons which companies gave for 'going international' was to exploit growth opportunities, cited by 84 per cent; followed by a desire to reduce dependence on the home market, 39 per cent; customer demand, 34 per cent, and a desire to reduce costs, 24 per cent. The most common reasons for not establishing foreign operations were that the risks were too high and thus likely profits too low, 23 per cent, or that companies could not find suitable joint venture business partners, which was the case for 16 per cent of the participants.

UNCERTAINTY AND RISK IN GLOBAL MARKETS

When a company becomes increasingly international in its perspective, a whole new range of issues will impact upon its operations. Though these issues may not initially be financial in origin, they will become financial in their impact on the organization, through such factors as changing raw material prices, growth of demand in particular markets and changing interest rates world-wide. All these factors can be expected to have an impact on exchange rates, which thus become a vital indicator for the international business to monitor.

Some of the issues facing the international company are similar to those facing companies solely operating in the domestic market, for example, the effect of political uncertainties on demand, or the likelihood of a change in interest rates. Others are entirely new, at least in terms of recent British experience, for example, political revolution, civil war and the expropriation of business assets. Moreover, the international organization has the additional complication of exchange rates which, due to their fluctuation, can wipe out in domestic currency terms an apparent profit in terms of another currency. Because of these fluctuations, and because the company will have receipts and expenditures to make in other currencies, the corporate treasurer's department must watch the FOREX (foreign exchange) market closely and be continuously active in it.

FOREIGN EXCHANGE RECEIPTS AND DISBURSEMENTS

A company operating in global markets will acquire assets and liabilities denominated in foreign currencies. These assets and liabilities are likely to involve receipts and payments at future dates, when the actual exchange rates in terms of the domestic currency cannot be known. Hence uncertainty and risk to the business is increased. The company operating overseas will be involved in FOREX receipts and disbursements for the following reasons.

TRADE

The company will buy raw materials and services, and sell products in overseas markets, sometimes for immediate payment, but often for payment at some time in the future. Other businesses with which it deals may be unwilling to contract in the organization's domestic currency, but only in local currency.

INVESTMENT

The global company may choose to expand by investing in a foreign subsidiary or branch operation. Initially the finance for such operations must be provided by the parent company in foreign currency, perhaps by borrowing in the UK or overseas. It may not only need to meet initial capital costs, but also day-to-day operating costs, such as wages and raw materials, for a considerable 'lead-time' before foreign currency earnings accrue in significant amounts. Moreover, once profits are earned, domestic shareholders require the profits, and hence their dividends, to be converted into the domestic currency, on the best possible terms.

BORROWING

Global companies may find it easier and/or cheaper to borrow in overseas markets rather than in the home market. Interest rates may be lower, and in some instances pockets of surplus loanable funds, or specific types of finance, may exist. However, the capital value of a foreign currency debt will increase in, say, sterling terms if that currency appreciates against the pound. So, too, will ongoing interest payments.

LENDING

Trading patterns may leave companies with surplus amounts of foreign currency which, rather than convert to the domestic currency, they may choose to lend in overseas markets. In addition, they may convert domestic currency surpluses to foreign currencies and lend them in markets offering relatively high interest rates. They should be aware, however, that if a foreign currency in which they have lent is subject to devaluation, this may well eradicate any interest premium earned. Often high yielding currencies are those that are weakest on the FOREX markets.

SPECULATION

Companies involved in global markets often speculate by buying and selling foreign currencies, in an attempt to enhance overall profits. Sometimes, but not always, this activity may be related to future anticipated foreign currency needs. Such actions may represent a relatively unique view of a particular corporate treasurer, or they may serve to reinforce market movements already under way.

A recent spectacular example of the profits that can be earned is provided by the Hungarian-American financier, George Soros. Soros believed that despite denials from the British government, the pound was likely to be forced into a devaluation in September 1992. Accordingly, he became a heavy seller of sterling, some of which was borrowed, and made almost $1 billion profit following the devaluation of sterling in mid-September, for the $6 billion of investment funds he managed.

FOREX MARKET BEHAVIOUR

One consequence of the growing strength of the Japanese economy in the last 40 years, and the movement of Europe towards an integrated economic block through the EC, has been that international currency markets have now evolved into three major currency blocs:

- the *dollar bloc* of countries in Central and South America and the Caribbean, and other parts of the world, whose fortunes are closely linked with those of the US economy and who usually denominate contracts in US dollars;
- the *Deutschmark bloc* of EC full and associate members who either formally through the European Exchange Rate Mechanism (ERM), or by informal government exchange rate shadowing, use the DM as a benchmark for their own currencies;
- the less established *yen block* of South-East Asian currencies, closely linked economically to Japan.

At the beginning of 1991, corporate treasurers may have felt justified in the view that there was little point in spending many hours analysing the Dutch guilder/DM rate, for example, because twitches in that exchange rate are more likely to be swamped by movements in DM/US dollar, yen/DM, and yen/US dollar rates, which had become the key indicators for MNCs to watch. However, it should be noted that other rates might be critical for smaller companies doing a large volume of business with one country. During 1991, however, the relative serenity of currency markets began to break down, and by September 1992, Britain and Italy had suspended their membership of the DM-dominated ERM, floating their currencies and suffering significant devaluations. Spain also devalued, but remained an ERM member.

During the first month after leaving the ERM, the pound at times fell as low as 82 per cent of its former ERM central parity rate of DM 2.95. This renewed volatility of the FOREX markets in 1991 and 1992 has made it essential that all corporate treasurers of companies with international interests monitor the currency markets much more closely. Only then can they develop appropriate strategies concerning currencies to hold, borrow and trade.

BUSINESS RISKS AND THE FOREX MARKETS

One way to identify the kinds of business risks inherent in the FOREX markets is to examine some of the key factors which have caused exchange rates to move during 1991 and 1992. Sometimes such movements offer companies with surplus currencies opportunities to benefit from rising exchange values or higher interest rates elsewhere in the world. In other cases, depreciation of currency in which contracts are denominated may cause a serious profit shortfall in terms of the domestic currency.

In addition, the depreciation of a domestic currency itself may greatly increase a company's outlay on vital raw materials. However, there may be countervailing benefits for exporting companies: a lower exchange value for the domestic currency will make exports more price-competitive in foreign currencies.

FUNDAMENTAL, TECHNICAL AND RANDOM INFLUENCES

Prices in all financial markets are determined by a mixture of three sets of influences affecting demand and supply for a particular currency. In the FOREX market, the price is the exchange value between one currency and another, and demand and supply for each currency will be affected by the actual performance of the economies involved, their perceived future performance, and special factors which may have both current and future impacts.

Fundamental factors are those which link the underlying performance of an economy to the value of its currency in the FOREX markets.

Technical factors represent the current attitude and perceptions of buyers and sellers in the market, sometimes referred to as the 'argument' between buyers and sellers. These attitudes will be related to the 'fundamentals' of the various economies, but sometimes the relationship is not easily apparent as markets develop their own momentum, often characterized by waves of optimism and then pessimism, which seem somewhat detached from current economic performance.

Random shocks and other *special factors* unsettle the markets by changing sentiment, perhaps through business perceptions of economic fundamentals in the future. These random shocks can include political unrest or uncertainty, wars and natural disasters such as earthquakes and typhoons.

ECONOMIC FUNDAMENTALS

The chief economic factors which affect the value of one currency in terms of another are as follows.

- *Relative goods prices* If the price of goods are higher in say Germany than the USA, more of the good will be purchased from the USA, whose exchange rate will appreciate against the DM. This is the so-called 'purchasing power parity' theory of FOREX values.
- *The level of domestic demand* The higher this is in one country, the higher will be its imports and the lower will be its exchange rate.
- *The level of world demand* If this is higher, then export demand, i.e. world trade, will grow faster. However, the way that this impacts on an individual economy and its currency will depend on the structure of its domestic industry and whether its products are 'income-elastic'. In other words, does it have a structure of output which will enable it to benefit from new patterns of growth of world demand? And does it produce 'superior' goods, sales of which will respond markedly to increases in world income? Or does it produce inferior goods, demand for which is little affected by income changes?
- *Relative interest rates* These affect exchange rates by attracting capital flows to centres with higher rates, providing exchange devaluation is unlikely.

COMPLEXITY OF FOREX MARKET BEHAVIOUR

By looking at the foreign exchange markets in 1991 and 1992 as a brief case study, it is possible to see how they have been affected by a mixture of fundamental, technical and random factors. It will be seen that it is critical for the corporate treasurer's department to watch a whole range of economic, political and social events unfolding on the world stage, and that knowledge of economic fundamentals alone may not explain market patterns. Corporate treasurers have to make their own assessments of what are acceptable risks for their companies to undertake, then adopt appropriate hedging strategies.

PERCEPTIONS OF GOVERNMENT POLICY

A key feature of the FOREX markets between February and August 1991 was the great strength of the US dollar. It experienced spectacular appreciation, rising by almost 30 per cent from trough to peak against the DM and related currencies. Corporate treasurers buying early in this upswing were able to significantly enhance the exchange value of dollar holdings, providing they switched currencies before the dollar depreciated again. From mid-August, the tone of the US currency weakened again, being exacerbated in late 1991 by a mini-US stockmarket crash, somewhat reminiscent of October 1987.

Underlying these movements in the dollar were perceptions of federal economic policy. Until August there was a belief that the Bush administration would actually take strong action against the twin US problems of a large budget deficit and a large balance of payments deficit. This could be expected to boost the dollar's external value, as the US supply of its own currency in exchange for other currencies would be constrained. However, by August it was apparent that the US recession was deepening, and the administration was expected to allow or encourage the dollar to fall in order to increase export competitiveness and reduce imports. Also, the Federal Reserve was expected to adopt a more lax monetary policy.

In fact, the markets' perceptions of federal policy was largely correct, although it is doubtful that actual economic fundamentals justified the big swings in dollar value which actually took place. However, it was important for the astute corporate treasurer wishing to trade US dollars to be aware of the perceptions, and to watch carefully for changes in trend which might dictate the best moment to trade. Thus he was likely to be able to buy on the dollar's upswing, and switch into other currencies before the dollar had moved too far on the downside.

RELATIVE INTEREST RATES AND CURRENCY STRENGTH

The US economy was not alone in being on the slide downwards in 1991. The European power-house, Germany, along with the weaker EC economies, was experiencing mounting economic difficulties. However, unlike the Federal Reserve, which was steadily cutting interest rates in the second half of the year to induce recovery, the Bundesbank continued to keep interest rates high, maintaining its overall objective to control inflation. The result was that the DM ended 1991 on a high compared to the US dollar, the yen, and most other major currencies.

Where a high interest rate is offered in a financial centre with a relatively strong currency, that will serve to increase the value of that currency still further. Corporate treasurers have to watch such market movements to know where to park short-term funds for greatest safety and return.

Some currencies are traditional 'high yielders', such as the Canadian and Australian dollars, both members of the US dollar bloc. Usually this is because there is a governmental desire to track some other, but stronger, major currency. In late 1991, given the level of German interest rates, the so-called 'high yielders' looked less attractive. The risks for companies holding these currencies were mounting, and there comes a point when high yielding currencies are dangerous to hold. They then become currencies under threat of significant devaluation due to an outflow of funds into stronger currencies.

THE DANGER OF 'THREATENED' CURRENCIES

Currencies likely to be most under threat are those which are members of some fixed exchange rate system, and which are seen to be progressively weakening against the system benchmark. Such benchmarks have included gold, under the gold standard system to 1931; the US dollar, under the Bretton Woods system to 1971; and the DM, under the European ERM.

Sterling, in September 1992, provided an obvious example of a threatened currency. Sterling had entered the ERM in October 1990, after a period of shadowing the DM at round DM 2.95, which became the UK's declared 'central parity'. After a honeymoon period of six weeks or so, life in the ERM did not prove easy for sterling. However, 'jawboning' by UK Chancellor of the Exchequer, Norman Lamont, managed to talk up the rate by leading markets to believe that:

- the UK Government was committed to a low inflation/high exchange rate strategy to be achieved through high interest rates;
- sterling was likely to enter the narrow band of the ERM at some point in 1992, reducing its volatility still further.

Events proved both intentions unrealistic. Continuing high interest rates, the length and severity of the UK recession, and weaknesses elsewhere in the EC, especially Italy, increased ERM volatility and put sterling into the firing line as a 'threatened' currency, which was likely to devalue. Speculative movements of funds out of sterling (such as those on which George Soros made spectacular gains) forced Britain to suspend its ERM membership and allow sterling to float downwards, as Italy had done with the lira shortly before. The markets had come to realize that fundamental weaknesses of the British and Italian economies no longer justified their declared ERM parities.

Corporate treasurers managing exchange portfolios thus have to decide whether the underlying strength of an economy justifies its current parities with other currencies, or whether government 'jawboning' lacks credibility and a speculative dam is likely to burst as market pessimism grows. High interest rates do not offer companies attractive returns on surplus funds deposited in a fundamentally weak currency, but the near certainty of capital loss in terms of other currencies following a devaluation. Moreover, when one currency gives way under a fixed exchange rate system, for example, Italy under the ERM, there is a possibility that other members will follow suit, for example Britain and Spain, or introduce new measures to limit the spread of volatility to their own currencies. An example of the latter case is Spain's reimposition of exchange controls in September 1992, creating renewed difficulties for converting peseta receipts into other currencies.

EXCHANGE CONTROLS

Exchange controls impose limitations or prohibitions on the movement of currency across national frontiers. This may not absolutely prevent companies taking funds from one country and converting them into other currencies, but they will need to get official approval to do so. At the very least, they will encounter new bureaucratic controls and red-tape to deal with, increasing delays and administrative costs. All industrialized countries have at one time or another enforced exchange controls. The UK abolished its controls in 1979, and progress to European Monetary Union was intended to lead to Europe-wide abolition by 1 January 1993. Even so, exchange controls exist elsewhere, creating difficulties for international companies, especially in the less developed world.

'OVERSHOOTING' AND HIGH-VOLATILITY FOREX MARKETS

It is often said that today's participant in the FOREX markets, both the professional trader and the corporate treasurer seeking to profit from his company's FOREX inflows and outflows, needs 'nerves of steel'. This is because in the last few years FOREX markets have shown high volatility, which is likely to increase following the September 1992 ERM crisis, and corporate treasurers and traders need to undertake 'technical analysis' of market trends. Technical analysts believe that price patterns recur over time and signals can be identified which show when to buy and sell for maximum profit. Even with a generally appreciating or depreciating currency, there will be fluctuations about the trend, giving opportunities for companies to make better or worse foreign exchange deals. Technical analysis of price patterns seeks to identify the best times to switch currencies.

Corporate treasurers can either undertake their own analyses, or more likely buy in technical analysis services. Services, such as those provided to corporates by Investment Research of Cambridge Ltd, offer daily fax services on currency movements, as well as published weekly and monthly chart-based currency commentaries for subscribers.

Often currency markets 'overshoot' or over-react to the available economic information. Thus a currency may suffer a dramatic reverse or devaluation with the markets overdoing the need for downward adjustment, and then rebound dramatically, at least for a time. Thereafter, there may follow a period of consolidated sideways trading at intermediate levels.

Taking the case of the US dollar in 1991: its DM/USA dollar exchange value was DM1.44 at its February low, but six months later the rate had improved 40 pfennigs or by 28 per cent. Thus the corporate treasurer with sufficient nerves and expertise to use his DM reserves to buy dollars at the low point could have enhanced the returns on them to his company by over a quarter. Knowledge of previous price trends, and how to interpret the buy/sell signals they offer using technical analysis, is an additional weapon in the corporate treasurers' armoury, although it will not be an invincible shield of protection.

RANDOM SHOCKS AND OTHER SPECIAL FACTORS

Corporate treasurers need to watch the world scene closely to see how sudden shocks, unique occurrences and political changes may affect key currencies.

ELECTIONS AND GOVERNMENTAL CHANGES

National elections can make FOREX markets nervous. This was the case with sterling in 1992 in the run-up to the April election, when in the UK opinion polls predicting a Labour election victory adversely affected the pound. Likewise, the growing strength in the opinion polls of Governor Clinton, regarded as more inflationary then Bush, was adversely affecting the US dollar prior to his election as President in November 1992.

THE MAASTRICHT TREATY

This Treaty represents an important milestone in the EC's progress towards European Monetary Union (EMU). However, by mid-1992, ratification of the Treaty was facing growing opposition and this was undermining confidence in the progress towards EMU and a single European currency. It was even becoming questionable whether the existing ERM arrangements would survive, thus increasing uncertainties about European currency alignments. This was intensifying the volatility of European FOREX markets and contributed to the crisis for sterling and the lira of September 1992. Such volatility is likely to worsen if the ERM collapses.

DEVELOPMENTS IN EASTERN EUROPE

The Soviet putsch of August 1991, the first stage in the demise of Mikhail Gorbachev, was deeply worrying for companies with investments in the USSR and the Eastern block and receipts in Soviet and related currencies. The subsequent break-up of the USSR has increased investment opportunities for companies to establish operations and joint ventures in the new eastern Europe. However, risks have also increased markedly in relation to the expropriation of foreign assets, civil war, currency collapses, currency inconvertibility and exchange controls. Likewise the break-up of the former Yugoslavia and the subsequent civil war between Bosnia and Serbia, has led to the collapse of the market for the Yugoslav dinar, grave risks of expropriation of foreign corporate assets by new governments in the former Yugoslav states, and the danger of outright destruction of such assets.

Foreign exchange risks have become intermingled with risks to physical assets, which create general uncertainties in the FOREX markets and specific problems for companies with close trading ties with the least stable parts of the former Eastern bloc. This point is illustrated in the case of Arthur Andersen.

CORPORATE RESPONSES TO FOREIGN CURRENCY RISKS

The survey of some of the features of two years in the FOREX markets has shown that MNC and smaller overseas traders alike need to watch vigilantly the fundamental, technical and special factors affecting these markets. The world is made

149

up of economic, political and social uncertainties which necessitate constant monitoring, and the development of strategic responses for companies with overseas interests. Some potential hedging strategies for such risks are now examined.

CATEGORIES OF CORPORATE FOREX RISK

Corporate treasurers and finance directors have three principal areas of foreign exchange risk to attempt to safeguard against.

- *Transaction risk* When the customer pays in three months' time in French francs, will this buy them sufficient DM to pay for components purchased in Germany? Or if settlement is agreed in US$, what will this be worth in terms of francs?
- *Translation risk* The company may well have assets and liabilities which face translation exposure. A factory overseas, or the balance sheet of a foreign subsidiary valued in a foreign currency, must be reflected in, say, sterling on the UK company's balance sheet.
- *Economic risk* The depreciation of, say, the lira may put up input costs for the Italian company, whether or not it sells overseas. Moreover, even a company which did no overseas buying or selling could be affected by, say, a strengthening of the lira, as competitor companies in Italy which utilized foreign raw materials would actually suffer a fall in input costs. Falling input costs were, of course, one justification for sterling entering the ERM at a relatively high rate in October 1990: they were a key part of the UK Government's anti-inflation strategy.

STRATEGIC RESPONSES TO FOREX RISKS

In view of the combination of risks that international companies face in the FOREX markets, it is vital that they are aware of the risks they are exposed to and develop a coherent strategy for risks they regard as unacceptably high. Possible strategies include the following.

MATCHING EXPECTED REVENUE FLOWS

A company may decide to cease borrowing in a weak, and probably high interest rate, currency and switch its borrowing into stronger currencies in which it expects revenue flows. These revenue flows can be used to pay off borrowings and bring benefit to the company from lower interest rates. Such a company might in 1992 have reduced its sterling exposure and taken out loans in yen, with repayments matched to expected revenue flows.

COMPLETE HEDGING

A company may decide that the best way to produce certainty is to hedge all foreign currency inflows and outflows. To do this it will use the forward FOREX trading. The forward markets give companies exchange values for the delivery of another currency at some future date, as opposed to the delivery price right now (the spot price). In other words, the bank providing the forward quotation is taking on the risk of delivering a currency, at a particular exchange rate, at some time in the future. A particular currency's forward quotation may be at a premium or at a discount to the current spot rate. The forward quotation will depend on the interest rate differentials between the two economies involved, and the view of the institution providing forward trading facilities as to the likely course of the exchange rates over the relevant period.

Interest rates are critical, as normally banks making forward transactions for, say, US dollar delivery in three months' time, will buy the dollars now and reinvest the proceeds in the US. Naturally, international companies can only hedge their risks in this way at a price. So the cost of hedging *all* transactions could put them at a competitive disadvantage. Such a strategy would involve buying sterling forward every time a contract is agreed for payment in another currency at a future date, and buying a foreign currency forward to match purchases of raw materials and other items overseas. Payment for currency bought forward does not take place until delivery of the currency actually takes place. Delivery between a range of dates is also possible, but the currency provider is then likely to base the quotation on the interest calculation for the end of the period.

SELECTIVE HEDGING

Few companies go to the lengths of complete hedging of all transactions, although it is a way to remove all uncertainty from FOREX transactions. Usually a company will use hedging selectively, to protect its position in what it regards as weak currencies or where it has especially large currency exposures. In fact, hedging itself can put a company at a competitive disadvantage, although it does give certainty for the transactions covered.

Visualize the case of a UK company which bought foreign exchange forward to hedge the value of, say, a shipment of computer components from Taiwan. It would lock itself into a particular sterling rate and a particular cost structure, and have given itself certainty on the cost side of its budgeting process. However, if sterling strengthened against the yen bloc, and the company's competitors had not hedged the value of their purchases, they would be able to buy the Taiwanese components much cheaper.

This leads on to another problem for the company, what size of inventories or stocks should it keep? Does it buy a large quantity of components because it believes the forward rate is currently favourable, or does it keep inventory size to a minimum, minimizing borrowing costs, and paying for shipments at prevailing spot FOREX rates?

METHODS OF HEDGING

In practice, companies will take a pragmatic approach to hedging and related questions, depending on their future view of world commodity and FOREX markets. They will accept a certain amount of risk and undertake selective hedging, where they believe key risk exposures lie. Once they decide to hedge, they have a number of possible alternative methods, which are outlined here.

NATURAL HEDGES

Such a hedge will be available if assets and liabilities in the same currency can be matched. For example, it has already been seen that expected foreign revenues can be matched by loan repayments on borrowings taken out in the same currency. Alternatively, purchases of raw materials in a particular currency can be set against sales to the relevant country. In the first case, the company must review its borrowing policy so as to place the maximum borrowings in the currencies it expects to receive revenues, subject to interest costs. The second strategy is only available to the company that both buys and sells extensively in the same market, unless it can induce other parties to pay or accept payment in some other currency.

FORWARD CONTRACTS

The value of using the forward market to 'fix' payments and receipts in sterling terms has already been discussed. Many smaller companies are happy to lock themselves into a price that they consider acceptable, although it is, of course, galling for the finance director when he discovers that changes in the spot rate have caused him to lose out by fixing the price, and he is forced to pay over the odds for a currency when the forward contract is closed out!

Multinationals may adopt other approaches and, because of the greater in-house expertise of their corporate treasury departments, may believe they have better insights into future market movements than FOREX dealers and economists. This could be true if they have especially good local knowledge about the fundamental situation of an economy in which they operate.

OPTION FORWARD CONTRACTS

These are the contracts which allow companies to take delivery of exchange within a range of specified future dates, rather than on a single set date, as with a standard forward contract. This is useful if there is uncertainty about the precise date when currency will be received or required, but it is generally more expensive than the standard contract. A superior strategy may be to enter into a standard forward contract for delivery at the earliest date the currency may be needed, and then place the funds on deposit until they are actually required.

CURRENCY SWAPS

These swaps usually cover a longer period and larger amounts. Essentially, a company will arrange through its bank to swap its debts with another company. Each company will pay the interest on the other's debt until an agreed date, and the swap agreement will set a rate at which the currencies will be exchanged until that time. The aim is to give the two companies a debt in their desired currency.

CURRENCY OPTIONS

Under a forward contract, a purchaser is obliged to buy or sell the agreed amount of currency up to or on the set maturity date. Currency options, on the other hand, do not have this obligation. The company pays a premium for the right to buy or sell the currency in the future, but if a deal falls through or the currencies move adversely, it can let its option lapse, losing only the premium it has paid.

FINANCIAL CONTROL OF OVERSEAS OPERATIONS

So far the discussion in this chapter has concentrated on identifying the factors which create foreign exchange risks for companies and discussing possible alternative strategies to deal with these risks.

Foreign exchange values are at the heart of international corporate activity because companies trade, invest, borrow, lend and speculate in other currencies. However, when expanding trading overseas or expanding in other countries directly through the acquisition of factories and other business premises, or through joint ventures, companies need to consider closely how other accounting, taxation, legal and regulatory practices will impinge on their plans. The purpose of this section is to indicate some of the issues to be considered.

INFLUENCES ON INTERNATIONAL CORPORATE REPORTING

Over the last ten years, the importance of international corporate reporting has grown significantly. The financial analysis and control of large corporations poses a number of intrinsic difficulties, which are intensified greatly when these companies expand and trade outside their own domestic origins. The problems can arise either by companies trading directly with overseas countries or indirectly though the establishment of subsidiary outlets. The financial implications of accounting for international companies are not only significant in the case of MNCs, but can also cause deep concern for smaller companies seeking to expand across national frontiers.

The difficulties that are common to all companies intent on operating in international markets are centred upon the calculation of costs and profits, currency translation, corporate taxation and the construction of group accounts. Additionally, major differences in legal and accounting systems can rapidly escalate to engulf the expanding company. The results of these various pressures will not only influence the financial reporting requirements of the company to the outside world, but also they have a related internal effect on the control of the organization from a management accounting perspective.

Many companies trading in the international arena now obtain their funding needs, not only in their home markets, but increasingly in international capital markets. The expansion of funding horizons has been caused by a number of factors including the deregulation of a number of the world's capital markets, the innovation of new financial instruments and the increasing attention which needs to be paid to foreign exchange transactions.

Additionally, from a practical viewpoint, the situation has been assisted by advances in technology whereby global equity and bond markets can be instantaneously accessed. The era when large companies solely tapped into the rather limited capital resources of their own national markets has disappeared.

LEGAL AND ACCOUNTING RULES

Financial reporting difficulties are magnified in the case of MNCs. These companies usually report their results in accordance with legal and accounting requirements of their home territory. Their place of origin will normally dictate the methods of accounting utilized, and the quantity and quality of information that needs to be publicly disclosed. The legal and accounting rules on corporate disclosure differ widely on a world-wide basis, causing enormous financial and analytical implications. These differences are centred upon a number of complex and interwoven factors and include differences in legal systems, in taxation requirements, in the nature of the providers of finance, and in national accounting practices and policies. The case study of Arthur Andersen illustrates some of these points.

It was stated in Chapter 9 that a major determinant of reporting systems is a country's legal system. For example, a number of countries including England and Wales and others that have been subject to English influence such as Australia and India, have a legal system that is based on common law. Many other legal systems are based upon codified Roman Law concepts, where detailed rules and codes are specified, such as those in France, Germany and Spain.

The practical implication is that companies operating in countries with common law systems normally have financial and reporting system that do not usually impose detailed and precise regulation. However, companies under a Roman Law system are subject to a more detailed statutory and accounting regulatory process concerning their financial reporting activities. For example, in countries such as France and Spain, corporate reporting is subject to a detailed and statutorily imposed accounting plan.

DIFFERING TAX SYSTEMS

The influence of countries' differing taxation systems can play a significant role in determining the locations in which companies choose to operate. By carefully planned corporate strategy, and by judicious use of a transfer pricing system, costs and profits can be discretely manipulated. In the case of MNCs, the high profits can be reported in countries with the lower taxation rates.

INFLUENCE OF LENDING INSTITUTIONS

The providers of finance can also effect the financial control and reporting procedures. In countries such as Germany, the large lending institutions commonly provide a substantial proportion of corporate funds. Consequently, the financial system of such countries is dictated by the overriding needs of the lenders, primarily the banks. However, in countries such as the UK and the USA, many of the financial requirements are imposed by the demands of shareholders.

ROLE OF ACCOUNTING PROFESSION

The varying power and influence of the accounting profession in different countries has a significant impact on a company's financial affairs. In countries with a more mature and long-established accounting profession, there are frequently detailed rules and relatively sophisticated accounting policies which are imposed on companies. Evidence of the application of these policies can be found in the USA, UK and in large areas of northern Europe. In other countries the accounting profession is relatively new and less influential, and hence it has produced less onerous and demanding requirements as regards accounting regulations.

The extent of the massive differences in international reporting is evidenced by the fact that no German company has been able to obtain a full listing on the New York Stock Exchange. The reasons are largely centred on the conceptual and practical accounting differences upon which German companies produce their financial statements. Many of the German accounting techniques are simply not acceptable, or even recognized, in the USA. Indeed, the extent of these differences can be found in the case of Mannesmann, a large German engineering company. It was estimated in the *Financial Times*, 19 March 1992, that Mannesmann's 1989 profits would have been over a third higher if the company had used US accounting principles. Moreover, the German car production company, Volkswagen, would have reported its 1989 profits to have been over 50 per cent higher if their financial statements had been prepared under UK accounting practices.

A company that undertakes international transactions will rapidly establish that there are important additional accounting rules to be considered. These rules are predominantly in the form of accounting standards, now termed 'financial reporting standards' in the UK, to which all company accounting statements must conform. These standards are implemented and monitored by accountants, and adherence to them is ensured in the form of verification by independent auditors.

LEGAL AND PRACTICAL REQUIREMENTS

Once a company has established subsidiary companies, there is, in the UK and in most parts of Europe, a statutory and accounting necessity to produce an annual summation of the subsidiary accounts with those of the parent company to form group accounts. The summation of the accounting statements of all companies in the group allows a clearer picture of the whole group's activities to emerge. It provides important information for external investors, as well as focusing management on the key issues faced by the company.

EXCHANGE RATES AND CORPORATE ACCOUNTS

The accounting transactions of a group can be further complicated in circumstances where a subsidiary's accounting records are expressed in a currency denomination that is different from the parent company. In these circumstances, the production of group accounts will necessitate the subsidiary company translating its accounting statements to the currency used by the parent company. This translation process will depend on the currency rates chosen and hence any gains and losses on translation will be incorporated into the group accounts. The case of Arthur Andersen addresses a number of these issues.

Additionally, foreign currency also causes significant problems where, for example, goods have been obtained from an overseas source and will need to be paid for at a later date in a foreign currency. During the intervening period between purchase and payment, changes in currency rates may cause gains or losses on currency movements to arise. As was seen earlier in this chapter, to help alleviate this risk of currency fluctuations it is possible to implement various currency hedging techniques in order to minimize difficulties of currency fluctuations. Failure to monitor and fully understand the implications of fluctuations in currency rates can provide companies with serious problems.

Evidence of the potential danger to investors of failing to fully understand the importance of currency translation losses, and the way the company treats them in its accounts, is all too clearly indicated with the collapse in 1990 of Polly Peck International. This company had deposits in weak, or soft, currencies paying high interest rates, but borrowed in hard currencies at low interest rates. The problem was that in the long run the soft currencies tended to depreciate against hard currencies, resulting in exchange losses. The company's 1989 accounts made a £10.5 million provision in the Profit and Loss in respect of unrealized currency losses. In addition, the group made adjustments directly reducing reserves by £44.7 million in 1989 and £170.3 million in 1988 in respect of 'exchange variances on net investments overseas'.

CONCLUSIONS

A company aiming at expansion into international markets is presented with considerable difficulties from many directions. The company hopes that the increased risks it faces will be more than adequately compensated for by increased profits. Day to day, it will need to monitor FOREX inflows and outflows, deciding what currencies to trade and hedge. The company must view the daily trading transactions in a framework of the overall corporate accounts. Finance department staff will need to not only monitor a comprehensive reporting and financial management system, but also understand the legal, tax and accounting framework in which the company operates. For companies heavily involved in intra-European trade, the movement towards a single market in financial services, with the harmonization of accounting practices that it is likely to bring, together with the establishment of a single European currency, are likely to greatly simplify the process of cross-border expansion within EC states. However, trade between EC countries only accounts for 25 per cent of world trade, and the problem of dealing with the rest of the world still remains.

References

1 *Why Companies Go International*, Touche Ross (DRT International), 1992.
2 *The Times*, Monday 26 October 1992.
3 Smith, T., *Accounting for Growth*, (Century Business, 1992).

Bibliography

Aliber, R. Z., *The International Money Game*, 5th edition, (London, Macmillan, 1988).
Allen, M., *The Times International Guide to Finance*, (London, Times Books, 1991).
Amlôt, R., *Guide to World Markets*, (London, Boxtree Ltd, 1992).
Cuthbertson, K., and Gripaios, P., *The Macro Economy: A Guide for Business*, (London, Unwin Hyman, 1988).

Goldman Sachs, *The Goldman Sachs Foreign Exchange Handbook*, (London, Euromoney, 1992).

Kaufman, H., *Interest Rates, the Markets and the New Financial World*, (London, I. B. Tauris & Co. Ltd, 1989).

Smith, T., *Accounting for Growth*, (London, Century Business, 1992).

CHAPTER FIFTEEN

SOME ISSUES IN INTERNATIONAL HUMAN RESOURCE MANAGEMENT

JILL PRESTON

INTRODUCTION

A major factor in the success of any organization is the best use of human resources, and this is particularly true of an international company. In any organization, the aim of having the right people in the right place at the right time is difficult to achieve. In an international organization, this aim is even more difficult to realize. In 1985 P. Enderwick identified a number of ways in which human resource management is affected by the internationalization of business activity.[1]

- International management requires awareness of, and sensitivity towards, differences in language, culture, and politics. Each of these affect the management of human resource practices.
- Personnel practices are usually subject to the influences of source nation values and procedures.
- The multinational structure of an international company may influence the human resource management process. For example, where the centralization of authority is high, local managers may be ineffectual in a collective bargaining role. However, multinational operations create the opportunity for cross-national comparison performance and the development and possible introduction of best practices.
- Internationalization brings with it issues that do not arise in the national context. For example, international companies have to develop policies in the area of the selection and management of expatriates, nationality composition and, frequently, transnational bargaining.

This chapter is divided into three sections: the first looks at communications and cultural issues involved in international management; the second examines the issues involved in staff mobility across national frontiers; and the final section looks at some of the implications of the internationalization of business in industrial relations.

COMMUNICATION AND CULTURE

In Chapter 8 Terry Mughan identifies some of the cultural issues involved in international business and how managers can respond in a positive way to cultural diversity. This chapter continues the general theme by looking at how culture affects communication and how culture has an impact on staff mobility, as well as industrial relations.

Effective communication is important in any organization, but it is particularly significant in international management. For example, problems of misinterpretation can be compounded at the international level. The communication process within an organization is normally influenced by cultural differences. For example, Richard Pascale, found that in comparison to managers in the USA, Japanese managers made much greater use of face-to-face contacts.[2]

In some countries the communication process involves very explicit communiqués, whereas in others communiqués are highly implicit. For example, in the USA managers are taught to say exactly what they mean, objectives are usually clearly stated in quantitative terms and the date for their achievement is established. In countries such as Japan and the Arab States, a more implicit approach is normally used. William G. Ouchi states that Japanese managers are intentionally ambiguous when it comes to assigning responsibility for tasks, as within this culture a team assumes responsibility.[3]

Cultural values indirectly and often directly affect communication between people from different countries. Cultural differences can cause misinterpretation, both in how others see expatriate managers and in how the latter see themselves. For example, US managers doing business in Austria often misinterpret the fact that local people conduct business in a highly formal manner.

Non-verbal communication is also affected by cultural norms. To take one example, it is good manners in the USA to look directly at the person being addressed. However, in other parts of the world this would be regarded as highly impolite.

The cases of the NEC Corporation, GH Neotech and Nissan show how a range of international organizations are dealing with the issue of communication.

STAFF MOBILITY ACROSS NATIONAL FRONTIERS

The type of training required by staff moving across frontiers is in part dependent on the organizations's overall philosophy of international management. There are four basic philosophical positions of multinational organizations.

- An *ethnocentric* approach is characterized by all key staff positions being filled by parent country nationals. This approach facilitates communication with the corporate headquarters, but it can result in an organization finding itself in conflict with a host government, if the latter places a high value on the localization of management.
- A *polycentric* organization places local nationals in key positions and allows these managers to appoint and develop their own people. This approach enables the organization to take maximum benefit of local knowledge but there can be difficulties in communications between staff at headquarters and those in subsidiary units. Nissan uses this approach.

- A *geocentric* approach involves a strategy of employing the most suitable people, regardless of nationality. This type of strategy can assist in the development of truly international executive teams. NH Geotech tends to use this approach, when possible.
- A *regiocentric* approach, which is a variation of internationalism, may be used when an organization requires regional or area expertise. In some situations, Arthur Andersen tends to use this approach.

With the growth of various types of international collaboration between organizations – for example, marketing and distribution partnerships, research consortia, licensing arrangements and joint ventures – there is a range of advantages in having multinational teams who are able to function across several cultures. Many organizations are investing heavily in the development of such teams. For example, in IBM all managers have training on the internationalization of the company, regardless of location.

Increasingly, the internationalization of business activity requires people mobility. For example, Shell have 5,000 expatriates world-wide. The internationalization of business activity, requiring people from different national backgrounds to work together, can result in problems, many of which can be traced back to cultural differences. To overcome these problems, many organizations are investing resources to understand cultural differences and its impact on business processes, as well as on team-building and communications.

Increasing importance is being given to expatriate selection, preparation and ways of reducing the failure rate. In expatriate selection there is some evidence to suggest that many organizations place too much emphasis on technical skills, rather than behavioural skills, such as the ability of managers to deal with customers, superiors and subordinates.

> *Indeed, a valid criticism of expatriate selection is that it tends to equate domestic success with likely overseas success.*[6]

Inappropriate selection is a major cause of expatriate failure, which can be defined as the premature return of an expatriate. The costs of such failure can be considerable. It has been estimated that failure rates can be as high as 40 per cent.[4]

Different posts demand different selection criteria for overseas postings, but there are a number of general factors which are taken into consideration by many organizations. Colin Coulson-Thomas identifies a checklist of qualities required for overseas assignments. He states that many of the skills required for international activities are similar to those required in a national setting, for example, the ability to communicate and the flexibility to learn and to change. However, success in the home situation does not automatically result in success in an overseas posting.

Qualities required for overseas assignments include:

- understanding of the business environment;
- sensitivity to customer requirements;
- open-mindedness;
- self-awareness;
- communication skills;
- team-working and networking skills;

- tolerance of diversity;
- commitment to life-long learning.[5]

Other related qualities include:

- adaptability to cultural change and linguistic ability;
- independence and self-reliance. Frequently, managers on overseas assignments have responsibilities which are at a higher level than those to which they are accustomed. At the same time, these people have fewer colleagues to call upon for assistance;
- physical and emotional health, 'sheer energy';
- motivation for an overseas placement. A manager must be convinced of the importance of the job;
- supportive and adaptable partners and dependants.

Preparation for overseas postings is crucial. For example, Shell works with the Centre for International Briefing at Barnham Castle in Surrey and claims to have achieved the very low failure rate of less than 1 per cent. It is significant that Shell provides all graduate recruits with compulsory cross-cultural training, whether or not they are likely to obtain a foreign posting.

Some companies have established there own cross-cultural training centres, for example, Scandinavian Airlines System (SAS) established a centre in 1984. The centre provides preparation for expatriate managers and their families. It has helped companies in intercultural productivity assessment and in analysing the way in which corporate cultures in Scandinavia and their overseas companies interact.

In the USA some organizations use the Graduate School of International Management in Glendale, Arizona, which provides courses in the linguistic and cultural aspects of doing business in other countries. Kevin Barham states that some areas of the world, such as Japan, present particularly difficult cultural problems.[7] Barham estimates that 90 per cent of managers are significantly less productive in Japan in comparison to their home country. A number of companies, such as Du Pont, Ford and Kodak, are introducing cross-cultural training specifically aimed at the problems of operating in Japan.

Japanese companies are likewise giving increased emphasis to the problems of dealing with foreign cultures, an issue which is discussed in the study of the NEC Corporation, for that organization has set up its own Institute of International Studies in Tokyo. Intensive six-day courses consist of business negotiations, cross-cultural communications, legal differences and Western business practices. In addition, a number of organizations are now providing some support for expatriates when they are in post; for example, Kleinwort Benson uses an informal mentor system.

Returning home from an overseas assignment can result in problems for the expatriate. Even during an 18 months or 2-year assignment abroad, changes can occur both at home and in how the individual perceives the foreign environment. The expatriate can experience difficulties in finding a proper place in the corporate hierarchy. If no provision is made, a returning manager can be caught in a holding position for a long time. Planning for repatriation is necessary; for example, some companies give the returning manager reasonable professional adjustment time and counselling for the whole family. Corporations such as Dow Chemical provide each manager embarking on an overseas assignment with a letter that promises a post of at least equal responsibility upon return.

In international business, the mobility of managers is becoming increasingly important, although many managers in subsidiaries are host-country nationals, especially in service industries. Some overseas assignments, particularly in the service sector, may be quite short-term. For example, many international hotel chains have established management contracts in China; the home country managers have the task of training local successors within three to five years. In the start-phase of an endeavour, headquarters' involvement tends to be high. For control and communications reasons, some companies always maintain a home-country national as manager in certain functional areas, such as accounting and finance. The case of Arthur Andersen shows how one organization in the service sector is preparing host country nationals to manage their offices in eastern Europe.

The reasons for recruiting host-country nationals include the increasing availability of local talent, corporate relations in the particular market and the economies realized by not having to maintain a corps of managers overseas. In addition, local managers are usually more familiar with environmental conditions and how they should be interpreted. This can be particularly important in a service industry such as financial services. By employing local mangement, the multinational is responding to host country demands for increased localization. This point is illustrated by the case of Nissan.

However, localization can go too far. If the company does not subscribe to a global philosophy, the manager's development is tied to the local operation. Without appropriate training, local managers may see things from a purely local perspective, which can jeopardize the co-ordination and control of corporate activities. Managers who outgrow the local operation may have nowhere else to go except to another organization. To develop language skills and to promote an international outlook in their management pools, multinational organizations are increasingly recruiting among foreign students at business schools in the USA, Europe and the Far East. The use of third-country nationals is most often seen in large multinational companies who have adopted a global philosophy. The practice of some companies, such as the Dutch Electronics giant NV Philips, is to employ third-country nationals as managing directors in subsidiaries. However, many third-country nationals are career international managers, and they may become targets for raids by competitors looking for high levels of talent. For example, they may be a considerable asset in regional development.

Most companies use a similar pattern of recruitment during the internationalization process. During the export stage, outside expertise is normally sought, but the company will usually develop its own personnel. Foreign entry through manufacture usually reverses this trend. The organization's reliance on home-country personnel diminishes as host-country nationals are prepared for managerial positions. The use of home-country nationals and third-country nationals is quite often restricted to special assignments, such as the transfer of technology, or specific expertise.

INDUSTRIAL RELATIONS

Industrial relations and processes can vary significantly from one country to another. These differences tend to result in a mainly advisory role for headquarters staff. However, many of the practices adopted in one market or region may easily come under discussion in another, making it necessary for multinational corporations to set general personnel policies. In some instances, multinational corporations have been instrumental in bringing about changes in the overall work environment in a country.

The relationship between management and labour varies considerably from one region to another. In most economies the role of the worker is changing both at the level of the job performed and in terms of participation in the decision-making process. The degree to which members of the labour force around the world can participate in corporate decision-making varies considerably. For example, rights of information and consultation can develop on three levels:

● the shop-floor level – for example, the right to be consulted in advance concerning transfers;
● the management level or through representative bodies – for example, works councils' participation in the setting of new policies;
● the board level – for example, labour membership on the board of directors.

The role of trade unions varies from one country to another. The variations include the extent of union power in negotiations and the activities of unions in general. For example, in many countries in northern Europe collective bargaining takes place between an employers' association and an umbrella organization of unions on either a national or regional basis, establishing the conditions for an entire industry. In contrast, negotiations in Japan tend to be at the company level and the role of larger-scale unions is usually consultative. The cases studies of Nissan and the NEC Corporation illustrate the role of trade unions in Japanese organizations.

The internationalization of business activity has resulted in a number of specific issues for trade unions. These include the following:

● the power of the company to move production from one country to another, if satisfactory terms are not achieved in a particular market;
● the availability of data, especially financial information, to support unions' bargaining positions;
● insufficient attention to local issues and problems, while focusing on global optimization;
● access to the main decision-makers.

Although all of these concerns are valid, the problems anticipated may not develop. For example, it is not possible to transfer production from one country to another in the short term. Individual unions can refer to contracts signed elsewhere when setting the agenda for their own negotiations.

References

1 Enderwick, P., *Multinational business and labour*, (London, Croom Helm, 1985).
2 Pascale, R., 'Communication and decision making across cultures: Japanese and American comparisons,' *Administration Science Quarterly*, March 1978, pp. 91–110.
3 Ouchi, William G., *Theory Z*, (New York, Avon Books, 1981) p. 39.
4 Buckley, P. J., and Brooke, M. Z., *International business: an overview*, (Oxford, Blackwell Business, 1992) p. 528.
5 Coulson-Thomas, C., *Creating the global company*, (London, McGraw-Hill, 1992). p. 172.

6 Buckley, P. J., and Brooke, M. Z., ibid., p. 527.
7 Barham, K., 'Developing the international manager' *Journal of European Industrial Training*, Vol. 15 No. 1, 1991, p. 13.

Bibliography

Adler, N. T., and Ghadir, F., 'Globalization and human resource management' in Rugman, A. M. (Ed.), *Research in global strategic management: a Canadian perspective*, (JAI Press, 1984).

Barham, K., and Oates, D., *The international manager*, (London, Ashridge/The Economist Books, 1991).

Bartlett, C., and Ghoshal, S., *Managing across borders*, (London, Hutchinson Business Books, 1989).

Brewster, Chris, and Tyson, Shaun, (Eds) *International Comparisons in Human Resource Management*, (London, Pitman, 1991).

Going global: succeeding in world markets, (Boston, Harvard Business Review Paperback, 1991).

Ratiu, I., 'Thinking internationally: a comparison of how international executives learn', *International Studies of Management and Organization*, Vol. 13, No. 1–2, 1983, pp. 139–150.

PART THREE

THE CASES

CASE ONE

ARTHUR ANDERSEN & CO. SC: AN INTERNATIONAL FIRM WITH A ONE-FIRM PHILOSOPHY

JILL PRESTON

ADVICE TO READERS

There is a wide variety of accounting systems and practices across the world and without appropriate advice and expertise, this could act as a major constraint to international business activity. This case shows how one international accountancy firm provides a wide range of financial and management advice services world-wide.

INTRODUCTION

Chapter 9 suggested that the globalization of financial services, including accountancy, is a vital element in the increasing level of business activity at the international level. World-wide six big firms dominate the industry. Ranked by world-wide fee income, they are KPMG, Ernst and Young, Coopers and Lybrand, Arthur Andersen, Deloitte Touche Tohmatsu, and Price Waterhouse. Exhibit 1.1 gives the world-wide revenues of these firms.

The wide variety of accounting practices across the globe could, without adequate advice and expertise, act as a major constraint on international activity. This variety of accounting methods and financial reporting practices makes it difficult for investors and businessmen to use accounting data to assess or compare the performance of companies in different countries.

Exhibit 1.1
The leading global accounting firms 1991

Accounting firms 1991	World-wide fee income $bn	Total staff (000s)
KPMG	6.01	76.2
Ernst & Young	5.41	66.8
Coopers & Lybrand	5.00	67.0
Arthur Andersen	4.95	59.8
Deloitte Touche Tohmatsu	4.50	56.00
Price Waterhouse	3.60	49.5

Source: Adapted from Lafferty Business Research as quoted in *The Economist*, 17 October, 1992.

The author would like to thank Ruth Granville and David Oliver, of Arthur Andersen & Co. SC, for the assitance that they have given during the development of this case study.

In recent years there has been a movement towards international harmonization of accounting, on an international basis as well as within groupings of countries such as the EC; one factor being the need for information to analyse the activities of MNEs. Harmonization aims to increase the comparability of accounting practices in different countries by setting limits to the extent to which they are allowed to vary.

On a world-wide basis the International Accounting Standards Committee (IASC), has contributed to standardization, but progress is slow. The main purpose of IASC is to formulate and publish the standards to be observed in the presentation of audited financial statements and to promote their world-wide acceptance.

The EC has gone further in achieving enforceable standards than has been obtained on a global basis. For example, the Fourth Company Law Directive stipulates the form and content of the annual accounts of limited liability companies; it requires the audit of such accounts and extended disclosure requirements. However, in spite of these developments, significant differences in accounting methods between European countries remain, and on a world scale the differences are wide. International users of accounting data need to be aware of national differences of accounting systems; if not, mistakes can be made about company performance. Clearly, in this situation expert advice is required.

The world is composed of separate tax authorities, and problems arise because the entity being taxed, or part of it, may fall under the jurisdiction of more than one tax authority. This problem has caused governments to provide credits for taxes paid abroad and to negotiate bilateral tax treaties. In addition, tax systems of different countries vary significantly, for example, in the treatment of who is taxed. For most organizations functioning across borders, international taxation advice and expertise is absolutely essential.

ORGANIZATION

Since 1989 the Arthur Andersen World-wide Organization has consisted of two business units – Arthur Andersen and Andersen Consulting, each of which has almost complete financial autonomy. The World-wide Organization has 318 offices located in 72 countries, with 60,000 staff involved. The organization is truly global, covering the Americas, Europe, the Middle East, India, Africa, Australia, the Far East and Asia.

Unlike other international firms of accountants, Arthur Andersen is a single world-wide organization, for AA has not been subjected to a major merger. Each member firm is privately owned by the partners in the country of operation. For example, personnel are recruited and promoted locally, but training is a constant across the organization. The firm operates a tightly knit network around the world. Offices share practice methodologies and technology, and co-ordinate their operations so that barriers to serving clients are normally removed, as far as national laws and professional regulations allow.

The firm does not have a headquarters, but corporate direction is provided by the World-wide Board of Partners. Each member of this Board is elected. The global organization is based on the five regional structures, covering the Americas, North and South; EMEIA covering Europe, the Middle East, India and Africa; Asia Pacific, covering Australia, the Far East and Asia. Within each region, the firm has an elected executive committee and within each country the lead is taken by the national managing partner.

In 1974 Arthur Andersen & Co. SC established its first Public Review Board. The main function of the Board is to advise the organization on how best to meet its responsibilities to the general public; it concentrates on the scope of its practice and quality control procedures. The Board has full access to information and may visit any office and talk to any employee in pursuit of these functions. Edward Heath, a former British Prime Minister, is a Board member, along with Gaston Thorn, who is a former President of the EC Commission and a former Prime Minister of Luxembourg.

In terms of policy-making, the World-wide Board of Partners is concerned with corporate decisions covering such areas as corporate culture and future directions – for example, the types of client to target – as well as audit methodologies and the overall direction of training practices; whereas national managing partners determine the overall framework of activity, including the financial targets for each partner.

FEE INCOME

Exhibits 1.2 and 1.3 provide data on Arthur Andersen's fee income for the period 1990/1.

AUDIT, TAX AND BUSINESS ADVISORY SERVICES

AA aims to provide a full business advice service to individual clients, including audit and taxation. The firm seeks to offer clients a co-ordinated, seamless approach. For example, in the area of tax advice the Andersen approach is first to obtain an understanding of an organization's overall position, rather than providing advice in an isolated way. A major aspect of this approach is that resources and expertise are available between one office and another, both nationally and internationally, where appropriate. The cases of News Corporation and TNT illustrate how AA operates on a global basis.

ARTHUR ANDERSEN AND NEWS CORPORATION

In February 1991 Arthur Andersen was appointed as world-wide auditor to News Corporation, the second largest media company

Exhibit 1.2
Revenues by business unit

	1990	1991
Audit and Business Advisory	$1,500.1	$1,808.4
Tax	$ 783.9	$ 883.1
Andersen Consulting	$1,875.5	$2,256.3
Total	$4,159.5	$4,947.8

Exhibit 1.3
Revenues by geographical area

	(in $ millions)	
Americas	$2,491.9	$2,714.6
Europe, Middle East, India and Africa	$1,358.5	$1,847.9
Asia/Pacific	$ 309.0	$ 385.3

in the world. The Corporation has major interests in Europe, the USA, and Australia. News Corporation owns *The Times*, the fourth national TV netwc ': in the USA and has a 50 per cent share in BskyB; Twentieth Century Fox is its film company.

AA's task was to audit the majority of this group world-wide but it had only 39 working days in which to complete the project. A team was put into place to perform the work and dedicated fax machines were installed in the partners' homes and offices. All key client personnel were linked into the international digital voice exchange network (DVX), the firm's electronic message machine which enables messages to be exchanged 24 hours a day all round the world.

The method used was that the lead partner in Sydney finished each working day with a breakfast call to the London office, who at the end of day handed over to the lead partner in the New York office. AA states that only by using this system of rolling control can it guarantee to beat the deadlines and keep pace with fast-moving business. Dealing with the competing demands of deals and near-simultaneous announcement of year-end results under different accounting principles in the UK, the US and the Pacific basin calls for strong project management skills.

ARTHUR ANDERSEN AND THE TNT JOINT VENTURE WITH GD NET

In July 1991 a joint venture was agreed between TNT and the GD net, to establish a major international postal and courier business. It has been estimated that this Group will take about 20 per cent of the international express delivery market. GD net is made up of the postal authorities in Canada, France, Germany, the Netherlands and Sweden.

AA was involved in this project in a number of ways; for example, tax planning and structuring advice was given to the five post offices involved. In addition, AA performed a due diligence review of the TNT courier and express parcel business for the post offices. TNT operates in over 140 countries and the review involved examining aircraft leases, statutory accounts and tax returns of 100 companies, as well as reviewing the underlying operations. The firm was also involved in assisting the legal firm Tory Tory to draft the agreements.

WORLD-WIDE INDUSTRY PROGRAMME

AA's world-wide industry programmes illustrates the range of business services provided by the firm. A significant element of business risk is related to the industry in which a company operates. Through this programme AA provides a general risk analysis, including current industry issues to clients, as well as providing additional information and advice, if necessary. In addition to an analysis of current business issues, the accounting issues, competitive environment, regulatory and technological changes that may affect the business are included. The processes and procedures were developed within the USA, but the approach is used by local offices in other countries.

THE GLOBAL BEST PRACTICES PROGRAMME

AA's global best practices programme is a diagnostic quality control approach where organizational performance can be evaluated in terms of global criteria. For a particular client the programme identifies world-wide best practices and best companies, as well as more specific performance measures.

EASTERN EUROPE

Chapter 5 suggested that privatization in eastern Europe is providing many companies with major business opportunities. These opportunities have been pursued by AA. The firm has opened offices in a number of east European countries. For example, they have been involved in privatizing programmes in Bulgaria, including the tourist industry as well as the cement industry. In Russia, the firm has been involved in the development of the banking system, whereas in Czechoslovakia the firm is assisting the government in a voucher scheme of privatization.

CLIENTS

World-wide Arthur Andersen has 85 audit clients in the Fortune 500 list of industrial companies and 163 in Fortune 1000; AA has 292 audit clients listed on the New York Stock Exchange.

World-wide clients include: Aer Lingus, Colgate Palmolive, Federal Express, Fiat, Hilton Hotels, ITT, Mitsubishi, Nissan, Peugeot, Texaco, and United Airlines.

ANDERSEN CONSULTING

Andersen Consulting provides technological solutions for clients, bringing together their information systems and corporate strategy. Andersen Consulting has developed the concept of 'total business integration', which involves a seamless approach to integrating strategy, people, operations and technology.

Andersen Consulting has market dominance in the USA and in the major markets of Europe, and plans are afoot to expand into Asia and the Pacific area. This part of the organization tends to concentrate on the top 100 companies in each country. More recently, the government services market, for example, defence, health care and telecommunications, has been targeted.

The two business units do not normally work together, although there was a joint project in assisting Moscow City Council to establish a scheme for the distribution of bread.

PRICING POLICIES

General guidelines on fee levels are determined nationally, but individual offices have some autonomy. The organization was not willing to disclose its pricing policies.

MARKETING OF SERVICES

The 'think global, act local' is a major theme running through AA's marketing strategy. This strategy involves emphasizing general concepts but also stressing local differences. Exhibit 1.4 illustrates this point.

HUMAN RESOURCES MANAGEMENT

It was stated in Chapter 15 that 'a major factor in the success of any organization is the best use of human resources'. International manage-

ment requires awareness of, and sensitivity towards, differences in language, culture and politics. Within the Andersen organization, most local offices are managed by local nationals. The main exception to this situation is the new offices being established in eastern Europe, where it has been estimated that it will take up to ten years before local nationals will have the appropriate expertise and experience.

Effective communication is important in any organization, but it is particularly significant in international business. AA's concept of a single firm, and the formal and informal links between managers and partners, assist in this process. For example, each year there is a world-wide meeting of all partners. In addition, AA's training programmes greatly assist in this process.

There is much international mobility, with all levels of staff moving between countries to work on assignments or undertaking transfers to other offices for periods of one or two years,

Exhibit 1.4
Company advertisement

Source: Arthur Andersen & Co. SC.

in response to the business needs of the offices concerned and the wishes of the individuals to broaden their work experience. For example, in 1991/2, 12.5 per cent of experienced seniors from the London Audit and Business Advisory practice transferred abroad.

TRAINING

AA puts much emphasis on its training programmes. In 1990 it spent $310 million, or 7 per cent of its revenue, on professional training. The training programmes, which are viewed by the organization as essential to its 'one firm philosophy', are common across the organization and people from different nations and different cultures train together. Training and staff development is seen as a continuous process for professional staff. On average, each professional within the organization receives 129 training hours per year. From the time of joining the firm, graduates are encouraged to think internationally. This approach enables a wide range of global networks to be established, thus enabling professional staff to draw upon organization-wide strengths to assist local clients.

Professional training within AA focuses on technical issues, but it is also concerned with the wider aspects of industrial and management issues. For audit staff, methodologies are developed on a world-wide basis, so that a manager could walk into any Arthur Andersen office across the world and be absolutely familiar with work practices. The firm has a world-wide training college on a 145-acre campus at St Charles, Illinois. In addition, it has training facilities at Veldhoven in the Netherlands, Segovia in Spain, and Manila in the Philippines. Partners and managers with current expertise in the subjects they teach provide most of the training.

QUESTIONS/DISCUSSION TOPICS

1 In terms of international business needs, evaluate Arthur Andersen's approach to training and staff development.

2 Are there disadvantages as well as advantages in Arthur Andersen's one-firm approach?

3 Evaluate the firm's approach to cultural issues.

4 With regard to the general eastern Europe market, carry out a SWOT analysis of Arthur Andersen.

CASE TWO
———

THE YEAR OF THE DRAGON: INTERNATIONALIZATION AND CORPORATE DEATH:[1] THE CASE OF THE MIDLAND BANK

STEPHEN REGAN

ADVICE TO READERS

Two of the most important elements in the internationalization of business in the 1980s were the rapid development of a global market in finance, and the frenetic pace of merger and acquisition activity, often of an international nature. The two trends were related.

The return of the world economy to growth and rising stock-markets after the stagflation of the 1970s, created in the 1980s the decade of the mega-takeover. The leveraged buy-out (LBO), the purchase of a company using borrowed money, known as leverage, became one of the buzz words of business schools world-wide, as deals in excess of $20 billion were swallowed by a financial system which seemed to have no limit on the amount of finance it could provide to international business. This type of financing created some very big businesses, many of which have now folded, such as the Bond Corporation, the Australian brewing concern; Maxwell Macmillan Communications, the media group; and many others which have survived the harsher régime of the 1990s, such as Rupert Murdoch's International News Group.

This case brings together two major issues: the globalization of finance and the creation of superbusinesses by international takeovers. It does this by looking at how and why a new global superbank was created by the merger of two regional banks.

Important themes in this case include the notion of internationalization as an inherently high-risk activity, to be underpinned by a coherent strategy in order to avoid disaster. There is also a suggestion that a strategy needs to be worked out within a culture which supports it, if it is going to be more than mere window-dressing. For example, the question of how best to internationalize a business's culture is pointed up in this case. Finally, the issue of the distribution of power within a global business is raised. A global business must achieve both a corporate identity and the heterogeneity to function in diverse business environments; this presents challenging contradictions.

INTRODUCTION: MIDLAND BANK PLC

By March 1991, Sir Kit McMahon, the Australian

economist and former Deputy Governor of the Bank of England, knew the worst. He was about to announce the Bank's profit's for the year to 1990 and with them his own resignation. Sir Kit had been recruited in 1985 to restore the fortunes of Midland Bank, which had begun by financing Victorian industrialists in Birmingham and had grown to become, at one stage, the world's largest bank.

Midland Bank PLC was a member of the FT-SE 100, one of the top 100 companies quoted on the UK Stock Exchange. Its market value in early 1992 was over £1.6 billion, and with 60,000 employees world-wide and over 100,000 share-holders, it was a major multinational in the finance business. However, Midland's figures over the previous three years made for depressing reading, as illustrated by Exhibit 2.1.

Midland would be cutting its dividend to ordinary shareholders: the first British bank in over 50 years to take such drastic measures. The price paid by Sir Kit would be the loss of his two jobs: one as Chairman, and the other as Chief Executive. In the first of these he was to be replaced by Sir Peter Walters of BP, and in the second by Brian Pearse, who was moving to the Midland after four decades with Barclays. There were grave doubts about what would become of the Midland Bank, given the weak state of the company and the competitive nature of the UK, European and world banking markets, in which Midland had once been such a strong force.

Sir Kit had pursued a strategy of innovation in his stewardship from 1985 to 1990, attempting to break the mould of UK banking. Despite constant experimentation, the alchemy had not worked, and much of the business remained the base metal the Australian wizard had inherited,

Exhibit 2.1
Midland's figures for the years 1988–1990

	1990	1989	1988
Market capital	1,617	2,852	2,330
Total assets	65,786	57,623	57,591
Profit (loss)	(349)	(353)	745

Note: All figures in £m.

Source: Adapted from Disclosure Europe.

rather than turning into the gold he had so confidently predicted. The reasons for the failure of the UK bank to revive itself were largely due to four costly mistakes at the international level.

UNSUCCESSFUL INTERNATIONALIZATION

The first and perhaps the most important of these mistakes, was the decision made in 1980 to purchase the California-based Crocker Bank. In those days Midland was a world leader in banking and was pursuing an aggressive expansion strategy into the lucrative US market, as part of its long-term plans to become a global bank. Unfortunately, Crocker Bank turned out to have a portfolio of bad loans to Third World borrowers; in effect, Midland had paid £1 billion more for the American bank than the bank was worth. In addition, Midland had its own large collection of loans to the same borrowers.

Midland had to write off these loans out of profits made in its UK domestic banking business, where it had a position of market leadership. However, the use of funds in this way meant the UK business was being used as a 'cash cow' and starved of the necessary investment to retain its pre-eminent position in the industry. Meanwhile, major competitors such as Lloyds, NatWest and Barclays were ploughing back profits to introduce cost-saving technology and lucrative new products. All this was essential, since the industry in the UK was entering a decade of intense competition: building societies and other interlopers had begun to compete head-to-head with banks in the UK high street.

In earlier times, a bank could recover from a costly mistake by recouping its losses through raising prices and reducing costs in the domestic market. Such action was possible because there was very limited competition between banks for each other's customers, and the industry of banking was so tightly regulated that there were unlikely to be any new entrants to the industry. The domestic banking industry in the UK was, in effect, a very profitable cartel.

However, the arrival of such aggressive and efficient competitors as the building societies had made the UK high street a banking battlefield by the mid-1980s and Midland could no longer write off debts against cartel profits.

Thus despite Sir Kit's frantic innovations, he just didn't have the necessary capital to prevent the Midland slipping from top to bottom of the pile. By 1990, the Bank had the worst cost structure of any of the Big Four, making it competitively the weakest in the UK industry.

A second international blow came from Midland's treasury division. Treasury is the function which controls the flow of funds around an international business. The aim is to minimize the costs of payments and receipt of funds by managing these transactions on a global scale. An example would be the receipt of dollars in a US subsidiary being used to pay in dollars an American customer of the Singapore subsidiary. The aim is to exactly match payments and receipts in their amounts, in their currencies and in their timing; this reduces costs. The two main types of costs are holding costs, essentially the rate of interest foregone by holding a low-interest currency, and transaction costs, the cost of switching out of one currency into another.

In 1989 and 1990, Midland's treasury division took a view that the UK interest rate would fall. When interest rates rose consistently over this period, the Bank lost £200 million. This further weakened the business's ability to compete and to invest.

The third international blunder was the attempt made by Sir Kit to establish a multinational senior management team at Midland Bank. The aim was to change the culture of the business which shared the inbred and conservative ethos for which British banking was now notorious. The revolving door at corporate HQ began to spin rather freely, as the new arrivals on one side of the door were matched by the departure of traditionalists on the other. Midland's UK retail banking business came to be headed by someone who was neither a banker nor British, but a highly respected American management consultant: Gene Lockhart; control of investment banking passed to the Dutch

banker, George Loudon; and Sir Kit himself was an Australian and an economist. This conscious strategy of internationalization at senior executive level may not have served the business well, since the middle and junior levels in the business were thoroughly located in traditional banking attitudes and liable to resist any attempts by an 'outsider' to alter their culture.

It is significant that the most successful bank in the UK in the 1980s was Lloyds, whose rise mirrored Midland's fall. Lloyds trumpeted their distrust of any such pretentious notions as internationalization and made great gains in profits by 'sticking to their knitting', focusing on cutting costs in their traditional businesses and keeping within a highly conservative corporate culture.

Sir Kit's final international problem was his failure to bring the Midland's long engagement with the Hong Kong and Shanghai Bank to a marriage. The relationship began in 1987 as a potential marriage of convenience, when the Hong Kong and Shanghai Bank (HKSB) bought a block of just under 15 per cent of Midland's shares. Midland had a £1 billion hole in its balance sheet from the mistakes of the early 1980s and Hong Kong had plenty of money, but wanted to put as much of it as possible outside Hong Kong, before the handover of power to Beijing in 1997. However, between 1987 and 1990 HKSB seemed to go cool on the deal and Sir Kit looked as though he was not going to be able to get his bride to the altar.

Sir Kit's problem was that Midland's shareholders needed the dowry, they couldn't pass up dividends forever; but the worse the Midland performed under his control, the less HKSB shareholders wanted to own them. It looked increasingly unlikely that he would be able to pull it off. Thus at the 1991 Annual General Meeting he announced his resignation as Chief Executive, in favour of Brian Pearse.

THE GRIFFIN LICKS ITS WOUNDS

At the time of Brian Pearse's arrival, it was clear that the Midland Bank was up for sale. In the meantime, Pearse's job was to reverse some of the more exotic changes of the 1980s. The Bank would return to the traditional virtues of British banking; after four decades at Barclays, Pearse was a banker to his fingertips, and a British banker at that. The Midland would be refocused on the UK market-place, its core businesses, and there would be a gimlet eye on costs. Moreover, the 'For Sale' sign went hand-in-hand with the planned restructuring, since Midland needed the money from the former to complete the latter, which was expected to take at least half a decade.

However, people in the industry other than HKSB could think of a good reason for buying Midland Bank. Sometime late in 1991 and early in 1992, there began secret talks between Lloyds Bank and Midland Bank, with a possible view to a merger or a takeover.

MERGERS AND ACQUISITIONS

The two potential buyers of Midland had rather different reasons for wishing to make the same purchase. HKSB had a rationale, which was based on creating a business with a global reach, whereas Lloyds believed the gains from any such globalization were illusory and that the real benefits were to be gained by concentrating into a superbusiness in the national UK market.

The theory behind mergers is quite simply that a merger makes sense if two businesses combined make higher profits than their aggregate profits apart. Thus mergers are based upon the pursuit of profit by shareholders looking for the highest return. The two ways that a merger can be justified are as follows.

1 The costs of the two companies combined are lower than their aggregate costs when they are separate.

This was essentially the strategy behind the Lloyds bid. The Lloyds thinking was that where two businesses operate in the same markets, there is considerable duplication of costs: there are two head offices, two branch networks, two advertising budgets, two product lines to be maintained etc. If such companies merge, profits will rise as the businesses are rationalized, since revenues will combine and remain the same, but costs will combine and fall.

2 The revenues of the merged business will be higher when they are combined than when they are unique business entities.

This was essentially the HKSB pitch. The idea behind the merger was not that there would be cost savings: there was little scope for redundancies and the closure of branches, as the two banks operated in different markets. HKSB was dominant in the Pacific-Asian region, whereas the Midland had strengths in the European market. Profits would rise because revenues would rise, and revenues would rise because the merger of two regional banks would create, not a large regional bank, but a new global bank.

HKSB was looking to put together a bank with 'global reach'. The logic was to be in a position to capture business on both of the world's two main trade flows. The first of these is the Atlantic trade, which flows principally between the USA and Europe. The second is the Pacific trade, which flows between the USA and the Far East. The distinguishing feature of this trade is that it is a flow between East and West, and that it accounts for over two-thirds of total world trade. The other third of world trade flows north to south.

Thus the HKSB strategy was to have a leading presence in each of the three zones of East-West trade. HKSB was already the strongest bank in the Far East outside Japan; it was also the bank closest to the heart of the potentially giant economy of China, where it had 15 branches. It had a major concern in the USA with its ownership of the New York bank, Midland Marine, and the purchase of an important UK/European bank would establish HKSB in every one of its desired market-places.

ENTER THE DRAGON

Such logic as this led William Purves, Chairman of HKSB, to announce a £3.1 billion bid for

Midland Bank on 14 April 1991. The offer valued Midland at 378p per share and was all paper. However, the City expected 400p a share and Lloyds took notice of this sentiment and began to prepare a counter-offer which exceeded HKSB's, although the latter had been recommended to the shareholders by the Midland Board.

As the City of London began to prepare for the almost unthinkable possibility of a hostile takeover of one UK clearing bank by another, Brian Pearse let it be known that any bid from Lloyds would be most unwelcome. His opposition rested on three arguments. First, the combined Lloyds Midland Bank would be even more UK-focused, since they would dominate the UK banking market and hardly need to compete overseas to increase profits. Second, the only benefits to the shareholders would come from massive redundancies in the UK. Third, the Lloyds bid for Midland would be unlikely to get past the Monopolies and Mergers Commission (MMC), which would view the new business as flagrantly anti-competitive.

On the other side of the coin, the wider international community seemed rather dubious about the Hong Kong offer. The Kuwaiti Investment Office became a heavy seller of Midland shares, and during April 1991 unloaded their 10 per cent stake in the business.[2] This indicated a reluctance by the Kuwaitis to buy into the global bank concept being offered by HKSB, since their early sale indicated a lack of interest in swapping Midland shares for HKSB scrip.

The New China News Agency, the official organ of the Chinese Government in Beijing, also seemed less than impressed, and questioned the soundness of such speculative gambles on globalization. Essentially, their position was the same as that of Lloyds, but they viewed this from a Far Eastern, rather than a European, perspective. Both China and Lloyds were convinced that businesses would do well to stick to the markets they knew. The Chinese news agency indicated that HKSB had responsibilities to the territory of Hong Kong and the region generally, and this was where its strengths lay. For instance, a Bank of China official was quoted as saying,

HKSB is the biggest bank in Hong Kong, it is a major note issuing bank, it is the clearing bank, and is also the government's main banker in the territory. How would its strengths justify investing in a European market where it had no such advantages?

HKSB'S GLOBAL STRATEGY

However, HKSB pushed ahead with its new strategy and gave some detail about how the new global group could operate. The deputy chairman of HKSB declared, 'We've been in international banking for over 130 years, and I think we've learned a few things.' The new business would have its corporate HQ in London – hence Beijing's concern – which is where the main executives of the global holding company would be based.

Below the corporate HQ the bank would operate with a 'global triad strategy' in three main regions. The European region would be spearheaded by Midland from the UK, but drawing on the strengths of the global business to sharpen its competitive edge. The North American bloc would be developed by the Marine Midland subsidiary. The Pacific-Asian region would be served by the HKSB. In each of these regions the relevant businesses would retain their local identities as they focused on retail or high street banking in these markets. Certain operations within the global business would, however, be passed from the regional businesses to global headquarters in London, and amongst these would be treasury and technology, both of which would be used to link up the three elements of the triad.

The new company would be able to offer a global service under one roof, which no other bank in the world could match. To this end, the new business would have a special division dedicated to meeting the needs of its top 300 corporate clients. For such clients, the global reach of the new HKSB would be an important improvement in the quality of service they received.

Where regional identities were not important to client service, they would be submerged into the new corporate identity. This would be the case in businesses where the clients themselves were sophisticated and global. For example, the UK brokerage firm, James Capel, would have elements of its activities merged with the Asian merchant bank, Wardley, since there were areas where the two businesses were duplicating each other's activities – for example, they dealt with the same clients.

HKSB was aware that they were putting together a bank which would enter the world's Top Ten, and would be the second largest in the world outside Japan. They were also aware that the costs of assembling this business would be significant, the merger itself would cost about £190 million, and there would be an increase in HKSB tax liability of about £200 million from the move to a UK headquarters. However, HKSB felt that the benefits would more than outweigh the costs, and most would come from synergies between the two businesses.

For instance, in trade finance HKSB felt they could teach Midland some important lessons which would increase their competitiveness in their UK market. The same was true of technology, where HKSB considered themselves to be a world leader. In investment banking, the new company would use a whole range of existing companies to attract business worldwide: Midland Montagu in the UK, Wardley in Asia, James Capel in London, Trinkhaus and Burkhardt in Germany, Euromobiliare in other parts of continental Europe, and in the US there was Marine Midland. The synergies would come from the creation of a global back office linking these front offices, which would have world-class resources and true global reach.

THE SIGN OF THE BLACK HORSE

The Lloyds bid eventually materialized, but in a conditional form. Lloyds tabled an offer in April 1991, which valued Midland at £3.6 billion: £$\frac{1}{2}$ billion higher than HKSB had felt able to offer. However Lloyds knew that its main problem would be to establish the credibility of the bid in the face of a certain referral to the competition policy authorities at either the European

Community or the UK level. It was just a case of which of these bodies would deal with the bid. The conditional nature of the bid was that Lloyds stated that they wanted both their offer and the HKSB offer to be referred to the EC competition authorities: if they were not both referred, the deal was off.

The European Commissioner who was head of Directorate General 4 (DG4) of the European Commission, and thus responsible for competition policy, was the British former Home Secretary, Sir Leon Brittan. The test he would apply was that if more than two thirds of the combined EC turnover of any two businesses proposing to merge was inside a single Member State, then this was not a matter for DG4 of the European Commission, but a matter to be dealt with by the government of that particular Member State.

Since banks don't have turnover in the conventional sense, the test would be applied to assets, and this, for a bank, means loans. It was likely that more than two thirds of the combined EC loans of Lloyds and Midland were made in the UK, but in the case of HKSB the position was less certain. Of its total EC business, HKSB made loans of £14.4 billion in London and only £604 million in the rest of the EC. From this point of view, it looked as if HKSB would be dealt with by the British authorities, as would Lloyds. However, nearly all of the £14.4 billion loans made in London by HKSB were made on the international money markets, typically to the UK branches of foreign banks. On this basis, it looked as though the HKSB bid would be referred to DG4 of the European Commission, since most of its loans were made in the UK, but not to UK customers. On the other hand, the Lloyds offer would be referred to the MMC, since this was a matter which primarily affected the UK market.

A referral to the MMC would have been disastrous for Lloyds, since any investigation at the European level would be likely to find either of the two proposed takeovers insignificant in terms of the huge European market. But any referral at the UK level would certainly find their offer to be a significantly anti-competitive move, and thus it would be blocked.

It eventually transpired that DG4 looked at the papers from both bids, and decided that the Lloyds bid was a UK matter, but that the HKSB bid was a matter for the Commission. From this point on, Lloyds were facing an uneven playing-field. Soon after the bid was referred back to the UK by Sir Leon Brittan, the President of the Board of Trade, Michael Heseltine, referred the Lloyds bid to the Monopolies and Mergers Commission. It seemed likely that the HKSB bid would be waived through at the EC level.

There was a degree of unreality about this, since the most significant of the two bids at the European level was the Lloyds bid. This was due to the fact that both Lloyds and Midland had significant overlapping interests in many European markets, which HKSB and Midland had not. For instance, in Germany, Lloyds owned 75 per cent of Schroder Munchmeyer, the powerful Frankfurt investment bank. On the other hand, Midland controlled 80 per cent of Trinkhaus and Barkhardt, an important Dusseldorf merchant bank. It was clear that if the merger of Lloyds and Midland went ahead there would be a major shake-up of the German merchant banking industry, involving both redundancies and branch closures. A merger between HKSB and Midland would not have had this type of impact at the European level. Yet, of the two bids, this was the one which was deemed to be the most European.

EXIT, PURSUED BY A DRAGON

By June 1991 HKSB had improved their bid to £3.9 billion, and Lloyds had been advised that they would need to offer 520 pence per share in order to complete the takeover. At such a price, it was not at all clear that the deal looked good value to Lloyds shareholders, even with the tremendous market share it would have created in the UK and the possibility that massive restructuring would offset some of these huge purchase costs.

Moreover, the bid was becoming increasingly unlikely to go ahead at any price, since the MMC was being assiduously lobbied by a spectrum of interest groups opposed to the Lloyds bid. Included amongst these groups were small businesses, who feared one less high street bank would reduce their choices and raise their bank charges in the midst of a long and difficult recession. Farmers had similar objections, and so did other consumer groups. The Banking Insurance and Finance Union were also strongly opposed to Lloyds' well known intention to cut 1000 branches and 20,000 staff. As a result, Lloyds withdrew their bid, and the HKSB offer of £3.9 billion was successful. By June 1992, Midland Bank was part of one of the world's biggest banking groups.

Sources

This case study was prepared from information published as follows:

The Economist

9 March 1991, p. 97, 'Midland minus McMahon'.

21 March 1992, p. 107, 'Hong Kong's Global Gamble'.

The Financial Times

15 April 1992, p. 1, 'Hong Kong and Shanghai Bank Offers £3.1 bn for Midland'.

30 April 1992, p. 24, 'German Subsidiaries Uncertain if Merger Succeeds'.

6 June 1992, p. 10, 'Hong Kong back with Final £3.9 bn'.

Footnotes

1 The symbol of the Hong Kong and Shanghai Bank is the Dragon. The symbol of Midland Bank PLC is the Griffin. The symbol of Lloyds Bank PLC is a Black Horse. Readers might like to reflect on the fact that both the Dragon and the Griffin are mythical creatures.
2 Kuwaiti Investment Office: A London-based organization which invests the Kuwaiti government's vast funds. They are one of the world's largest investors, and have been so successful in their investment strategy that the Kuwaiti Investment Office now earns more for the Kuwaiti government than that country's oil revenues.

QUESTIONS/DISCUSSION TOPICS

1 You work for the merchant bank advising HKSB on its bid for Midland. You have been asked to produce a summary, for the shareholders of Midland Bank, of the reasons why the HKSB merger will produce higher profits for them than the Lloyds merger. Your summary will be used as a full page advertisement in the business sections of all the Sunday papers.

2 Is Midland a case of a company destroyed by its international strategy? If so, how could they have pursued a more effective programme?

3 How, if at all, could Sir Kit have been more successful in tackling the proposed changes in corporate culture at Midland. Was it worth trying?

4 Are there any generic threats and opportunities inherent in a programme of internationalization which you could deduce from this case?

5 What are your views on the way HKSB is intending to distribute power and control around the business? For instance, why are technology and treasury to be centralized? Can you suggest a corporate structure which will meet the opposing needs of autonomy and control in a more efficient way?

CASE THREE

—

BMW: NICHE MARKETING IN A GLOBAL ECONOMY?

RON ALLISON AND ERWIN BLUM

ADVICE TO READERS

Until 1992, when a decision was made to build a production plant in the USA, BMW was a national car producer. The South African factory is small and just assembles cars on a completely knock down (CKD) basis. This means that the parts were made at the HQ and just assembled in the South African factory. BMW competes vigorously in the global market for cars and this study illustrates some of its international aspects. The company is at the leading edge of recycling technology and claims to have a regard for the protection of the environment in this and other areas.

INTRODUCTION

By 1992 there were over 4,000,000 BMW cars and 400,000 motor cycles on the road world-wide. Up to the end of the Second World War, the company was also a substantial manu-facturer of aircraft engines. After a lapse of nearly 45 years, aircraft engine production began once again in 1990, with the formation of a joint venture with Rolls Royce PLC.

The Bayerische Motoren Werke was founded in 1916 by Gustav Otto, the son of the inventor of the internal combustion engine, and Karl Rapp. The first products were aircraft engines and BMW's famous blue and white propeller symbol dates back to the beginning of the company. The original plant was in Munich-Oberwiesenfeld. Following the end of the First World War, new plants were bought at Eisenach in Thuringia and Spandau in Berlin. The first car was built in the Eisenach factory and was built under licence from the Austin Motor Company of Britain. One of these models – recognizably an Austin Seven – may be seen in the motor car gallery in the Deutsches Museum in Munich.

After the Second World War, the Eisenach site was in the DDR and no longer available and reconstruction started in Munich and Spandau. As an aftermath of the War, the production of cars and motor cycles was initially forbidden in Germany, and so small appliances and equip-ment were made. It was not until the 1948 currency reform that vehicle production recom-menced. For many years the company was undercapitalized and the financial situation was precarious until the late 1950s. The turning-

The authors would like to thank Frau Helga Raddatz, Head of Public Relations at BMW, for her assistance in the writing of this case study.

point in the company's fortunes was 1959, when a majority shareholding was acquired by Dr Herbert Quandt. The Quandt family still own 70 per cent of the shares and this provides protection from a hostile takeover bid. A substantial injection of capital was provided and from then the company has flourished and expanded.

The Glas company in Lower Bavaria was purchased, along with its two plants, located in Dingolfing and Landshut, and the Spandau motor cycle plant was greatly enlarged, as was the assembly plant in South Africa. A new engine factory was constructed at Steyr in Austria and a new car factory was opened in Regensburg in May 1987. Following reunification, a new factory for producing tools was built in Eisenach.

THE PLANTS

LANDSHUT

Hans Glas GmbH, producers of the Goggomobile, was acquired in 1967 and one of the assets acquired was the Landshut plant. The extensively altered and extended plant employed over 3,000 people by 1992. Plastic parts such as instrument panels and bumpers were made, as well as propeller shafts and exchange engines. An important milestone was the completion of a new aluminium foundry in 1991, which replaced the outdated foundry in Munich. Landshut now has 60,000 inhabitants and the company is the biggest employer in this medieval town.

DINGOLFING

Dingolfing is a small town of around 16,000 people and the number of employees working within the factory is greater than the population of the town. However, the social structure has been relatively unaffected, because residential accommodation has not been built around the town. BMW's personnel department and Dingolfing's town planners have worked closely together to preserve the dimensions and characteristics of the town and many workers travel considerable distances to the plant.

MUNICH

The BMW headquarters are still at Milbertshofen, the site of the original factory. Series 3 cars as well as various engines are produced here and over half of the total workforce of more than 60,000 employees work in Munich. A new Research and Development centre to the north of this site has been under construction since 1980 and ultimately thousands of engineers and technicians will work here.

BERLIN

This plant employs about 1,700 people and now makes all the motor cycles with more than 110 being produced each working day. About two thirds of these are destined for export. Parts and components for the cars are also produced. Since the early 1980s, over 500 million DM have been invested in the plant

STEYR

This plant was built in 1979 and until 1989 employed 1,900 people, working solely on the production of engines. The third phase was completed in 1989 and 100 more people found work there. Altogether, 1,500 million DM have been invested. BMW Motoren GmbH in Steyr has its own development centre responsible for developing all the diesel engines for the BMW group. It supplies engines to other customers and companies all over the world. The plant is highly versatile and both diesel and petrol engines can be built at the same time by the same machines. The annual capacity is 300,000 units and engines are sent daily, mostly by rail, to Munich, Dingolfing and Landshut. The purchasing office of the Munich Headquarters for Austrian suppliers is located here and BMW say that this shows that its business concept works in both directions: successful business means selling and purchasing alike.

REGENSBURG

This is BMW's latest factory and production started in November 1986. By mid-1988, 240 cars were being produced daily in one shift on six days a week. It concentrates entirely on the top (ie 6-cylinder) models of the Series 3. Over 1,400 million DM have been invested and more than 6,000 people are employed. As well as jobs at the factory, jobs have been created elsewhere, as numerous suppliers have either moved to the region or expanded existing facilities.

EISENACH

A total of 120 million DM had been invested in this plant by 1992. It employs around 200 workers and produces tools for both internal and external demand.

WACKERSDORF

This site employs around 260 people and produces bodies for the Series 3 cabriolets.

THE SOUTH AFRICAN PLANT

This is an historic acquisition, obtained with the purchase of the Glas company. A South African Government requirement is that 60 per cent of the parts must be sourced locally. A major component, the engine, comes from Germany and the factory may be classed as a completely knocked down (CKD) assembly plant. Until recently, the products assembled here could not be exported to other African countries, but exports are now increasing, as apartheid breaks down.

THE LOCATION STRATEGY

Until 1967, BMW produced only in Berlin and Munich. By this time the company was prospering, and production facilities were facing capacity strains. A move beyond Munich was indicated. By the mid-1960s Hans Glas GmbH, with plants in Dingolfing and Landshut, was experiencing financial difficulties, because it was producing too many models in too small numbers. The group was acquired in January 1967.

The takeover yielded approximately 300,000 square metres of land, a well-trained workforce of 3,700 people and production facilities in Dingolfing and Landshut. Support for the takeover came from the Bavarian State Government, which provided a guarantee of 50 million DM, although in the event this did not have to be taken up. A comprehensive investment programme was immediately set in train, a programme that has continued to this day. Over 40 million DM had been spent by the end of 1968 alone and two new production buildings, with a total area of 20,000 square metres, were built, which allowed some production to be moved from Munich.

Originally, it was planned to make Dingolfing a parts supply centre only, but the rapid development of the company caused a strategic rethink in relation to the role of plants. The growing demand for BMW cars, coupled with insurmountable capacity constraints in Munich, meant that a new factory had to be built. Although there were other alternatives, Dingolfing was chosen. Earlier (and wisely, as it turned out), BMW had purchased 600,000 square metres of land just north of Federal Highway 11 and the new plant was built here, coming on-stream in September 1973 when the first of the Series 5 cars rolled off the assembly lines.

Production and employment grew rapidly. Daily production in 1974 was 100 cars a day, built by a workforce of 6,000 employees. By 1977, with the launch of the Series 6 and 7 models, 10,000 people were employed. The original planned capacity was 400 vehicles a day and 8,000 employees. In the mid-1980s the capacity level of the site – 1,000 cars a day – was reached and a new plant at Regensburg was constructed. This was opened in May 1987 and here the production of the Series 3 range was concentrated.

Development is still happening in Dingolfing as technological change continues apace. New models, which are more complex and labour-intensive than their predecessors, require new, more, and often better qualified, employees than before. New production methods and technologies are constantly being introduced as well.

After the Glas takeover, production of motor cycle and car parts was started in Landshut, using the existing facilities. A substantial investment programme was quickly initiated on this site. In 1971, Hall 1 of the Landshut factory was opened and in 1973, the production of plastic parts began. The total workforce at Landshut increased rapidly and had reached 1,000 by 1979.

In 1980 a further production hall was opened and this enabled the entire flow of production to be restructured. The next major building project was a new warehouse, which opened in 1984. Hall 3, where plastic bumpers are made, also opened in 1984. Bumpers are produced and painted and moved to Dingolfing, just in time for assembly. In 1986 the factory area was further expanded by the construction of a multi-purpose hall. Originally, it produced machined parts, but subsequently it was converted and enlarged for injection casting of plastic components.

A new aluminium foundry, embodying state-of-the-art technology, was commenced in 1986 and finished in 1989. This replaced the outmoded foundry on the Munich site, which was almost 60 years old and unable to be efficiently modernized to cope with the introduction of four-valve technology. The new foundry has a total area of 36,000 square metres and uses three casting techniques – sand casting, low pressure and pressure casting. The total production of aluminium castings is approximately 20,000 tonnes per year. Sophisticated quality control mechanisms are used and electronic data processing systems (EDP), such as statistic process control (SPC), are employed. During production, the castings are constantly monitored by other measures such as X-ray examinations, crack inspections and the measuring of combustion chamber volume by laser scanners. A consequence of this sophisticated quality control is that there is no need for any further inspection of incoming components at the other factories before the castings are further processed.

The Landshut factory produces four main types of components:

- machined parts;
- exchange parts;
- plastic parts;
- aluminium parts.

Ready-made parts and components, such as bumpers, are supplied for installation at BMW's assembly plants, whilst parts requiring further machining and processing go to the engine plants.

THE FACTORY NETWORK

A deliberate decision has been made to concentrate production in a relatively small geographical area, centred on Lower Bavaria. The network of factories is highly integrated, each factory supplying parts and components to the others. For example, the chassis and suspension parts of all BMWs are produced in Dingolfing. The plants in Munich and Steyr produce all the engines, which are then delivered to the other factories. Landshut supplies all of the factories with plastic components and propeller shafts. The Berlin plant, although concentrating mainly on the production of motor cycles, also produces some parts for the cars made elsewhere.

The widespread use of Just in Time (JIT) production techniques is one of the reasons why the BMW plants are located comparatively closely to one another. Another location factor is that labour can be moved quite easily between the production centres according to the demand for the various models. In this way, flexibility can be obtained without laying workers off as demand fluctuates.

Some parts and components are produced by BMW, but about 60 per cent by value are bought in from a network of independent suppliers, who have also located themselves in a small geographical area. This facilitates the use of JIT. For many of the parts and components, a maximum of one day's production is held as stock. In the case of seats, literally only a few minutes' production is held and this shows in the constant stream of lorries that flow into the plants each day. With a few components, such as engines and tyres, several days' stock are normally held. Some parts are bought in from outside the immediate geographical area, but there are dangers in this sourcing strategy. The civil war in the former Yugoslavia is a vivid example of how supplies could be disrupted, if components are sourced from another country.

The use of minimal JIT periods has several consequences. The logistics must be carefully thought through. For example, in times of severe weather the lorries leave the supplying plants a little earlier. The quality of components is obviously important and BMW closely supervises its suppliers. So far there have been no major problems.

The important Dingolfing plant was not linked to the German autobahn network until 1987/88, when the A92 linking Munich-Deggendorf-Passau was completed. This link had two important consequences. First, it greatly helped the movement of parts and cars to and from the plant. Second, it allowed most of the 17,000 employees, about 75 per cent of the Dingolfing workforce, to commute daily over a distance of up to 110 kilometres.

Both road and rail transport is used to move parts and cars. One train a day takes cars to the ports for export. One train a day carries cars to Cologne for markets in the western regions of Germany. The Ford plant in Cologne uses the same train, on its return journey, to move its cars to the south of Germany. The service provided by the railway system is not ideal, however, as it takes two days, for instance, for car bodies to be moved between the Dingolfing and Regensburg plants.

THE USA PLANT

A major change in location strategy was announced by BMW in June 1992. In what is seen as a gamble by some commentators on the car industry, BMW will build its first-ever assembly plant outside Germany on a greenfield site in South Carolina, in the USA. The initial investment is $400 million and the plant will produce a new model for both the new North American free trade area market, and world markets. Eberhard von Keunheim, Executive Chairman of BMW, said that a major reason for this strategy change was to avoid possible trade restrictions and exchange rate fluctuations. Changes in exchange rates can have a considerable impact on companies such as BMW, where export earnings are significant. For instance, the effective devaluation of the British pound of 15 per cent in September 1992 against the Deutschmark meant that BMW would have to increase its prices by this amount to maintain revenue; in a competitive and depressed market, this was not possible.

The US market is important. In 1991, BMW sales there declined by 16 per cent to 53,343 vehicles. In part this was due to a new luxury tax on cars costing over $30,000, and in part it was due to the recession. But in the first five months of 1992, sales grew by 24 per cent to 25,000. The best year for BMW in the US was 1986, when 96,000 cars were sold. The USA is the world's largest car market and BMW considers it essential to maintain a strong presence there. Production is at the limits of capacity in the German plants and the new factory in South Carolina will allow the company to retain and strengthen its market share. The plant will come on-stream in 1995 with a daily production of 300 cars. Eventually, 2,000 people will be employed. A number of incentives were reported to be offered by the State government, including a 20-year freeze on taxes, which is worth $150 million.

VW, which is Germany's largest car producer, shut its loss-making Pennsylvania subsidiary in 1987 and supplies the US market from a plant in Mexico. Audi, the luxury arm of VW, is considering sites in the new free trade area of Canada, Mexico and the USA. Mercedes-Benz, the main German competitor of BMW, said in response to the BMW announcement, that it had no plans to build any assembly plants outside Germany, although the US market is also important to it. Mercedes suffered a decline in sales in 1991 in the USA – from 78,000 to 59,000, but it, too, reported a growth in the first five months of 1992, up 18 per cent to 28,000 units.

185

This diversification strategy represents a significant change to BMW's long-established 'build local' policy. Apart from the reasons already given for the change, there were worries about high wage costs in the German plants. There are also worries about Japanese competition and the decision shows that BMW will fight hard to keep a major presence in the US market. Honda, Mazda, Nissan and Toyota all have plants in the USA and between them will soon have 30 per cent of the market.

The experts in the car industry who criticize the BMW decision point out that the US market, even when the new free trade area is taken into account, is not large enough to provide the volume necessary for low-cost production, for example, scale economies are important in the car industry. This implies that the plant will have to produce cars for export outside the USA and this will have implications for the jobs of German workers. The concern about costs in the Bavarian plants has already led to economic measures that will result in 3,000 jobs being lost in 1992. Wage costs are about the same in South Carolina as they are in Germany, but there will be a saving on transport costs and BMW will be immune from exchange rate vagaries.

PRODUCTION AND TECHNOLOGY: AN OVERVIEW

The continuous and substantial investment programme has resulted in modern buildings, a highly trained workforce, and state-of-the-art machinery. The lead time for a new model is about five years and starts in the Munich Research and Development centre where around 6,000 scientists and engineers are employed. Here the cars are designed, prototypes built, tested and further developed, before they are built in the Munich, Dingolfing and Regensburg plants. Information Technology is extensively used. For instance, computers at the R&D centre for the Series 5 and 7 and the new Series 3 models are connected with computers in Dingolfing to ensure a smooth and direct transfer of all data on the car to the responsible departments at the Dingolfing factory.

Although the computer link up is virtually foolproof, a full-scale model is built first, as even the best computer-generated drawings lack the spatial dimension of an actual vehicle. The mould production shop in Munich builds the prototype by applying computer data and drawings. Then the styling and appearance of the new car is fine-tuned by designers, stylists and production specialists, who add the final touch round all the edges and body contours and make sure that the parts and components can be made easily and efficiently.

The design and pre-production phases are complemented with expensive and modern equipment at the production plants. The production of just one part, the bonnet for instance, utilizes tools that cost 3.8 million DM. These high-quality tools must be backed up with other capital items to apply the tool properly. In the Dingolfing press shop, there are machines with a capacity of more than 900 tonnes of sheet metal a day. These machines produce an average of 500 parts per car. These parts are not made on a daily basis, but are produced in batches for between 15 and 30 working days, depending on size, in order to reduce costs to a minimum.

A good example of state-of-the-art technology is the transfer press at Dingolfing which was installed in 1986. This and the other automated press lines produce large body parts such as floor pans, side frames, doors, bonnets and roofs, fully automatically in large numbers (optimum batch sizes). This transfer press, because of its sliding carriage, can be retooled in only 10 minutes as the new tool just has to be pushed into position on the carriage. A conventional press machine without the sliding carriage takes, on average, 90 minutes. The transfer press cost 25 million DM, but the new technology it embodies enables great efficiency to be obtained. This cuts costs and enables production to be very flexible. Costs are also reduced because the machine operates very quickly, about twice as fast as a conventional press. In effect, capacity is greatly increased. Further economies are obtained from the fact that it takes up less space than the conventional tool. This is a good example of the scale economies available to the large organization through the use of specialized capital equipment.

After the parts have been pressed, they are visually checked by a quality controller and then stored for assembly in an immediate-retrieval, high-rack, storage area. During the pressing process, specimens are taken off the production line and carefully measured and checked by computerized equipment. Any deviations are determined and eliminated by suitable adjustments. Thus optimum ongoing quality control is achieved.

The techniques and machinery used have implications for the workforce. The jobs of the workers on the pressing line are much easier than they were just a few years ago. The new machinery is quieter and easier to use, but it does demand more highly qualified workers. Specialists maintain the machines, supervise the production process, set the machine and operating data and carry out minor repairs. Working conditions are much less monotonous than they once were.

A feature of contemporary car production is the widespread use of plastics. Production technology is being constantly improved, as is materials technology. Plastics provide the possibility of designing different shapes and structures and because plastics weigh far less than the metals they have replaced, fuel consumption is reduced. The interior of a car is totally dominated by plastic and many exterior parts are now made of plastic, too. Examples of external parts made of plastic include the bumpers, front and rear ends, hub caps and sometimes wings, bonnet and boot lids. At the Landshut plant, over 500 workers are employed in plastics production, compared with about 200 in 1984.

PRODUCTION AND TECHNOLOGY: PRODUCING A VEHICLE

Most BMW cars are manufactured to specific order and this requires high-level logistics, a sophisticated EDP system and a highly qualified workforce. The technology employed ensures a high degree of flexibility. For instance, a single model can be built in large numbers, one after the other. Alternatively, completely different models and model series in any order can be produced. Formerly, a separate body production line was required for each individual model; now a single production line only is needed and used. The new technology yields several advantages. One is the flexibility already mentioned; the system is so flexible that individual customer requests can be quickly incorporated, without the extra work and retooling needed in the past. Another is the very high standard of quality, as all operations on the line are constantly monitored and rectified, where necessary. The production robots are programmed not to accept even a slight deviation from the target. For example, the maximum body shell tolerance allowed during production is not more than one tenth of a millimetre.

There was automation in the past but at a much lower level. Until the end of the 1980s, most of the pressed parts were still welded and bonded by hand – a monotonous process for the workers. Now 94 per cent of all welding spots are applied automatically by robots, which are more reliable and do not suffer from fatigue. The widespread introduction of robots did not lead to job losses. About the same number of workers are still required, but their job description has changed. Workers now supervise the robots, check the programmes applied in the production process, and carry out repairs, if there is a defect.

The end destination of each car is known early on in the production process, when the bonnet has been attached to a further 134 major, and 378 minor, body components. Even when the pressed parts are being fitted together to form the basic bodyshell, it is known whether the car will have left-hand or right-hand drive, whether it will be fitted with a sun roof or air conditioning, whether it is a US model or a Japanese model, etc. The robots are programmed with instructions providing the exact specification for each body shell.

By the time the body is complete, the exact colour of the paintwork is known and all the other steps required for completing the body are determined by the PREMIT electronic data processing programme, attached to the body in a small box, which specifies all the customer's requests. Before the topcoat can be applied, the bodyshell has to undergo 12 further processes in a cleaning, degreasing, and phosphatization regime. After the final coat has been sprayed on, the car goes through the drying ovens for the last time, and then the hollow cavity protection is applied before the remaining components are fitted.

PRODUCTION LOGISTICS

The production of a car is a very complex operation, requiring great co-ordination: all of the components supplied by BMW itself; engines from Steyr and Munich; bumpers from Landshut; transmissions from Dingolfing; and the parts supplied by more than 1,000 suppliers from all over the world have to be available on the production line exactly on time, without delays or long periods of storage. In the case of the Dingolfing plant, more than 200 lorries and 40 railway wagons ferry in the parts. Sometimes helicopters are used.

Over 1,750 engine variants are available and there are more than 800 types of seats. These, and all the other component variations, must be fed on to the assembly line at exactly the right time, according to the specification of the vehicle being produced. A comprehensive data processing system links the various factories and it provides the logistics experts with exact information on the current production status.

Within the factory, parts and components are delivered to the assembly line in electrical suspension tracks, chain conveyors and hoists. This ensures that all high-quality parts are efficiently protected from damage and environmental effects, thus aiding high-quality production. Regardless of their origin, all parts and components are subject to consistent quality control upon receipt. Swivel-joint conveyors, which are still not common in other manufacturers' plants, were introduced into the Regensburg plant in 1987. These machines ensure that workers are not required to bend down or work above head height, and this is another example of how state-of-the-art technology improves working conditions.

A large number of pre-assembly processes are conducted away from the production line on 'assembly islands' or at pre-assembly work stations. An example is the separate assembly of doors. Immediately after the paintwork line, the doors are removed from the body and fitted with all their components on a pre-assembly line. Other components which are pre-assembled are the instrument panel, roof lining, heating, steering column, and wheels. While these parts are being assembled separately, the remainder of the body is being completed on the main assembly line. In BMW's view, this technique provides optimum facilities and working conditions for all operations and aids the quest for perfect, all-round quality.

As the car is being built, quality control measures are in force, but once the car has been finished it is again thoroughly checked, before being driven to the shipping area. Here the ignition, emission control, brakes, and all electrical functions are given another check before the car is given final approval to leave the factory.

THE REGIONAL IMPACT

The Dingolfing plant provides a useful example of the impact of BMW on the regional economy. This is the factory for the whole of Lower Bavaria. Only a small number of employees, 3,000 out of 17,000, come from the immediate vicinity of the plant. About 30 per cent come from a distance of up to 40 kilometres, another 30 per cent travel up to 70 kilometres, and the rest travel up to 110 kilometres.

Most of the employees come from the region around the Bavarian forest and Passau, where the ground is poor and employment opportunities have always been limited. BMW Dingolfing is the largest employer in the region and pays almost 1 billion DM annually in wages and salaries. This provides both considerable purchasing power and tax revenues and has greatly helped the financing of public projects. Altogether, there is a substantial regional multiplier effect, with bus companies that drive two thirds of the employees to work, butchers, bakers, and small house construction companies being obvious beneficiaries.

The company has a 'good neighbour' philosophy and an important task of the PR managers is to maintain good relationships with the regional media and local opinion leaders. The company also supports cultural and sports activities in the Lower Bavarian region.

HUMAN RESOURCE MANAGEMENT

BMW regards training and ongoing education as very important. At the Dingolfing plant over 800 apprentices are trained, and more than 200 positions are provided each year for trainees from the Fachhochschulen and Universities. Training is offered in 16 different careers, with a concentration in technical professions. All training stations are equipped with up-to-date electronic and mechanical facilities, which the apprentices will later use on their jobs. Training of this calibre does not come cheaply and the cost per apprentice in Dingolfing is about 25,000 DM per year.

Each apprentice must remain in training between 3 and 3.5 years. Additional to training in the apprentice workshop is training on the job, which anticipates the tasks and activities that will be a standard requirement in later employment. One of the benefits of this thorough programme is that apprentices gain a feeling of responsibility, a willingness to co-operate, a sense of quality, and genuine dedication to their jobs. Another benefit is that the firm is able to train its own skilled manpower and thus remain largely independent of the job market. This is particularly important in special professions such as steel mould production, model making, and foundry operation. The apprentice programme in Dingolfing has now been operating for more than 20 years and during this time jobs have been offered to almost every successful apprentice.

There is a large measure of decentralization, with plant managers being given a great deal of freedom. One important reason is that whilst centralized decision-making is easy, these decision-makers do not have to take the responsibility for their decisions.

ENVIRONMENTAL ISSUES

In recent years, respect for the environment has been growing and this has a number of manifestations. Two important aspects in which BMW has taken a particular interest are the development and application of production processes that are friendly to the environment, and the recycling or reprocessing of materials used in old cars. This is a good example of existing and anticipated future legislation, and the requirements of customers being viewed as a business opportunity, rather than a threat to the business to be resisted by all means possible.

In the 1970s, plastics were mainly used in cars for functional components. Even then, and increasingly in the 1980s, manufacturers were looking for ways of making plastic parts that were kinder to the environment. BMW, for instance, deliberately decided not to use fluorchlorohydrocarbons (CFCs) as a propellant for PU foam. The waste generated in the production of plastic interior panels was reduced by more than 50 per cent by optimizing the tools and process technologies. Significant improvements were also achieved with the separating agents required for plastic part production. The introduction of robots using optimized spray systems has reduced the consumption of separating agents by a substantial amount. Another example is the replacement of separating agents containing solvents by systems soluble in water.

The process of painting plastic parts is now more environmentally friendly. New types of paint with lower drying temperatures have led to the introduction of the so-called two-component system. The result is a substantial saving of energy. The general improvement in paints has led to smaller amounts of solvents being used. This, together with new plant technologies dealing with such items as escaping solvents which are burnt, ensures significant energy saving.

Substantial progress has also been made in recycling waste material in injection casting. Rejects and other waste material are fully recycled back into the production process. The plastics are cut up into their original grain structure in large mills and then fed back into the new material. Thus no plastics have to be dumped on waste sites. Painted plastic, i.e. thermoplastic, is a crucial component of modern cars and can now be recycled too, thanks to advances in technology.

Chemicals are used on the paintwork line to help protect the environment. The water used is recycled in a special effluent plant and the paint residue is removed as special industrial waste. The Dingolfing factory overfulfils the legal requirements for environmental protection. A group of specially trained chemists has just one task – to take care of pollutants and, where possible, to avoid their generation right at the outset.

Sales of motor cars are still growing worldwide and this means an ever-growing number of old cars. As natural resources become more scarce, the recycling of the materials used in cars becomes more important and cost-effective. It is for this reason that BMW has installed a 1,000 square metre pilot plant at the Landshut factory to try out special technologies for disassembling and stripping old cars. The help of universities and other companies is being enlisted to determine the best ways and means of solving the recycling problems.

Another environmental aspect is the increased use of electronic control systems. All BMW cars with petrol engines are fitted with catalytic converters and diesel cars can be supplied with an uncontrolled catalytic converter.

OUTPUT AND FINANCIAL PERFORMANCE OF THE BMW GROUP

From Exhibit 3.1 it may be seen that sales of the BMW group increased by 2.5 per cent from 1989 to 1990. The declining exchange rates of the currencies of the USA, Canada, and Japan, with which sales in foreign currencies were converted into Deutschmarks, counteracted higher growth.

In Germany, which is still the most important market for BMW, total sales of 191,000 units equalled the record total of the previous year. In Europe as a whole, 370,000 cars, i.e. some 70 per cent of production, were sold. The North American market posed some problems, with demand being affected by the economic climate and taxation, and the sales figure of 68,000 was about the same as the previous year. In East Asia sales rose by 9 per cent to 50,000 units. The Japanese market continued to grow, with sales reaching a new record level of 36,500.

In 1991 car sales rose by 5 per cent to the highest level ever of 553,000 units. Development in individual markets was influenced by the availability of the new·Series 3 model. Deliveries in Europe began in the spring, but overseas markets were not supplied in any scale until the second half of the year. In Europe as a whole, the overall market was stagnant, but despite this sales rose by 14 per cent to 422,000.

Exhibit 3.1
Sales by value

Sales	1989	1990	%change	1991	%change
Domestic	9,184 (35)	10,453 (38)	13.8	12,955 (43)	23.9
Foreign	17,337 (65)	16,725 (62)	– 3.5	16,884 (57)	–1.0
Total	26,515	27,178	2.5	29,839	9.8

Notes: 1 Sales figures in DM millions.
2 All figures rounded off to nearest whole number.
3 Figures in brackets are percentage of total sales.

Source: BMW Annual Reports (Abridged Version) 1990 and 1991.

Exhibit 3.2
Sales by volume

Sales	1989	1990	%change	1991	%change
Cars					
Domestic	190,363 (36)	200,418 (38)	5.3	238,030 (43)	18.5
Foreign	332,658 (64)	325,448 (62)	−2.2	314,630 (57)	−3.3
Total	523,021	525,866	0.5	552,660	5.1
Motorcycles					
Domestic	7,486 (28)	8,127 (27)	8.6	10,919 (34)	34.4
Foreign	19,319 (72)	21,574 (73)	11.7	21,268 (66)	−1.4
Total	26,805	29,701	10.8	32,187	8.4

Note: All figures rounded off to nearest whole number

Source: BMW Annual Reports (Abridged Version) 1990 and 1991.

Exhibit 3.3
Production figures

	1986	1987	1988	1989	1990	1991
Series 3	328	312	272	271	265	324
Series 5	93	76	163	202	212	184
Series 7	28	57	61	50	49	45
Total	449	445	496	523	526	553

Notes: 1 All figures in 000s.
2 All figures rounded off.

Source: BMW Annual Reports (Abridged Version) 1990 and 1991.

Exhibit 3.4
Workforce, investment and net income

	1989	1990	1991
Workforce at Year end	66,267	70,948	74,385
Investment in tangible and intangible assets	1,820	2,066	2,123
Year's net income	558	696	783

Notes: 1 Rows 2 and 3 in DM millions.
2 All figures rounded off.

Source: BMW Annual Reports (Abridged Version) 1990 and 1991.

Exhibit 3.5
Statement of income of BMW AG (in DM thousand)

	1989	1990	1991
Net sales	**20,957,814**	**22,147,126**	**24,476,510**
Change in product inventories and other company-produced additions to tangible fixed assets	80,223	277,007	217,373
Total value of production	**21,038,037**	**22,424,133**	**24,693,883**
Other operating income	423,478	538,805	677,568
Expenditure on materials	12,727,647	13,723,108	15,132,747
Expenditure on personnel	4,126,617	4,594,755	4,942,730
Depreciation on intangible assets and on fixed assets	1,233,325	1,441,052	1,395,773
Other operating expenditure	2,677,119	2,623,845	3,481,874
Income from investment in subsidiaries and associated companies	80,136	82,769	199,906
Interest income	196,558	223,590	157,942
Income from normal business	973,501	877,537	776,175
Tax and income and profits	509,405	389,371	227,852
Other taxes	78,134	90,408	99,049
Year's net income	**385,962**	**397,758**	**449,274**

continued

Exhibit 3.5 (continued)
Statement of income of BMW AG (in DM thousand)

	1989	*1990*	*1991*
Transfer to profit reserves	192,981	198,879	224,637
Net income available for distribution	**192,981**	**198,879**	**224,637**
Intangible assets	7,467	1,781	–
Tangible fixed assets	3,638,171	3,861,317	4,034,034
Financial assets	626,654	962,011	962,284
Fixed assets	**4,272,292**	**4,825,109**	**4,996,318**
Inventories	1,018,386	1,255,866	1,470,625
Trade receivables	341,444	391,186	572,769
Receivables from subsidiaries	1,412,672	1,427,890	1,737,936
Other receivables and miscellaneous assets	821,112	661,742	518,844
Marketable securities and notes	1,129,273	1,428,839	1,543,029
Liquid funds	1,136,937	849,570	517,020
Current assets	**5,859,824**	**6,015,093**	**6,360,223**
Prepaid expenses	**690**	**3,736**	**7,163**
Shareholders' equity and liabilities	**10,132,806**	**10,843,938**	**11,363,704**
Subscribed capital	790,600	793,690	896,078
Capital reserve	749,332	774,793	795,949
Profit reserves	2,118,660	2,317,539	2,442,965
Net income available for distribution	192,981	198,879	224,637
Shareholders' equity	**3,851,573**	**4,084,901**	**4,359,629**
Registered dividend right certificates	**105,717**	**104,534**	**103,161**
Pension fund provision	1,066,659	1,236,310	1,356,356
Other provisions	3,719,545	3,733,382	3,488,237
Provisions	**4,799,951**	**4,955,855**	**4,844,593**
Due to banks	96,388	118,658	110,874
Trade payables	1,023,634	1,154,902	1,210,731
Liabilities to subsidiaries	29,919	159,370	370,537
Other liabilities	225,624	265,718	364,179
Liabilities	**1,375,565**	**1,698,648**	**2,056,321**
	10,132,806	**10,843,938**	**11,363,704**

Source: BMW Annual Reports (Abridged Version) 1990 and 1991.

The important German market continued to develop, with registrations increasing by 20 per cent to 232,000 units.

The North American market was affected by the 10 per cent luxury car tax on cars costing more than $30,000. Total sales fell to 53,000 units. In Japan the slow-down in economic growth and the model change-over in the Series 3 led to a decrease in sales to 33,800 units.

MARKETING STRATEGIES

Another aspect of decentralization concerns advertising and promotion. Once this was devised centrally and sent out for distribution to showrooms and centres, but it has been recognized that this centralized approach was not too successful. Increasingly, localized material is being used. In this way the special knowledge of the people on the spot, and the local culture, may both be used with advantage.

Niche marketing strategies were employed in the past, but total production is expected to reach 600,000 vehicles in 1992. Of this, 40 per cent will be sold in Germany itself. This is an awkward size for the company to be: it is too large to view as being in a market niche and too small to compete with the volume car producers, such as Fiat, Ford and Renault, whose cars are largely aimed at a different market anyway. Mercedes-Benz is seen as a major competitor, particularly if the 190,000 Series 3 cars are looked at. In Germany, Mercedes is considered to be slightly upmarket from BMW. Mercedes sell well in the 'fleet car' market but a drawback is that if an economic downturn causes firms to keep their cars for a longer period of time, the fall in sales might have a serious effect on sales and cash flow. In contrast, BMW sell mainly to individuals. The Series 7 was introduced mainly to compete with Mercedes and their strategic response was the 190 model.

Japanese competition is now being experienced at a significant level for the first time in this segment of the car market. The top-of-the-range Japanese competition is underpinned by huge mass market sales, which BMW doesn't have, and this has enabled the Japanese to price very keenly. There is a potential drawback for the Japanese, though: their strategy is based on ever increasing sales and if the market slumps to any extent, then they are in trouble.

BMW sold 36,500 cars in Japan in 1990 and 33,800 in 1991. On 14 February 1992 Herr Siegfried Richter, the BMW Japan president, was quoted in *The Guardian* as expecting sales to reach 39,500 cars in 1992 in this market. He thought the launch of two new models in Japan would contribute to this growth. BMW cars in Japan are very highly equipped and much business is conducted from the cars. It is perhaps an interesting statistic to note that a BMW Series 7 contains more space for an executive than that available in the average Japanese office.

A possible new niche is the electric car. Prototypes of the E1, a small town car, are running, but there is a serious problem, that of battery technology. Despite advances in technology, batteries are still both expensive and heavy. Some idea of the problem may be gained from the fact that 40,000 DM of the total cost of 75,000 DM of this car is accounted for by the battery.

CONCLUSION

BMW has progressed a long way since it was on the point of bankruptcy in 1959. Sales have grown steadily in recent years and in 1992, for the first time ever, are expected to be greater than those of its arch rival, Mercedes-Benz – 560,000 against 538,000. A major change in strategy is the decision to establish production facilities outside Germany and this may have far-reaching consequences. BMW is a firm that has grasped the opportunities made available by customer and government concern about the environment, and is well placed to profit from anticipated legislation about the recycling of cars. Perhaps the major problem facing the company is large-scale Japanese competition in the luxury car market, but the indications are that they intend to meet it head-on.

QUESTIONS/DISCUSSION TOPICS

1 Do you consider BMW to be a national company functioning in an international market, or an international company?

2 How does the decision by BMW to build production facilities in the USA relate to the theories outlined in Chapter 11 of this book?

3 Using appropriate ratio analysis, comment on the performance of BMW in recent years.

4 Obtain a recent set of accounts for Rover and compare their performance with that of BMW. Which company do you consider to have the better long-term future?

CASE FOUR

NISSAN MOTOR MANUFACTURING (UK): A SUCCESSFUL MIXED MARRIAGE

RON ALLISON

ADVICE TO THE READER

Reading the chapters on the multinational enterprise, environmental issues and technology, before you start on this case study, will be helpful, as the case illustrates many of the concepts and themes discussed.

INTRODUCTION

The Nissan Motor Company Limited was established in 1933 and is the second largest car maker in Japan, and the fourth largest in the world. It produces and assembles in 21 countries and its cars, buses, and trucks are sold in more than 150 countries. It is the largest selling Japanese car in Europe, with over 500,000 sold in 1991. Some statistics that illustrate its global presence are provided in Exhibit 4.1.

Nissan Motor Manufacturing (UK) Limited was established in the Sunderland area of England in 1986. The 750-acre site contains an assembly plant, an engine manufacturing plant, aluminium casting plant and a plastic injection and blow-moulding facility. There is also a major Research and Design (R&D) presence in England with the Nissan European Technology Centre Ltd established in Sunderland and Cranfield. Nissan Yamato Engineering is also located in the Sunderland area and this joint venture supplies small chassis pressings to the main plant on a synchronous basis. The main site includes a 12,000-square metre administration block and a 20-acre vehicle distribution centre for the UK dealer network.

Employment, investment, output and cars exported have risen steadily since 1986, as shown in Exhibit 4.2, on p. 204. By 1993, 4,600 people will be directly employed by the company and over 1,000 other jobs will exist in associated enterprises in the Wearside area. By 1993, total investment in Wearside will be £900 million and this represents the largest single foreign direct investment by a Japanese firm in Europe. The increase in output since 1989 has been remarkable. In 1991, 125,000 Nissan Primera cars, an upper-middle range model, were built. In 1992, 175,000 cars were made. Of these, a new model, the Nissan Micra – a small car especially designed for Europe – accounted for 130,000 units. This planned target was achieved in mid-November, only 14 weeks after the first Micra was completed. The company claims that this is the fastest production build-up for a new model ever achieved in Europe.

Total production is planned to rise to 270,000 units in 1993. Around 600 new staff will be recruited for these targets to be realized. Exports to Europe began in 1988, and in 1989,

44 per cent of the plant's production of 77,000 cars were exported to Europe. In 1991, there was a a huge increase in exported cars to 112,000, which accounted for 90 per cent of total production. Cars from the plant are exported to 30 markets world-wide, including Japan. The target for exports in 1993 is 60 per cent plus of total production.

EMPLOYMENT

Many of the management and working practices which are common in Japan have been introduced to the Sunderland plant. The aim is to produce a workforce that has a high level of team spirit and motivation. This is achieved by thorough training and committing workers, through an innovative management policy, to be fully involved in many aspects of the business. As Peter Wickens, the Personnel Director, said, 'If you can hire good people, train them well and give them real responsibility, you are well on the way to success.' If workers are motivated to do the best possible job, the end quality of the product will also be high. A side-effect is that traditional practices such as clocking on are unnecessary.

The traditional divide between management and workers, still common in much of European industry, is largely absent in the company. Everyone has the same terms and conditions of employment. Everyone is paid by the month and encouraged to progress up the appropriate salary scales at a rate which is determined by individual performance. All employees use the same car-park and eat in the same canteen, benefit from the same sickness scheme, can opt for private medical insurance and take advantage of an assisted car purchase scheme.

Production teams are used on the shop floor. Typically, these consist of a supervisor and 20 manufacturing staff, 2 of whom are team leaders. The supervisor and team leaders know every job function in some detail. The supervisor has the responsibility for all aspects of the team's area of operation. The responsibility is very wide and includes selection, training, all communication, line layout, the process, line balancing, preparing, and improving the standard operation. In 1992, the salary scale for supervisors ranged between £20,000 and £25,000. The scale for manufacturing staff was £11,764 to £13,593, exclusive of the 16.6 per cent shift premium.

Another innovative aspect relating to employment was the introduction of a single union deal. The union that was successful is the Amalgamated Engineering Union (AEU). All staff are encouraged to join, but membership is not compulsory and about half of the production force are members. The firm is keen to point out that, contrary to some opinions, the agreement is not a 'no strike' deal.

Unique to the British car industry is the company council, although these exist in the German car industry. Within Nissan, the council consists of 10 elected representatives from all areas of the plant and 6 company appointments, meeting 4 times a year and reporting to the workforce twice a year. The council operates as a consultative forum which discusses aspects of company business, including quality, production levels and market share. In addition, it is a negotiating body which considers issues referred to it under the procedure agreement, covering individual and collective grievances. Unresolved issues are referred to the Arbitration, Conciliation and Advisory Service (ACAS).

Recruitment and training is taken very seriously. Before manufacturing staff are appointed, they are assessed; tested for numeracy, literacy and mechanical aptitude; and interviewed. Total time for this procedure per applicant is at least six hours. An important aspect of the recruitment policy is that the final decision on whether to employ is taken by the supervisor of the team in which the candidate will work. After selection, new employees receive a full induction programme before training is started. Training is seen as vital by Nissan in ensuring that all employees are able to be efficient and effective workers. As an indication of the importance attached to training the proportion of the total payroll costs of this process was 14.5 per cent in 1991. Peter Wickens points out that the company actually does a lot of training as opposed to just talking about it and integrates training courses, so they do not appear to be aimed exclusively at production or at management/indirect staff.

The need for more skilled staff as production levels rise over time has been anticipated and a programme has been developed with local FE colleges to provide training courses for school leavers. Trainee technicians have also been sponsored to attend a full-time undergraduate engineering course at Sunderland University.

Thus formal on- and off-the-job training is taken seriously. Equally important is the development of Nissan's overall philosophy of team-working, quality consciousness and flexibility and the giving of responsibility to people to enhance the status and authority of production management. In contrast to many other UK employers, production managers are given the same authority, responsibility and salary ranges as professionals in engineering, finance and personnel.

THE PRODUCTION PROCESS

The first stage is the press shop, and the technology employed here and in the remainder of the production processes is state-of-the-art. In the press shop, 67 highly skilled staff work with 300 different dies on a five-day cycle in three dedicated press lines to produce around 7 million panels a year. Some of the die sets can be changed in less than three minutes which allows shorter panel runs, greater schedule flexibility and lower inventories. There is a clean air environment in the shop. Although no special technology is used, most of the dust particles that would normally be found are absent. This is important, as any dust particles of around 15 microns, the thickness of a human hair, leave an impression on the pressed panels which would have to be filled by the subsequent surface coatings. Prevention, rather than cure, enhances the quality of the final paint finish.

After straightening and cleaning, the steel coils from which the panels are made are blanked in a high speed Hitachi Zozen press which works at up to 60 strokes per minute.

A specially made, side-piling unit enables the blanks to be stacked very quickly and a total of four special blanking-die carriages allows rapid tool changes of around 16 minutes. This specialized and expensive machinery significantly reduces costs at this stage of the operation. The blanks then go for further processing onto one of four high-speed press lines. One is a Komatsu tandem press line, comprised of one 1,000 tonne double-action press, two 800 tonne and three 600 tonne machines. A panel turning operation is needed, and this means the running time is only about four strokes per minute. Die changes take between 8 and 25 minutes.

The Hitachi Zozen 3,200 double-action press runs at up to 15 strokes per minute and uses a very advanced, computer-controlled, three-axis transfer system, which grips the panels by their sides and carries them between the stations at high speed. Between 1988 and 1992 die change times have been reduced from 130 minutes to 10 minutes.

There is a Komatsu, 2,700 tonne, single-stamping cushion press on the third line which runs at up to 18 strokes a minute. Die change times have been reduced from 50 minutes in 1988 to 5 minutes in 1992. A 5000 tonne press, which Nissan believes is the first of this capacity to be used in Europe, came into use in mid-October 1992. This machine was installed exclusively for Micra production and is able to stamp out a complete body side in one operation.

The body and assembly shop is linked directly to the press shop. A total of 86 robots are used here in Primera body-in-white (a traditional term in the car industry for an unpainted body shell) production which provides an automation level of over 70 per cent. Midway through body production, each body is given its production identity and fitted temporarily with an electronic transponder chip which contains all the information about the customer's order and which can be read by process control instruments and related to the specific body during the remainder of the production process.

After the body has been assembled, it goes to the paint shop, where there is an advanced, multi-stage paint system operating in a semi-sealed, clean-air environment, with double-door pressure locks at all ground-floor entrances. Bodies are brought in by overhead conveyors. An unusual zig-zag flow sequence is used, with the four treatment ovens and two topcoat ovens located in specially insulated blocks at one end of the building, in order to conserve energy and reduce operating costs. An important objective is to provide trouble-free corrosion protection throughout the six-year body warranty period applicable to all Nissan cars.

Before they are painted, the shells are prepared by a total immersion in an automatic, 11-stage process which cleans, degreases and etches the surface of the sheet metal with zinc phosphate. This allows for maximum adhesion of the subsequent electrocoating and spray-coating process. The paint facility is very versatile and paint is applied by a combination of high-speed, rotating bells and pneumatic spray nozzles, which are able to handle 6 different primer surface colours, 11 different topcoats, and a clearcoat, ultra-violet, screening lacquer. Unique to Nissan is the way the overhead paint guns follow the moving shell, which improves the paint coverage of the body profile.

In the engine machining shop, aluminium head castings, intake manifolds and chilled-iron camshaft castings are received as raw materials and fully machined before assembly. An advanced, fully-automated, engine head transfer line has been installed, together with nine, multi-headed, manifold milling machines and milling, turning and grinding machines for camshaft production. Spark-plug tapping, valve-bore guides and valve seats are machines using fully-programmable numerical control (NC) equipment, which allows high precision and quality standards to be maintained, along with full flexibility and maximum process control.

Machining operations on 500 individual tools are monitored by a total of 50 robot scanning video cameras, which compare digitized images with a master map stored in a controlling computer and shut down any machine if a fault or defect is detected.

Engine assembly started in 1988. Cylinder heads, camshafts and intake manifolds are combined with parts bought in from European

suppliers or shipped from Nissan plants in Japan. The build specification for different engines is derived from the Central Control Room (CCR), which regulates the supply of parts and integrates engine assembly with the trim and chassis to minimize the storage inventory. Each completed engine is transferred to an automatic, rail-guided trolley, which takes it to the 'hot test' area. Here ignition timing is set, idle speed checked and carbon monoxide emission level confirmed. Other checks are carried out to ensure that the engine is operating correctly and sample engines are regularly selected at random from production to make sure that design specifications are being met.

A plastics moulding facility was also opened in 1988. Bumpers, radiator grills, fascia parts and fuel tanks are produced, using two basic moulding processes and six different machines. All the flash removed from the mouldings, plus any scrap parts, are ground and recycled into the material supply stream. Fuel tanks are blow-moulded in a special machine developed jointly in Japan between Nissan and Japan steel works. The curing stage of the process can take place outside the moulding machine, which significantly reduces the cycle time required. Scrap from the fuel tanks is also recycled into the material supply system. The process can be operated with up to 30 per cent of recycled waste material and this enables all offcuts to be utilized. The finished tanks are stacked by a computer-controlled crane in overhead racks, where they are automatically retrieved as required by the build specification of each car.

Production lines for trim and final assembly have been specially developed for the Primera and Micra models. Very high quality standards are achieved with specially trained manufacturing staff. The line is fed with minimum-inventory components using the Just-In-Time (JIT) concept. For a description of JIT, see the Appendix.

As the painted body shells leave the paint store to travel to the final assembly line, the transponder fitted during the body-in-white assembly is scanned and replaced by a build sheet printout, detailing the specification and customer order details. Contemporaneously, the CRC computer broadcasts the scanned information of each vehicle's specification to the various sub-assembly stations and component supply points around the plant, so that all the parts needed for final assembly will arrive at the right station at the right time.

Five special final inspection bays are provided at the end of the line, where sample cars are pulled off the line for a detailed audit every 8–10 hours. They are equipped with high-intensity lights and white floors, for maximum visibility. After completion, all vehicles pass through a wheel alignment station and a roller test booth, before engine idling and exhaust emission checks are performed.

The final stage is a water-leak shower and short test drive. After any rectification and post-process work that may be necessary, finished cars are placed into storage, prior to shipment to dealers in the UK and the various distributors in mainland Europe, Japan and the far East.

PRODUCTIVITY AND EFFICIENCY

The standards of productivity and efficiency being set in the Sunderland plant are unmatched anywhere else in the European car industry and are as good as many plants in Japan. It is accepted that international comparisons of car plant productivity are far from easy; no two plants are the same, model specifications produced in different plants vary considerably, and levels of integration differ likewise.

The concept of 'hours per car' expended in the production process is gaining wide acceptance as a basis for comparison. Nissan claims that it requires 12.5 hours per car for its Primera large family car and only 10.5 hours for its new, small, European car, the Micra. Basically, the hours measure the so-called 'direct labour' in body welding, painting, and final trim and assembly parts of the operation. Even allowing for differences between car makers as to how they measure the hours, the competitive gap between Nissan UK and other makers in Europe is very large. According to Mr Ian Gibson, the Managing Director of Nissan (*Financial Times*, 23 September 1992), the best of the European

models (Vauxhall Cavalier, Ford Sierra, Peugot 405 and Volkswagen Passat) which compete with the Primera need around 20 hours per car, whilst the European average is closer to 30 hours.

The Nissan performance may be explained by a combination of sophisticated technology and machinery, advanced production techniques and a highly trained and motivated workforce. The huge and complex presses already mentioned are one example of technology. Whilst their exact costs are a commercial secret, they are measured in tens of millions of pounds, rather than millions. The use of these and other hardware, combined with advanced techniques such as synchronous supply or delivery, not only permit considerable cost savings to be made, but also enable production to take place that could not with older equipment. For instance, the use of ever more complex and sophisticated IT hardware and software has been an important factor in the move from large batch production. Transponder chips, the CRC computer, presses with very quick die-change times, skilled workers, and synchronous delivery allow small numbers of different models to be produced economically and efficiently.

The capital, labour and production techniques which are employed provide great flexibility in output, but there are still constraints. For instance, the top-of-the-range models require 50 per cent more time to assemble than the standard basic models. If a batch of, say, 12 top-of-the-range models were to be assembled, they could not be completed in the time allowed for 12 cars. Similarly, if there were a batch of 12 basic models at one time, there would be idle manufacturing staff. Thus there has to be a judicious mix in production. What has definitely been abandoned is the old idea, based on economic ordering quality (EOQ), of large production runs of the same model. The EOQ concept is redundant in modern car production.

Synchronous delivery is a technique that concentrates on supplier scheduling. Under this system, suppliers start making the parts only when notified by the Nissan computer and they are delivered just as they are needed. As an example, the stock-holding time for carpets is less than 10 minutes and only 42 minutes elapse from the time the supplier, in a nearby plant, receives the order from Nissan and the carpet is installed in the car. The same is true for other parts, such as seats. Typically, these components are made in small batches of 1–20, which reflects the cars going through the plant. The operation is obviously very complex and a high level of co-ordination and scheduling is required for the system to work. The benefits make it worthwhile. There are no 'on site' inventory costs and the operation is not cluttered up with the storage of parts and materials. Synchronous delivery is concentrated on parts which are relatively bulky and difficult to store, and which are supplied in many varieties, such as the seats previously mentioned.

COMPONENT SOURCING

Only two major components are imported from Japan, the engine block and transmission system. The remaining components are purchased from nearly 200 European companies and of these 130 are British. Twelve of these suppliers are either wholly owned, Japanese firms or joint ventures with Japanese firms. At the time of the introduction of the Micra model in 1992, annual expenditure on European-sourced components was £575 million. By 1993, this will have risen to £850 million. The cost of the components imported from Japan, including freight and insurance, will be £240 million in 1993. The European content of the Micra, according to the government's formula of factory-gate price minus the value of the non-European components, is greater than 80 per cent.

Nissan buys each individual component from just one supplier. Whilst this policy offers suppliers great opportunities, it means that they must be willing and able to develop long-term relationships with the company. They are required to work closely with Nissan's engineers, starting at the concept and ending with the product. The end result is the production of cost-effective components on time, with no

defects. Potential suppliers are surveyed with regard to their facilities, manufacturing processes, and quality assurance procedures. After they have been selected, suppliers are involved with engineers and designers from Nissan at the very earliest concept stages of a new project. After the specification tender, describing the part that is required, has been drawn up by Nissan, the supplier's role is to enter into joint design and development work and produce the part. This early involvement is for two reasons: the first is that lead times for new models is reduced by the development process of simultaneous engineering and the second is that quality is designed and developed-in by dealing throughout with parts that are fully representative of production components.

As Peter Hill, the Purchase Director, commented in a press release in early 1992:

> *Nissan has been able to accelerate its location programme as a result of positive improvements in quality standards achieved by our suppliers. Our increasing international manufacturing presence put those companies who can demonstrate an ability to meet our standards in a very good position. In the coming years, Nissan is going to be spending a great deal more money in Europe and we are currently working on developing world-wide standards for component and materials suppliers, incorporating a common evaluation standard that will allow both Nissan and its suppliers to clearly understand what is required, in terms of cost, design and engineering facilities and product quality.*

CORPORATE PHILOSOPHY

Nissan is proud of its claim to place the customer first. A cornerstone of its philosophy is localizing all aspects of its operations, from vehicle design and development through production to marketing and finance. By doing so, it brings itself closer to the markets and customers it serves. It also improves its ability to anticipate changes in customer needs and to contribute to the communities in which it operates. To quote from the 1991 Nissan Motor Company Limited Annual Report:

> *Our globalization and localization philosophy is to be at home world-wide as an integral and contributing member of the local community. This policy stems from our overall, corporate philosophy. Our first commitment is to customer satisfaction. Through diligent efforts to develop new customers and expand our customer base, we are contributing to the ongoing progress and enrichment of society.*

Thus the decision to set up a production facility in Europe may be viewed as strategic, since it aims at maximizing the advantages inherent in Nissan's position as the biggest Japanese marque in Europe. The clear and stated strategy is to develop an autonomous European operation, encompassing component design and manufacture as well as complete vehicle design, engineering and manufacture.

Consistent with this philosophy is a considerable degree of autonomy for the British operation. Discussions between the author and two senior managers appeared to indicate that corporate and strategic decisons were largely determined at Board level in Japan, but that there was a great deal of operational freedom for the Sunderland plant. Nissan Motor Manufacturing (UK) Limited is run as a profit centre, although this must be qualified in that the operation doesn't have full control over pricing. A business plan is prepared each year, which is sent to Japan for approval. Once this has been gained, the UK operation is free to make many business decisions. One aspect of the philosophy of localizing plants, production and management is the small number of Japanese personnel working in the Washington plant. The managing director is British and there are six other British directors. There are just two Japanese line managers, the deputy managing director and the finance director. This hands-off philosophy is very different from that of another major Japanese car producer, Toyota: in its US plant there are literally hundreds of Japanese personnel, and it is likely that this will be the case once its British plant near Derby comes on-stream.

Another aspect of localization is the very different managerial style, culture, and organization operating in the UK and Japan. Even allowing for the fact that Nissan in Japan employs over 65,000 people, the UK operation has a very flat management structure. At the top is the managing director and underneath in successive layers, the eight directors followed by senior supervisors/engineers, supervisors/ engineers and manufacturing staff. This means that the lines of communication and times of communication are short. The lean organization ensures that senior colleagues all know one another. A point of similarity between the UK and Japan is that the working day begins with a meeting of each shift to review the previous day and anticipate the coming period of production. This is paid for, and thus is an integral and important part of the day.

DESIGN AND ENGINEERING

The localization concept shows up prominently in the design and engineering function. The Primera was designed especially for the European market, in contrast to the Nissan tradition of designing their export models to satisfy world markets as a whole. The process began in 1985 and by mid-1986 Nissan's British staff were working with Japanese colleagues to develop the image of the European car. An important part was to identify key aspects of design or equipment thought to be desirable, necessary or essential. Specific European features included ABS braking, analogue-type instruments, four- and five-door derivatives, plastic fuel tanks and flush glazing for low drag coefficients.

The ABS braking system is a good example of how suppliers were involved at an early stage in the development process. Lucas Girling developed a European four-channel braking system that was very different from the Japanese market specification. The skills and expertise of the European supplier base were utilized to achieve Nissan specifications on a truly European product. UK design engineers took prime responsibility for the local development of Japanese ideas on interior and exterior trim, body components and the chassis. The steering wheel looks identical to the Japanese unit, but is, in fact, a totally new design. The headlining in the roof is manufactured from resin felt in Japan, but specified in polyurethane in the UK.

Late in 1989, Nissan announced a £31 million investment to establish two permanent sites for Nissan European Technology Centre Limited (NETC). This company is now the European link in Nissan's global research and development. Over 250 high-technology jobs were created at the new centre in Cranford to support this global strategy and a further 100 jobs were created in the Northern centre near the Washington plant. This European design capability means Nissan is a truly global company in the 1990s with sales, production, and design facilities in each of the three major world markets of Western Europe, Japan, and North America.

THE NISSAN APPROACH TO QUALITY

Quality is a philosophy that runs right through every aspect of the business: the way the plant is run and the way in which the cars it produces are built. According to Keith Jones, Director of Quality Assurance, total quality:

> ...means that we plan to do things correctly to ensure that quality is considered at every stage of the design and manufacture of our products. It also means that we ensure everything at the plant is done in the most effective way in respect of quality. We set quality standards and targets, and then we monitor the plant's performance against these. We feed back the results of the monitoring process and use them to help improve individual processes from what we have learned. We also ensure that we get the maximum amount of customer feedback and comments, and again this is incorporated into the way in which we do things at the plant.

Thus quality is not something that is left to quality controllers, it is the responsibility of every single person in the organization.

Quality is designed into the product. Prior to the introduction of a new model, a number of trial builds are made. Targets are set, a trial car is built and then the results are reviewed to see where standards need to be improved still further. After each trial build, the quality assurance department chairs a review of the concepts standards in the areas of design, engineering and manufacturing. Only after this department is satisfied is production allowed to proceed. No other department has the authority to start production.

Quality in manufacturing has four main features. The first are the help lamps, operated by a wire running the length of the production line which can be pulled at any time by an operator who has a 'quality concern'. This activates a siren and flashing light and draws the attention of a supervisor, who investigates and takes appropriate action. The use of these lamps is positively encouraged.

The second is a philosophy that no defect shall pass on from one part of the process to the next. In a series of 'neighbour checks,' whenever one component is to be passed on to the next station or 'neighbour', it is checked by the operator concerned. By building up this network, the integrity of the manufactured quality is continuously developed within the process.

The third feature is the visible management system, comprising large display boards on every supervisor section. On these boards quality data and performance are displayed. The graphs and charts on these boards are completed by the individual sections and this continuously enhances the awareness of the need for quality.

The final feature is the quality targets, which are divided into supervisor sections, so that each team of people in the production process has a defined quality target to aim at and monitor. The targets are constantly changed and are aimed at continuously improving the product. They are important in that they make everyone aware of their own individual contribution to the overall quality philosophy.

The vehicle evaluation system (VES) is another facet of the importance placed on quality. The quality of the cars being produced in the UK plant, as measured by this system, is at least as good as those produced in Nissan's other plants, and in some cases it is higher. Through the VES, the product is viewed by staff trained to look through the eyes of the most critical and knowledgeable of customers, and a numerical value is given to faults, depending on their nature and severity.

The 'failsafe' system is a means of improving product quality by preventing, or 'failsafing', defects from occurring in the first place. An example is the building of complex welded assemblies, where a number of different brackets have to be spot-welded in exact positions. If one is missed or wrongly placed, it is unlikely to be noticed until the car reaches the final assembly line. It would then be difficult or impossible to remedy. To prevent this, micro-switches are utilized to detect the presence or omission of brackets. Nissan is also encouraging its European suppliers to operate similar schemes.

The company has a small team whose job is to work with suppliers, both to help them improve their quality and to help them improve their productivity. 'Kaizen' is a concept of continuous improvement at every level in the company, which seeks to involve every individual in finding better ways of doing the job. It involves continuously seeking to find small improvements in quality, productivity, ease of working, or simply making a better working environment. Anyone who has an idea is given the opportunity and facilities to work the idea through. For larger projects, Kaizen teams are set up.

TRAINING

Nissan takes training very seriously and it is given a high priority. There are personalized individual continuous development programmes and every staff member has a programme of development of their own. Over 1,200 key elements of job skill, knowledge, and ability have been identified, enabling an individual development matrix to be created for every member of staff.

The programme starts with an induction course for all employees, which covers subjects such as Kaizen, the company philosophy, and the main production process. Next there is a 'core skills' programme, developing skills common to a group of employees. The professional part of the programme is related to skills required to carry out a specific function within a specific department. Finally, the personal programme develops employees in a variety of personal skills, tailored to their individual needs.

The idea behind all this training is that employees can sit down with their line managers and go through their personal continuous development plan to ensure that, over a period of time, they will have covered all the various aspects of their job to a validated proficiency level. This approach is unique in the motor industry and unusual in most other sectors of British industry. This is emphasized by Peter Wickens, the Personnel Director, who has said in a 1992 information leaflet:

Not only is this approach unique in the motor industry, it is also unusual within Nissan – we are the only company within the group addressing our training needs in this way.

ENVIRONMENTAL ASPECTS

The company says it is committed to producing products and using processes which conserve energy and resources and are environmentally responsible. Environmental concerns at the UK plant fall into three major areas: working environment for staff; energy, natural resource and raw material conservation in production; and the impact of the plant on the local economy.

The creation of an excellent working environment requires investment in the best technology available and careful planning of its use before installation. An example is the press shop, which is both very efficient and quiet. This was achieved by investing heavily in the latest, high-speed automatic transfer lines. Staff do not have to operate between the units in a noisy and difficult environment, as they would on a conventional press line; instead, the technology allows them to inspect and stack finished panels at the end of the line.

Another example is the aluminium casting shop, where a purpose-built filtration plant cleans all the exhaust gases to remove fumes and dust from the working environment. Clean air is discharged into the atmosphere.

Nissan's strategy in production is to minimize the amount of waste at every step of the production process. Where there is waste, it is monitored and disposed of in an environmentally friendly way. There is a growing awareness about the harm chlorofluorcarbon (CFC) gases are doing to the ozone layer. The Sunderland plant has never used CFCs in plastics processing and is working to remove them from vehicle air conditioning systems and a non-CFC refrigerant was introduced for the Primera in 1992.

A returnable or reusable packaging has been developed for use with its European suppliers, and the target of 95 per cent returnable packaging was achieved in 1992. Since 1991, components arriving from Japan have arrived in packaging, which is virtually 100 per cent returnable. The use of wooden cases has almost ceased. If used in 1992, they would have weighed more than 1500 tonnes.

In 1992, 20,000 tonnes of scrap steel will have been baled for recycling. Where possible, office staff use both sides of the paper when photocopying, and this saves over one million sheets of paper a year.

Energy is saved in a number of ways. Automatically controlled sensors turn lights off in certain production areas at the end of each shift and during breaks, saving over £15,000 per year. In storage areas, lights switch on only when activity is detected. In key parts of the plant, energy-saving circuits close down equipment during production breaks. The large, paint-drying ovens use a great deal of energy. In 1991 the thickness of the insulation layer was increased, and this saves over £26,000 a year. Along with other large UK companies, Nissan has signed the government's 'Declaration of commitment to energy management', which

commits the firm to regularly review the progress of improvements in energy conservation and to set performance targets which will be monitored and reported to employees.

There is concern about overall environmental impact. As far back as the planning stage in 1984, Nissan worked closely with the local water authority. In 1991, £1.7 million was spent in the latest water purifying technology and the quality of the water discharged from the plant is considerably better than the water authority requirements.

Another aspect of the company's concern for the environment is a reduction in the number of deliveries made by lorries. In December 1991, the pilot phase of a new logistics strategy was introduced. The haulier collects components from 33 Midlands-based suppliers for same-day delivery to the plant. This project reduces the number of road miles required by 3.9 million annually, which represents an 80 per cent reduction. Prior to this, each supplier delivered parts individually on a daily basis. Once the pilot scheme has been perfected, the approach will be extended to other road deliveries.

CONCLUSIONS

In the car industry, the move away from highly vertically integrated operations began in the early 1950s, with the initiative being taken by the fledgling Japanese producers. Nissan Motor Manufacturing (UK) Ltd is a good example of a modern, entirely integrated manufacturing facility, where efficient and lost-cost production has been achieved by heavy capital investment, advanced production techniques, and a skilled and motivated workforce. The productivity and quality standards being achieved in the Sunderland plant are both a threat and an opportunity to other European car manufacturers.

APPENDIX: JUST-IN-TIME

This very important concept is much more than just delivering materials on time. It is a management philosophy, and is essentially concerned

Exhibit 4.1
Output and other statistics

	1987	1988	1989	1990	1991
Japan	999,993	1,144,731	1,155,981	1,371,171	1,381,118
North America	908,373	695,103	693,925	669,018	592,090
Europe	460,368	486,214	521,130	521,130	502,587
Middle East	40,679	51,284	49,601	56,599	65,688
South East Asia	33,398	46,301	88,309	70,926	78,370
Africa	29,758	35,276	56,906	13,938	15,126
Latin America	101,082	110,355	117,860	134,788	159,073
Oceania	54,392	60,339	101,381	95,549	85,908
Others	5,456	6,805	4,248	941	1,134
Total	**1,633,506**	**1,491,677**	**1,633,360**	**1,563,555**	**1,499,976**

Note: Figures include both cars and commercial vehicles.

Source: Nissan Annual Report 1991.

Exhibit 4.2
Employment and production in Britain

	Employees	Domestic production	Export production	Total
1986	470	5,139	nil	5,139
1987	1,100	28,797	nil	28,797
1988	1,800	45,664	11,080	56,744
1989	2,500	42,827	34,164	76,991
1990	2,700	16,451	59,739	76,190
1991	3,000	11,800	112,700	124,500
1992	4,600	20%	80%	175,000
1993	4,600	35%	65%	270,000

Notes: 1 The percentage figures are estimates.
2 The total production figures for 1992 and 1993 are planned figures.

Source: Nissan Motor Manufacturing (UK) Ltd Fact File 1992.

Sub-assemblies that are incorporated into the final product arrive at the final assembly point just-in-time to be used. Finally, the finished goods are produced just-in-time for them to be sold. A consequence of this technique is that there are minimal amounts of stock and work in progress.

This concept and process may be compared and contrasted with the traditional Western approach to production management, which can be summed up as just-in-case. Here large amounts of components from outside suppliers are bought and stock-piled until needed in production; sub-assemblies are produced and stored as buffer stocks until they are required by the final assembly process; and finished goods are produced and stockpiled just-in-case there will be a buyer for them.

This, in outline, is the concept. A more detailed account is outside the scope of this book. A useful and approachable beginning to the technique is Oliver, N., *Productivity and Performance in the Japanese Car Industry*, Business Studies, November 1990. There are many more detailed accounts available. One is to be found in Dilworth, J., *Operations Management: Design, Planning, and Control for Manufacturing and Services*, McGraw-Hill, 1992.

with minimizing waste and maximizing added value. This approach to production management was pioneered by Japanese firms and is only slowly being adopted by European and North American companies.

The idea behind the concept and practice is very simple: parts which are made by outside suppliers arrive just-in-time to be incorporated into sub-assemblies or the final product.

QUESTIONS/DISCUSSION TOPICS

1 Does this case study tend to support the beneficial or deleterious view of the multinational enterprise?

2 Why did Nissan build a car plant in Europe and why did it locate this plant in the Sunderland area?

3 To what extent has Nissan adapted 'traditional' Japanese management practices to cater for the British cultural environment?

4 Should/could European car makers adopt the Nissan philosophy and manufacturing techniques?

CASE FIVE

GLOBAL TYRE WAR: PIRELLI VERSUS CONTINENTAL

LEIGH DAVISON, ALAN MARCHANT, RUDI GRUNWALD

ADVICE TO READERS

This case examines competitive interaction within the tyre industry, emphasizing the importance that all major players give to the achievement of global scope in all aspects of their operations as a prerequisite for success. This has provoked a spate of transnational mergers since the late 1980s, which have reduced the number of major manufacturers from ten to six as they have sought to establish or enhance their positions as global players.

The protracted and unsuccessful attempt by Pirelli to acquire Continental, its German rival, illustrates how differences in national business cultures and environments can frustrate globally-orientated strategies. For example, the development of a *level playing field* for international merger activity can impede.

THE GLOBAL TYRE INDUSTRY

In the summer of 1992, there was little sign that the global tyre industry was recovering from a severe recession characterized by over-capacity: tyre producers being squeezed by recession-hit car producers; bouts of price warfare; and, last but not least, further concentration within an industry already dominated by a small number of major players. Exhibit 5.1 illustrates world tyre market shares by volume.

Two propositions have been put forward to explain the vicious price wars of the late 1980s and early 1990s.

- Goodyear in North America, and Michelin in Europe, specifically instigated a downward fall in price; the aim being to dissuade Japanese tyre producers from expanding overseas. If this had been the aim it failed.

Exhibit 5.1
World tyre market shares by volume, 1990

Manufacturer	% share
Michelin	21.5
Goodyear	19.0
Bridgestone/Firestone	16.5
Continental	7.0
Pirelli	6.0
Sumitomo	6.0
Yokohama	4.5
Toyo	2.0
Cooper	1.5
Others	16.0

Note: The total market for car, bus and truck tyres in 1990 was estimated at 750 million units.

Source: Fundamental Research Incorporated, as quoted in the *Financial Times*, 2 December 1991.

- The 'beggar-thy-neighbour' philosophy prevailed, namely, if prices are kept low enough for long enough, the result is further concentration within the industry, and therefore when the recession lifts, profitability will be helped by this decrease in competition.

The spate of international mergers which erupted in the second half of the 1980s produced a further and dramatic increase in concentration within the industry. In 1978, for example, the five largest tyre manufacturers held 55 per cent of the market but by 1990 their share had risen to 70 per cent, confirming the impact of what had become a global tyre war.

The companies acquired during this period are summarized in Exhibit 5.2. The purchase of Uniroyal-Goodrich by Michelin, the French tyre giant, concluded this initial merger battle in 1989. Whilst Michelin, Bridgestone and Continental had emerged as clear winners, Pirelli had failed to acquire its prime target, Firestone.

In 1980 Bridgestone, a Japanese tyre concern, had only a small presence overseas, exporting tyres in the wake of emerging Japanese car sales. In 1988, however, its acquisition of the ailing US tyre giant, Firestone, boosted its share of the international tyre market from around 9 per cent to over 16 per cent. By gaining

manufacturing plants in both America and Europe, Bridgestone became a global player and, in so doing, had thwarted Pirelli's expansionary strategy.

Pirelli had been seeking to boost its very weak position in the US tyre market via acquisition of Firestone. If successful, this acquisition would have resulted in further production capacity in Europe and elevated Pirelli to the global 'big league', alongside the likes of Michelin and Goodyear, in addition to making it a major player in the USA. Although this prize went to Bridgestone, in 1988 Pirelli did succeed with a bid for Armstrong Rubber in the USA. The latter was but small fry compared to Firestone, but the acquisition represented for Pirelli an important bridgehead in the US market.

Like Bridgestone and Pirelli, Continental, the German tyre manufacturer based in Hanover, regarded a strategy of global expansion via acquisition as a critical requirement for its future success. This was confirmed in 1991 by Horst Urban who, at the time, was Continental's Chief Executive:

Throughout the 1980s we made great efforts to move from the purely nationally-oriented Conti [Continental] of the 1970s to create a global concern.

Horst Urban quoted in The *Financial Times*, 13 March 1991.

Exhibit 5.2
Principal tyre industry acquisitions, 1986–1989

Company sales[2]	Acquisition	Year	Cost[1] ($m)
Michelin (2,200)	Uniroyal-Goodrich	1989	1,500
Bridgestone (3,900)	Firestone	1988	2,260
Pirelli (469)	Armstrong Rubber	1988	200
Continental (1,100)	General Tire	1987	650
Sumitomo (450)	Dunlop	1986	240

Notes: 1 Cost refers to the purchase price.
2 Sales are those of the acquired company one year before purchase.

Source: Barclays de Zoete Wedd as quoted in the *Financial Times*, 14 July 1992.

This strategy manifested itself in the purchase of two European-based tyre producers, Uniroyal in 1979 and Semperit in 1985, together with the fifth largest American tyre producer, General Tire in 1987. Despite being in financial difficulties, General Tire gave Continental what was seen as vital access to the US, Canadian, and Mexican markets. By 1990 it also made Continental, the fourth largest tyre producer with over a 7 per cent share of the global market. This was a significant improvement on its 1985 position of 4.5 per cent, but its global scale was still dwarfed by each of the 'big three' (see Exhibit 5.1).

In 1990 Continental acquired a controlling interest in Mabor, a Portuguese company, and a 49 per cent equity holding in Nivis, a

Scandinavian organization, both of which were tyre manufacturers. Nivis owned the Oslo-based tyre dealership chain of Olrich A/S, together with a small number of other outlets. Nivis had been targeted for acquisition, because it was seen by Continental as a means of enhancing its competitive position.

Continental had also won either majority control or ownership influence in a number of other tyre dealerships in both Europe and the USA. In 1989 it acquired Heinrich Maurer GmbH in Germany, as well as minority interests in Glasgow-based Birkenshaw Tyre Ltd, which had 45 sales outlets, and Big 'O' Tires Inc. of Englewood, Colorado, which had 315 sales outlets. In 1990 it successfully bid for control of National Tyre Service of Stockport which, with control of over 408 outlets, was the second largest dealership chain in the UK.

THE PROTAGONISTS

THE PIRELLI GROUP

The ownership structure of Pirelli is illustrated in Exhibit 5.3. The Pirelli family, Leopoldo Pirelli being the group's Chairman, held around 10 per cent of Pirelli & C.'s equity. By acting in co-operation with other major share-holders, such as Mediobanca, the Agnelli family of Fiat and De Benedetti of Olivetti, the family had established a syndicate which collectively held the majority (about 57 per cent) of the company's equity.

Pirelli's manufacturing activities, formerly three divisions of Pirelli S.p.A., had recently been converted into legally separate entities. Pirelli Tyre Holding was listed on the Amsterdam Stock Exchange in late June of 1989, with 62 per cent of its equity being held by Pirelli S.p.A. and a further 15 per cent being controlled by Société Internationale Pirelli S.A.

PIRELLI TYRE

Pirelli Tyre was the world's fifth largest tyre manufacturer, behind Michelin, Goodyear, Bridgestone and Continental. Its products were manufactured through factories in Argentina, Brazil, Greece, Spain, Turkey, Italy, the UK, the USA and Germany. Tyres were sold predominantly under the Pirelli trade mark, for which it paid a licence fee under a contract with Pirelli

Exhibit 5.3
Pirelli ownership structure

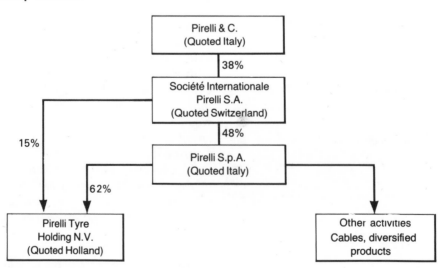

Source: Continental AG's letter to shareholders, 20 January, 1991.

S.p.A., and its largest markets included South America and Southern Europe.

CONTINENTAL AKTIENGESELLSCHAFT

Exhibit 5.4 illustrates the range of Continental's tyre and non-tyre activities, the latter comprising a range of rubber and plastic products manufactured by the ContiTech group for industrial usage. Between 1989 and 1990, ContiTech's share of total group sales increased from 20.8 per cent to 25.2 per cent. As from 1 January 1991, ContiTech's seven business units became separate legal entities.

The supervisory board and the management board

The title 'Aktiengesellschaft' (AG) indicates that Continental is the German equivalent of a British public limited company (PLC). Continental, like other AGs, had both a supervisory board and a management, or executive, board, (shown in Appendix 1); this 'two-tier-structure' is strikingly different from the British PLC, with its single board of directors.

The management board of directors is appointed by the supervisory board and, as well as conducting the business, the directors have to report to the latter regarding:

- the planned and intended business strategy and other fundamental aspects regarding the future development of the AG;
- the profitability of the AG and the return on equity;
- the current development of the business and sales development;
- any other 'important incidents'.

The following extract from Continental AG's annual report for 1989 illustrates the nature of the relationship between the company's supervisory board and its management board and confirms that the final word regarding company policy rested with the former:

At its meetings during the past year, at individual conferences, and through oral written reports, the supervisory board was provided regularly with detailed information about the company's position and progress, which it then discussed with the executive board.

These joint discussions were primarily concerned with the budget, medium- and long-term corporate planning, including capital investments, and basic questions about business policy and corporate structure. The supervisory board also ruled on those issues, which require its approval under the applicable statutory provisions ...

The primary task of Continental's supervisory board, as was the case for such boards of other AGs, is the control of management to ensure the successful performance of the AG and to enable them to carry out this obligation, the

Exhibit 5.4
Continental AG – group structure by sales acitvity

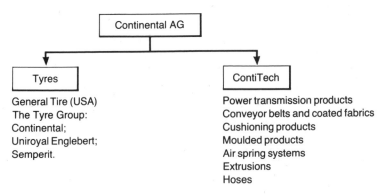

members of the supervisory board were empowered to:

- have access to all the company's books;
- call an extraordinary shareholders' meeting, whenever they regard it as necessary for the company's wellbeing;
- judge, and thereby decide upon, business matters that the management board cannot unilaterally engage in, for example, the closure or acquisition of a plant, or the sale of a subsidiary;
- dismiss one or all members of the management board 'if there is just cause'.

By employing more than 2,000 people on a regular basis, Continental AG automatically came under Germany's 'enlarged co-determination' rules, the significance of which was that 50 per cent of the members of its supervisory board were elected by a majority vote of shareholders at the annual general meeting. The remaining 50 per cent was a mixture of employees and trade-union representatives, chosen by the company's employees.

Shareholders

Shareholders in an AG have the right to dismiss members of the supervisory board. In most instances a 75 per cent majority of the votes cast is required, so that a 'blocking' vote only requires a minimum of just over 25 per cent of the vote. However, Continental's Articles of Association state that a simple majority vote of the shareholders present is all that is required to remove any member of its supervisory board. This can prove to be of vital importance to any predator seeking to gain control of the company.

Shareholders own the assets of the company and, under German rules, a predator can buy up to 25 per cent of an AG's equity without having to inform the AG. Moreover, as the ownership of bearer shares (the most common type of share in Germany) is not registered with the AG, the company may have little knowledge of the scale of the predator's equity holding until the 25 per cent figure is reached. For Continental and AGs in general, this

accumulation of equity by a predator will probably not be viewed as a serious cause for concern. This is because Continental, like other AGs, has stipulated in its Articles of Association that a shareholder – irrespective of the size of their equity holding in the company – can have a maximum of only 5 per cent of the voting rights. This is usually referred to as the '5 per cent rule'.

Continental's chief advisor during the Pirelli affair publicly sought to defend the 5 per cent rule, claiming that it certainly did not make a company 'bid-proof'. In fact, only one German company has ever succumbed to a hostile takeover: Feldmühle Nobel's acquisition by Stora. This method, although imperfect, does ensure that any predator must have the support of other shareholders for it to be able to gain control. The 'rule' is there to protect the interests of minority shareholders – or, more likely, to afford the same power to the management and supervisory boards.

Further support for the keeping of the 5 per cent rule came, not surprisingly, from Urban himself. In echoing Continental's advisers, Urban argued that, in the absence of takeover rules in Germany and without a voting rights limitation, Continental could be vulnerable to a 'secret takeover' that the shareholders did not necessarily want.

Germany could be some sort of Wild West, or if you like a Wild East, for all takeover attempts – be they friendly or hostile.

Urban, as quoted in *The European*, (15–17 March 1991)

Despite such arguments, and before Pirelli came onto the scene, a group of Continental shareholders supporting a national pressure group in favour of the principle of 'one share, one vote', known collectively as the Deutsche Schutzvereinigung Für Wertpapierbesitz, or DSW, had actively sought removal of the company's 5 per cent rule. At the annual general meeting in 1990, the DSW put forward a formal motion to eliminate the voting rights limitation, which received the support of 49 per cent of those votes represented.

WHY CONTINENTAL? – THE VIEW FROM MILAN

Given the difficulties inherent in any unwelcome attempt to acquire a German AG, Pirelli's motives warrant closer examination. Both Leopoldo Pirelli, the Chairman of Pirelli, and Carlo Banchieri, its director of tyre production and a leading player in the merger attempt, sought to demonstrate why the proposed takeover made strategic sense in the context of the global tyre industry. Their arguments in favour of a takeover focused upon three key areas: research and development; marketing and production technology; and geographic spread.

RESEARCH AND DEVELOPMENT (R&D)

According to estimates presented by Pirelli, neither Continental's nor its own spending on R&D matched that of their bigger rivals, Michelin, Goodyear, or Bridgestone. However, Pirelli claimed that R&D expenditure was of ever-increasing strategic importance, due to the growing diversity of tyre types and sizes demanded by high-performance car manufacturers; so that any company offering less than the full range of tyres would lose market share. The apparent drawback of this stance is the associated R&D costs, which could be a considerable burden for mid-sized tyre producers such as Continental and Pirelli. A merger between them would generate significant economies of scale, according to Pirelli.

MARKETING

Pirelli argued that, unlike its own tyres – the bulk of which were marketed under its own name and were clearly perceived as occupying a niche in the premium tyre sector – Continental's three marques, Uniroyal, Semperit and Continental, were viewed as having a more diffuse image. The merger, Pirelli claimed, would enable the establishment of a more coherent marketing strategy, with each marque being targeted at a particular market segment. Some overlap would be tolerated to give an impression of inter-brand competition and retain the illusion of consumer choice.

PRODUCTION TECHNOLOGY

Pirelli argued that considerable benefits could be derived from sharing tyre-making knowledge with Continental, and by using the combined resources of the merged companies more efficiently. In particular, Banchieri claimed the merger would allow Continental access to Pirelli's technology for the automated production of premium quality performance car tyres. This, Pirelli held, could be of considerable value to Continental, for the German company could then improve its established, but underexploited, presence in the high-performance tyre market.

GEOGRAPHICAL SPREAD

The Italian camp contended that in Europe the two companies are tailor-made for each other, with Continental's strength lying north of the Alps and Pirelli being dominant to the south. Concerning the US and Latin American markets, Pirelli asserted that the 'fit is even more complementary'. In the USA, it claimed that the Pirelli and Continental subsidiaries, Armstrong Rubber and General Tire respectively, were individually 'small beer', demanding considerable investment. Together, however, they would represent a significant bridgehead, having over 15 per cent of the replacement market for tyres and approximately 10 per cent of the market for 'original' tyres supplied to US car makers.

Given the broad segmentation of the US market, Pirelli went even further regarding benefits that would accrue from this link-up of forces. Like Michelin, their arch rival, the merged group would be able to furnish a multi-brand marketing strategy in the USA. Banchieri declared that: 'it makes a very complete package – full brand, full product, full segmentation.' (Quoted in the *Financial Times*, (13 March 1991).

In the Latin American market, where Pirelli operated a plant in both Brazil and Argentina,

Continental had no real presence. Pirelli feared that Bridgestone could use its ownership of Firestone, which was active in the region, to introduce Bridgestone tyres. Banchieri argued that this challenge could be met by Pirelli using its plants to introduce Continental's marques into the region. In the case of the Mexican market, Pirelli claimed that the situation is reversed, in that Pirelli's tyres could be manufactured in the factories of General Tire, itself a Continental subsidiary.

THE WARBURG ANALYSIS – IN SUPPORT OF MILAN

The financial outcome of the proposed merger between Pirelli and Continental was effectively given the 'thumbs up' by the Warburg Bank. Its report estimated the value of the resultant synergistic effects, after allowing for a transitionary phase, at about DM 400 million per annum, quantified as follows:

- DM 100 million, arising from increased market share, enabling the new group greater influence on pricing;
- DM 100 million, because of higher revenue or reduced costs on account of optimizing the range of products offered – taking regional tastes into consideration of course;
- DM 100 million, resulting from improved standardization of production across plants and on account of improvements in purchasing;
- DM 50 million, cost savings by merging the two companies' respective research and development operations;
- DM 50 million, cost saving to be achieved by greater co-ordination of distribution and marketing functions.

THE RESPONSE FROM HANOVER

Urban Horst, Continental's Chief Executive, was instrumental in forging and strongly advocating what became known as Continental's 'stand alone policy', adopted by the company's management as the response to Pirelli's

unwanted overtures. In rejecting Pirelli's so-called 'friendly' intentions and, at the same time, claiming that the proposed takeover was most definitely not in the best interests of both shareholders and employees, Continental's management – and in particular Urban – defended their chosen stance with a range of arguments as detailed below.

GLOBALIZATION AND GEOGRAPHIC FIT

Thanks to its existing strategy of acquiring carefully selected companies, Continental already regarded itself as being well on the way to becoming a major global player in the tyre business and did not envisage a role for Pirelli in that process.

In Europe, this strategy included its takeover of Mabor, a Portuguese tyre producer, in 1989, and in 1990 its purchase of a 49 per cent stake in Nivis, a Swedish company owning two tyre producers, Gislaved Daeck Production of Sweden and Viking Dekk Produksjon of Norway. The following comment by Wilhelm Winterstein, Vice-Chairman of Continental's management board, reveals the underlying logic: '... European south-west flank covered by joint venture factory Mabor ... northern flank secured by Nivis ...'. (Wilhelm Winterstein, quoted in *Tyres & Accessories*, August 1991).

In its analysis of the move, the trade publication reached exactly the opposite conclusion: 'Mabor alone cannot 'cover Europe's south-western flank', Nivis does not 'secure the northern flank'...'. (*Tyres & Accessories, ibid.*)

Regarding the liberalization of eastern Europe, Continental stressed that it had already taken steps to ensure the company was positioned to take full advantage of these emergent markets. As evidence of this, it cited its talks with Barum, a Czechoslovakian tyre manufacturer, and its recent agreement with Stomil, a Polish tyre producer, whereby the Polish concern would in future manufacture Continental tyres under licence.

What, then, of Turkey and South America? Continental's position was highlighted in a letter written by John Craven, the Chairman of

Morgan Grenfell Bank, to the *Financial Times* (14 February 1991). The Morgan Grenfell Bank, which is owned by Deutsche Bank, acted as an adviser to Continental in its efforts to repulse Pirelli's unwanted takeover attempt. The Deutsche Bank is represented on Continental's supervisory board. The letter reads:

> ... there is not a 'good business fit' between the two groups [Continental and Pirelli]. Apart from anything else, Pirelli has a major exposure to Turkey and South America and a merger would therefore detract from Continental's strong focus on the important markets of Europe, North America and the Far East.

A month later, at an extra-ordinary shareholders' meeting called by Alberto Vicari, Horst Urban argued that, due to the inherent political and economic instability of South America, Continental had no strategic interest at all in the region.

TERMS OF THE PROPOSED DEAL

In September 1990 Pirelli officially notified Continental of its proposals for merging the two groups. After due consideration, the management of Continental was extremely critical of the terms of the merger proposal. Pirelli proposed that the initial phase of the merger process would involve Continental purchasing Pirelli PTH, at an estimated price tag of around DM 1.85 to 2.25 billion. Continental was to finance the purchase by increasing its borrowings and, secondly, by undertaking a rights issue. Thereafter, Pirelli would form a syndicate of shareholders to give it control of the merged company.

Continental justified its rejection of the Pirelli proposal on the following grounds.

- Continental would have had to take on substantial loans – estimated by the company at between DM 0.4 to 1.25 billion – at a time when conditions in the tyre industry had deteriorated markedly.

- Continental was informed by each of its two advisers, Morgan Grenfell and Goldman Sachs International, that the true value of Pirelli PTH was its then market capitalization of DM 0.73 billion. In other words, Continental was being asked to pay a huge premium of more than DM 1.0 billion over and above the market value of the Pirelli PTH. This led John Craven of Morgan Grenfell to declare:

> This must be the first time a company has expected to pay a massive premium to lose rather than acquire control of a business.
>
> Quoted in the *Financial Times*, (14 February 1991)

SOLE SUPPLIER

Continental asserted that the proposed deal with Pirelli PTH could result in a net reduction in tyre sales for the merged company. It claimed that German car producers, fearful of over-reliance upon one tyre supplier, had in the past sought to ensure that their purchases were spread across a number of suppliers. The merger might lead to some car producers being too highly dependent upon the new company, an imbalance they would probably seek to correct.

FINANCIAL STRENGTH

Continental further stressed that it, and not Pirelli PTH, was by far the stronger of the two in financial terms. The direct inference was a questioning of the competence of senior management at Pirelli PTH. To support this view, in a letter to its shareholders, dated 12 January 1991, Continental pointed out that:

- despite the poor trading situation which prevailed in the tyre market, it was still expecting to make after tax profits for the second half of 1990 of around DM 40 million, whilst Pirelli PTH was anticipating a loss of about DM 36 million;

- whilst its shares had fallen in value by 36 per cent since 30 June 1989, those of Pirelli PTH had dropped by a staggering 66 per cent.

SYNERGIES

Continental sought to refute Pirelli's assertion that the synergies resulting from the proposed merger would amount to additional profits before tax of DM 400 million per annum. It contended that a realistic figure was about DM 100 million per annum because:

- the merger would not, given the highly competitive nature of the tyre business, enable the new group to have a greater influence upon pricing, as originally claimed by Pirelli;
- the merger could lead to a reduction in tyre sales;
- the highly complex job of integrating the two groups would be costly and detract from fighting the opposition.

FUTURE CO-OPERATION

Having firmly rejected Pirelli's proposal for merger, Continental did offer co-operation:

> ... we informed Pirelli that, under the given circumstances, we are not prepared to engage in further discussions of a merger, but offered at the same time to join them in investigating whether synergies could be achieved through co-operation, without running the risks inherent in a merger.

> Continental Aktiengesellschaft
> Annual Report, 1990

THE ATTEMPTED TAKEOVER: A CHRONOLOGY

On 15 September 1990 Pirelli formally advised Continental that it intended to take control of the German company by instigating a 'friendly' merger. Just over a week later, on 24 September, Continental's executive board openly rejected what it described as a 'hostile' takeover by Pirelli, but indicated that the door remained open for co-operation between the two groups.

By the end of September, Pirelli declared to the press that the company and its allies, known as a 'concert party', held over 50 per cent of Continental AG's voting equity. Given the German rules on the disclosure of share ownership in an AG, Continental was not in a position to either refute or verify Pirelli's claim. At one time or another during the attempted takeover, Pirelli's 'concert party' included:

Concert party member of Continental AG	Equity stake in percentage
Pirelli	5
Mediobanca	5
Sopaf SpA	5
Intalmobilare	3
Fiat	less than 4
Riunione Adriatica di Sicurta	2.5

It has been alleged that the response from some of the 'big players' in German industry and banking was to set up a concert party, or defence pool, to protect Continental AG. Urban vehemently denied that he, acting on behalf of Continental, organized such a defence pool. This denial is not surprising, as the existence of a defence pool could be seen as a breach of the law. On the other hand, it seems probable that Continental had the support of the following equity holders: Deutsche Bank, Nord-Deutsche Landesbank, Daimler-Benz, BMW and Volkswagen.

The next major event in the saga came on 12 December 1990 when Alberto Vicari, representing the required 5 per cent of Continental's equity, asked for an extraordinary meeting of shareholders so that, amongst other things, the uncertainty surrounding the future of Continental AG could be resolved. The meeting was arranged for 13 March 1991. Vicari, somewhat of a mystery figure from Wiesbaden, claimed that he had no interests in the Pirelli group, although he openly admitted that he was prepared to support a merger. He was duly disowned by both Pirelli and Continental. The following critical resolutions were to be voted on at the meeting.

1 The revision of the voting rights limitations will henceforth require a majority of at least 75 per cent of the votes cast and the equity present at the meeting.
2 The removal of members of the supervisory board who have been elected by the shareholders will require a majority of at least 75 per cent of the votes cast and the equity present at the meeting.
3 The elimination of the voting rights limitation.
4 The management board are instructed to take all the necessary steps to enable the next ordinary shareholders' meeting to adopt a resolution 'that Continental AG shall acquire the tyre business of Pirelli Tyre Holding NV, Amsterdam, . . .' [in other words, to merge].

On 21 January 1991, in a letter to the shareholders accompanying the invitation to the extraordinary meeting of its shareholders, Continental's management put forward its recommendations on how the shareholders should vote. Somewhat surprisingly, and for reasons that are not wholly clear, the management advocated that shareholders should vote against resolution number 2 on the agenda. It also recommended that shareholders should reject both the resolution seeking to remove the voting rights and that instructing management to prepare the ground for a merger with Pirelli. The management, however, was in favour of resolution number 1.

THE EXTRAORDINARY MEETING OF SHAREHOLDERS

On 13 March 1991 approximately 2,000 people, representing 79 per cent of Continental's equity, gathered in the Congress-Centrum Stadpark, Hanover, to listen to nine hours of speeches before deciding upon Continental's future. Included was a virtuoso performance by Urban in forceful defence of Continental's 'stand alone policy'. From the ranks of the opposition came Gert Silber-Bonz, Chairman of Pirelli Deutschland, who, after re-stating Pirelli's friendly intentions towards Continental,

went on to assert that the merger made strategic sense and that Pirelli would not have shown any interest in Continental if it had not first had the support of important representatives of German industry. Vicario, the instigator of the meeting, attacked Urban by accusing Continental's chief executive of having actively sought to create a defence pool – a charge which Urban, of course, denied. Vicario then advocated that, if the voting rights limitation were dropped, Continental should be reorganized and Pirelli should take control of its supervisory board.

When, at last, it was time for the shareholders to vote, 66 per cent of the equity present voted for the removal of the voting rights restriction. In the case of resolution number 4 – instructing Continental's Management Board to prepare the ground for a merger with Pirelli, which would be voted on at the next annual general meeting – 46 per cent of the equity present abstained from voting. Of those who did vote, 89 per cent were against the motion whilst only 11 per cent supported it. Prior to the meeting the Pirelli camp, on the grounds that it wished to keep the negotiations friendly, made it known to the press that Pirelli would abstain on resolution 4. The fact that the abstentions equalled only 36 per cent of Continental's voting stock, led the management and its advisers to conclude that Pirelli lacked sufficient support from the shareholders to take control of Continental. Resolutions 1 and 2 were heavily defeated, very much against the wishes of Continental's management.

Continental's shareholders had voted to maintain the status quo, whereby a simple majority of the equity present at a meeting was all that was needed to alter the voting rights limitation. They did, however, support the management view to retain the rule that a simple majority was all that was required to remove a member of the supervisory board.

AFTERMATH

Pirelli had failed in its attempt to gain control of Continental, but even in January 1992 it still held shares and options amounting to around 39 per cent of Continental's voting equity. In a letter to its shareholders, Pirelli revealed that it had expended over $106 million to give it the right to purchase options on 32 per cent of Continental's equity held by allies. In other words, it had paid a premium of $37 per share for the option to buy them at any time during the next five years. This expenditure and other costs incurred in the attempted takeover of Continental pushed Pirelli's financial position deeper into the red.

> *Together, capital losses on PTH's own Continental shares, legal costs and acquisition of the options account for around L340 bn of Pirelli's estimated L590 bn loss for 1991. A further L240 bn stems from restructuring costs in the tyres and cables divisions, while operating losses account for L110 bn.*
>
> Financial Times, 14 January 1992

To shore up its ailing finances, Pirelli has since been forced to take a number of steps including a rights share issue, a L1,500 billion loan arranged by Mediobanca and Credito Italiano, and an attempted sale of its diversified products division, the latter including activities in shoes, clothes and industrial and automotive components. Somewhat ironically, Continental has expressed interest in some of the concerns involved.

For the Pirelli camp, the major gain made at the critical extraordinary meeting of shareholders in March 1991 was the removal of the voting rights restriction. However, the legitimacy of this resolution was subsequently contested in a Hanover court. Towards the end of May 1992, the court annulled the motion, ruling that in March 1991 Pirelli had failed to disclose

that it controlled over 25 per cent of Continental's equity. This directly led Pirelli to attempt to get a similar motion passed at Continental's next annual general meeting, which was timetabled for 3 July. Continental's counter-blow came on 2 July, when it sought a definitive ruling from the court, limiting the Pirelli camp as a whole to a 5 per cent voting right. Pirelli immediately contested the legality of Continental's stance.

At the annual general meeting, Ulrich Weiss, chairman of Continental's Supervisory Board and member of Deutsche Bank's Executive Board, ruled that Pirelli and its associates would remain limited to a 5 per cent voting right. Otherwise, he claimed, Pirelli 'would have control of the company' (quoted in the *Financial Times*, 4–5 July 1991). Pirelli's response was to declare that it would challenge Weiss' ruling, and all other decisions made at the meeting in the courts. This signalled that relations between the two groups had hit a new low.

The world tyre industry continues to be plagued by overcapacity, fierce competition and, for some companies, onerous debt and stock levels. During 1992 new car sales worldwide fell by over 3 per cent, the largest sales reduction since the recession of 1980–81, with the US and most European markets experiencing their third year of cumulative decline. All leading tyre makers have continued to see profits slump as their industry has become locked into a seemingly endless spiral of declining demand, leading to cut-throat competition to preserve market share. Although the initial battle between Pirelli and Continental is over, in such a hostile environment the global tyre war is set to continue and further dramatic restructuring of the industry appears unavoidable.

APPENDIX 1: SUPERVISORY AND MANAGEMENT BOARDS

Exhibit 5.5a
Membership of Continental AG Supervisory Board 1990 (excluding employee representatives)

Ulrich Weiss	Member of Board of Managing Directors, Deutsche Bank AG
Hans H. Angermueller	Shearman & Sterling, New York
Werner Breitschwerdt	Member of the Supervisory Board, Daimler-Benz AG
Hans Detlev von Garnier	Director of Deutsche Bank AG
Wilhelm Helms	Legal Counsel and Notary Public
Hans-Olaf Henkel	President IBM Deutschland GmbH
Ernst Pieper	Chairman of the Managing Board Preussag AG
Klaus Piltz	Chairman of the Managing Board Veba AG
Friedrich Schiefer	Member of the Managing Board Allianz AG Holding

Source: Continental AG Annual Report, May, 1991.

Exhibit 5.5b
Membership of Continental AG Executive Board 1990

Horst W. Urban	Chairman
Wilhelm Borgmann	Vice Chairman
Haimo Fortmann	Tire Manufacturing
Peter Haverbeck	ContiTech
Hans Kauth	Director of Personnel
Ingolf Knaup	Corporate Finance
Günter H. Sieber	Tyre Marketing and Sales
Wilhelm P. Winterstein	Controlling and Logistics

Source: Continental AG Annual Report, May, 1991.

APPENDIX 2: PERFORMANCE INDICATORS

Exhibit 5.6a
Western world tyre market percentage shares

By manufacturer:		By product:		By area:	
Sumitomo	4	Car	46	Europe	29
Goodyear	17	Motorcycle	2	North America	38
Bridgestone	19	Van	14	Japan	13
Pirelli	6	Truck	31	Latin America	7
Continental	7	Agricultural	4		
Michelin	21				
Cooper	1				
Others	25	Others	3	Others	13
	100		100		100

Source: Adapted from the *Financial Times*, 14 July, 1992.

Exhibit 5.6b
Estimated share of world tyre market by company

Company	% Share:	
	1980	*1989*
Pirelli	6.5	6.3
Continental	3.9	8.1

Source: Derived from company reports.

Exhibit 5.6c
Share price indices as at January 1991 (June 1989 = 100)

Continental	64
Michelin	37
Pirelli Tyre	34
Goodyear	33
Bridgestone	58

Note: Based on prices quoted on the Amsterdam Stock Exchange.

Source: Information supplied by Continental AG to its shareholders on 20 January, 1991.

Exhibit 5.6d
Sales analysis by product and geographic region, 1989

	Continental % of total company sales		Pirelli Tyre % of total company sales
By product:		*By product*:	
Cars	42	Cars	54
Agricultural	2	Agricultural	7
Trucks and CVs	29	Trucks and CVs	24
Other tyres	6	Other tyres	11
ContiTech	21	Motorcycles	4
By region:		*By region*:	
Germany	35	Western Europe	50
Rest of Europe	28	North America	23
North America	33	South America	17
Other	4		

Source: Company reports.

QUESTIONS/DISCUSSION TOPICS

1 Appraise the contention that the German business environment was responsible for destroying Pirelli's ambition of expanding its global presence.

2 Evaluate the relative strategic logic of the cases presented by Continental and Pirelli regarding the proposed merger.

3 What role did financial institutions play in the attempted merger?

4 If the merger had been agreed, what do you consider would have been the major problems involved in integrating the global operations of Continental and Pirelli?

5 How do you envisage the global tyre industry is likely to develop in the future?

MARCONI RADAR SYSTEMS LTD/ NOBELTECH SYSTEMS AB: INTERNATIONAL COLLABORATION IN THE MARKET FOR AIR TRAFFIC CONTROL SYSTEMS

ELIZABETH HILL, JOHN MACDONALD AND MARGARET ROBINS

ADVICE TO READERS

This case illustrates how changes in the technological and political environments of companies can lead to collaboration rather than competition.

THE STRUCTURE OF THE MARKET

Air Traffic Control (ATC) is a process for enabling the safe passage of aircraft across national boundaries and is therefore, by definition, a matter of international interest.

Hence the market for air traffic control systems, namely the hardware and software which facilitate this process, is interwoven with a diverse range of interested parties, including commercial and industrial institutions, financiers and governments from a wide geographical base. In terms of market segments, there is a broad division between civil and military ATC systems, but in both cases, the products which are serving the market are at the forefront of technological development.

INTERNATIONAL COMPETITION

Much of the market for ATC products exists in western Europe and the USA. Until the 1980s, supply to these markets had been dominated by domestic manufacturers. However, as market saturation approached, with the emphasis of demand turning to 'renovation' rather than replacement systems in the West, suppliers were looking further afield for their new business. US companies began looking to world markets for their expansion. Raytheon and IBM, leading players in the US air traffic control market, have both formed international ATC units, following estimates that over $2 billion will be spent outside the USA on acquiring or upgrading ATC systems during the 1990s.

A significant proportion of this demand is likely to come from the growing east European markets. Whilst little finance is being made available, a few new initiatives are beginning. An Italian firm, Alenia, has already received approval to work with a variety of institutes and production factories in the

Commonwealth of Independent States (CIS) to develop a new ATC system which will improve long-term, international air services across the region. Because Alenia moved quickly to establish a presence in the market, competition for this bid was limited, but the company anticipates a much tougher battle for business in the future, as other international players enter the ring. The US Department of Commerce has already organized an aerospace trade mission to Hungary, Poland and Czechoslovakia, and US export legislation is being relaxed for many non-military high-technology items, including radar.

Several other developing markets are also prompting a move towards international competition. The Asian/Pacific rim markets, traditionally the stronghold of Japanese companies, are being targeted by European firms. Evidence of this emerged at the Asian Aerospace '92 show in Singapore, where these companies had a strong presence. Alenia decided to forego direct participation at the Farnborough Air Show in England in favour of the Singapore Show. French companies were also present, with Thomson CSF having already won a variety of civil and military contracts in South East Asia.

CIVIL AVIATION IN EUROPE

The management of civil airspace in Europe involves a number of international institutions.

THE EUROPEAN CIVIL AVIATION CONFERENCE (ECAC)

This is an intergovernmental organization comprising 28 states (see Appendix 3 for a list of members), each Member State being represented by its Transport Minister. Active since 1955, the remit of ECAC is to promote the co-ordination, better utilization and orderly development of European civil aviation in the economic, technical security and safety fields. In practice, this means that ECAC provides a forum for international debate and decision-making, but with each ECAC member defending its own airspace sovereignty, political interests can influence proceedings. Lacking any financial or organizational powers, ECAC normally works through Eurocontrol to develop operational requirements for advanced air traffic systems.

EUROCONTROL

The European Organization for the Safety of Air Navigation comprises aviation experts from 12 Member States (as listed in Appendix 2), whose role is to promote the safety and efficiency of air traffic flow throughout Europe. More specifically, its primary tasks are as follows:

- to analyse the future needs of air traffic and new techniques necessary for meeting such needs;
- to develop and adopt common long-term objectives in the field of air navigation;
- to co-ordinate the medium-term, national plans of Member States, in order to establish a common plan in respect of air traffic services and facilities;
- to promote common policies for ground and airborne navigation systems and the training of the staff of Air Traffic Services;
- to study and promote measures for improving cost-effectiveness and efficiency in the field of air navigation;
- to promote and conduct studies, tests and trials relating to air navigation;
- to examine matters in the field of air navigation being studied by the International Civil Aviation Organization, and other organizations concerned with civil aviation;
- to study amendments to the Regional Air Navigational Plans to be submitted to the International Civil Aviation Organization;
- to assist Member States, and interested Non-member States, in the institution and operation of an international, air traffic, flow management system;
- to establish and collect charges levied on users of air navigation services in accordance

with the Multilateral Agreement relating to Route Charges, and on behalf of the Member States and of Non-member States who are parties to that Agreement;

- to concert any other measures that the Member States deem necessary to ensure the safe, orderly flow of air traffic.

Financing of Eurocontrol is via contributions from Member States, the size of these contributions being determined in accordance with a formula which is based on their Gross National Product and their annual costs for air traffic services purposes.

EUROCONTROL AGENCY

This is a branch of the main Eurocontrol Organization. In addition to undertaking tasks connected with planning, studies, engineering, air traffic flow management and the collection of route charges, the Agency is also entrusted with providing air traffic services in the airspace of certain Member States. In all these tasks, it co-operates closely with the national civil and military authorities, in order to achieve its aims as efficiently and economically as possible.

THE EUROPEAN COMMUNITY

Although the European Community has no specific remit in the context of air traffic control, because it embodies the formal union of European sovereign states it is an important catalyst for interactive dialogue between Member States. It also provides some funding for national ATC research in parallel with Eurocontrol projects. Arguments have been put forward for the EC to manage and operate the entire European ATC network, but this is resisted by many because of their allegedly bureaucratic systems.

These organizations have different institutional, political and financial powers in the geographical areas they cover, so interaction and collaboration between them is a prerequisite for any pan-European ATC developments.

THE HISTORY OF COLLABORATION IN THE ATC INDUSTRY

POLITICAL ORIGINS OF COLLABORATION

As long ago as 1963, when the Eurocontrol Convention relating to co-operation for the safety of air navigation came into force, the foundations were laid for collaborative partnerships in Europe between industries and countries. The impetus for collaboration at this time was mainly political, with consortia from a spread of EC Member States being favoured for early Eurocontrol projects. For example, one such project for a simulator system at Bretigny was awarded to a consortium of companies from Germany, Belgium, France, and the UK.

A MOVE TO COMPETITIVE TENDERING

In the early days, true competitive tendering was rare. Even if lip-service was paid to the process, the governments who financed the projects expected a return in the form of contracts to their domestic industries, so political pressure was brought to bear on any purchasing decisions. However, as more companies entered the market, the criteria for awarding contracts had to be made explicit and by the late 1970s, competitive tendering had been reconsidered, with sealed bids being invited for the major projects. This caused serious problems for the industry, for several reasons.

Firstly, the process of bidding itself was very costly. Bids had to be 'compliant', that is conform to specification, before they would be considered. In many cases, in an attempt to prove compliance, there was a requirement to undertake a significant amount of research and development before a bid could be submitted. If no bids were fully compliant, which was often the case, then the percentage compliance against price had to be considered. These factors greatly increased the risk and cost of failing to secure the contract. Consequently, companies started to submit bids at minimum prices and profits fell as customer requirements became more complex.

Many of the companies who successfully landed contracts found that these would be completed at a financial loss, as the cost of development often exceeded original estimates. Newly designed, unproven systems often proved problematic, and the customers were subjected to late deliveries and products which fell short of their specifications. As a result of this, manufacturers often fell foul of financial penalty clauses written into the contracts.

If the investment cost in research and development for a particular bid could have been spread across future similar contracts, perhaps these issues would have been less problematic. However, at this time air traffic control systems were specified by national authorities in such a way that they had to be tailor-made, so the individuality of each system solution precluded any economies of scale in future development work.

All parties seemed to be suffering under the sealed bid system. Some companies left the industry, whilst others suffered acute financial hardship. The customer was supplied with non-compliant projects, which were completed late as a result of underfunding. The industry had become cautious, and new ways had to be found to enable technically advanced systems to be built efficiently, economically and with an acceptable level of risk for all concerned.

DEVELOPMENTS OF THE 1980s

To overcome the problems of the previous decade, a new pattern of competition had to emerge, which addressed several of the key issues.

COMMONALITY OF ATC SYSTEMS

If the investment in development for a major bid could be spread across a series of similar projects, the financial incentive for up-front research would be far greater. This investment represented a 'sunk cost' in the event of failure to win a contract. To achieve this situation required the national authorities to come to an agreement on a standardized ATC system to be used by all.

OFF-THE-SHELF COMPONENTS AND SUB-SYSTEMS

Even if complete systems for an individual customer require a substantial bespoke element, it is likely that the component parts of those systems can be designed to standardized specifications, thereby minimizing the new development work required for any project.

CO-OPERATION OF NATIONAL AUTHORITIES IN SYSTEM SPECIFICATION

A lack of communication between customer and manufacturer when the original tender was written had led to difficulties, or even inability to comply with specification. In addition, it had required the dissipation of effort into technical development which could perhaps have been avoided altogether if a more continuous dialogue were maintained between the parties. Co-operation at this stage had the potential for helping both manufacturers to understand customer objectives and expectations, and customers to understand the technological limitations facing their suppliers.

SHARED DEVELOPMENT COSTS

For companies to work autonomously and simultaneously, with identical project objectives, implies duplication of effort and cost. Shared development could reduce this overlap and minimize cost for all parties.

SPECIALIZATION

To produce complete systems in-house requires heavy investment and thus implies substantial risk. Focus on a narrower product range in a field in which a company holds specific technical expertise is more desirable from a commercial point of view, as this improves the potential for greater financial returns. However, the consequence of this type of specialization is that an individual company is unable to pursue projects alone, because of its inability to supply all the necessary component parts and expertise. Collaboration with a partner then becomes a prerequisite for submitting a bid.

THE GROWTH OF INTER-COMPANY ALLIANCES

In response to the changing nature of the market, brought about by the system of competitive tendering, companies in the industry started to look to each other to fill gaps in their portfolios. Many were only in a position to bid for a contract in alliance with a partner possessing complementary skills, products and expertise. These alliances took one of two general forms.

1 MERGERS AND ACQUISITIONS

In the 1980s mergers and acquisitions became more common, in particular across the Atlantic. The European and US segments may not have held the greatest potential for growth in the world market, but their financial strengths relative to other territories made them attractive propositions. Companies interested in pursuing opportunities across the Atlantic started to recognize that the workings of each other's markets showed some significant differences. For example, in the USA, it is common for the Federal Aviation Administration (FAA) to undertake its own engineering research and development, and then present a detailed tender document outlining its specific needs. The contractor that wins then builds to specification, but in some cases the FAA will fund the initial development as far as the third prototype phase. In Europe, research and development has traditionally taken place at the suppliers' expense, and even then at the risk of failing to win a contract on price grounds.

It was recognized that to compete in these transatlantic markets required local knowledge, and also that the markets were too heavily competitive to profitably allow room for numerous foreign entrants. Hence the flurry of acquisition activity from the mid-1980s onwards; for example, US-based Raytheon acquired Cossor of the UK, and Hughes Aircraft took over UK manufacturer Rediffusion. In the reverse direction, Thomson-CSF bought out US ATC manufacturer, Wilcox, and Siemens bought Cardion.

Already a major multinational, IBM was an interesting exception to this. Choosing to grow organically, the company established a working group in Europe to bid for contracts in that area.

If the trend towards acquisition and merger continues, it seems likely that the 1990s will see the emergence of just a few multinational companies to dominate the ATC market.

2 JOINT VENTURES

Whereas merger and acquisition imply permanent collaboration, other co-operative activity started to develop on a project basis, with companies forming one-off alliances to bid for specific contracts. Often, a smaller company with specific knowledge in a limited field could help a larger organization win a contract by this type of joint venture. This was a particularly popular route if a potential partner existed in the country offering the contract; the likelihood of success increased if there was a link with a domestic organization. One implication of this type of joint-venture was that a company could be bidding with a partner for one contract, but against that same organization in the next.

Whom to choose as a partner for any particular bid was a tricky decision. Client preference is a major consideration, with some customers influencing companies towards a specific partner, often on nationalistic grounds. It then has to be decided whether the partner should be an equal or a sub-contractor. Even if equal partnership is agreed, there is a tendency for one company to take the lead. Joint ventures are not necessarily limited to one partner either, and multi-company consortia are sometimes appropriate on large contracts, though the costs involved in managing these network alliances normally preclude them on smaller projects.

Sometimes, even if a potential partner appears to offer appropriate expertise and products, they may be ruled out on the grounds of financial risk, political instability or even managerial ability. The strength of the international planning and control process can make or break a project. Communications have to take into account language barriers, time differences and geographical distances, and deadlines may be affected by cultural factors such as summer holiday periods or religious festivals. Contracts between partners have to be highly formalized, covering issues such as product ownership, financial arrangements and logistical responsibilities, to prevent subsequent disputes between the parties.

In the final analysis, the choice of partners is influenced by a variety of factors, especially:

- customer preference;
- product;
- technical performance and reliability;
- background/expertise;
- commercial/financial suitability;
- political implications.

Basically, all large companies would prefer to go it alone, retaining profits and control, but at times a careful choice of partner is beneficial to the winning and delivery of a contract. From the small enterprises' point of view, the best opportunities they have for involvement in large-scale projects is to be a part of a contract gained by a larger competitor.

TWO MAJOR SUPPLIERS

MARCONI RADAR SYSTEMS

The Marconi Company was founded by the Italian Guglielmo Marconi in 1897 and was the world's first radio company. Shortly after the Second World War, it was bought by the English Electric Company, who set up a number of product divisions based on specialist knowledge and experience in a specific branch of electronics. Service equipment, subsequently renamed Radar Division, was one of these divisions, specializing in what was then a comparatively new technology. It quickly established for the company a world-wide reputation as a leading supplier of radar equipment and systems for both military and civil roles.

The merger between the General Electric Company and English Electric in 1968 led to the formation of Britain's largest electronics group, GEC-Marconi Electronics Ltd. The following year, the radar interests of the two groups were concentrated under single management, and Marconi Radar Systems Ltd was born, thus creating the largest ground radar organization in Europe. The company became responsible for all GEC business in radar and data handling for air defence, shipborne defence, air traffic control and for military applications of control engineering. Queen's Awards for both export achievement and technological achievement were bestowed in the 1980s.

The year 1991 saw the merger of Marconi Radar with Marconi Command and Control Systems Ltd, to form Marconi Radar and Control Systems Ltd. This subsidiary is but one of over 30 companies which form the Electronic Systems Division of GEC. In 1991, this division showed a turnover of £2,811 million and a profit of £263 million, with the order book at year-end standing at £4,720 million. Marconi Radar Systems contributes to these figures. Only half of the turnover of the division was attributable to UK customers, with the rest coming from a wide variety of world markets.

Marconi Radar is the largest radar manufacturer in the UK, and has its products in use in over half the countries in the world. The company describes itself as producing a range of primary and secondary radars, display and data systems of civil and military air traffic control. Commitment to product support service is seen as a major strength. Installation, maintenance, refurbishment, repair and training are all provided world-wide. Research and development is also given the highest priority. High proportions of turnover are invested in future developments, and the research facilities of the GEC group are available for use. Marconi Radar employs just over 2,000 people, with more than 400 engineers involved in hardware and software development. Quality is also emphasized. This is partly driven by the demands of the military markets, where products must conform to standards laid down by NATO.

NOBELTECH SYSTEMS AB

The origins of Nobel Industries date back to the 19th century, when the scientist Alfred Nobel, the founder of the Nobel Prize, built up a large industrial empire following his invention of dynamite. Nobel Industries is Sweden's largest chemicals and ordnance company, together with a significant interest in high-technology electronics. In the 1980s the group underwent substantial change during a period of very rapid growth. The group's strategic objective is to be active in those areas in which competitive advantages for international expansion can be achieved from a Scandinavian base.

A number of areas have been identified for further development. These include consumer products, such as adhesives, paints and toiletries; chemicals for the pulp and paper industries; niche products in specialist hi-tech markets, such as biotechnology and explosives; and electronics and electro-optical products, including defence systems and civil air traffic control.

NobelTech Systems AB is one subsidiary of Nobel Industries, having evolved from the acquisition of Philips Electronikindustrien in 1989 and a subsequent acquisition of shares in the Command and Control Systems Division of Ericsson Radar Electronics AB. Ericsson had historical links with Marconi, dating back to the 1920s. (The history of links between Marconi and NobelTech are illustrated in Appendix 1). Thus the company is currently 100 per cent owned by Nobel Industries, making it an all Swedish company, with its headquarters near Stockholm.

Defence electronics form the core of the company's activities, the main domestic customer being the Swedish Armed Forces. A major Swedish defence contract called STRIC is currently under way, with Marconi operating as a sub-contractor. However, international trade with 20 countries accounts for about two-thirds of sales, with clients ranging from

Exhibit 6.1
The concept of multi-radar tracking

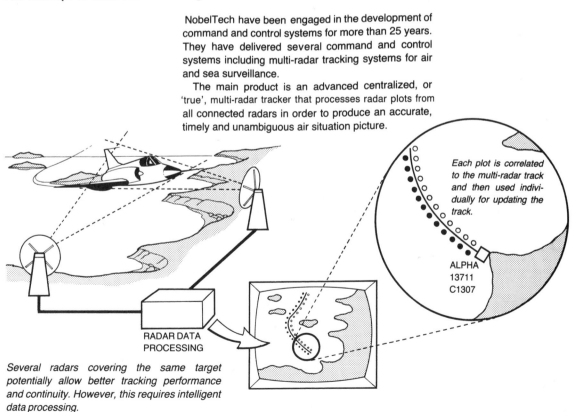

NobelTech have been engaged in the development of command and control systems for more than 25 years. They have delivered several command and control systems including multi-radar tracking systems for air and sea surveillance.

The main product is an advanced centralized, or 'true', multi-radar tracker that processes radar plots from all connected radars in order to produce an accurate, timely and unambiguous air situation picture.

Each plot is correlated to the multi-radar track and then used individually for updating the track.

ALPHA
13711
C1307

RADAR DATA
PROCESSING

Several radars covering the same target potentially allow better tracking performance and continuity. However, this requires intelligent data processing.

defence organizations and local governments to shipyards, aircraft manufacturers and civil aviation boards. The company has 1,100 employees, and in 1991, invoiced sales stood at £188 million and the order book stood at £619 million.

In the field of air traffic control, the company is recognized as having specialist expertise in a number of areas. In particular, its Multi-Radar Tracker is one of the most advanced systems in the world, integrating the radar data supplied by a number of individual radars to provide clear, unambiguous, air pictures. This system is illustrated in Exhibit 6.1.

International recognition has also been achieved for the development of effective tools and methods for air traffic controller training. This has stemmed from development emphasis on ergonomically designed work-stations, which focus on the man/machine interface, aiming to offer the controller comfort whilst keeping him or her alert and receptive. All NobelTech ATC products make use of advanced computer software, which is based on international standards to provide flexibility in application and allow the upgrading or exchange of related hardware.

A PAN-EUROPEAN ATC PROJECT

A DRIVE TOWARDS INTEGRATED ATC SYSTEMS

At a meeting of the transport ministers of ECAC member states in Paris on 24 April 1990, attention was drawn to the substantial growth which is forecast in air traffic demand in the ECAC area to the end of the century and beyond. It was also noted that considerable efforts were being deployed throughout the Continent to expand the system accordingly and to reduce air traffic congestion in Europe. In order to unite and accelerate these efforts, they announced the launch of the EATCHIP programme (European ATC Harmonization and Integration Programme). The objective of the programme was for the progressive integration of ATC systems to be completed by 1995 in high-density traffic areas, and by 1998 in other areas.

Eurocontrol was deemed to have the required expertise to implement an action plan working towards the establishment of a pan-European system for the management of air-space. Thus it was invited to set up the institutional and financial arrangements for the management of such a plan.

PRODUCT REQUIREMENT

One of the problems facing Eurocontrol was the diversity of ATC systems in operation in the region. Practically all ATC operators had different radar data processing systems, with different levels of sophistication, different hardware and software, and different performances. Most systems had been developed to operate autonomously. However, because several national governments were planning and studying the replacement and update of their present equipment, Eurocontrol commenced the search for systems which could be standardized across Member States. One example of this project is the provision of an ATC Radar Tracker and Server (ARTAS).

The project was put up for tender, with Eurocontrol Member States eligible to bid, though members of ECAC could be sub-contracted.

ARTAS

Marconi, as part of their normal marketing function, maintain good channels of communication with Eurocontrol and were thus well able to follow closely the progress of ARTAS. As the project developed and drew nearer, Marconi approached NobelTech regarding a possible collaboration. Within a month of that first contact, a mutual agreement to jointly pursue the project was reached. It was estimated that roughly 50 per cent of the work would be carried out by Marconi and 50 per cent by NobelTech.

In May 1991, approximately 11 groups, including some consortia, were invited by Eurocontrol to a series of pre-selection meetings. Of these, three were selected to take part in the bid: Thompson CSF/NLR; Hughes/Alcatel and Marconi/NobelTech. The final decision by Eurocontrol is expected in March 1993.

APPENDIX 1

THE HISTORY OF LINKS BETWEEN MARCONI AND NOBELTECH

1920

Svenska Radio AB

LM Ericsson	Marconi
50%	50%

EARLY 1950s

Svenska Radio AB

LM Ericsson	Marconi
70%	30%

LATE 1950s

Swedish government awarded Marconi Radar a large and prestigious defence contract. Svenska Radio were also associated with this work.

EARLY 1980s

Marconi sold their shares to LM Ericsson who now own 100 per cent of the company which is now re-named Ericsson Radio Systems AB. Datasaab AB was acquired to strengthen and complement the business activities.

Ericsson Radio Systems AB

100% Ericsson	Datasaab

LATE 1980s

The Swedish government commenced discussions on an update to the 1950 Defence contract and opened a channel of discussion with Ericsson and Philips. Marconi approached both Ericsson and Philips with a view to collaboration on this project.

1990s

Bofors Electronics AB (part of the Nobel Group) acquired first Philips, and secondly the Command and Control Division of Ericsson. The Swedish government awarded Bofors Electronics AB the STRIC Project. The newly merged company is re-named:

NobelTech Systems AB

Nobel
100%

NobelTech Systems AB awarded a sub-contract to Marconi to carry out work on the Swedish Defence Project.

APPENDIX 2

THE 12 MEMBER STATES OF EUROCONTROL

Belgium	Luxembourg
Germany	Netherlands
France	Portugal
United Kingdom	Cyprus
Greece	Malta
Ireland	Turkey

APPENDIX 3

THE 28 MEMBER STATES OF ECAC

Finland	Norway	Czechoslovakia	Italy
Iceland	Hungary	Austria	Cyprus
Poland	Sweden	Switzerland	Malta
Romania	Yugoslavia	Denmark	Turkey
Germany	France	UK	Greece
Ireland	Luxembourg	Netherlands	Portugal
Monaco	Bulgaria	Spain	Belgium

QUESTIONS/DISCUSSION TOPICS

1 Identify the benefits and drawbacks to both Marconi and NobelTech in collaborating on this project.

2 What do you foresee as the major project management difficulties?

3 Assess the value of joint ventures in the markets for technologically advanced products. In what other contexts might strategic alliances prove beneficial?

CASE SEVEN

NH GEOTECH: AN INTERNATIONAL CORPORATION'S RESPONSE TO A CONTRACTING MARKET

JILL PRESTON

ADVICE TO READER

This case shows how one international corporation within the Fiat Group has responded strategically to a major contraction in the European market for agricultural machinery. It also illustrates certain aspects of operational management at the international level, including human resources management and product development.

INTRODUCTION

In May 1991 the farm and industrial machinery company of NH Geotech was formed as a result of a merger between Fiat Geotech and Ford New Holland. This case study focuses on the process of the merger, which was in part a strategic response to the declining world market for agricultural machinery. The new company intends to keep its separate brand names and sales networks:

The company views its brand names as its most valuable asset and these will continue and compete in the market place.
Peter Quaglia, Vice-President

Whilst keeping its brand names, the company aims to obtain synergies and economies of scale in areas such as common purchasing, R&D, engineering and production. In addition, both the Fiat and the Ford New Holland organizations had a range of joint ventures and alliances in many countries and it has been agreed that most of these will continue.

BACKGROUND

The Fiat Group, which controls the new

I should like to express my thanks to Mr Peter Quaglia, Vice-President, Communications and External Relations, NH Geotech Ltd, for his enthusiastic help and advice in the development of this case study.

company, holds 80 per cent of its shares; in addition, it has a four-year option to take over the remaining 20 per cent. NH Geotech is one of the world's three leading manufacturers of farm and construction equipment, with a turnover in 1991 of over $4 billion, and approximately 30,000 employees.

Both Fiat and Ford were involved in the mechanization of the agricultural industry in the early part of the 20th century. For example, Ford began manufacturing tractors in 1917, and the first Fiat tractor appeared in 1919.

From the 1920s both companies gradually developed their global positions in tractors and each made the necessary acquisitions to offer a wide range of products. Fiat acquired the Hesston Corporation, a well-known name in the hay and forage handling and harvesting machinery business. This part of the Fiat organization grew rapidly, especially in the years from 1945 to the early 1970s. In addition, Fiat designed track-type farm equipment for use as heavy duty quarry and construction-site machinery. With the establishment of FiatAllis and Fiat-Hitachi brands, the organization developed a complete line of products ranging from intermediate and heavy track-type vehicles to wheeled loaders and excavators. Under the FiatAgri brand name were incorporated Laverda, which was founded in 1874 and acquired in 1975; Braud, founded in 1854; and Hesston, founded in 1947.

In the period from 1945, Ford had concentrated on the development of light versatile machines, for example, the tractor loader backhoe. In 1986 Ford acquired New Holland, a company formed in 1895 in the Pennsylvania town of the same name, and then acquired Versatile, a Canadian corporation formed in 1954.

In global terms, Ford's world-wide organization outside Europe was larger than that of Fiat; the latter had tended to concentrate mainly in Italy, France, Germany and Switzerland. Significantly, it had not been highly successful in the UK market. In addition, the Fiat Group had a presence in eastern Europe, with permanent representative offices in some COMECON countries.

SOME ISSUES WITHIN THE SECTOR

By the late 1980s, the market for agricultural machinery, both in Europe and in much of the rest of the world, was in decline. For example, during the period 1986–1991, the demand for tractors and combined harvesters saw an overall drop of 40 per cent in the Western world. This situation was caused by structural changes in agriculture, especially in Europe. Therefore it seems unlikely that the situation will improve in the short or medium term.

During this period, the world industry overall has seen the disappearance of a volume of sales equivalent to about 180,000–190,000 tractors. To take one example, of the 1200 dealers in France in 1991, 100 had gone out of business and at the time of writing it was estimated that in 1992 another 200 would follow.

In May 1992 the EC Agricultural Ministers reached agreement on the reform of the Common Agricultural Policy (CAP), the main objective being to reduce the prices of produce to competitive world market levels. The subsidies, which had encouraged farmers to produce more, were in part substituted by a sort of rental income for land 'set aside' or left untilled. For example, 15 per cent of Britain's agricultural land will be set aside.

The reforms of the CAP had become urgent as the system, based on price guarantees for an unlimited amount of produce, weighed more and more on the EC budget. Measures taken during the 1980s, such as the introduction of milk quotas, had failed to solve the problems. The CAP had become increasingly difficult to administer and certain excess products, such as meat, oil and wine, failed to find an outlet, and to stock the surpluses was becoming increasingly expensive. International pressure to reform the CAP had also grown with the Uruguay Round of the GATT trade negotiations.

The main feature of the reforms is to reduce the production of some items and to bring the industry more in line with modern environmental requirements. For example, the removal of grain subsidies will have a severe impact on those countries, such as Italy and Spain, which have a large proportion of small farm holdings.

European farmers have only been given four or five years to absorb a revolution: for a group who thinks in terms of generations, this period of time is somewhat short.

Riccardo Ruggeri, Chief Executive of
NH Geotech

The reforms in the CAP will result in a dramatic decline in the demand for tractors and combines and most other forms of farm machinery. During the 1980s the demand for tractors fell, from 300,000 to 150,000 in 1992, and this decline is likely to increase during the last decade of the century. In continental Europe, the aggregation of farming properties will result in a substantially lower demand for tractors, but these will require increased power.

In the last 20 years the average size of French farms has doubled and by the early 1990s was 30 hectares. The average size of British farms is around twice that size, but that is only one-fifth of American holdings. The extent of the Italian problem is illustrated by the fact that, on average, the size of farms is one-tenth that of British farms.

The larger farms will be most affected by the 'set aside' rule and the demand for agricultural machinery will be radically affected. Countries in southern Europe will be able to convert to specialized fruit and vegetable crops because of their climate, but advantages will only be gained by these farmers if they are able to improve their distribution networks. Riccardo Ruggeri has suggested that, apart from the small specialized manufacturers of farm machinery, only the large producers will survive.

The reconstruction of eastern Europe is a major opportunity for the agricultural machinery sector. In this part of Europe, land is being returned to farmers, as a come-back from large, state-owned properties to individual properties is occurring. Many of these farm holdings have low-quality agricultural machinery; for example, a 30 per cent grain loss on a combine harvester is not unusual. A major problem, of course, is that these countries lack the resources to acquire modern machinery in sufficient numbers. Joint ventures in all areas, including agricultural machinery manufacture, are difficult and expensive for Western companies, because there are few entrepreneurial skills within these countries.

Semi-developed countries, such as Malaysia, Thailand and Indonesia, as well as countries in the Middle East and South America, have large potential markets for agricultural machinery. For example, India has not only reached self-sufficiency for food, but by the early 1990s had become a food exporter. In India, the demand for tractors is increasing steadily and is served by local manufacturers with foreign participation. Through a joint venture, NH Geotech holds a significant share of this market.

One of the problems facing many developing countries is that they are very dependent on aid-funding, and by the late 1980s much of this aid had been reduced and was being funnelled into eastern and central Europe. In addition, from the mid-1980s many semi-developed countries, such as Brazil, made attempts to develop their own industrial sector; NH Geotech owns a manufacturing company in that country. The Group holds a number of licensing agreements with other developing countries, whereby the assembly of tractors takes place on the ground, and these licensing agreements often include a local content clause. Although this is business for NHG, it has only a limited value.

At the time of writing, a number of countries in South America were in the process of forming a free trade area. In addition, the USA, Canada and Mexico were establishing a free trade zone. NHG sees these developments as major marketing opportunities.

The North American agricultural economy has gone through a slow and constant process of restructuring and by the early 1990s had stabilized. At the time of writing, the GATT negotiations had not reached settlement; the results of these negotiations may have a major impact on this area.

THE MERGER

During the post-war period, Fiat grew mainly in Europe, especially in Italy, France, Germany

231

and Spain, and by the 1970s it had obtained the number one market-share for tractors. In addition, the company had interests in Argentina, Central Africa and the Middle East, but it had few outlets in the Americas or the Far East.

During the 1980s, Ford had taken a strategic decision to concentrate on its core business of cars, trucks and financial services. The company disposed of its aerospace and steel divisions in 1990 and 1991 respectively. The acquisition of New Holland in 1986 was part of this process of rationalization.

Thanks to complementary world market cover, product range and location of its plants, along with various types of joint ventures, the merger with Ford New Holland was the opportunity Fiat was looking for. For example, FNH had a strong presence outside Europe, especially in North America, Brazil and the Far East. In addition, the American company had valuable know-how in the highly specialized sector of agricultural machines and its sales force had extensive international experience.

Fiat sees the agricultural sector as an integral part of its core business and views the establishment of NHG as part of its strategy to expand quickly and to compete as a world market-leader. The Group intends to reach higher production volumes in order to achieve maximum economies of scale and obtain a more balanced market coverage.

The merger negotiations began in the Spring of 1990 and from the earliest stages, plans were being developed so that once the contracts were signed, the strategy was very close to being ready for implementation. The first six months of the new Group was a period of high risk. Not only was the world going through a major recession, but its main competitors were subjecting NH Geotech to fierce competition by taking advantage of the inevitable uncertainties associated with the merger. For example, a number of competitors suggested that the separate brand names within NHG would soon disappear.

To obtain the necessary economies of scale as quickly as possible, the Group adopted strategies to cut production volumes fast. For example, the workforce was cut drastically

from 30,366 employees in December 1990 to 24,108 by the end of 1991. The Group used a wide range of policies to cushion the social costs of this process.

ORGANIZATIONAL STRUCTURE

What kind of organization is required to cope with an increasingly complex and fast-moving international environment? Many companies recognize the need to speed up decision-making by reducing bureaucracy and flattening the organization. A complementary approach is to develop more flexible structures, by experimenting with task forces and project teams. Decentralization to focus resources on particular markets is an additional way which companies have developed to cope with the international environment. However, some companies are taking a very different route; in effect, they are increasing the degree of integration of their international organizations.

NH Geotech is a holding company established under Dutch law, but the parent company of NH Geotech has its world-wide co-ordination offices in London. During the restructuring process it was decided to establish a number of 'operating divisions'. These divisions were given responsibility for products, manufacturing and marketing respectively.

The 'co-ordination centre', was established in London, because this was seen as an ideal, 'neutral' location for a small group of managers from the two groups to consolidate the company, co-ordinate operations, prepare plans and blend the different organizational cultures which had been combined. The company argues that London has established itself as a crucial 'meeting table' at which positions are compared and consensus reached.

The new NH Geotech structure was in place by January 1992. Exhibit 7.1 illustrates the organization of the Group as of October 1992. But it should be remembered that the principal feature of the world of NH Geotech is 'change' and therefore obsolescence is built into the system. Exhibit 7.2 outlines the main committees within Geotech.

Exhibit 7.1
The organizational structure of NH Geotech, October 1992

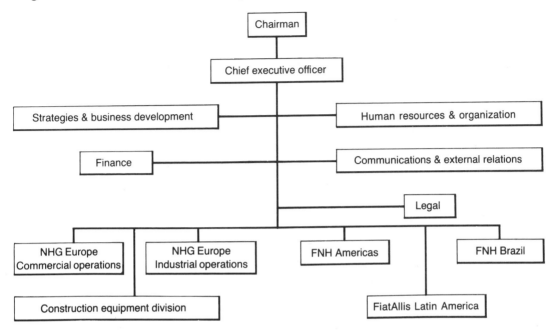

Exhibit 7.2
Committees within NH Geotech, October 1992

The company has five companies/operating divisions, and 18 manufacturing plants located in the USA, Italy, Great Britain, Brazil, Belgium and France. There are five research and development units, located in Italy, the USA and Belgium.

Gradually, the major factories are being transformed into workshops, as processes such as administration and finance are centralized.

Clearly, the management information system (MIS), is crucial to all of this.

The sales and service network operates in 130 countries through more than 6,000 outlets, which include branches, importers and dealers. In addition, through various types of joint ventures and licensing agreements, NH Geotech operates in such key markets as Turkey, Pakistan, India, Mexico and Japan.

OPERATING DIVISIONS

These consist of the following:

1 strategies and business development, product planning operations for all lines and manufacturing/marketing systems relating thereto, strategic marketing, logistics, quality, manufacturing policies and purchasing policies;
2 finance;
3 human resources and organization;
4 communications and external relations;
5 legal.

233

The headquarters is responsible for co-ordinating the various operating divisions. The headquarters is responsible for:

- the definition of objectives and policies;
- the allocation of resources;
- the promotion of synergies;
- the evaluation and control of business performance.

The decision-making body of NH Geotech is the executive committee, which meets monthly and draws on the co-ordinating committee, which in turn includes the heads of the functions listed above and the heads of the four operating divisions, as follows.

NH GEOTECH EUROPE – COMMERCIAL OPERATIONS

This division is in charge of marketing, sales and service for the FiatAgri and FNH product lines in Europe and world-wide, except for the Americas. This unit uses the commercial organizations based at Modena in Italy and Basildon in England. The head of this operation reports directly to the Chief Executive Officer and co-operates with the central 'Strategies and business development' function with regard to product market and quality aspects.

NH GEOTECH EUROPE – INDUSTRIAL OPERATIONS

This unit is responsible for the designing, testing, manufacturing and purchasing of all FiatAgri and FNH product lines in Europe and world-wide. This includes the various licences and industrial co-operation agreements, except for the Americas. As well as running the factories, the division also has engineering centres in Modena, Basildon and Zedelgem, Belgium. It is also responsible for Sicurcab of Turin, Italy, which specializes in the construction of driver modules.

The head of these operations reports directly to the Chief Executive Officer and co-operates with the central 'Strategies and business development' function for industrial policies, purchasing and quality issues.

FNH AMERICAS

This division has overall responsibility for the production and marketing operations for the FNH product line in the Americas (except Brazil) and for the FiatAgri line in North America, with the exception of Quebec. It also supervises the Woods Division (lawn and garden machines) and the Mexican joint venture. The headquarters of the division is at New Holland, Pennsylvania. The head of these operations reports to the Chief Executive Officer and collaborates with the various central functions.

FNH BRAZIL

This unit is responsible for all production and marketing operations in Brazil for the FNH line of both tractors and combines, which have been concentrated in the Curitiba factory. The head of these operations reports to the chief executive officer and collaborates with all the central functions.

FIATALLIS, FIAT-HITACHI AND BENITA

The construction machinery division (FiatAllis, Fiat-Hitachi and Benita) with headquarters in Turin and FiatAllis Latin America, Brazil, is the fifth unit within the corporation. Negotiations were in progress during 1992 to develop joint ventures with experienced, specialist partners, in order to relaunch this highly specialized field of operation. This strategy is a continuation of the joint venture developed with Hitachi in the hydraulic excavators business.

The structure is functional and integrated for Europe, and divisional and decentralized for the Americas. This organization structure responds to the objective of achieving the maximum flexibility required by markets which differ deeply in structure, product types and commercial traditions.

Joint ventures within NH Geotech are more concerned with looking at longer term aims, which is similar in style to typical Japanese joint ventures.

THE MANUFACTURING ORGANIZATION

Each of the operating divisions has been given specific missions in terms of product development and engineering, with clearly defined geographic marketing responsibilities. The Group aims to achieve manufacturing integration, from components to finished machines, with the allocation to the factories of specific product missions. Economies of scale are being achieved by plant saturation, rationalization of factories and 'make or buy' policies and purchasing. In addition, human resources are being used more efficiently, for example, by concentrating on clearly defined missions and by bringing together forces which had previously worked separately and on parallel lines.

ENGINES

Iveco, a Fiat Group company and a world leader in trucks and diesel engines, provides product engineering support. The future engines of NH Geotech will consist of both the Iveco 8000 series with three and four cylinders, and the Genesis series with four and six cylinders, naturally aspired and turbo-charged, covering the power range from 45 to 240 CV.

FACTORIES

The NH Geotech Group includes the following factories.

Modena Final assembly of FiatAgri tractors: medium-low, medium-high and high horsepower ranges; machining and production of components such as transmissions, drive shafts and hydraulics.
Basildon Final assembly of low and medium-low HP range Ford tractors; production of Genesis engines.
Jesi Final assembly of small tractors and 'special' tractors for vineyards and orchards and crawlers.
Antwerp Production of gears, transmissions and axles, and final assembly of Ford series 8030 tractors for the markets of Europe and the rest of the world; and the TLBs.

Zedelgem Production of combines, hay and forage machines and components for back-hoe loaders.
Breganze Production of Laverda combines.
Coex Production of self-propelled and pull-type grape harvesters and hay and forage machinery.

Production and marketing are handled by the Operating Divisions, based at Modena and Turin in Italy; New Holland, Pennsylvania; Curitiba in Brazil; and near Brussels, in Belgium.

ORGANIZATIONAL PROCESSES

The primary requirement when the new Group was formed was to guarantee the smooth continuity of day-to-day production and commercial operations. At the point of merger, the Group faced major problems for, in addition to the major recession in agricultural machinery, the two organizations were very diverse in terms of history, culture, processes and procedures.

These two organizations had to be integrated as quickly as possible in order to achieve the economies of scale required to meet the Group's targets. The background to the factory in Belgium was Flemish and although the Fiat Group had tackled alliances with diverse organizations, Ford had only limited experience in this area and was far less adaptable.

One of the problems facing the new organization was that the merger between Ford and New Holland had not resulted in anything like full integration. New Holland was a harvester company, whilst Ford was a tractor company. 'The Ford tractor was really a carbon copy of their car.' Therefore, in reality, the corporation was concerned with integrating three companies, not just two.

Fiat emphasizes the concept of the project team. Teams within the Group include finance, marketing and purchasing people as well as engineers. Early on in the development of the organization, working groups were established for four areas:

- manufacturing;
- product development;

- systems;
- legal issues.

Each of these areas benefits from seminars with participants from the Group's world-wide organization; encouragement is given to the development of professional families across borders.

Peter Quaglia argues that, in a major corporation, terms such as 'line' and 'staff' are largely obsolete. A modern organization is process-driven with a range of activities going on simultaneously.

When two groups of companies come together a range of problems have to be addressed. To take one issue, product development has a range of different meanings within organizations. A similar point can be made about purchasing; for example, in Fiat, purchasing is a corporate function, therefore purchasers are prime movers in the organization.

A major issue within any international organization is the relationship between the HQ and other units. Within NHG, decisions on strategic issues are taken centrally, but after much discussion within the Group, a consensus is usually reached. Decisions such as make or buy, and investment decisions, are taken centrally.

During the development of the Corporation two or three levels within the hierarchy were removed. Senior management argues that there is a high degree of accountability but at the same time substantial autonomy, of local units:

> ... in decision making we view ourselves as one organization in partnership, not as HQ and separate subsidiaries.
>
> Peter Quaglia

The style of decision-making in NHG is illustrated by the way budgetary decisions are taken. Between September and November the budgetary process is very much one of continuous discussion between the central and the operating units. The agreed budget is not an authority to spend, but a guideline or ceiling. Every major project developed at the local level requires the authorization of the co-ordinating committee.

The accountability and control processes in FNH were very different from those found in Fiat. Once the budget for the following year had been agreed within FNH, things went ahead with no questions asked. There was a kind of contract, but very little direction. 'In FNH people in the field were left alone, but many felt that no one cared,' said a senior spokesman.

HUMAN RESOURCES MANAGEMENT

The Group covers a wide range of nationalities and attempts to manage cultural diversity effectively. For example, Geotech people move from one country to another for a significant period of time – not just for the duration of an individual project, which tends to be the more usual American practice. This mobility is happening at the managerial level; by 1992, it was also beginning to happen at lower levels within the hierarchies.

NHG rates the following attributes as essential for the international manager within the Corporation:

- intelligence;
- honesty and openness to change;
- good interpersonal skills and the ability to work in a variety of different groups;
- international awareness: 'We do not want people who are encapsulated in some kind of ecosystem, Americans even bring their own water';
- the ability to correctly interpret the values of the company culture and the ability to hold a dialogue with other cultures;
- good leadership skills;
- good communication skills.

There is a general belief within the organization that no one should stay in a staff position for more than two years and the Corporation is very much results-orientated; status symbols are not important.

> *People within this type of organization must have grown up in areas other than those benefiting from constant growth. They must have experienced recession and crisis. Darwinism must have touched them directly.*
>
> Peter Quaglia

In all plants there are active trade unions, especially in Belgium, Italy and the UK. In general terms, employee relations are good; for example, in June 1992 a three-year agreement was reached in the UK, with few disputes; and in February 1992 managers within the corporation agreed not to take a salary increase. It has been agreed that all sections of the organization should show a willingness to make sacrifices, shareholders as well as managers and other staff.

The integration of the new Group by the use of effective communication procedures was a major priority in the early days of its establishment. 'We have a high degree of transparency.' For example, every month senior executives record on video the problems and the results. This video is disseminated to all factories within 48 hours. Peter Quaglia argues that this approach has been very well received.

We are very visible in all locations. [The Chief Executive has the policy of visiting one location each month in turn.] People visibility is regarded as very important.

A major organizational focus of the Group for integration is the co-ordinating centre in London. Peter Quaglia argues that communication is a crucial aspect of integration. For example, the co-ordinating committee, which is composed of corporate senior managers as well as the heads of the operating units, meets once a month. The staff at London number only 50, but people throughout the organization use it as a 'cultural bridge': 'If there are difficulties, we offer London as a forum'.

The reduction of staff from 30,000 to 22,000 was both painful and costly, but plant closures have been kept to a minimum, as the Group is very aware of the political repercussions of closures.

MANAGEMENT INFORMATION SYSTEMS

Matching the MIS of two Companies is very difficult. The system reflects the business practices of organizations and these can be very different, as was the case with FNH and Fiat. One issue is that within one organization some element of an IS will be old, and some will have been more recently installed. At any one time there is likely to be a complete mix of old and new elements.

In any organization, a common MIS is essential for effective integration, but it represents a major cost. For example, Fiat and FNH had quite different ways of costing products and without harmonization, it would have been quite impossible to compare costs. During a short transitionary period, the corporation kept two systems going, whilst at the same time developing a common system in areas of high priority. A major issue is to try to ensure that living data is not lost during this process, but it is crucial that work goes on whilst these new systems are developed and implemented.

If we waited until we were ready, we would be out of business.

Eugene Alacevich, Vice President,
Information Systems

The MIS within the corporation is viewed as being pro-active. This section has the task of identifying problems and suggesting ways to overcome them. In the development of the new MIS, NH Geotech set up a list of fundamental priorities which would require a high degree of harmonization early on in development. For example, the warranty of products was given high priority. Information on claims is a critical part of quality control within the organization, so early harmonization in this area was essential. Some options are, of course, too expensive, but others are absolutely essential – for example, information must be in a wide range of languages.

The product lines in Ford and Fiat were quite different, and there were two quite separate coding systems. It was decided that both of these two systems must operate for a transitionary period. This is satisfactory whilst the two product ranges are quite separate, but harmonization will be crucial when, for example, some of the FNH and Fiat tractors start to have common components. As far as the dealers are concerned, as long as there are two distinct networks of dealers the MIS can be separate, but when individual dealers hold both franchises the two systems will have to be harmonized.

NH Geotech has attempted to overcome some of the resistance often associated with the implementation of new systems. For example, the technical IS staff prefer to involve the users in helping to train colleagues. There have been times when the technology was used as an excuse for not implementing an unpopular decision.

MARKETING

During the first year of operation there was much uncertainty, which was not helped by a number of the competitors suggesting to dealers that the FNH and Fiat brand names would soon disappear. The competition in the USA was particularly aggressive at this time – for example, there was a very aggressive programme of promotion and stock liquidation to exploit these uncertainties.

At an early stage, it was decided to continue with the two brand names (although where possible unified components will be developed), a major factor being that in this sector consumer taste is conservative. In addition, the relative strength of the two former companies in different parts of Europe was an important element in this decision and it was agreed that customer loyalty to the trade marks must be fully exploited. 'We can attack our competitors on two fronts by our marketing.'

It is clear that by the mid-1990s, and certainly by 2010, the European market will be very small. The objective of NH Geotech is to position itself as a product leader, in terms of innovation and quality, while at the same time achieving maximum efficiency. A number of strategic marketing decisions will have be taken as the decade develops. For example, will it be appropriate for the Group to continue with two separate brands, in all or any of its markets?

Western industry has gone for greater sophistication and greater horsepower in agricultural machinery. This development has tended to ignore the large, but less sophisticated and cheaper markets of the developing world, for example, India and Mexico. The Indian Government is highly protectionist, although its market for tractors by the early 1990s was higher than that in Europe. During the 1980s this market had been growing at a rate of 10 per cent per annum.

Prices of products are determined by the individual market:

1991 Sales
Tractors   70,809
Combines   4,327
Agricultural machinery   13,452
Industrial tractors and construction machines   13,971

The consolidated balance sheet for 1992 is likely to show a sharp increase over 1991.

PURCHASING

One of the main aims of the merger was to achieve economies of scale. Substantial economies are being obtained in the area of purchasing; for example, tyres, wheel rims and other common, multi-purpose parts, such as batteries and instrumentation, are purchased externally.

The Group is planning to adopt common components such as axles – virtually doubling the volumes formerly handled separately. Previously, Ford purchased from outside and Fiat produced on its own account. In the medium term, the production of gears and hydraulics will benefit from greater economies of scale, as the specialization missions of each factory gradually come into effect. In addition, economies of scale are being achieved gradually by the structural integration of future products. Major launches of future products are planned between 1993–7.

The size of the corporation gives it great clout in the market-place of purchasing. By 1992, the new Group had doubled the purchasing power of the old. As a result of the merger, the Group has rationalized the number of its suppliers and it has been able to negotiate reduced costs, whilst at the same time increasing the quality of supplies. A number of these suppliers have had to invest additional resources to meet the stringent requirements of NH Geotech.

PRODUCT DEVELOPMENT

The Group feels that its success is dependent on its competitiveness and the state-of-the-art technology of its products. During 1991, the Group spent about $200 million in R&D, involving the development of new products, such as the new Winner range and Series 40 tractors, as well as on more general technological innovation. In addition, Ford New Holland Americas has access to complementary products, such as vineyard and orchard tractors provided by Fiat, and intends to cover market segments not previously served. In 1992, $109 million was allocated for R&D, which equated to more than 3 per cent of turnover.

In August 1992, the product development plan was agreed; it involves the complete renovation of all product ranges between 1992–7. By adopting methods of product development used in the Japanese car industry, the company has speeded up the time from product concept to market to less than three years. The support given to product development is illustrated by the fact that in June 1992 the shareholders injected a further $600 million into the organization. This type of support was something quite new to the FNH side of the organization.

PRODUCTION

Since the merger, there has begun a process of re-allocating manufacturing and engineering to sites, based on centres of excellence. Anything that is redundant is eliminated. One of the principles behind this process has been to bring manufacturing as close as possible to the customer, one issue being the fickle nature of the exchange rate.

QUALITY CONTROL

Quality control is an area which exemplifies the advantages of integrating different cultures and traditions. Prior to the merger, Fiat had a total quality programme of Group-wide application, with emphasis on continuous improvement and on processes. On the other hand, Ford New Holland had in existence a quality development programme (Q1) aimed principally at its manufacturing sites and, significantly, its suppliers. These two approaches have been combined in an NH Geotech total quality programme (QUALITAS), supervised by a total quality coordinator reporting to the executive committee.

THE QUALITAS PROGRAMME

Peter Quaglia argues that FNH in Britain, the USA and Belgium were slow both to develop strategy and to aggressively pursue opportunities. However, a major strength of that organization was its implementation of quality control procedures, whereas the Fiat approach is more aggressive and creative, 'because we are Italian'. In Fiat, the implementation of decisions was much more fragmented and the control procedures 'left much to be desired'.

In Ford, its concept of Q1 quality was implemented across all sections. This was regarded as absolutely relevant for the production of cars, but not so necessary for the production of tractors. Fiat had been very active in quality control and especially in the area of automation, but its experience in joint ventures with Japanese manufacturers raised questions about the extensive use of robots: 'We had too many robots, we are now back to people'.

In many areas of activity the methods of Fiat have been used in the new Group but in the area of quality control the approach of total quality, developed by FNH is being applied pragmatically.

CONCLUSIONS

NH Geotech has responded with great speed to its rapidly changing international business environment. It seems likely that, to survive and flourish in this sector, change is likely to be a constant factor in the structure and processes within the organization. In the future, a number of major strategic decisions will have to be taken as a result of the radical change in market demand. For example, is the retention of two separate brand names an appropriate strategy for the late 1990s and early 21st century?

QUESTIONS/DISCUSSION TOPICS

1 Is NH Geotech an international corporation or a national corporation functioning internationally?

2 In view of the contraction of major markets, especially in Europe, should the Company continue to market under separate brand names?

3 'The whole concept of "line" and "staff" is largely redundant in a corporation of this type.' In the light of this case study, comment on this view.

4 Looking specifically at the European market for agricultural machinery, carry out a SWOT analysis of NH Geotech.

5 Evaluate the Corporation's management of cultural diversity.

6 In the light of NH Geotech's rapidly changing business environment, evaluate the Corporations organization structure and processes?

CASE EIGHT

STRUCTURE AND STRATEGY IN A GLOBAL ENVIRONMENT: THE CASE OF THE NEC CORPORATION

ALAN GRIFFITHS AND TORU NAKAKITA

ADVICE TO READERS

This case study illustrates the general rationale behind multinational activity in the world's electronics industry. It shows that multinationals must be prepared to change their organizational design and strategies in an ever-increasing competitive environment. Furthermore, it provides an insight into the important variables which determine competitiveness, and discusses briefly the general experiences which multinationals face when operating across international boundaries.

INTRODUCTION

One of the most significant industrial developments since the Second World War has been the phenomenal growth of the electronics and communications industries. It has enabled the creation of new products and processes and has also altered the nature of company strategy. The creation of the first transistor at the Bell Telephones Laboratories in the USA in 1948 meant that the valve or vacuum tube would soon become mere exhibits on the shelves of industrial museums.

Basically, a transistor was a solid state device made with materials such as silicon which could, with certain modification, act as a semiconductor of electricity. Some ten years after the development of the transistor came the integrated circuit (IC), consisting of a number of transistors connected to each other on a single piece of silicon, i.e. the silicon 'chip'. A further decade saw the development of the microprocessor which was, in essence, a number of sophisticated ICs on one silicon chip, which could act as the central processing unit of a computer. The applications of such new, miniaturized technology to industries ranging from consumer products, such as cars and calculators, to sophisticated communications and defence equipment has assured the sector of the title of the world's leading industry.

The electronics industry tends to be dominated by a number of large global companies, which have invested significant amounts of capital in order to produce competitive products. Most of the competition is between companies whose headquarters are in the USA, Japan or Europe. Companies which compete in the diverse area of electronics and communications include such well-known names as IBM, Hewlett Packard, DEC, AT & T, and Texas

Instruments from the USA; Alcatel, Siemens, Olivetti, Group Bull, and Philips from Europe; and NEC, Toshiba, Hitachi, Fujitsu and Matsushita of Japan.

GLOBALIZATION OF THE JAPANESE ELECTRONICS INDUSTRY

The first movement towards globalization of the world's electronics industry began in the 1960s, when US producers began setting up subsidiaries abroad. However, by the 1980s the world pattern of production had changed fundamentally, as companies from Europe and Japan began to compete with the USA on a world-wide basis. By 1990, Japanese companies had begun to dominate some sectors of the industry, with a combined market share of 43 per cent in the semiconductors, IC and microprocessors division, leaving the shares of the USA (26 per cent) and Europe (12 per cent) some way behind. Meanwhile, in the production of DRAMS (Dynamic Random Access Memory) the Japanese share of world production had reached over 88 per cent. What general factors have determined the shift of Japanese electronics production overseas as a means of maintaining their competitiveness?

The first set of reasons relate to the comparative advantage of producing abroad. Such advantages include the securing of cheap raw materials and labour supplies which help reduce production costs, thus allowing companies to penetrate world markets. However, it should be remembered that the reasons for such comparative advantage can change over time and may be accelerated (as in the case of Japan) by specific events, such as the appreciation of the Yen after 1985. The location of production abroad also provided Japanese subsidiaries with preferential tax status and investment incentives offered by host countries. This process was further accelerated by the tight labour situation in Japan, which increased the wages of Japanese workers in the electronics sector.

Secondly, many Japanese companies in the electronics industry shifted their emphasis from domestic exports to overseas production as a

means of reducing various risks related to direct exports. For example, export transactions from Japan involve the use of different currencies, duties on components and products, and difficulties with transportation and communication across long distances. Despite the fact that some of these problems have decreased with improvement in global communication and lower tariffs, Japanese corporate managers, like others, still have to deal with foreign exchange risks and uncertainty of long-distance transportation. Overseas production is one way of minimizing such risks.

Thirdly, the growth of intensive competition between global companies during the 1980s led to an increasing awareness of the importance of global markets. With income levels rising, product life cycles shortening, and consumer tastes becoming more sophisticated and diverse, Japanese electronics companies felt it increasingly more important to locate production and marketing facilities near to product markets. In this way, effective market intelligence could be gathered and used to modify products to local tastes as efficiently and rapidly as possible.

Fourthly, local production was also viewed by Japanese electronics companies as a countermeasure to the protectionist sentiments espoused by different trading blocs. The growth of Japan's trade surplus in electronic goods with the rest of the world during the 1980s led to the imposition by the USA and Europe of high tariffs, quotas and other forms of anti-dumping duties, in addition to various 'local content' requirements. The natural way for Japanese companies to overcome such a threat was to 'internalize' it by producing within the overseas area concerned. In this way, they could overcome the 'imperfections' (e.g. tariffs etc.) in the world market for electronic goods and components.

Finally, from the supply side, the motives for Japanese production overseas also emanated from their desire to use more effectively the accumulated managerial and technical expertise which they had acquired during the rapid growth of the Japanese economy after the Second World War. During that period of growth, many of the major Japanese electronics companies had changed their organizational structures from a purely 'functional' form to a more appropriate 'divisional' structure. In addition, they had refocused their corporate culture on the so-called 'pillars' of Japanese corporate behaviour, i.e. stress on management philosophy and management objectives, long-term employment policy, job rotation and multi-skilling, collective decision-making and responsibility, and small group activities with a high regard for quality and human relations policies. It seemed reasonable to think that these important qualities could be 'transplanted' to foreign soil (together with the necessary technology) in order to ensure more competitive production.

JAPANESE MULTINATIONALS IN THE ASIAN CONTEXT

The development of Asia as a base for Japanese trade and production needs no complicated explanation. The geographic location of the Asian economies meant that economic relations would inevitably become increasingly important over time. By the early 1990s, over a third of Japanese exports were destined for Asian economies and nearly half of Japan's imports were obtained from these economies. As Japan's economy grew rapidly after the 1950s, it was inevitable that its need for raw materials and for markets would lead it to focus some of its activity in this area, e.g. raw materials from Australia.

The growth of trading linkages was followed by flows of direct investment and the setting-up of overseas subsidiaries designed to take the international economic division of labour one step further. Between 1945 and 1990, some 45 per cent of all Japanese companies' overseas subsidiaries were set up in Asia, compared with 25 five per cent in the US and 17 per cent in Europe. In the electronics industry, the concentration of Japanese companies in Asia was even greater. For example, by the late 1980s some 60 per cent of Japan's overseas plants producing electronic components were located in Asia.

Most of the dynamic activity in the Asian region is between Japan and two groups of countries, the Asian Newly Industrializing Economies (ANIEs) and the Association of South East Asian Nations (ASEAN).

The nature of the Japanese multinational activity in Asia can be gauged from Exhibit 8.1. The number of cases of Japanese direct investment in the area amounted to over 17,000 between 1951 and 1990. By the early 1990s Japanese subsidiaries in Asia employed some 13,000 Japanese staff and 860,000 local employees. Manufacturing employment was important in all the countries concerned, with the electrical machinery subsector as an important component of employment in over half the countries. The weight of Japanese involvement in the top five sectors varied from country to country, according to the various aspects of comparative advantage noted previously.

The aim of the following account will be to investigate the behaviour of Japanese companies in the electronics sector by tracing the structure and general strategies of the giant NEC Corporation; particular, but not exclusive, attention will be paid to the SE Asian context.[1]

BACKGROUND TO THE NEC CORPORATION

There are three important aspects of the NEC Corporation which have combined to give it a strong position in the world of electronics and communications equipment, and which have helped to define its subsequent strategies.

First, Nippon Electric Company Ltd (today's NEC Corporation) was founded in Tokyo on 17 July 1899 as Japan's first 'joint venture' company with foreign participation. In effect, NEC had been set up by Western Electric of Illinois (now AT & T Technologies Inc) as its plant for the Far East market, with 54 per cent of the start-up funds being supplied by Western Electric and the rest from Japanese sources. By 1925, the foreign subsidiaries of Western Electric had been acquired by International Standard Electric Corporation (ITT). This company remained NEC's most significant

Exhibit 8.1
Employment and investment in Japanese subsidiaries in Asia

	ANIEs				ASEAN			
	Hong Kong	S. Korea	Singapore	Taiwan	Indonesia	Malaysia	Philippines	Thailand
Total employment (000s)	53.8	188.7	82.0	135.2	90.1	101.5	58.7	159.0
Manufacturing	22.8	112.3	54.4	113.5	56.7	67.2	23.6	86.9
(Electrical machinery)	(6.7)	(42.2)	(33.5)	(65.8)	(4.3)	(39.6)	(11.6)	(25.8)
Foreign direct investment No. of cases 1951–90 (000s)	3.7	1.8	2.6	2.4	1.9	1.5	0.8	2.5
No. of Japanese staff (000s)	2.5	0.6	2.3	1.9	1.0	1.2	0.3	2.4
TOP FIVE SECTORS	Wholesale (incl electric) Trade Finance/banking Storage	Electric Chemicals Machinery Textiles Auto/parts	Wholesale Electric Chemicals Finance/banking Storage	Electric Wholesale Chemicals Machinery Auto/Parts	Chemicals Finance/banking Auto/parts Machinery Electric	Electric Wholesale Chemicals Service Trade	Trade Chemicals Electric Service Food	Wholesale Electric Food Chemicals Textiles

Note: All figures are rounded.
Source: Tachiki (1990, 1992).

single stockholder until 1971, although it had gradually reduced its holdings during the 1960s. NEC's various links with foreign companies continued in the 1980s, with cross-licensing of patents and copyrights between its own computer operations and those of Honeywell (US) and Bull of France being introduced in 1984. By 1991, NEC had exchanged its 15 per cent interest in Bull HN Information Systems for a 4.7 per cent stake in Compagne des Machines Bull, the parent company of group Bull, so as to strengthen the co-operative arrangement.

Secondly, NEC was a major supplier of communications equipment to Japan's Ministry of Communications during the interwar. This trend continued after the war, when NEC became the leading supplier to Nippon Telegraph and Telephone (NTT), Japan's state-owned corporation, until its privatization in 1985. In terms of a popular expression used in Japan in the early years of the 20th century, NEC was a 'Goyo Kojo', or a quasi-official company providing goods to the government. NEC's strong links with NTT provided the base for its expertise in the area, since the demanding specifications laid down by NTT for any equipment which it bought ensured that NEC's standards were high.

Thirdly, NEC as a foreign-financed company had found itself beset by management difficulties during the interwar period, due to both the world-wide economic recession and the emergence of nationalism in Japan. As a way out of this dilemma, NEC's foreign investors entrusted the running of the company to the massive Sumitomo industrial group. This link continued from the 1940s to the early 1960s, with each succeeding president of NEC being nominated from one of the major companies in the Sumitomo Group. It was only in 1964, when Koji Kobayashi became president that NEC nominated a president, who had risen through the ranks of the company. The links with the Sumitomo group still continue, in that 25 per cent of its stock are held by Sumitomo companies and 33 per cent of its funds, in the form of short- and long-term loans, are provided from financial institutions belonging to the

Sumitomo group. The company is therefore embedded in the Japanese corporate system, which helps to provide a stable and relatively supportive environment.

NEC AND THE ELECTRONICS INDUSTRY

Based on annual sales of $28,374 million in the fiscal year ended March 1992, NEC is the 39th largest industrial corporation in the world and the 7th largest Japanese company. Within the electronics and electrical equipment sector, it is the 8th largest company in the world. If we divide this sector into some of its major sub-sectors, we find that NEC has the following world ranking: semiconductors (1st); information systems (4th); personal computers (4th); and telecommunications equipment (5th). These basic statistics show that the company has grown to become one of the world's largest industrial corporations, with particular competitive strengths in the electronics, computing and communications sector.

NEC employs a total of some 117,000 workers, with its overseas affiliates employing 24,500 (Asia and North America employ over 7,000 workers each and Europe employs 3,500). Its productivity, in terms of sales per employee, was $221,000 in 1991, which is equivalent to its Japanese competitor, Matsushita, and higher than Hitachi and Toshiba of Japan, IBM of the USA, and Philips Electronics of the Netherlands.

Basically speaking, NEC's main competitive power lies in what may be called the computer and communications fields, which are known within the company as its C & C operations. Its C & C operations are composed of communications systems and equipment, computers and industrial electronic systems and electron devices. The communications systems and equipment sector produces such products as fibre-optic transmission systems, digital switching systems, space electronic systems, radar equipment, mobile and portable radio equipment, and installation and maintenance of communication systems.

The computers and industrial electronic sector includes the production of mainframe computers, PC workstations, industrial robots and VAN information systems. Finally, its electronic devices sector produces semiconductors, integrated circuits, electron tubes, colour LCDs and electrical connectors, etc. Outside its C & C operations, its other operations include the production of colour TV receivers, VCRs, compact disk players and video games units.

By the late 1960s and early 1970s, Koji Kobayashi, the NEC President, had identified the vital importance of the interface between computers and communication. Historically speaking, this was not surprising because the Japanese computer industry, unlike its US and European equivalents, had its roots in communications and had developed out of communication technology. In the USA and Europe, the computer industry often grew out of the office equipment sector. As a result, Japanese entrepreneurs such as Kobayashi were able to see quite early on the increasing importance of integrating computers and communication systems.

Technological innovations, such as the digitalization of communication, means that communications technology is now on a par with computer technology. As computers come online they begin to use communication circuits, which means that not only the human voice, but also data and images, can be transmitted. NEC's basic strength in communications equipment, derived from its close contact with NTT, meant that it could capitalize on the increasingly important links between computers and communications. It is not surprising that NEC also developed the building blocks on which all C & C operations are based, i.e. the electron device sector producing mainly semiconductors.

As can be seen from Exhibit 8.2a, the breakdown of sales by product in 1992 shows that the largest section was computers at 52 per cent of total sales, followed by communications systems and equipment (27 per cent), electron devices (16 per cent) and others (5 per cent). This pattern of production follows the declared aim of Kobayashi: 'I consider it my duty as an industrialist to develop C & C so that it can contribute to society and the human race.'

Exhibit 8.2a
Sales by product (1992)

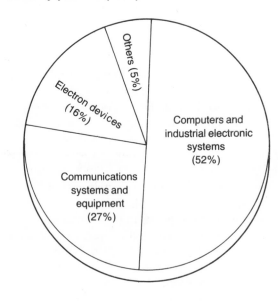

Exhibit 8.2b
Sales by market (1992)

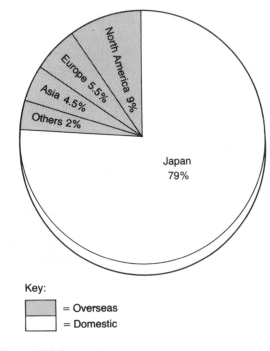

Key:

☒ = Overseas
☐ = Domestic

Source: NEC Corporation.

Exhibit 8.3

NEC world-wide: manufacturing and non-manufacturing subsidiaries and affiliates (31 December 1991)

	MANUFACTURING		MARKETING, SERVICE AND RESEARCH	
ASIA	Thailand	3	Thailand	3
	Malaysia	3 (4)	Singapore	2
	Hong Kong	1	Hong Kong	2
	Singapore	1	Taiwan	2
	Taiwan	1	Malaysia	1
	Philippines	1	China	1
	China	2		
		12 (13)		11
OCEANIA	Australia	2	Australia	1
	New Zealand	1		
		3		1
NORTH AMERICA	Canada	1	Canada	1
	US	3 (6)	US	9
		4 (7)		10
EUROPE	UK	2	UK	3
	Ireland	1	Germany	3
			France	2
			Italy	2
			Spain	1
			Netherlands	1
			Sweden	1
			Finland	1
		3		14
LATIN AMERICA	Mexico	2	Chile	1
	Argentina	2	Argentina	1
	Brazil	1	Colombia	1
			Venezuela	1
		5		4
MIDDLE EAST			Saudi Arabia	1
				1
AFRICA			Nigeria	1
GRAND TOTAL		**27 (31)**		**42**

Notes: 1 Subsidiaries are wholly owned while affiliates indicates ownership interests of between 20 per cent and 50 per cent.
2 Figures in brackets indicate number of plants.
3 Less than half of the manufacturing subsidiaries also undertake some degree of marketing function.

Source: NEC, Tokyo, 1991.

Exhibit 8.2b shows NEC's sales by market and geographic region. Basically, the huge home market means that in 1992 some 79 per cent of total sales were sold in Japan itself. However, the overseas market had increased to 21 per cent from a figure of 10.5 per cent in 1966. In this sense, NEC had doubled its share of overseas sales in 15 years, to become a world player in the electronics sector.

As early as the mid-1960s NEC, with the strength of the home market behind it, began to look more closely at the world market in terms of direct sales from Japan and in terms of direct foreign investment abroad in the form of new overseas subsidiaries. The first overseas manufacturing subsidiary of NEC was NEC de Mexico SA de CV, established in Edo de Morelos, Mexico in 1968.

From this start, NEC set up an increasing number of overseas subsidiaries which, by 1991, had grown to the extent shown in Exhibit 8.3. Out of a total of 69 overseas subsidiaries, some 23 (or about one-third) are located in Asia. Some 40 per cent of the manufacturing plants are located in Asia, but only 26 per cent of its marketing service and research subsidiaries are in this area. In general, the relatively lower cost production units are located in Asia, while the marketing, service and research affiliates are more concentrated in the higher per capita income countries of USA and Europe, which account for 65 per cent of NEC's overseas sales.

DIVISIONAL STRUCTURES AND CHANGE

Like any competitive company, NEC's organizational structure changed over time, as the needs of the industry dictated. The Korean War created a procurement boom in Japan and this occurred as Japan's Telegraph and Telephone Corporation introduced a five-year development plan. Both of these facts created increased demand for communications equipment and other devices. As a result, NEC reorganized its product line and introduced production management techniques and quality control. As far as its organizational structure was concerned,

it divided its factory production units into either radio or wired communication systems, while the sales, finance and personnel activities were centralized at head office.

Between 1955 and 1964, investment in radio communication and electronic appliances increased and the range of products expanded. As a result, instead of having factory units with a general manager in charge of a wide product-base, the idea was to create divisional managers in charge of research and production in each product line. However, the sales function was still concentrated at head office and the idea of profit responsibility was not clarified. Despite these changes, it was difficult to decrease costs and so, in 1961, a multidivisional structure was formed in which each division handled its own technology, production and sales in each product line.

By the mid-1960s, the growth of the communications equipment industry, computers, electronic components and the consumer electrical sectors gave an impetus to further structural change within NEC. These changes occurred at the same time as the nomination of the dynamic K. Kobayashi as president of NEC. He developed a reorganization plan which laid the foundations for NEC's future. Basically, he reinforced the divisional structure, which had only been half-heartedly introduced in 1961.

Under the new arrangements, four groups were formed, based on the nature of the technology. These groups were composed of 14 operating divisions, each having its own engineering, manufacturing and marketing functions and acting as a profit centre. At the same time, there were formed one central research laboratory, three development laboratories, two further marketing divisions, to deal with special customers, and an overseas division.

By the 1970s, the number of divisions in NEC was growing; the complex interaction between the communication equipment sector and the computer section was becoming more evident, and the need to improve the interaction between complementary technologies was growing more intense. As a result, a divisional matrix-type of system emerged, where the

Exhibit 8.4
NEC Corporation, top management organization

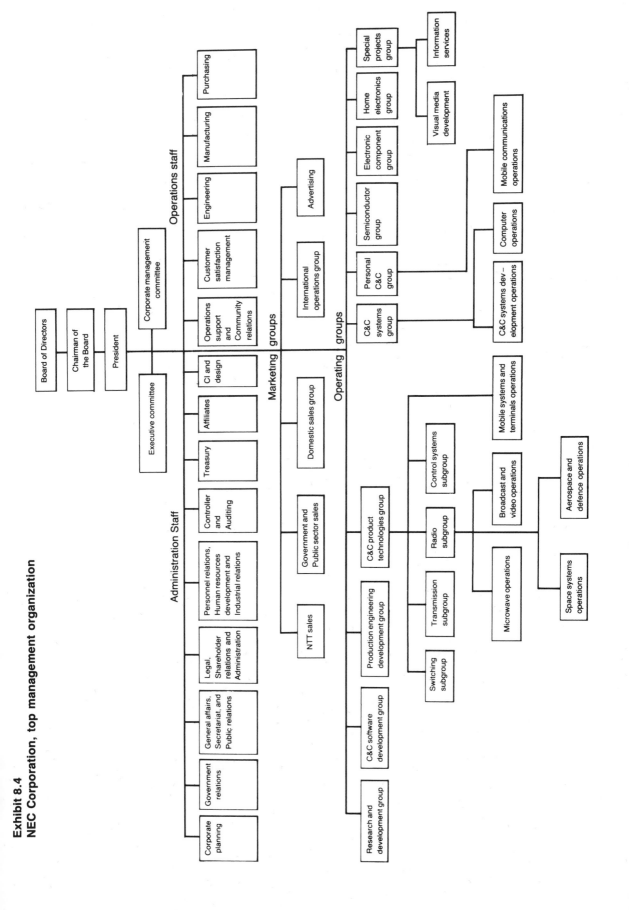

general managers of each division were encouraged to take an active interest in technology, manufacturing and marketing practices in other divisions adjacent to their own. Also, the heads of each operating division and marketing division were responsible for the joint co-ordination of the complicated relationships between production and marketing divisions over a wide range of products and markets.

The changes in the structure of NEC, which were implemented in July 1991, have resulted in an organizational chart illustrated in Exhibit 8.4. The main change was to establish a more market-orientated organization for the business C & C systems market in Japan. In essence, the new changes have meant the dismembering of various pre-1991 operating groups and their reorganization into three new groups under the heading of C & C group, and the formation of a new 'customer satisfaction management' department at head office. Basically, the drive to meet an increasing demand for customized products, and the growing requirement to meet the challenges from the convergence of technologies in communication and computers, have demanded a more integrated approach to the market-place. The aim of the new groups is to integrate the former separate groups into a market-orientated and technologically compatible, new group structure in C & C products.

Like any large corporation, NEC has an international dimension to its organization. In Exhibit 8.4, the most active, overseas-orientated section is the international operations group, which deals with the planning of international operations and co-ordinates and promotes NEC products and production in various world markets. At the same time, overseas affiliates also come under the influence of the appropriate operational subgroup, for example, NEC Technologies Hong Kong Ltd is obviously closely linked to the personal C & C group, while NEC Technologies, Philippines, comes under C & C product technologies group. Overseas subsidiaries are also supported by staff departments at headquarters such as personnel and finance (treasury).

RESEARCH AND DEVELOPMENT

The R & D function is important to any company's long-term survival and no more so than in the electronic and communications sector. NEC set up its first research laboratory in 1936. By 1961, it had already set up research groups in the fields of transistor, computer and integrated circuits. In 1965, the central research laboratories and developmental laboratories were formed, but by the 1980s they had become inflexible, with the central research laboratories tending to dominate research policy. In 1980, the further development of C & C systems needed a more flexible R & D structure and so the research and development group was reorganized with the dissolving of the central research laboratories and the formation of five new laboratories, covering fundamental research, optoelectronic research, C & C research, software production research and environmental production research. This organizational change brought research closer to the individual production groups and to the market for the final products.

The central research and operational divisions are brought together for research evaluation before a project starts and the group planning divisions attached to each operating group prepare market studies of their area, which is circulated to R & D workers. Exhibit 8.4 shows the operating groups. Within NEC, the effective interaction between R & D, production and the market are considered of paramount importance. For example, in 1991 the R & D and engineering expenses of NEC amounted to 17 per cent of net sales, with the growth of R & D between 1988 and 1992 being around 6 per cent per annum.

In terms of its global strategy, the R & D work contracted out depends on the distribution of overseas knowledge and skills. NEC's strategy has followed a relatively consistent path with much of the high value-added R & D being done at home, while any perceived gaps in such research and development work may activate the setting up of an overseas facility. The R & D group carries out long-term projects, which require 10–20 years to bear fruit, whilst shorter term R&D activities are handled by each operating group. For example NEC's Computer Systems Research Laboratory in Tokyo is working on circuits which are capable of self-learning which could lead to the production of personal computers more powerful than present supercomputers. In the superconductor field, where NEC is the world's leader, their Kanagawa Laboratories near Tokyo are researching on a new 3-D fabrication technique for making integrated circuits. On the other hand, the lack of basic science-based research in Japan (for example, only 8 per cent of all scientific and technical literature published in the late 1980s came from Japan, whilst the figure for the USA was 35.6 per cent) galvanized NEC to create a research institute in Princeton in 1988 in order to tap the skills and talent of US academics and engineers.

While most high-technology R&D is focused on Japan, it should not be forgotten that an important part of the R&D process does not always come from the large, home research laboratories. In SE Asian subsidiaries, R&D activity still occurs, but the nature of the R&D is different. It is often geared to adapting the main technologies to local conditions; for example, research on translation packages into local languages or development of connectors and adapters which facilitate local use of computers. Basically speaking, in NEC's subsidiaries in this area, the objectives of R&D are to invent new processes, to apply technology properly and to increase the quality of the product. In other words, the accent of R&D in countries such as Thailand, Malaysia and Indonesia is most often on improving process adaptation technology.

A warning should be given here about general ideas relating to the geographic location of R&D processes explained above. The only certain aspect of successful corporate strategy in companies such as NEC is attention to ever-changing circumstances and opportunities. For example, although we have seen that NEC has tended to be involved in the production/assembly of components and final products which are relatively less intensive in new technology in Malaysia and Thailand, this is not necessarily the whole picture. In Singapore,

for example, where relatively high engineering skills are available, there is a design centre which supports the development of semi-customized LSI (e.g. ASIC and microcomputers).

PRODUCTION

The strategy for international production of an organization such as NEC has followed relatively closely the reasons given earlier, regarding the general movement of Japanese electronics companies abroad, i.e. cheap raw materials and labour costs, high value of the yen after 1985 and the desire to get closer to the consumer in order to increase market share.

In South East Asia, NEC produces a range of products from semiconductors and other electronic devices to colour TV sets. If we take the production of semiconductors we find that the types of semiconductors which are mainly used for home electronics, such as TVs, are produced in Malaysia and shipped to other parts of SE Asia, such as Thailand, for incorporating into consumer products. On the other hand, Singapore acts as an assembly stage for memory chips, with the components often produced in the USA and the final chip being exported back to that country. Therefore, if we investigate the 'division of labour' concept in NEC's DRAM production between its home plants and the rest of the world, we find that the upper, and more complicated, high value-added stage of the DRAM production cycle is more likely to be carried out in Japan, USA, and the EC, while the lower value-added stage, which includes assembly, is carried out in countries such as Singapore. In the PC printer market, there is a tendency for NEC subsidiaries in Asia to produce dot matrix printers and the home factories to produce the laser printer end of the market.

The division of production shown above is the result of NEC strategies relating to costs, technology and skills, as well as market and political forces. For example, contrary to many accepted ideas, the major costs of various consumer electronic products are often the material rather than labour costs. In some cases, the costs of materials are a significant part of total costs, so that the low costs of raw material and components in SE Asia, for example, which are 30 per cent cheaper than Tokyo, are a powerful reason to site production overseas. Also, tariff rates for imported raw materials and components are low in some Asian countries, which facilitates the assembly industries in those areas.

Companies such as NEC have not been slow to realize that the market in the Pacific rim (excluding Japan) comprises 1,500 million people, with per capita incomes beginning to show sustained increases. The number of people per personal computer varies from 7 in Australia to 2,286 in China, so that market potential is enormous for certain kinds of electronic products. The Asian market for colour TV sets is worth £113 billion, i.e. ten times larger than the US and five times larger than the EC!

It is important to note that inter-regional trade in Asia has progressed in a more confident manner during the early 1990s, with the announcement in January 1992 of an agreement to introduce AFTA (Asean Free Trade Agreement), aimed at substantially reducing tariff rates for goods produced and traded among ASEAN countries. The importance to NEC and other companies of being within such trading blocs is substantial, although full account will be taken of political factors, for example, political instability as well as economic factors, when determining the location of plants.

PRICES AND COSTS

Strategies relating to prices and costs are of paramount importance to any company wishing to increase market share and maintain profits. There are no fixed theories of how prices should be determined, as differing costs and demand conditions will alter the nature and direction of prices. In this context, NEC has followed the general strategy of lowering costs by introducing high production runs of basic components and finished products – the application of the 'learning curve'. The critical approach

which NEC and other companies take on costs and cost management is an important part of their eventual pricing strategies. There are two aspects of NEC's cost management approach, i.e. cost reduction and cost control. Cost reduction stems from improvements in design and production technologies, which results in lower costs, while cost control is achieved by lowering 'standard costs' by reducing error/defect rates and lead times and by introducing flexible manufacturing systems.

Companies such as NEC tend to set a price based on what they think the consumer will bear, given the specific characteristics of the product and its market. From this price, a certain amount of desired profit is deducted, leaving a 'target cost' which designers and engineers have to meet. Therefore, a cost reduction exercise takes place before the manufacturing stage (i.e. in design and engineering) in order to meet the target cost. This process is often called 'design to cost'. Once this stage is complete, the manufacturing stage begins and, here again, the aim is to decrease costs wherever possible. During this stage the target cost may be revised downwards, if competition from other companies emerges. It is interesting to note that at NEC, the target cost calculation is not based on current retail prices and competitors' costs, but on what these are likely to be in six months to a year when the product comes onto the market! In other words, the target cost calculations try to anticipate future market and cost conditions.

Therefore it can be seen that this form of target cost pricing is a powerful method of maintaining competitive advantage. In the past, many of NEC's competitors in the West did not always engage in the design-to-cost strategy, thus giving designers and engineers more freedom of action. This often gave rise to designs which were too costly and resulted in an inflated final price. However, as intense competition increased during the late 1980s, most of the large, Western-based multinationals began to become more cost-minded.

Obviously, this obsession with costs is one of the most dynamic aspects of Japanese competitive strength. This is not to say that other major multinationals from USA and Europe are not cost-competitive, but it does ensure that Japanese companies such as NEC will place continuous pressure on costs, and therefore on their competitors whenever they can. The use of overseas production bases in SE Asia can often provide the extra opportunities to lower costs even further. In order to improve the flow of low-cost raw materials and parts to the relevant production and assembly sites, NEC set up International Procurement Offices (IPOs), in Boston, London, Hong Kong and Singapore, to ameliorate this aspect of cost competition. From this cost perspective, NEC's pricing policies can be more flexible, depending on market conditions.

HUMAN RESOURCE MANAGEMENT

In 1965, K. Kobayashi laid the foundations of his future vision for NEC with the comment, 'A properly employed workforce is the ultimate source of corporate growth'. In any corporate body, he believed that company profits arose from its line operations and that the function of the staff was to support these line operations. An important function of management was to show affection and consideration for the people who worked under them and the essence of leadership was to bring out the latent ingenuity and individual abilities of company personnel. In conjunction with these general ideas, Kobayashi felt that managers and workers should be flexible and not assume that they were capable of doing only one job or function. A staff employee qualified in finance should not mean exclusion from learning and understanding aspects of research, or marketing, or production. Similarly, the production engineer should be aware of marketing or sales. Thus one of the essential aspects of corporate management was to develop the innate flexibility of people through training and teamwork.

The aim of these policies towards human resource management in NEC is to create what economists call an 'internal labour market', i.e. a permanent, flexible and well-trained workforce, whose aim is the achievement of quality

products. Communications between employee and employer are based on a long-term or 'permanent' relationship, as reflected by the Japanese name for a company, 'Kaisha', which has a strong connotation of 'community'. The fact that the Japanese trade unions are based on the enterprise means that grievances are quickly dealt with in the interests of the company as a whole, i.e. both employer and employee. A great deal of the vocational training is done in-house so that workers learn from their seniors in a 'mentor' type situation. Stress is also laid on the concept of job rotation and the assumption is made that staff and line operators should be flexible in terms of job assignment.

This internal labour market system has been criticized by many Western writers because it seems to be an insular system where management has the real power. It is pointed out that the privileges of being a permanent employee of a company like NEC are not enjoyed by the hundreds of small companies which work on sub-contracts to large Japanese multinationals. However, a detailed discussion of these issues is not the primary aim of this chapter.

THE INTERNATIONALIZATION OF JAPANESE CORPORATE CULTURE

LABOUR/MANAGEMENT

The more interesting question at this stage is, to what extent do Japanese companies attempt to transfer their indigenous Japanese-style management to their overseas subsidiaries? Obviously, the degree to which they can transplant their model of corporate organization depends on economic and cultural forces in such different areas as the USA, Europe and Asia. As much research has been done on Japanese companies in Western nations, the next few paragraphs will concentrate on the general behaviour of Japanese multinationals in the SE Asian context, with references made to NEC only where specifically relevant.

As far as the ideology of Japanese management is concerned, many Japanese companies have sometimes found it difficult to imbue local

SE Asian managers with the strong, managerial philosophy of responsibility to the corporation. This is because the benefits of shared customs and background between employers and employees and the view of the company as part of their 'common destiny', so strong in Japan, are often less apparent in some ASEAN or ANIC countries. For example, Japanese managers of SE Asian subsidiaries, who are engaged in hiring local managers, often think in terms of 'Japanese' criteria such as 'effort', 'sincerity' and 'a team player'. Over time, however, these criteria have had to be complemented by valuations based on more objective skills, such as merit and behavioural work standards, in order to adapt the Japanese approach to the different situation in SE Asian countries.

This type of complication percolates down to the management employment level, where the Japanese experiential or job-rotation approach to training managers (which takes longer than usual to cultivate) means that many local managers do not always stay with the company very long. However, it should be noted that the higher turnover rate is also due to the ample employment opportunities which exist in the rapidly developing SE Asian economies. On average, the median turnover rate among local managers in Japanese subsidiaries in SE Asia is 12–20 per cent, which is higher than back in Japan. To counteract this trend, Japanese companies have had to be pragmatic and promote appropriate staff from entry level to subsection chief ('kakaricho') in 12 years instead of the 17–20 years it would take in Japan. NEC has been very progressive in this context, with promotion to subsection chief being achieved in the relatively short period of 8–10 years.

There have been more attempts by Japanese companies to introduce some of the more basic elements of 'lifetime' employment,[2] seniority wages and labour unions based on the enterprise, wherever possible. Also, the stress on production methods, technology and improved quality systems is an important part of the Japanese managerial brief. The following sections will look at these aspects within the SE Asian context.

For example, the Japanese trade union type structure, based on the company, has been rather difficult to transfer to SE Asian subsidiaries. This may be due to the fact that Japanese companies actually prefer to operate non-union plants in cultures which have not been affected previously by modern industrialization. Joint labour management committees have been formed in some Japanese subsidiaries to discuss areas of employer/employee interest and a 'suggestion' system has been introduced, so that workers can communicate their ideas on various aspects of company operation to higher management. Also, there has been some attempt to introduce the lifetime employment and seniority wages systems, but success varies with individual SE Asian countries. For example, in Thailand, Malaysia and Indonesia, these systems are adopted to a greater degree than, say, Singapore where job-hopping is common to all classes of workers.

Where there is a strong 'external' labour market, for example, where workers change jobs relatively frequently, it is difficult to build up the sort of typical Japanese corporate mentality based on the 'internal' market philosophy. All in all, what we see is that Japanese companies have to try to introduce incentives, such as higher basic pay and conditions of service, to attract the most valuable workers.

PRODUCTION

As far as overseas production is concerned, the subsidiaries of many Japanese companies try to create a basic manufacturing consciousness through the three S's movement, i.e. *seiri*, discarding unnecessary items; *seiton*, arranging things in good order; and *seiso*, cleaning and checking the condition of something. Although this seems like mundane housekeeping, it is very important, especially when efforts are made to cut inventory costs and to use factory space more effectively. The second phase is the automation of sub-assemblies requiring precise manufacturing. To achieve this, managers and engineers have to learn about industrial engineering, for example, process analysis and work measures, quality control such as work-flow and control charts, and other specialised topics, such as value engineering.

Since its establishment in 1983, the NEC Institute of Management has provided systematic training and educational programmes, which enable employees of NEC and its subsidiaries to improve their managerial skills. NEC also invites managers from overseas subsidiaries, such as SE Asia, to Japan to study NEC's management philosophy and diverse operations, as well as Japanese culture and society. The degree of help which NEC headquarters in Japan provides for overseas affiliates depends upon the nature of the products and processes. For example, the degree of sophistication in terms of production and hardware systems, such as machinery and design work, depends on whether NEC is producing colour TVs at its Siam NEC subsidiary in Thailand, or electronics components at its NEC Electronics, Singapore, subsidiary.

QUALITY

As far as the transference of a 'quality' mentality to its SE Asian subsidiaries is concerned, the aim is to follow NEC's corporate motto of 'Better products, better services', which was adopted when the company was founded. In fact, NEC was the first Japanese company to introduce statistical quality control programmes in 1946. By 1952, it had won its first Deming prize for such activity and in 1972, it introduced its company-wide 'Operation quality' movement. Also complementing such quality aspects was the introduction of a zero defects (ZD) movement in the middle of the 1960s, which was designed to eliminate any mistakes and the root sources of such errors. Some of the ideas behind the ZD programme at NEC were taken from the Hughes Aircraft Company of the USA, with which NEC had close connections. Since 1982, NEC has held international conventions in Tokyo to discuss quality-related issues and activities of subsidiaries in Japan and overseas.

In their overseas subsidiaries in SE Asia, NEC found that, on average, the product quality of its subsidiaries was roughly equivalent to its home plants in Japan. This has been achieved by investing in on-the-job training for workers and the organization of small group activities, such as quality circles and zero defect programmes where possible.

The aim of introducing such activity is not only the more technical function of pooling ideas to improve products, but also to help management to create a more corporate consciousness within its foreign workforce. The effectiveness of such movements is often modified by the higher mobility of the labour force in SE Asian countries, but as far as the future is concerned, the improvement in general quality consciousness may accelerate, as local quality control organizations are formed to increase the overall awareness of the value of quality in SE Asia. For example, the National Productivity Board (Singapore), National Productivity Centre (Malaysia), Technology Promotion Association (Thailand), Indonesian Quality Management Association (Indonesia), Productivity and Development Centre (Philippines) and the Hong Kong Productivity Centre, all have well-equipped training facilities and programmes modelled on Japanese and Western quality control methods. As a result, the diffusion of modern ideas of quality through such activities is slowly making it less difficult for Japanese companies (such as NEC) to build further workforce skills.

TECHNOLOGY

Japanese companies have been accused of not transferring sufficient technology to their SE Asian subsidiaries and keeping the more advanced technology in Japan. This idea is partly true, but it is also an accusation which misunderstands the nature of 'technological transfer'.

Real technological transfer involves two main phases. First, what can be called the early phase, which involves the transference of such processes as operating technology, maintenance, quality control, production management and improving technology. The later stage of technological transfer involves processes such as moulding, design, product development and equipment development. NEC has placed importance on developing the early stage of technological transfer and is transferring the later stage when it sees fit. NEC's vision of the future in SE Asia is to gradually introduce the later stages of technological transfer, when the skill levels and the market demand dictate. This is the pragmatic approach to the transference of technology.

CONCLUSION

Global competition in the electronics industry will continue to remain intense for the rest of the 1990s. In such an environment, companies will have to be dynamic enough to modify their corporate structure and strategies, as market conditions dictate. This brief discussion of the Japanese presence in the electronics market has attempted to explain the factors which affect competitiveness in the electronics industry. On a more specific level, the growth and adaptation of the NEC Corporation over the last 30 years is a testament to the major role which Japanese companies will continue to have in this market for years to come.

Footnotes

1 For an in-depth discussion of the general behaviour of Japanese multinationals in the Asian Pacific region, see Dennis Tachiki's articles quoted below. The authors are grateful to Mr Tachiki for access to his work in this area.
2 Strictly speaking, the 'lifetime employment' concept covers the permanent workforce of large Japanese companies, and usually means employment from the time of entry into the company until the age of around 58 years.

Bibliography

Emmott, Bill, *Japan's Global Reach*, (London, Century Business, 1992).
Kobayashi, K., *The Rise of NEC*, (Oxford, Blackwell Business, 1991).
Morris, J., (Ed.) *Japan and the Global Economy*, (London, Routledge, 1991).
This is NEC, (Tokyo, NEC Corporation, 1991).
Tachiki, Dennis S., *Going Transnational; Japanese subsidiaries in the Asia Pacific Region*, (Tokyo, Mitsui Research Institute, November 1990).
Tachiki, Dennis S., *The Movement of Japanese Production and Personnel Overseas; Human Resource Development Implications for PECC Member Countries*, (Tokyo, Sakura Institute of Research, 1992).

QUESTIONS/DISCUSSION TOPICS

1 What factors would lead Japan's manufacturers to change the focus of their overseas production?

2 Why do companies such as NEC have to modify their organizational 'design' over time?

3 What are the strengths of the Japanese companies such as NEC in the areas of production and research?

4 Why is it difficult for multinational companies to transplant their domestic 'corporate culture' to overseas subsidiaries?

PHILIPS: A DUTCH ELECTRONICS GIANT, A MULTINATIONAL OR A GLOBAL?

MIKE HEWINS

ADVICE TO READERS

This study is written to illustrate two aspects of business management, citing a large international company. Firstly, how it has altered its organizational structure to meet the new challenges of internationalization: particular attention should be paid to changes brought about in management structure and operation that support its strategic objective of expanding its global position within selected core competencies. The conflicts between local autonomy and central control, and their resolution, should be considered. Secondly, how technology has formed both its strategy and the competitive environment within which it trades: these issues have already been drawn out in Chapter 6. Particular attention should be paid to the strategic management of research and development, the use of joint ventures and the role of technology transfer in international trade.

PHILIPS, THE COMPANY

How has Philips organized itself for the international business environment? What type of company is it? This study, based on published information, shows how the company is evolving to meet the new challenges in international trade. Philips has been international for many decades, with operations stretching from China, the Pacific rim, through America and on to Europe. Its organizational structure has been very different from that of, say, the major automotive manufacturers. Compared with large companies in other industries, it showed markedly less integration of logistics and manufacture, maintained a high diversity of products and services and encouraged a strong national independence within its constituent companies.

There was no analogy within Philips, for example, to General Motors' world-wide integration of manufacture. One of its passenger cars, known in England as the Cavalier but internationally dubbed the 'world car,' is assembled in several countries from common components and only given its local market image at final assembly. The components for each local model come from the same specialist manufacturing plants, regardless of where in the world they are to be assembled. Engines manufactured in Brazil, body panels in Spain and transmission units in Germany are all shipped and brought together for assembly in

England, in France, in Brazil and elsewhere, with a General Motors final assembly operation.

Philips' business environment is different, of course, but its response to changing international trade is now clearly established as one of integration across national boundaries. It will differ from General Motors' response as befits its very different markets, but the broad picture will be integration of markets, logistics, manufacture and their supporting infrastructures of finance, new product development and technology. Its trading profits had for some years signalled problems and some financial analyses had traced these to the dominant position of its national companies. Hamel and Prahalad, in 1985, had described Philips' national managers defending single country autonomy in marketing and strategy, and unable to analyse global competition.[1] For Philips, 'multinational' had come to mean a loose federation of national companies, each fostering the trade of its parent country, possibly to the detriment rather than the health of the corporate whole.

This study discusses the new organizational structure evolving within Philips, as it follows its objective to change from a multinational to a global company.[2] Beginning with an outline of the scale of Philips, in terms of the breadth of its business, its geographical extent, and its competitive environment, it then goes on to what Philips calls 'the global perception'. The case examines the problems of federalism addressed in the 1980s. The new business strategy of global perception, set in motion in the latter half of the 1980s, is reviewed in terms of organizational and operational responses. Particular attention is paid to international research and development (R&D) both as driving forces of the change and as vehicles for this new global perception. (Chapter 6 has already outlined these issues.) The study ends by commenting on some issues and problems.

A word first on terminology. 'Multinational' and 'global', although everyday terms, have no strict technical definition. For the purpose of this book, a multinational company is defined, at its simplest level, as one which operates in several countries simultaneously. Individual countries retain their own companies, each operating with varying mixtures of autonomy and dependence, but identifiable as part of a large group sharing similar business aims.

In the global companies human, financial, marketing and R&D resources are grouped independently of national boundaries. Under the influences of technology, IT and logistics, this developed into integrated operational structures, which crossed not just national, but continental, boundaries and hemispheres. In practice, most companies are some way along a continuum moving from global to multinational.

In the 1970s Philips was something of a hybrid between a global and a multinational organization; but 'multinational' had become for Philips synonymous with 'federalism'. Federalism suggests a high degree of autonomy from the centre. This federalism within the organization increasingly hindered the development of the efficient trading company. There is a parallel here to the struggles of the EC as it evolves in the closing decade of the 20th century. Perhaps this should not cause surprise in a company so closely linked into European life.

THE SCALE OF PHILIPS

The most commonly used description of Philips, at least in the media, is 'Philips, the Dutch electronics giant'. This description, used even in the *Wall Street Journal*, is misleading. It highlights a misconception about the company's business which lies close to the heart of one of its problems: inadequate attention to customer needs when developing new technologies. Philips has not been, for many decades, merely a Dutch electronics giant. Its major interests in such non-electronic fields as software and music, plus major manufacturing operations around the world, demonstrate the fallacy of such a description. So what is the true business of this 'electronics giant'?

HOW PHILIPS EVOLVED

It was established just over a hundred years ago, when Frederick Philips and his son Gerard began making light bulbs in Eindhoven in 1891. The light bulb, so well understood today, is an early example of the bringing together of separated technologies to make a new product (this has been explored briefly in Chapter 6.) Manufacturing an incandescent lamp was complicated, combining together for the first time into a single consistent process glass blowing, metallurgy, chemistry and electricity. This business unit is one of Philips' most successful enterprises and today runs as a discrete financial activity. It is the world leader in the lighting sector, holding about 20 per cent of the world market, and pioneering new lighting forms for domestic and commercial use with 40,000 separate products.

By the mid-1980s Gloeilampenfabrieken had expanded to a 68 billion guilders (1986) turnover, derived from 345,000 employees. In comparative terms, the scale of Philips is vast. By 1987, it had the second largest consumer electronics turnover in the world, second only to Matsushita, taking some 12.5 per cent of an estimated 150 billion guilders world market. In lighting it was, and still is, the largest company in Europe and second in size to General Electric, USA. Its size is illustrated in Exhibit 9.1, which shows on an annual basis for 1985 to 1991 the net sales per major activity and the total staff employed.

One of the world's largest companies, it is also one of the most international, covering in 1990 some 60 different countries around the world. Wholly owned national organizations and affiliated companies were to be found in all European countries, North America, Mexico, Brazil, Japan and Taiwan. Affiliated companies, often owned 100 per cent, were to be found in many other countries in every major land mass of the world; for example, in Central and South America, the Near and Far East, Africa, the Indian sub-continent and Asia. Of particular note is the large number of affiliated companies in emerging trading powers, such as China.

Exhibit 9.1 also shows the picture changing by the beginning of the 1990s. There was a fall of 105,000 (30.4 per cent) in staff employed between 1986 and 1991, but the geographical spread of the company did not alter significantly. There was a change in the pattern of net sales reflecting the concentration of activities into core businesses. Consumer electronics, comprising a vast array of different products, was established as the major business activity by the early 1990s. It accounted for 47 per cent of total sales, up from 28 per cent in 1985. Professional products fell from 29 per cent to 22 per cent of total sales in the same period, whilst defence and major domestic appliances fell more sharply. Lighting and components remained unchanged, however, at 13 and 14 per cent respectively over this period.

Exhibit 9.2 shows that sales patterns have changed little on a geographical basis over three

Exhibit 9.1 The scale of Philips

Sales breakdown (billions of guilders)	1991	1990	1989	1988	1987	1986	1985
Net sales to all sectors	57.0	55.8	57.2	56.1	52.2	55.5	–
Made up of:							
Lighting	7.4	7.0	7.5	6.9	6.5	6.8	7.9
Consumer electronics	26.9	25.4	23.5	18.2	16.5	16.8	16.7
Professional systems	12.5	13.1	15.8	15.1	–	–	17.5
Components and semiconductors	7.8	8.2	8.5	7.8	7.3	7.4	8.1
And others	2.4	2.1	2.0	8.1	–	–	9.8
Staff employed (in 1000s)	240	273	305	310	336	345	–

Source: Compiled from Philips' Annual Accounts & Reports.

Exhibit 9.2
Sales pattern on a geographical basis

	1991	1990	1989
Europe	59	61	57
North America	23	21	24
Asia	10	9	8
Others	8	9	11

Note: Percentage total sales in each year attributable to the named geographical areas

Source: Philips' Annual Reports & Accounts.

years, except perhaps in Asia, notwithstanding this change in core activities. Some of the unconsolidated activities have now been brought within Philips. Outstanding US Philips stock was bought-out in 1986, for example, as its importance to turnover increased from 3 per cent to 30 per cent over 15 years. Investments in Japan and China have increased steadily over the years; for example, radios are manufactured in China, and Marantz, which is owned by Philips, makes hi-fi systems in Japan.

The scale of Philips can be described in two different dimensions: in effect, two descriptions running, like the axes on a graph, at right angles

to each other. The axis just described is in terms of geography and size (net sales and staff employed). The other axis is in operational terms of products, manufacturing, marketing, logistics and R&D. This axis is showing a significant change. Exhibit 9.3 shows a selection of products which have either been discontinued since 1987 or introduced after 1987. This list is far from exhaustive and merely serves to illustrate the point.

As can be seen in the table, the mid-1980s product range included many items not found in the early 1990s, for example, defence systems sold in 1989 to SGS Thomson. In 1991 alone the company divested itself of businesses employing 10,000 people and worth 2.2 billion guilders. This dispersal continues in 1992, with Philips transferring cables and optical fibres to Siemens[3] and selling most of its information systems division to DEC.[4]

Alongside these disposals, selective acquisitions are also taking place, such as a 25 per cent stake in Whittle Communications USA,[5] which specializes in teaching technology. These disposals and acquisitions are part of a programme of concentration on core activities, or business areas which offer the greatest growth potential. The product range, in accordance

Exhibit 9.3
Products manufactured in 1986 and 1992

Products manufactured	1992/91	1986/85
Cables	X	/
Defence	X	/
Fibre-optics	X	/
High-definition video	/	X
Information production:		
Office systems	X	/
Personal (e.g. mobile phones)	/ + JV	X
Information applications		
e.g. learning systems	JV	X
Major domestic appliances	JV	/

Notes: X indicates not manufactured.
/ indicates in manufacture.
JV indicates manufactured by another organization as part of a joint venture.
This list is indicative only and many other products show significant changes in sales turnover.

with the new strategy, is becoming centred around four major areas:

- lighting, a separate business and technology;
- components, fundamental to all other activities;
- consumer electronics, the major activity;
- information technology and communications.

This shift to core businesses is extending the number of soft products. Trimmer (Philips' President) is quoted as saying 'software distribution is very important for our future products ... we must develop a better equilibrium of our portfolios'. Soft products such as record titles, publishing rights and computer software itself are essential to the sale of new product systems, such as laser disc players and interactive video. These are worthless without the rights to the music or film titles, because customers buy entertainment, not technology. By the year 2000, soft products are expected to account for 25–30 per cent of total sales.[6]

Operationally, manufacturing, marketing, sales and new product developments are increasingly being funded and carried out by joint international ventures with other companies. Prior to the 1980s, joint ventures were uncommon, but they became increasingly necessary and larger in scale towards the close of the 1980s and will become even more so in the 1990s. Joint ventures formed with Siemens, Grundig, Matsushita and others are explored in greater depth later. Allied to this, many of Philips' manufacturing and R&D operations are being closed down, regrouped or relocated, on a world-wide basis. Video-player production is being set up in Malaysia (a joint venture with JVC), computer monitor production has been closed down in Canada and semiconductor production halted at Orem, Utah, after 25 years. This closure and regrouping on a world-wide scale supports the concentration of activities called for in the new global perception.

THE COMPETITIVE ENVIRONMENT

Organizational and operational changes are explored further under the heading A global perception, but first a look at the competitive environment within which Philips operates. The European market alone for consumer electronics totalled ECU30.6 billion in 1988 and the industry is predicted to become the biggest single manufacturing industry in Europe by the year 2000.[7]

The largest single influence in the competitive environment is new technology, specifically that technology which supports professional and consumer electronic products. Chapter 6 has explored technology's impact on strategy in broad terms. For Philips and its competitors, this impact is caused by four factors:

- more and more product features in ever smaller devices;
- rapid falls in market price per function;
- rapid escalation of R&D investment and hence risk;
- increasing demands for standardization of information exchange.

The technological aspects are discussed later. Of first concern is the response to these factors by Philips' competitors, companies such as AT & T, General Electric, Hitachi, IBM, Matsushita, NEC, Siemens, Sony and Toshiba. It was Japanese companies, and later the NICs (newly industrialized countries) which set the competitive pace and determined the new environment. Along with most other Western electronics companies, Philips failed to respond at first to the scale of the changes. Many companies failed altogether and large sections of consumer electronics production were closed down in Europe – for example, TV production. The central theme of Japanese competition from the 1960s through to the 1980s has, in consumer electronics, centred on:

- investing in and creating world class technical competence;

supported by

- aggressive overseas sales and logistics.

In the 1960s, Japanese companies moved away from their low-cost labour, copycat approach to consumer electronics. Further examples can be seen in the case studies of Nissan and NEC. These companies saw that technology not only gave birth to new products, but also could be used to produce those same products more cheaply. Between 1977 and 1987 the productivity of Japanese labour rose two-fold, largely by applying technology to production, and was some 50 per cent greater than that of Philips. European and American consumers were offered electronic products at lower prices than their domestic manufacturers were capable of achieving. The home industries had failed to use technology to improve productivity and margins. Japanese products did not rely solely on a pricing advantage, however. Such an advantage rapidly brings demands for tariff barriers, anti-dumping laws, etc., as from American semiconductor manufacturers in 1991, when Japanese companies were accused of dumping computer components onto the US market.

Market analysis had shown that customers wanted increased product reliability and would pay a premium for it. Technology was the vehicle for improved reliability, initially in TV sets, but Western companies again failed to respond quickly enough and consumers bought still more Japanese products. Improved reliability carries the risk of market saturation as products last longer, but technology can offer better products. Customers wanted new features such as high quality audio, sharper pictures, in-car entertainment, physically smaller products and automatic control. Japanese companies used technology to meet these needs and consumers replaced old, reliable and still-working products with new ones. In ten years new products had proliferated tenfold.

This integrated application of technology, with lower cost production, greater reliability and frequent product updates, created the new competitive environment for American and European manufacturers. It is to this environment that Philips, with its tremendous strengths in R&D, is responding. Technology, however, presents new problems when it creates opportunities. The components needed for the new consumer products required R&D investments typically equalling 45 per cent of annual revenue. The lifetime of technology is typically five years and each new technology

takes twice as much capital investment as its predecessor. The competitive environment is becoming, in consequence, a high volume, co-operative environment. Competitors share investment and development, as potential individual company earnings become smaller than development costs. Production is concentrated into a few international supply centres and products are distributed on a world-wide basis. In 1986, for example, 88 per cent of all Japanese copiers were exported and 79 per cent of microwave ovens.[8] Many other products showed similar patterns.

There are many contributing factors left out of this analysis of the consumer electronics environment. It has concentrated on technology and touched briefly on the world-wide marketing essential to any recovery of the capital employed. Certainly, factors such as low finance charges, closed home markets, tax treatment of depreciation and many others have helped Japanese companies. These are, however, secondary to the combined influences of technology and world-wide marketing.

Reference was made earlier to the influence of newly industrialized countries (NICs) on the competitive environment. The discussion has centred around high technology, which represents Philips' main market area and the target of Japanese competition. NICs such as South Korea, Taiwan, Hong Kong and Singapore, have concentrated on the lower technology end of the consumer electronics business, such as 14-inch TVs and low-cost watches. They have saturated these areas and are moving up-market, especially in personal computers. NICs such as China are entering the field, with almost unlimited cheap labour. A combination of cheap labour and new production technology opens the possibility of NICs attacking the higher technology end of the market. At the present time, major companies such as Philips are using NICs as production centres and helping them develop their own markets, which are virgin soil for consumer electronic products. China has 1.35 billion people, who save a third of their income and have few consumer goods available for purchase.

A GLOBAL PERCEPTION

When in 1987 Mr C. J. van der Klugt, President and Chairman of Philips, spoke of changing Philips from a multinational to a global company, he was setting the scene for a new strategy and a major change to the organizational structure.[2] The existing structure had evolved over many years to support federalism. Resources were duplicated in many countries: for example, production of televisions and washing machines in both England and mainland Europe or production of computer monitors in northern America and the Far East. Operational decisions had often reinforced national boundaries as, for example, component sourcing from within the local country, rather than from within Philips itself. New technologies, often well researched and understood, were underutilized for corporate growth and prosperity. The technologies for personal computer development and production were, in the 1980s, within the competence of both Philips and IBM. Only IBM took an initiative on a global scale and developed markets and the technology of production. Philips limited itself to national initiatives. The new strategy needed, above all, to avoid such duplication of costly production and support. It is cheaper to move finished goods from one country to another than it is to install parallel production and fragment the markets.

A new organization was required that brought together, under one management, the information and decision-taking functions needed to optimize development and production across a world-wide stage. Such an organization could facilitate utilization of capital regardless of national boundaries, optimize currency and cash flows on an international basis, and be effective in forming strategic partnerships. In short, the strategy demanded:

- a new management or organizational structure that transcended national boundaries;
- a new operational structure that focused on products and their world-wide markets;
- a concentration of resources into selected technologies and a shedding of several activities.

THE ORGANIZATIONAL RESPONSE

Organizational or management structure can be described as the co-ordination of all the ways in which labour and resources have to be divided up to achieve different tasks. Three key factors in this co-ordination are:

- *environment* external factors such as markets, finance, technology and politics;
- *goals* mission and culture (the internal environment);
- *history* the organizational past with which we live.

Changes in the first of these, the environment, have been reviewed in the competitive environment. Philips was renowned for its slow response to change. Weaknesses were apparent to it in terms of declining profits, new competitors and new technologies in the mid-1980s. Lighting, the most competitive of businesses, had raised its margins to just over 11 per cent by the late 1980s, from a trough of 8 per cent in 1986. Consumer electronics, the major activity of the company, had, on the other hand, achieved a margin of less than 2 per cent by 1988. The components division had seen its margins slump from 14 per cent in 1984 to 4.5 per cent by 1988.[9] By 1988, core businesses accounted for 70 per cent of revenues but only 60 per cent of the profits (see Exhibit 9.3). The existing organizational structure seemed unable to co-ordinate a response, being locked into the third key factor of co-ordination, its own history.

The most significant elements of the changing competitive environment, given the historically slow response of Philips, were to be its speed, its direction and – perhaps most important of all – its priorities, i.e. which changes were relevant and which could be ignored. How was the company to reorganize its management to respond? What were the new goals of the company to be (the second key factor of co-ordination)? Three elements could be isolated from the environment to help define new goals and structures, the same three used earlier by Japanese competitors:

- falling product life cycles (see Exhibit 9.4);

- increasing capital investments in new technologies (see Exhibit 9.5)
- falling market prices (see Exhibit 9.6).

Together, these exert a tremendous pressure on capital employed in the business. There was an ever-increasing demand to use more capital for new product development, accompanied by less time to recover it and lower margins with which to pay for it. The magnitude of this effect can be judged by looking at product life cycles, development costs and market prices in the electronics industries. The shortening life-cycle of consumer electronic products is graphically illustrated in Exhibit 9.4, where model life has fallen by half in 10 years. The trend has not yet levelled out and industry sources predict that by 1995, 65 per cent of all consumer electronic products on sale will be new. Capital investment in new technologies is rising more rapidly than product life cycles are falling. An eleven-fold increase in development costs for computer memory occurred in only four product generations, rising from the equivalent of 100 million guilders to 1.1 billion guilders (1985 base). Integrated circuit development costs show a similar pattern.

Market prices for products using such technology none the less continue to fall. Super-

Exhibit 9.5
Rising investment costs

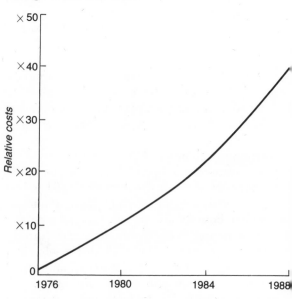

ficially, this appears to have reversed on occasions, in products such as car radios, but this figure is misleading. Many new features are combined into products, initially with small increases in real price.[3] A car radio in 1980 had no automatic, station-seeking capability, no memory of broadcasting stations and none of the other features deemed essential by consumers in the late 1980s for car stereo systems.

In practice, consumer electronics either decline sharply in price or gain a host of new features, sometimes both. Video-player prices have declined to 35 per cent of the 1980 price in 11 years, but added a host of new features. Some companies, such as Japan's Matsushita, even achieved a 20 per cent price fall for video players in 1985/87, whilst the yen appreciated 46 per cent against other currencies.

Philips estimated in 1989 that, since the invention of the first silicon chip, the number of functions on it had risen by a factor of 250,000, while the cost per function had fallen by a factor of 40,000.[10] Profit in such a situation could only come about by increasing volume and simultaneously reducing operating expense. Larger volumes require larger markets. Lower operating

Exhibit 9.4
Falling product life cycles

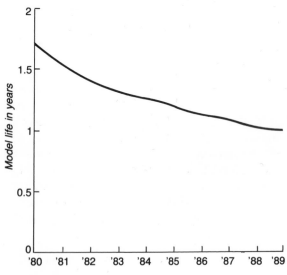

Exhibit 9.6
Falling market prices

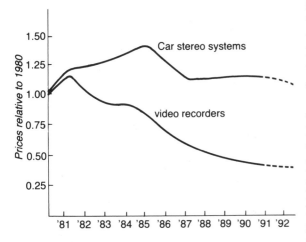

expenses require a concentration of activities in geographical and business terms.

Corporate management responded and a new profit-centred goal was in place. It was based on world-wide markets served from a reduced number of production facilities. Performance and customer orientation were the new culture, with an emphasis on rapid response to new innovations. Good internal publicity, higher public profiles for corporate management (including video presentations by the Chairman), new business targets, annual performance reviews and extensive senior management training were all used to promote the new goals.

By themselves, goals and culture could not yield significant results; the organizational structure itself had first to be changed. It was gradually changed from the nationally dominated federalism of the 1970s to a structure in the late 1980s which was more evenly balanced between product orientation and national leadership. National leadership, which led to duplication of facilities, had unique strengths in local markets and local infrastructures. The new balance sought to combine this strength with a product-orientated view of world markets.

Product orientation calls for integrated production on a world scale. Even more importantly, it integrates different technologies together to

give new products and services at competitive prices. It brings about international standards for information exchange and it brings joint ventures. These things could never be achieved under nationally dominated leadership. Pressure from shareholders at the slowness of the change forced a more rapid pace, which is still going on at the time of writing.

The 1987 Board of Management consisted of a Chairman, two vice-chairmen and six Board of Management members (see Exhibit 9.7). Most of these were responsible for not only one or more product divisions, but also national organizations and several staff functions. For example, Mr Heessels was responsible for Elcoma Lighting and Components, as well as staff functions and national organizations. The Chairman, however, of Elcoma product division was not on the Board of Management; nor was the Chairman of Consumer Electronics, the largest of the product divisions.

In September 1987 this was changed to a more classical structure (see Exhibit 9.8) with a strengthening of central authority. It has similarities to the structures used by many international competitors. A group management committee (GMC) now sets company general policy, but the product divisions themselves are directly responsible for all world-wide activity and profit. The chairmen of components, IT and communications and consumer electronics product divisions are now included on the GMC. A new post with responsibility for the organizational structure has been created and technology, finance, industry and control are directly represented. The GMC now mirrors the external environment and can better control its own competitive strategy. Indeed the success of any organization can probably be best gauged in terms of how well it mirrors the external factors affecting it.

The product domination of the market-place is mirrored in the enhanced role of the product divisions, ensuring that market needs are clearly visible. It has been further strengthened by merging related product divisions, such as audio with video, and telecommunications with data systems. The strengths of the national companies (known in Philips as

Exhibit 9.7
A functional view of the management structure prior to September 1987

BOARD OF MANAGEMENT

PRESIDENT Coordination, Press, Legal, Management Development, etc.	

VICE PRESIDENT Manufacturing, purchasing & shipping coordination, standards, organization, efficiency & others		VICE PRESIDENT Two major product divisions Polygram, Industrial Design, Regional Bureau & others

BOARD MEMBERS

Coordination of matters relating to new product developments	Financial & Pension Affairs	Three major product divisions, miscellaneous and national organizations
Three major product divisions, China national organizations & others	Information, corporate accounting and information systems	Two major product divisions, cable & wire international projects & national organizations

Source: Annual Reports

national organizations) have been retained, but redirected towards a global perception. They are now responsible to the product divisions, which limits their autonomy, but each is still the corporate presence in its own country, managing primarily distribution, social policy and conditions of employment. Production, along with sales, has become the responsibility of the product divisions. The national organizations for key countries use their integration into local economies to good effect, by serving as part of a product divisions' policy team. By 1990, a product division-dominated structure was in place, in which federalism was giving way to global perception.

THE OPERATIONAL RESPONSE

The second demand of Philips' strategy was for a new operational structure. This can be seen both as a focus on products and world markets,

and as a move away from Taylor's scientific management, with its emphasis on mass production.

Jaikumar has argued that there have been six phases in technology and process control since the Industrial Revolution, of which Taylor's is the third.[12] Philips appears to be combining elements of the remaining three into a single strategy. Returning to the question of focus, the company had operated for four decades under dual-headed commercial and technical matrix management, each of which had a large degree of autonomy, but restricted international co-ordination. The boundaries between individual product divisions were rigid and high-level decisions had been needed as to who should be responsible for products which spanned different divisions. This led to some odd criteria, such as a separation of integrated audio/video systems based on the size of the combination, rather than on the products and their markets. Communications between

Exhibit 9.8
A functional view of the management structure after September 1987

GROUP MANAGEMENT COMMITTEE

PRESIDENT
Shared responsibilities for
strategies, human resources
core technologies &
priorities

VICE PRESIDENT
Shared responsibilities
for strategies, human
resources, core
technologies and
priorities

VICE PRESIDENT
Shared responsibilities
for strategies, human
resources, core technologies
& priorities

BOARD MEMBERS

Technology Development	Finance & Pension Affairs	Organizational structure
Control	Information Technology Division	Industrial Affairs
Joint Ventures & I & E	Components Division	Consumer Electronics Division

Source: Annual Reports

divisions and organizations were tortuous and often indecisive (see earlier comments on IBM and the PC market).

The new operational structure, put in place from about 1987/88 and still evolving, has fewer staff and fewer managers. This makes faster, clearer decisions at lower cost. By the late 1980s, a single director replaced the dual technical commercial management of the product divisions. Many staff departments and specialized services, formed over the preceding four decades, were abolished, floated off or merged into slimmer centralized services. Some of the 95,000 staff lost between 1987 and 1991 were a result of this, others a result of factory closures or business disposals. Some 80 factories had been closed by 1987, for instance. The end result is fewer staff needed, now and in the future, to run the company, leading to lower expense and more efficient operation.

In support of this change, operational responsibilities were defined more clearly for products and budgets. Product divisions were made responsible for product and market strategies within their own business areas, regardless of country. They determine resources and, where relevant, manage activities from development, through production, logistics and on to sales. Investment, divestment and profits are amongst their deliverables. They are made up of smaller business groups, which either link related activities to improve efficiency, or support individual activities when the market is sufficiently large. The Audio Business Group, an example of the latter, was in 1990 the second largest within the Consumer Electronics Product Division. The Business Group for Personal Information Products, on the other hand, formed in 1990, links together PCs, printers, fax, telephones, CD-ROM and interactive video.

National organizations remain, at the operational level, the public face of Philips within individual countries. They are 'Philips' to shareholders and governments and the local legal entity. Although the role of these organizations is still evolving, they were made operationally responsible for identifying market opportunities, for financial reporting and for locally implementing resource, finance and management policies. They also advise the GMC and product divisions on policy. Precise responsibilities are determined partly by their country's importance, in business terms, to Philips and partly by contractual agreements with product divisions to manage activities on their behalf.

Perhaps the simplest model is to regard national organizations as a provider of services to product divisions and as a manager of any operations which are independent of them. In both product divisions and national organizations, a centralization of decision and control is emerging. In apparent contradiction of this centralization, independence and financial autonomy have been granted to one group. This apparent contradiction in transnational companies was described by C. Bartlett as 'striking a balance between global integration and national responsiveness in order to maximize the trading response'.[13] The largest decentralization to date has been the separation of lighting products into a separate company, to allow it to respond to its own specialized markets without hindrance.

JOINT VENTURES AND STRATEGIC PARTNERSHIPS

The first two demands of Philips' strategy, new organizational and operational structures, have already been discussed. The third demand was for building core competencies, that is, using resources to support those technologies most likely to contribute to future growth. The extremely high investments required for developing new technologies and new markets, such as the high-definition TV or the digital compact cassette launched in Europe in April 1992, call for investment to be shared on an international basis.

A project to develop a new electronic memory chip to hold over one million bits of information, the Mega-Project, was reported by Philips to require a 2.5 billion guilders investment in 1987. This was jointly funded by Philips, Siemens and Dutch and German governments. Such core competencies cannot be funded adequately by Philips on their own. Even switching funds away from non-core activities, such as major domestic appliances, or selling off activities such as fibre-optics to Radiale of France, does not liberate sufficient funds. Strategic partnerships, Philips' term for joint ventures, embodies the resources management policy to resolve this dilemma. In effect, it extends the resources available to partners when one or more of the following is present:

- complementary expertise to other partners;
- need to share risks on capital or technology;
- need to find additional capital;
- need for assistance in penetrating new markets.

An alliance with SGS-Thomson to develop silicon technology (0.5 micron CMOS) meets these criteria, for instance, and should shorten the time to market. Beside this basic technology, Philips also seeks out partners for component development, such as in interactive video.[14] At the applications level, Philips has entered into joint ventures such as that with Whittle Communications USA in 1991, to develop an interactive video system for schools.[5] Joint ventures in applications will be increasingly common in the 1990s, driven not so much by high development costs as by the need for expertise associated with the end-use of systems. Systems, rather than free-standing components, will form the IT products of the future and Philips sees a need to get closer to the end user.

Co-operation is not confined to new technology or markets and can be built around comakership. Here sub-assembly, or complete product assembly, is shared with another company. It offers improvements in quality, cost and delivery by concentrating production into larger units. A partnership has been formed with Grundig of Germany to merge the entire Philips' VCR business into a joint venture.[15] A joint venture to make high-fidelity VCRs from October 1992 had already been announced with JVC Malaysia. Such ventures, it may be noted, can be organized in several different ways: between large companies, they may take the form of an agreement for a specific project, perhaps even with government collaboration, as in the Eureka programme to develop very high speed electronic components (gallium arsenide chips).

Eureka is a pan-European, EC-funded, research programme which involves 12 EC Member States, 7 other European nations and the EC Commission itself. In other cases, a separate company, jointly owned by the venture partners, may be formed to develop a new product. In yet other cases, the venture may involve equity purchase, as in the case of Whittle Communications USA, where Philips has a 25 per cent equity holding, and Grundig, where Philips has a minority equity holding. An alternative form of risk-sharing can be seen in an agreement between Philips and Sony. Both world players have developed competing digital audio systems and it is unlikely that both will find markets. However, each has a share in the other's technology, limiting the downside to the risk.

Such international co-operation is not confined to investment and production. Products built around sound, vision or data require protocols or standards to allow, for instance, audio tapes to be played on machines from different manufacturers, without tedious and expensive conversion to different formats. Consumers demand compatibility between products from different manufacturers, so that they retain freedom to update their entertainment by purchasing from whomsoever they choose. In international markets, competing manufacturers must agree world-wide standards for such exchange protocols. Philips lost a share of the international video recorder market, and a technically superior product, by ignoring standards with its V2000 video recorders, which were incompatible with the VHS format. In order to prevent similar problems occurring with CDs, which store full-length movies, an international standard has been agreed in advance with the Moving Picture Experts Group.

INTERNATIONAL RESEARCH AND DEVELOPMENT

Products are becoming interactive, smaller, lighter and less power-demanding, as technologies converge. The CD is one such product, formed by the convergence of optics, electronics, music and video. Convergence is visible in telecommunications and computing, which are joining together to become IT, the information technology industry. Such areas have been very clearly identified by Philips as part of their core competency and they are underpinned by joint ventures. The company is actively using technology to earn market share and meet customer needs.

This convergence, where engineers continuously combine different technologies together, offers several other advantages to Philips beside new products and services. By providing more efficient ways of doing things, such as serving a world-wide market from one or two production centres, it offers lower cost, as has been discussed in Chapter 6. Information technology can reduce the risks from political and economic instability. Product technology, or even the production processes themselves, can be transferred from one country to another which offers more congenial conditions.

Information technology also supports sourcing partnerships by world-wide transfer of designs, specifications and orders. As more and more functions are put onto individual electronic chips, components become unique to a particular product or company. Increasingly, they are used to give the resultant product either its individuality within the market-place or, more fundamentally, its operational features. Sourcing for such key components can be concentrated into a few specialized production facilities which ship them, automotive style, to product assembly centres located in other parts of the world. The remaining electronic, mechanical and optical components of the products are also out-sourced from specialists and shipped to assembly centres. This type of technology transfer demonstrates why it is essential for sourcing partnerships to extend not simply to supply of components, but also to the design of the product itself. When the product character depends so heavily on individual components, the product and components must be developed hand in hand, regardless of national boundaries.

So how has Philips organized its R&D activities to meet these needs? In 1990 it reported spending some 4 billion guilders, 7 per cent of annual sales, on R&D, of which 0.66 billion guilders was spent on research and the rest on development.[16] Research is mainly centralized in Holland and almost 60 per cent directed towards technologies significant to product divisions, reflecting the market orientation. For example, the 1990 Annual Report lists exploratory research in silicon-germanium technology (to support telecommunications), flat screen technology (to replace current VDUs), conducting polymer technology (to replace some silicon devices) and artificial intelligence. Some research is carried out in local centres, such as work on magnetic-head technology for video recording and play-back, reflecting the existence of specialized skills and knowledge.

In keeping with its policy on strategic partnerships, which effectively extends available resources by bringing in joint venture partners, Philips collaborates in research with universities, governments and other companies. Within EC-sponsored framework programmes for collaborative research, work has been carried out in 1990 in telecommunications under RACE (Research and Development in Advanced Communications in Europe), in very small electronic chips under JESSI (Joint European Submicron Silicon Investigation), in high-definition TV under Eureka and in IT under Esprit. Esprit is the best known, EC joint research programme and is specifically targeted on IT.

Research is concentrated into the three areas; fundamental knowledge, the application of it and automation: but the pressure on projects is for a faster transfer of technologies to products. Most of the R&D budget is spent, not on long-term research in technologies, but on medium- or short-term developments of products and their production. This work, on products such as high-definition TV lighting, medical diagnostics, IT for banks, shops, office and home, etc., is usually placed locally according to expertise. Again, joint ventures are used to extend the available resources, such as in the case of Grundig and VCRs mentioned earlier. Production and development technology is centrally supported under the three distinct headings of fundamental knowledge, application of new know-how and major automation projects. This work is located in CFT Eindhoven, but supported by locally based projects and implementations.

Much research, and a significant amount of development, is centralized and the relevant technologies transferred to the production facilities for further development; but this picture is a generalization. Almost all development of professional equipment is carried out on a local basis, even when initiated by technology transfer. This arises because of the specialized nature of the work which demands collaboration with local professional users. Overall the picture is one of centralized research, but decentralized development.

Technology transfer appears to have a lower profile within Philips than other companies, but perhaps this is because transferring information is taken for granted. Information has always been transferred between research and development and between development and production. Traditionally, the transfer paths have been short, by virtue of geographical location. In the new global company, these paths are much longer and standardization of information transfer, supported by electronic data protocols, is being urged upon national organizations. Transfer will increase in importance, but Philips' business does not demand the massive investment in transfer that characterizes automotive and continuous process industries. A new area of technology transfer is cross-licensing and sale of technologies between companies. Philips and Matsushita, who jointly manufacture the digital compact cassettes, have offered licences on the process to other companies.[17]

SOME ISSUES AND PROBLEMS

If success is growth of business and profits in international markets, what problems might Philips face? The company is clearly slimmer and has reduced its operating costs. By 1991, sales per employee were 13 per cent higher, despite lower volumes. Its new organizational and operational structures are strengthened and concentrate on core competencies. For each competency, all factors about technical possibilities, market needs, competitor strategies, size of world markets and financial resources can be brought to the same discussion table.

The potential to make informed decisions on a global basis is there. Take, for example, the question, should a market such as personal computers be abandoned so that the resources it uses can be concentrated on other consumer electronics? This has many facets, such as integrated manufacture for world-wide markets, cost of developing a world market share, likely developments by international competitors and possible joint ventures. Technological issues are raised, such as whether the core competencies include the necessary skills and whether the technology will be unique to PCs or become integrated into other products.

Finally, there is the issue of whether PCs are becoming an integral part of future consumer products. The structures are being put in place to provide genuinely international answers to such questions. The retained strengths of R&D support this, as do national organizations which influence policy whilst remaining fully accepted and integrated within their local economies.

The difficulties which have yet to be worked out are large. Some will centre around situations where marketing opportunities cross boundaries. Domestic products are becoming less differentiated from professional products. For example, the personal computer discussed above can no longer be classified as simply professional or domestic. A product life cycle model is now established, whereby new products in electronics, especially those concerned with information handling and visual display, are launched first into a professional niche environment. Here a product meets a need, where cost considerations are secondary to professional problems. This phase is characterized by high margins for the developer, but it is rapidly followed by cost reduction of production and mass exploitation in the consumer market. Once accepted in this mass market, the product is taken up again professionally, but by those whose businesses are more cost-sensitive. The distinction between consumer and professional markets is thus blurred, at least for the primary supplier. How will this be perceived within national organizations? Will they identify the different stages of the model sufficiently clearly to advise on policy?

The product divisions must disentangle the conflicting signals from national organizations, many of whom will be at different points in the product life cycle. Other difficulties will centre around political issues, such as demands for indigenous manufacture by emerging nations. Such demands may conflict with integrated manufacturing policies.

Philips is catching up on the Japanese and SE Asia but it started a long way behind. Coming from Taylor's scientific management to a modern, applications driven, reactive management style is a long haul, which took the Japanese 15 years or so. How long will Philips take? More importantly, what new Japanese and Asian strategies are being put in place whilst Philips is changing? Will it still be a step behind the competition?

CONCLUSIONS

The strengths of the company have been supported by a concentration of technical, financial and other resources into a narrower base of business activities. This strategy has the potential for success and prosperity in the new, international trading environment. The question that still concerns many of its shareholders in the early 1990s is whether it can achieve quickly enough the integration of technology, finance, logistics and marketing that was singled out in Chapter 6 as the key that turns potential into reality. As the *Wall Street Journal* said in mid-1987 'If Philips manages to transform itself ... it could become a model for the global corporation of the 1990s'.

References

1   Hamel, G., and Prahalad, C. K., 'Do You Really Have A Global Strategy?', *Harvard Business Review*, July-August 1985, p. 146.
2   Klugt, van der, C. J., Speech to Harvard Business School by the President and Chairman of the Philips' Board of Management, 27 October 1987.
3   'Philips Bows Out Of Cables and Optical Fibres', *Electronics*, March 1992, p. 25.
4   'US Maker Purchases Information Systems Divisions', *Office Equipment and Products*, January 1992, p. 34.
5   'Whittle Communications to be 25 per cent acquired by Philips Electronics for $175m', *Electronic Times*, 13 February 1992, p. 6.
6   Timmer, J., *Philips Annual Report For 1991*.
7   *Source*: European Association Of Consumer Electronic Manufacturers.
8   *Source*: Ministry For Trade (Japan).
9   *Philips*, London, James Capel and Co. September 1989, p. 4.
10 Klugt, van der, C. J., Speech to European Parliament, Brussels, 7 March 1989.
11 Bartlett, C. A., Doz, Y., and Hedland, G., (Eds) *Managing The Global Firm*, (London, Routledge, 1990) Chaps 5 & 9.
12 *Manufacturing Renaissance*, KPMG Peat Marwick McLintock, 1990, pp. 4, 5.
13 Bartlett, C., and Ghoshal, S., Managing across borders, (London, Hutchinson Business Books, 1989).
14 'Philips to Pick CD-I Partner', *Electronic Engineering Times*, 16 March 1992, p. 2.
15 'Philips-Grundig bei Video gemeinsam', *Suddeutsche-Zeitung*, 24 March 1992, p. 28.
16 *Philips Annual Report And Accounts for 1990*.
17 'Makers Begin DCC Licensing', *Journal of the Electronics Industry*, January 1992, p. 11.

QUESTIONS/DISCUSSION TOPICS

1 Discuss the competitive environment within which Philips found itself. How would you keep track of changes in competitive strategies?

2 What strengths and weaknesses in Philips were key in its response to its environment? How could they have been differently utilized and with what potential benefit?

3 Discuss the significance of technology as a driver of competitive strategies within the electronics industries. Which other industries might show similar dependencies?

4 Describe Philips' response to its perceived problems and highlight areas that seem to you worthy of special note.

5 Discuss the use of joint ventures as a means of extending resources. What problems might flow from such ventures and how might they be limited?

6 Explain core competencies and discuss what factors determine which skills become core for a business.

7 Discuss the impact of different management styles on a company's strategic thinking.

CASE TEN

NORTHERN FOODS: A CASE OF DEINTERNATIONALIZATION

SARAH GRIBBIN

ADVICE TO READERS

There are sound economic reasons for certain products and services to be standardized on a global basis, but it can be argued that this model does not fit all markets, products or peoples.

Within certain industries, there are constraints which, by their very nature, may dictate that the industry or product remain within certain geographical boundaries. These constraints include:

- technology;
- the culture of the market-place;
- the production process;
- the nature of the product;
- the links between the organizational culture and management style and the nature of the product;
- climate;
- geography;
- consumer tastes and preferences.

The case shows how Northern Foods is concentrating on a national market and not actively looking to expand globally. The main question

that the reader should address is, will Northern Food have to change this strategic decision in the light of the increasing internationalization of the sector?

INTRODUCTION

Northern Foods is one of the FT-SE 100 share members and in 1991 had a turnover of £1.4 billion and an operating profit of £137.5 million. This is illustrated in the Appendix. Since its takeover of Express Dairies in 1992, it has become the seventh largest food manufacturer in Europe – not bad for a company that few members of the public would have heard of, but which is Marks and Spencer's largest fresh food supplier and has many well-known brands of its own.

The company's 1992 Annual Report opened with the following statement:

> Northern Foods is the United Kingdom's most broadly based, fresh food manufacturer. We produce a wide range of high quality, chilled foods under the 'own labels' of major retailers

The author would like to thank Alec Horsley and Chris Haskins for their help and support in writing this case study. Any inadvertent inaccuracies within the text are solely the responsibility of the author, rather than that of those who so kindly gave their help and advice.

and leading brands, including *Ski, Eden Vale, Pork Farms, Bowyers and Hollands. We are also Britain's largest supplier of liquid milk to households and shops under the Dale Farm and Express brands and retailer labels. Our grocery interests include Fox's, the leading name in premium quality biscuits.*

We produce foods to the highest standards of quality and reliability and are skilled in the handling of short-life products. Our commitment is to customer service, product freshness and innovation, supported by investment in new facilities and technology.

We will continue to grow by meeting our customers' increasing demands for consistent quality, variety and value.

The company's objective in implementing these policies is to improve the prospects of shareholders, employees and the communities in which we operate.

Northern Foods started life in 1936, when Alec Horsley and his father merged their family firm of Pape and Company with Southwicks Dairies. Alec Horsley was the prime mover in establishing Northern Dairies and during the 1940s, 1950s and 1960s built up the organization with a string of enterprizing deals and takeovers with other dairy companies. In 1956, Northern Dairies went public, with Alec Horsley as its Chairman, and he remained so until 1970, when he retired and was succeeded by his son, Nicholas.

Alec Horsley's active Quaker beliefs played a crucial role in the company's early days. This manifested itself through a concern for individual employees, first names being used throughout the organization, and the establishment of an active welfare and sports association for employees and pensioners. An education trust was established to aid those with financial difficulties in the funding of their studies, and many local charities and 'good causes' were and are continually supported. This was, however, balanced by an exceptionally sharp sense of good business and an attention to quality, value and systems that have had a lasting effect within the organization. Stories still circulate in the dairy division of Mr Alec's visits to milk

delivery depots that would include a rummage through the dustbins to make sure that no unbroken milk bottles were unnecessarily and wastefully disposed of.

During his period as Chairman, Northern Dairies was not Alec Horsley's only interest. His 'spare time' was devoted to helping in the formation and growth during the 1950s and 1960s of Campaign for Nuclear Disarmament (CND), a cause still supported by the current Chairman Chris Haskins, Alec Horsley's son-in-law.

The 1960s and 1970s saw a period of diversification away from the core dairy business into many unrelated areas – for example, consumer finance, painting and decorating, car sales and the making of retread tyres. By 1971, 40 per cent of its profits came from consumer finance. However, the 1980s witnessed a move away from unrelated diversification to a point where today the only non-food interest Northern still have is Turners Decorating.

In 1970 Chris Haskins, then Deputy Managing Director of the Irish operation, chanced to be seated next to an executive of Marks and Spencer during a plane journey to Belfast. This was the beginnings of an important relationship for both organizations. The initial outcome of this meeting was that Northern began making St Michael trifle, which in 1990 was still sold in large quantities.

The 1970s saw a considerable increase in the intensity of the relationship existing between Northern and Marks and Spencer. Northern bought several existing Marks and Spencer suppliers, Avana and Park Cakes, to be followed in 1977 by the upmarket Fox's Biscuits, and in 1978 the meat processor and pie maker Pork Farms, who were also suppliers to the supermarket chain, J. Sainsbury.

Until the late 1970s, Northern's only international interests lay in a dairy concern in the West Indies. However, during the 1970s international expansion came about through several US acquisitions. The first was a pork processor called Bluebird. Unfortunately, Northern entered this cyclical, undifferentiated commodity business at the top of a boom and the whole venture was fraught with problems. The second venture, Keystone, ought to have been more promising; Keystone were meat processors, as well as being large suppliers to McDonald's. This area of close customer relationships was one that Northern knew well. The experience of person-to-person marking for special customers, with contacts from chairman to development chiefs in individual plants, had brought great benefits to its UK business. It was anticipated that this experience of closeness and trust, would greatly help in their US business dealings.

However, within the very nature of McDonald's conservative and restricted product lines lay the seeds of some of the issues that were ultimately to contribute to Northern's withdrawal from the US market. Northern's entrepreneurial and innovative style, which had helped to develop and cement the relationships with its main UK customers, were thwarted by McDonald's reluctance to introduce new product lines.

After six years of involvement in the US, Northern eventually sold back to its original owner his 80 per cent share in Bluebird. The experience could not be deemed a resounding success: different management styles, consumer tastes, markets and cultures all combined and led to what Chris Haskins has been known to refer to as 'the American cock-up'. However, many valuable lessons were learnt:

.. not to be naive; not to assume that a shared language means shared assumptions; and how to go about it next time ... there is little doubt that NF will take another bite at the American cherry — when that huge market is ready to accept UK-style high quality, high added-value fresh products rather than the current dreary engineering dominated prepared foods.[1]

CURRENT OPERATION

During the 1980s and early 1990s, Northern's portfolio became increasingly focused, reflecting the sentiment that Northern knew what its type of business was and how to effectively and efficiently manage it. The organization has four operating divisions: dairy, convenience, meat and grocery.

DAIRY

Two million customers a day have fresh, 'Dale Farm' (Northern's brand name) milk delivered to their homes by Northern Dairies franchisees or dairymen. Within the dairy sector, 1,750 of its own milk rounds have been franchised and the acquisition of Express Dairies virtually doubled Northern's dairy sales and made it into one of the three largest players in the UK market.

In addition to the profitable and efficient doorstep delivery and process sides, Northern is also a leading supplier of milk to many of the large supermarkets. It even exports British milk to France through its connections with Marks and Spencer, through its Ashby Dairy Company it produces a growing range of specialist milks for a variety of customers, from flavoured milks for Thornton's through to Pedigree Petfoods Whiskas drink for cats.

The 1992 acquisition of Express Dairies is all part of the strategy intended to guarantee Northern's position of strength in the UK dairy industry, when the much anticipated structural changes to the industry occur in the 1990s. The milk market is one of the most regulated and complex markets in the UK. The Milk Marketing Board, which is at the heart of the system, is under much pressure from the EC to change. These changes, on top of the changes in consumption and distribution patterns, pose a further threat to the current structure of the whole dairy industry.

The European dairy industry is dictated to by the EC's Common Agriculture Policy which, through the use of milk quotas, encourages farmers to 'pour away good milk' rather than risk being fined for over-production. The trade in milk quotas distorts the quantities of milk that would otherwise have been produced in a more 'normal' market system.

The supply of raw milk is totally controlled by the Milk Marketing Board (MMB), which is in effect a producers' monopoly. This monopoly insists that, except for farmer/processors, all dairy farmers must sell their milk through the

MMB, which collects, pools and distributes the milk to the dairies. They operate a highly restrictive system, whereby the price of milk is set according to what it is going to be made into. They permit no discount for volumes, so the price of one gallon is the same as the price of a million gallons. This price is also influenced by the EC. The EC fix a floor-price for butter, below which it may not fall. Northern hope that their policy of being close to not only their employees and customers, but also their suppliers, will help ensure that whatever the outcome of the reorganization of the MMB, their relationship with farmers will be positive and close.

The total liquid milk market can be said to be mature and relatively stable. In 1984/85, total liquid milk sales were 6,055 million litres, and in 1989/90 total liquid milk sales stood at 5,927 million litres, a 2.1 per cent drop in volume terms. However, the 1989/90 figure actually represents a year-on-year increase of 0.5 per cent over the 1988/90 figure.

Nevertheless, these figures disguise an important trend within the market for liquid milk. There has been a marked move away from whole, full-fat milk towards the low-fat, semi-skimmed or skimmed milks. In 1983, only 3 per cent of household milk consumption was of low-fat milks, but by 1990 this figure had risen to 39 per cent and it is predicted to reach 48 per cent by 1992.

A further, and equally dramatic, trend is the change in purchasing habits of consumers. Exhibit 10.1 shows the percentage of households buying milk, by source of purchase, in the previous week. The numbers do not add up to 100 per cent, reflecting the fact that many customers are 'dual purchasers', i.e., they buy milk from both the milkman and the shop. This shift in source of supply is attributable primarily to two main factors. Firstly, there is the issue of

Exhibit 10.1
Source of purchase of milk

Year	Doorstep	Supermarket	Small shop
1985	82%	27%	20%
1990	68%	45%	25%

convenience for the purchaser: the whole week's shopping can be done at one time and in one place, the supermarket. The second, and increasingly important, issue is that of price. The price differential between a pint of pasteurized whole milk delivered to the doorstep, and a 4-pint plastic container purchased from the supermarket, has increased from 12.3 per cent in 1985 to 20.5 per cent in 1990.

CONVENIENCE

The convenience foods sector produces a wide range of high quality, fresh foods for leading stores and supermarkets, but it could be said that it was Marks and Spencer and Northern Foods between them that virtually invented the market for recipe dishes. Northern have three whole factories devoted to creating and producing chilled 'recipe dishes' for Marks and Spencer and it is the European leader in this specialist market. The very nature of this market demands constant, new product development, the highest quality and service standards and regular investment in new capacity to keep pace with the increasing demand. Examples of the diversity of the product range include fresh soups and pasta dishes for Marks and Spencer.

The more 'traditional' product lines within convenience foods include fresh pies, quiches, sausage rolls, pizzas, cakes and breads. Northern has, however, avoided entry into the cut-throat, undifferentiated, mainstream bread market, by concentrating on the demand for speciality breads and filled buns and sandwiches. Since the acquisition of Falconis, who supply Marks and Spencer with speciality breads, Northern have consolidated and built up their presence in this niche market.

During 1991, Northern bought Kara Foods, again increasing their product range and customer base within the speciality bread market, and in 1992 they bought a strategic shareholding in yet another speciality baker. Northern now concentrates on supplying Marks and Spencer and other retailers, and the restaurant and hotel trade, with their speciality breads. Park Cakes operates as both a supplier to the main retailers and in its own right; again, the emphasis is not only on quality, but also constant innovation and investment. The convenience food section also includes factories making yogurts and dairy desserts, as well as a salad produce grower and the fast-growing NFT distribution, which works for all Northern's companies as well as retailers and other food manufacturers, including Sainsbury and Asda.

MEAT

Pork Farm, Hollands, Fleur de Lys, Bowyers, Trafford Park Banker, Palethorpes, Trentham and Savoury Foods, Parrs, Mayhew Chicken, Dorset Chilled Foods and Binghams all combine within the meat sector and make Northern Foods the UK's leading manufacturer of fresh meat pies and savouries. Once again, they produce Northern's own brands and serve the needs of such retailers as Tesco, Sainsbury and Marks and Spencer.

GROCERY

The grocery sector represents Northern's longer-life food businesses. Fox's are the UK's leading, premium quality, biscuit brand and Elkes produce sweet and semi-sweet biscuits, both for retailers and under their own name. The other members of this group are Smiths Floor Mills and the Irish Batchelors and Poldy's, Batchelors being brand leaders in Eire and Poldy's being a fast-growing frozen foods business.

STRUCTURE

Northern Foods have 30,000 employees within the UK. The company is organized into 60 profit centres which are responsible, not only for its operating decisions, but also for balance sheets, cash flow and return on assets. These centres each have their own managing director or general manager, and are also responsible for close customer contacts and new product and market ideas and developments. This structure allows staff, even at a relatively junior level, to be given positions of responsibility, a situation enjoyed in few organizations.

Managers are encouraged to develop their individual skills and careers and gain as much experience in different parts of the organization as they can. These opportunities for responsibility are intended to encourage the flair, the initiative, and the individuality that help to maintain Northern Foods' reputation as the market leader.

This highly decentralized structure is managed from the Hull head office. The Board of Directors takes responsibility for overall strategic direction of the group, with a group executive committee, made up of three main executive Board members and other senior managers, who are responsible for operational decisions. Although the company has grown and developed considerably from its early days, the management style remains largely unchanged. The ethos is very much one of team effort, the importance of each individual's contribution being stressed and valued. The hands-on, close contact style of all the management is reflected in the members of the main Board of Directors. The top management team are not remote head office recluses; their names and faces are well known throughout the Northern empire, and they make frequent site visits. The first-name terms, and the apparent informality and openness within the organization, are features that strike outsiders and new employees alike.

Profit-sharing schemes and share-save schemes are available to employees. The welfare and pensioners' associations continue to flourish, with events like the group sports day and Christmas parties proving very popular. *Employee Reports* and the internally produced *Northern News* newspapers are available to all employees. Even customers such as franchisees and bottle milk buyers receive their own newspapers and regular flows of information and access to social events.

With its special customers, Northern has developed a system of person-to-person marking with personal contacts from company Chairman down to development chiefs in individual plants. Although time-consuming, and seen by some as unnecessary, this policy, which is a manifestation of their closeness to customers, paid dividends in 1988 during a threatened takeover of Northern by the smaller Hazelwood Foods. Although Hazelwood were not seen as plausible owners of Northern and were possibly more interested in breaking up Northern or selling it on at a profit, a turning-point in their hostile stake-building campaign came on 3 May 1988 when Northern's largest customer, Marks and Spencer, issued a statement saying:

> We would like Northern to remain independent. They are a highly innovative company and very important to us. We have had very good relations with them for 20 years.

This message was further driven home to Hazelwood by Chris Haskins saying that there was no contractual obligation on Marks and Spencer to buy Northern's products. The relationship was based on trust.

THE UK FOOD INDUSTRY

The nature of the UK food industry has changed dramatically in the 1980s. A report in 1992 from the Corporate Intelligence Group, the retail consultants, showed increasing concentration of retail power in the UK. The ten largest retailers accounted for more than a third of all sales and during 1991 increased their combined market share by 2 per cent. The top six grocery retailers accounted for 75 per cent of all food sales.

The report supports the view that, for the retail trade as a whole, there is increasing polarization between the strong, large chains who benefit from economies of scale and bigger efficiencies and the greater flexibility of the small chains. Between them are sandwiched the middle-ranking multiples, whose position looks increasingly precarious.

An article in the *Financial Times* in December 1991 examined the relationships between retailers and producers.[2] Technological and logistical advances have revolutionized the relationship between stores and their suppliers. The large retailers have invested heavily in new technology, which enables them to bring the

principles of 'just in time' production systems to the supermarket floors. These technological developments take three main forms.

- *Distribution systems* Until recently, most retailers relied on manufacturers to deliver products to the shops. Now retailers do much of the distribution themselves, with manufacturers delivering only to centralized warehouses. This, combined with powerful computer DRP systems, gives retailers a far higher degree of control over deliveries. Marks and Spencer can have their shelves restocked within 12 hours of placing an order.
- *Electronic point-of-sale scanning systems* These provide the retailer with fast and detailed information on product sales, and it is intended that eventually these systems will transmit replenishment orders automatically.
- *Electronic data interchange* These will eventually replace paper orders and invoices to allow automatic transmission between retailer and supplier.

Combine these features with the more accurate forecasting techniques now used by the retailers and the result is a system which considerably reduces lead-times, and passes down the supply chain many of the risks and problems inherent in food retailing. For an organization like Northern Foods, whose current success is due in part to the very specialized skills that they developed in the delivery and handling of fresh milk, exploitation of fast, accurate and safe delivery and process systems is second nature.

Coupled with the shift in power from the independents to the large multiple retailers is the growth of private label (own brand) products as a proportion of the retail food sales in the UK. Research published in 1991 showed that these private-label goods now account for a third of all UK packaged grocery sales and the number of lines and the amount of advertising expenditure is increasing fast.[3] This point is illustrated in Exhibit 10.2.

In 1990 J. Sainsbury introduced 1,300 new lines, bringing their share of private-label goods to some 40 per cent, whilst Tesco has increased their advertising expenditure on private-label

Exhibit 10.2
Private-label products as proportion of total UK retail foods sales

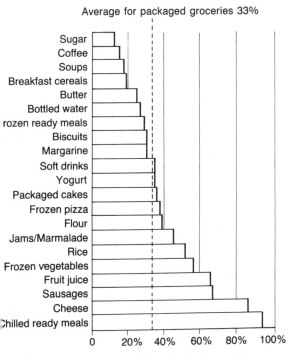

Average for packaged groceries 33%

Sugar
Coffee
Soups
Breakfast cereals
Butter
Bottled water
Frozen ready meals
Biscuits
Margarine
Soft drinks
Yogurt
Packaged cakes
Frozen pizza
Flour
Jams/Marmalade
Rice
Frozen vegetables
Fruit juice
Sausages
Cheese
Chilled ready meals

0   20%   40%   60%   80%   100%

Source: Adapted from *Financial Times*, 31 October, 1991.

ENVIRONMENTAL FACTORS

Since the 1960s, there has been a considerable shift in the life-styles and expectations of people, not only in the UK, but in the whole of Western society. Several factors have combined to bring about the changes:

- dual-income families, working wives, increasingly affluent young people and growing affluence amongst the large numbers of 'young at heart' people over retirement age; added to these, the general increase in wealth by society as a whole;
- the considerable increase in foreign travel by the population as a whole, which has increased the interest in foreign foods and eating habits;
- technological developments, such as microwave ovens, and awareness of more controlled production techniques.

The combined effect of these demographic, economic and technical factors has been the development of new eating habits, resulting in a higher demand for more sophisticated food products.

brands from £191,000 in 1986 to £13.5 million in 1990. Although the average proportion of private-label products of all retail food sales is a third, there is a wide variation in the relative strengths of private-label, depending on the product.

The supermarkets also adopt differing images for their 'own brand' products. At one end of the scale is the 'no-nonsense', good value bargain, and at the other end, for example, Marks and Spencer, where 'own brand' high quality markets is the image. However, the image which is portrayed should, and indeed must, complement the overall image and strategy which the supermarket chain attempts to pursue.

In a research project carried out by Kingston Business School, it was found that people ranked quality and choice as the major reasons for using out-of-town stores. These factors were less important for people using stores within town centres. Exhibit 10.3 illustrates this point.

THE WORLD FOOD MARKETS

THE EUROPEAN MARKETS

Europe's food industry is highly complex, fragmented and regionalized, the 20 largest food manufacturers only accounting for 12 per cent of the market.

The fragmentation of the market reflects the nature of the European-wide market, with very diverse tastes conforming to national and even regional boundaries. There are few 'Euro-products' and those aspiring to that title are often obliged to have slight regional/national differences. Nescafé, for example, comes in 50 different combinations of strength, taste and flavour.

Certain product categories are more prone to concentration than others. The European market for edible fats is dominated by Unilever and they have a fair percentage of the market

Exhibit 10.3
Why people like supermarkets

	WHY PEOPLE LIKE SUPERMARKETS						
	Quality, Choice	Convenient location	Easy parking	Good value	Convenient opening	Clean	Friendly
Tesco	53	40	26	22	22	8	7
Sainsbury	70	32	23	25	14	14	3
Safeway	46	55	23	14	25	14	9
Asda	55	39	30	25	9	9	11
Gateway	34	68	20	17	12	2	7
Others	26	52	28	32	11	9	9
Mean	48	45	25	24	16	10	7

Response in percentages

Source: Adapted from *The Independent*, 26 November, 1991.

for ice-cream. Kellogg's have a commanding hold over the breakfast cereal market, whilst within the chocolate market four companies, Mars, Nestlé, Suchard and Cadbury, dominate.

Some of the problems facing European food manufacturers are well illustrated by one of the largest multinationals, Unilever. In an article in the *Financial Times*, Guy de Jonquières showed how Unilever is attempting to reshape its food business:

by eliminating inefficient duplication, rationalising manufacturing, strengthening internal collaboration and extending products and marketing concepts faster across borders.[4]

This response to the changes in the European market is considerably less dramatic than the restructuring of their detergents division. This is a reflection of Unilever's view that, whilst European consumers are far more likely to try exotic new dishes, these are likely to remain niche products.

Allan Price, Chairman of Birds Eye Wall's, reckons that there are about five varieties of staple food accounting for three-quarters of sales in every national market, with the rest divided between ten or more niche products. Lasagne is one of the few products that is a staple food in many European and American households.

Unilever's attitude to new product development is now leaning towards the development of international products, with modifications only if there is a strong regional difference in taste. Recent examples of this strategy include Ragu spaghetti sauce and the Magnum ice-cream bar. However, even within Europe, markets do vary considerably. For example frozen herbs, Unilever's most profitable frozen product in Germany, flopped in the UK, as did the seven attempts to introduce the Continental ice-cream Carte d'Or into the UK. The degree of harmonization that will eventually be possible is open to debate. Some believe that there will always be major national and regional differences, whilst others believe that it will be the nature of the product that will eventually dictate the degree of harmonization. Basic products, such as edible oils, are capable of a high degree of harmonization, whilst in other cases it may be easier to export concepts such as 'healthy eating', as opposed to the products themselves.

The issues of branded versus private-label products, and the relative power of retailers and manufacturers, are also relevant to the European markets. It is still rare for European supermarkets to have a sizeable presence outside their home markets. Their buying power relative to that of the manufacturers is continuing to grow.

During the late 1980s, the food manufacturing industry saw a flood of mergers as companies fought to ensure brand leadership and scale of operation. Antoine Riboud, Chairman of the French company BSN, is quoted as saying:

In this business, the Number 1 makes a lot of money, the Number 2 can make a decent living, the Number 3 just suffers.

Regardless of size, food manufacturers tend to be highly specialized. For example, Nestlé's businesses tend to be concentrated around coffee and milk-based products, whilst Unilever specializes in edible oils, ice-cream and tea. The European food market is, however, character-ized by the large number of small- and medium-sized companies concentrated within their own home-base. Even quite large companies can have strong regional tendencies; BSN, for example is highly concentrated in France and Italy. There are also various large American companies, such as Philip Morris, PepsiCo, Sara Lee and Campbells Soups, which are also keen to prioritize the European food markets. However, virtually all the large food manufac-turers are concentrated within the processed, long-life product ranges. Few are competitors within the market of processed fresh products.

The European supermarkets are still strongly biased along national lines, with large national chains still cautious about venturing away from home. The most notable exception to this is Aldi and Netto's attempts to conquer the discount end of the European supermarket business. Their expansion into virtually every European country has challenged the established chains at a time of economic recession, when the con-sumers are at their most sensitive to price com-petition. Their market positioning in relatively barren, warehouse-type buildings, reverting to a 'pile it high, sell it cheap' philosophy, keeping product choices to a minimum, concentrating on long-life as opposed to fresh products, keeping staffing levels and general overhead costs as low as possible, has made an impact in the markets they have so far entered.

At the other end of the spectrum, Marks and Spencer has its ambitions firmly set on European expansion. In 1992, when it had 17 European stores, it announced that it intended to build 23 new stores, increasing its selling space during 1992 by 40 per cent and quad-rupling it over the next four years. They intend to concentrate their expansion in the Nether-lands, Belgium, France and Spain, countries where they are already successfully established. It has already franchised retail outlets in Scandinavia and Portugal. It has no immediate plans to open stores in Germany and Italy. Its food sections in Paris have already started introducing the French to the very 'English' products of cakes, marmalades, breakfast milk and recipe dishes, all relatively unknown to the French culinary palate until the Marks and Spencer introduction.

THE NORTH AMERICAN MARKET

The North American food and retail market, as Northern Foods and others have discovered, is a different animal from that of Europe. In May 1992, Marks and Spencer announced that they are to pull out of their loss-making Canadian subsidiary. Many UK retailers, including Dixons, John Menzies and The Sock Shop, have been attracted to the United States for the very same reasons that Northern Foods was – the apparently common language and culture – and have learnt to their cost that these factors do not ensure success.

There are marked differences between North American consumer tastes and retail distri-bution systems and their UK equivalents. The recent advent of discount warehouses has put pressure on the already different, and less pro-fitable, cost structure of American super-markets. Distribution patterns are different from the centralized systems being developed by UK stores. Store layout has a tendency to be cluttered, opening hours tend to be longer and the range of goods available in US stores is traditionally wider. Customer tastes also vary considerably. Branded goods in the UK are widely perceived as being far superior to the supermarkets' private-label products, which are seen as being of low quality. Sales of private-label goods in the US are less than 15 per cent of sales compared to the rapidly approaching 40 per cent in Sainsbury's stores in the UK. The US brand manufacturers are reluctant to relinquish any of their power and are not interested in supplying private-label goods for the supermarkets.

Sainsbury's foray into the American supermarket business was through the acquisition of Shaw's, a New England supermarket chain. Their experience in attempting to transfer their skills at being one of the most efficient and profitable retailers in the UK to the relatively low-profile, US market has shown that there are considerable differences in the two apparently similar markets. They shift the management of the stores towards a product-based system, installing new computerized systems, and attempting to change the distribution of the goods towards a more UK-based approach. In addition, they are also attempting to change the American perception of private-label goods by emphasizing their high-quality specifications. However, they not only face refusal from some reputable manufacturers to supply the goods, but also scepticism from other, well-established, supermarket rivals. Safeway, for example, consider any growth in the volume of their private-label goods as merely a reflection of the economic recession, rather than any change of heart by the consumers.

CONCLUSIONS

It could be argued that the increasing inter-nationalization of many industries and markets would appear to be a tide against which it is difficult to swim. Increasingly, a whole range of goods and services are becoming standardized and national tastes, histories and preferences are being subjugated.

The 1990s are seeing a fundamental change in world food markets, and the subsequent restructuring of the industry is still continuing. However, the question as to how far the internationalization of food markets can go must be asked. Northern Food's continuing success within their current markets seems to have secured their place as a player within the UK food markets. Growth within other markets is not seen as an immediate priority within the organization. Is this policy a reflection of the fact that there are natural limits to how far other nations' food preferences can be standardized or, which the nature of the markets that Northern have concentrated on does not easily allow? Have Northern's experiences in the apparently very different markets of the USA so coloured their attitude towards international expansion as to deter them from trying it again?

References

1 *Management Today*, 1988.
2 *Financial Times*, December 1991.
3 OC & C Strategy Consultants, *Just When You Thought It Was Safe To Put Brands On The Balance Sheet*.
4 *Financial Times*, 28 November 1991.

QUESTIONS/DISCUSSION TOPICS

1 Assess the threats to Northern Food's present portfolio of products.

2 Given the fragmented nature of the international food industry and markets, how realistic is Northern Food's policy of home-based expansion?

3 Analyse the importance of developments in related industries to Northern Food's future prospects.

4 What are the strengths and weaknesses of Northern Food's style of management?

5 The dairy industry is undergoing fundamental structural changes. Assess the importance of this for Northern Foods.

APPENDIX
NORTHERN FOODS PLC – EXCERPTS FROM ANNUAL REPORTS

CONSOLIDATED PROFIT AND LOSS ACCOUNT
FOR THE YEAR ENDED 31st MARCH 1992

	1992 £m	1991 £m
TURNOVER	**1,444.2**	1,187.0
Cost of sales	**(1,056.4)**	(874.9)
GROSS PROFIT	**387.8**	312.1
Distribution costs	**(181.2)**	(144.9)
Administrative expenses	**(71.7)**	(57.8)
Other operating income	**2.6**	2.2
OPERATING PROFIT	**137.5**	111.6
Investment income	**1.9**	2.6
Interest payable	**(9.7)**	(6.1)
Allocated to profit sharing	**(3.5)**	(2.7)
PROFIT ON ORDINARY ACTIVITIES BEFORE TAXATION	**126.2**	105.4
Taxation on profit on ordinary activities	**(32.7)**	(28.4)
PROFIT ON ORDINARY ACTIVITIES AFTER TAXATION	**93.5**	77.0
Extraordinary items	**–**	1.1
PROFIT FOR THE FINANCIAL YEAR	**93.5**	78.1
Dividends	**(41.6)**	(32.2)
RETAINED PROFIT FOR THE YEAR	**51.9**	45.9
EARNINGS PER ORDINARY SHARE	**38.31p**	32.79p

Earnings per share for both the current and comparative years have been adjusted to reflect the bonus element of the rights issues.

CONSOLIDATED BALANCE SHEET
AT 31st MARCH 1992

	1992 £m	1991 £m
FIXED ASSETS		
Tangible fixed assets	**560.2**	400.2
CURRENT ASSETS		
Stocks	**73.1**	54.2
Debtors	**227.2**	142.9
Cash at bank and in hand	**45.8**	20.1
	346.1	217.2
CREDITORS: amounts falling due within one year	**558.3**	292.5
Net current liabilities	**(212.2)**	(75.3)
Total assets less current liabilities	**348.0**	324.9
CREDITORS: amounts falling due after more than one year	**9.0**	7.0
	339.0	317.9
PROVISIONS FOR LIABILITIES AND CHARGES	**62.0**	12.5
	277.0	305.4
CAPITAL AND RESERVES		
Called up share capital	**70.6**	55.6
Share premium account	**0.2**	61.3
Revaluation reserve	**12.1**	12.3
Other reserves	**4.1**	4.1
Profit and loss account	**190.0**	172.1
SHAREHOLDERS' FUNDS	**277.0**	305.4

FIVE-YEAR RECORD
YEAR ENDED 31st MARCH

£m where applicable	1988	1989	1990	1991	1992
Turnover	1,019.2	1,041.3	1,094.4	1,187.0	1,444.2
Profit before tax	77.3	85.3	90.2	105.4	126.2
Earned for ordinary shareholders from operations	54.4	60.7	64.9	77.0	93.5
Extraordinary items	(13.6)	(9.2)	(5.9)	1.1	–
Ordinary dividends	(22.1)	(24.9)	(27.8)	(32.2)	(41.6)
Retained in the business	18.7	26.6	31.2	45.9	51.9
*Number of ordinary shares in issue (millions)	233.6	234.1	234.6	235.1	282.4
*Earnings per ordinary share (pence)	23.36	25.95	27.67	32.79	38.31
*Dividends per ordinary share (pence)	9.46	10.64	11.83	13.72	15.75
Dividend cover (times)	2.5	2.4	2.3	2.4	2.4
Retained profit plus depreciation	42.0	52.7	60.1	79.6	93.3
Capital expenditure	49.0	66.0	75.9	60.7	93.1
Shareholders' funds	276.4	296.3	314.2	305.4	277.0

* Figures have been adjusted to reflect the bonus element of the rights issue.

FIVE-YEAR RECORD
YEAR ENDED 31st MARCH

£m where applicable	1984	1985	1986	1987	1988
Turnover	1,319.8	1,293.3	1,514.0	1,348.2	1,019.2
Profit before tax	54.3	56.6	67.4	75.2	77.3
Earned for ordinary shareholders from operations	39.8	41.4	43.6	49.9	54.4
Extraordinary items	(34.8)	(0.8)	(1.6)	20.1	(13.6)
Ordinary dividends	(14.2)	(15.4)	(17.1)	(19.8)	(22.1)
Retained in the business	(9.2)	25.2	24.9	50.2	18.7
Number of ordinary shares in issue (*millions*)	215.2	217.1	218.5	220.3	221.0
Earnings per ordinary share (*pence*)	18.65	19.11	20.01	22.70	24.69
Dividends per ordinary share (*pence*)	6.75	7.25	8.00	9.00	10.00
Dividend cover (*times*)	2.8	2.7	2.5	2.5	2.5
Retained profit plus depreciation	14.8	50.3	52.5	80.6	42.0
Capital expenditure	46.1	70.0	58.7	55.6	49.0
Shareholders' funds	208.4	213.1	227.4	263.3	276.4

NOTES TO THE ACCOUNTS

TURNOVER AND SEGMENTAL ANALYSIS

	1992 £m	1991 £m
ASSETS		
Dairy	**212.4**	114.8
Convenience Foods	**189.4**	128.6
Meat	**120.8**	108.6
Grocery	**93.6**	91.5
Operating assets	**616.2**	443.5
Non-operating assets and liabilities	**(339.2)**	(138.1)
Net assets	**277.0**	305.4
ASSETS ANALYSIS		
Tangible fixed assets	**560.2**	400.2
Stocks	**73.1**	54.2
Debtors	**215.0**	142.9
Creditors	**(232.1)**	(153.8)
Operating assets	**616.2**	443.5
Cash at bank and in hand	**45.8**	20.1
Borrowings	**(244.8)**	(73.5)
Current taxation	**(64.3)**	(53.3)
Deferred taxation and other provisions	**(49.8)**	(12.5)
Dividend payable	**(26.1)**	(18.9)
Net assets	**277.0**	305.4
Net gearing	**71.8%**	17.5%
Return on sales	**9.5%**	9.4%
Return on average operating assets	28.1%	25.2%

ANALYSIS OF ACTIVITIES

	1988 £m	1987 £m
TURNOVER		
Dairy Group	450.0	433.4
Convenience Foods Group	206.4	197.1
Meat Group	231.8	240.3
Grocery Group	121.4	105.3
UK turnover	1,009.6	976.1
North America	9.6	372.1
Group turnover	1,019.2	1,348.2
PROFIT		
Dairy Group	38.0	31.9
Convenience Foods Group	13.3	10.2
Meat Group	13.2	13.1
Grocery Group	12.6	10.0
UK operating profit	77.1	65.2
Related company	–	4.0
UK finance charges	(0.5)	(2.5)
Profit sharing	(2.1)	(2.1)
UK profit before tax	74.5	64.6
North America	2.8	10.6
Group profit before tax	77.3	75.2
ASSETS		
Tangible fixed assets	268.9	257.7
Stock	46.2	46.7
Debtors	113.4	101.5
Creditors	(145.7)	(146.9)
UK operating assets	282.8	259.0
North American operating assets	10.5	29.4
Cash and short term investments	14.9	17.3
Borrowings	(9.4)	(21.5)
Deferred taxation	(9.7)	(10.4)
Dividend payable	(12.7)	(10.5)
Net assets	276.4	263.3
Net gearing	–	1.6%
Return on UK sales	7.6%	6.7%
Return on UK operating assets	27.3%	25.2%
Return on net assets	28.0%	28.6%

CHANGING CORPORATE IDENTITY TO SUCCEED: THE CASE OF TYPHOON INTERNATIONAL LTD

JILL PRESTON

ADVICE TO READERS

By the end of the 1980s Typhoon International, a producer of wetsuits and drysuits for the leisure market and of protective clothing, was faced with a changing business environment and the recession, which was resulting in a major clear-out of sports clothing manufacturers. In response, the company changed its corporate identity and developed a radical new range of products; the aim being to reposition Typhoon as a producer of contemporary water sports gear and equipment in a young, fashion-conscious market. This case study tells the Typhoon story.

TYPHOON'S BUSINESS BACKGROUND

Typhoon International is a producer of wetsuits and drysuits for the leisure industry and the survival/protective clothing markets. Typhoon is an independent, UK, private limited company, with approximately 60 employees and an annual turnover of £2.2m. The headquarters are located in East Sheen, London, and the Company's 24,000 square feet factory is situated in Redcar, Cleveland. About 25 per cent of turnover is realized by exporting activity.

The company has four main areas of operation:

- wetsuit manufacture;
- drysuit manufacture for sports and safety and survival;
- injection-moulded thermal footwear;
- accessories for the sports diving market, such as masks, fins and snorkels.

Typhoon concentrates on those products where it can control the design and manufacture.

Typhoon was set up in 1946 by Oscar Gugen. At that time, the company traded under the name E. T. Skinner and was primarily

---

I should like to express my thanks to Roger Gugen, Director of Typhoon International Ltd, for the assistance that he has given during the writing of this case. The study was developed from work carried out as part of the EC Commission's EuroMarketing Project in 1992. The project was carried out for the WPP group, which includes Hill & Knowlton International, Belgium.

concerned with the importation of general goods, including sports equipment, and later, sports diving equipment. Gugen, who later founded the British Sub Aqua Club, saw the market potential in diving and he proceeded to develop a range of equipment, including masks, fins, and snorkels. In turn, this led to the development of protective clothing for divers and in 1952 the company launched the first British drysuit for diving.

During the 1950s Gugen worked on the development of protective garments for divers. The Typhoon wetsuit was launched, which was the first wetsuit in the UK and one of the first in the world.

When windsurfing became a popular sport in Europe, existing wetsuits, which had been developed for other sports, were used, but these were not entirely suitable for the type of physical activity involved in the new sport. In the mid-1970s, the company was approached by Peter Brockhaus, who at that time was Ten Cate importer for Germany; later he set up the Mistral company and then F2. In conjunction with Brockhaus, Typhoon developed a new range of suits and became one of the first European companies to produce a range of wetsuits specifically designed for windsurfing.

One of the problems with the early wetsuits was that the type of stitching used to sew them together made them uncomfortable to wear. The German sewing-machine company, Mauser, was approached and as a result it developed a machine which could sew a strong stitch which was also soft to the skin. Previously, wetsuits were glued and taped.

The original Typhoon drysuit was heavy and therefore only suitable for divers. Gugen realized that a lightweight wetsuit would be of great benefit to surface watersports enthusiasts. In 1977 Typhoon launched the lightweight drysuit, which incorporated a butyl/nylon laminate, a material used in assault craft.

The lightweight drysuit was further developed for water-skiing and other surface watersports, and retails under the name Typhoon Drystyle. Further development of the suit resulted in a model for use by dinghy sailors and windsurfers. From the original drysuit, the Sport Diving Drysuit was developed for sports divers and the Pro-Diving Drysuit, for commercial divers. In addition, the Front Entry Survival Drysuit was developed for the rescue services, including the United States Coastguards and the Royal National Lifeboat Institution.

In 1979 the company decided on a name change. The name 'Typhoon', which had been used as a brand name, became the company's new name.

During the recession of the early 1980s, there was a major clear-out of sports clothing manufacturers, especially at the lower and middle ends of the market. It was during this period that the company felt that a different approach was required for the sports side of its business. Typhoon had developed its products from the diving side, rather than from the leisure clothing side of the industry. Typhoon's suits were regarded as technically sound, but lacking in fashion sense and flair.

By the end of the 1980s, Typhoon had changed its corporate identity and the company was relaunched in 1989. The new corporate identity not only involved a change of image with a new logo, but also a radical change of product on the sports side of the business. In effect, the company moved from the middle to the upper end of the market. In 1987, Typhoon had purchased the footwear division of a French company which had developed a range of specialist thermal footwear for watersports. In 1988, a completely new product was designed, the Typhoon Flexboot, and by 1989 Typhoon was the brand leader in this sector.

THE WATERSPORTS MARKET

Since Typhoon was founded, the watersports market has changed dramatically. In 1946, this market was characterized by a handful of enthusiasts, with divers requiring performance, as opposed to aesthetically pleasing, products. Until the mid-1960s, divers were the main users of wetsuits, but this market began to develop when dinghy sailing became popular. This growth expanded dramatically with the increased popularity of windsurfing in the 1980s. By the

1990s the market for wetsuits included wind-surfers, Typhoon's most important market, together with surfers, water-skiers, jet-skiers, canoeists and dinghy sailors.

TYPHOON'S MARKETING RESPONSE

In 1988 Typhoon commissioned Sports Marketing to carry out a quantitative and a qualitative research survey of the UK end-users of its products. The survey showed that Typhoon was the second largest operator in the wetsuit market. It also showed that Typhoon's products appealed to the older end of the market, those who were aged 35 and above, although 80 per cent of this market was found in the 18–35 age group. The company's visual image was considered to be old-fashioned, with none of the colour, and vibrancy of competitive logos which appealed to younger people. It was obvious to Typhoon that they were unsatisfactory to their existing market.

It was at this time that the company decided to change its corporate identity. Typhoon commissioned the consultants, Coley Porter Bell, to develop a new corporate image, the objective being to reposition Typhoon as a producer of contemporary watersports wear and equipment in a young, fashion-conscious market. This identity in turn spearheaded the relaunch of the company. Coley Porter Bell's research revealed that Typhoon had a number of strengths and opportunities. It had a well-known name, which associated it with the strength and power of wind and water. It had a sound reputation for quality at a reasonable price and the company was perceived to have a good sales force, administration and distribution network. This research revealed some weaknesses, one retailer describing the logo as 'cheap and tacky'. The company was also considered to have a conservative approach to change.

In comparison with its competitors, Typhoon's promotional material, including its corporate image, was not easily recognizable on clothing and could not be seen clearly in publicity or advertising shots. The research confirmed that

the typical watersports enthusiast was young, with a relatively high disposable income, and was fashion-conscious; 'they want to be seen wearing the right brands of sports clothing'. It was clear that the long-term prospects for Typhoon were bleak unless they took prompt action. The object of the exercise was for Typhoon to obtain the status of brand leader by 1991. The new corporate image as the catalyst for change was central to Typhoon's identity and business plan.

This, as an expression of its culture , would be core to its success. It would set a new tone for the company and its products, giving both a higher profile and providing the opportunity for a new public relations and advertising campaign.

Coley, Porter & Bell design initiative report to
Typhoon International Ltd, August 1989

The new logo represented a flexible visual identity. Exhibit 11.1 shows both the old and the new logos.

The design of the new logo is a symbolic representation of a sail cutting through water, 'giving a feel of speed and excitement'. The new logo enabled the introduction of the latest fashionable colours and the facility to update them as fashions change. This was a vital part of Typhoon's strategy, since the watersports market is fashion-led. The logo was used across stationery, promotional material and products.

A business strategy was drawn up, focusing on the design, manufacture and marketing of wetsuits, drysuits and moulded footwear. The diving market, once the core of the business but now static, was given lower priority. Typhoon would manufacture a limited number of products and completely withdraw from the wholesaling of diving equipment.

MARKETING WETSUITS

The main theme of the business plan was the development of separate suits for different sports.

Exhibit 11.1
A The former logo
B The new logo

Stop Playing... Start Performing

Source: Typhoon International Ltd

We can't sell a windsurfer's suit to a bike rider, you could two years ago but not now. The product wouldn't perform in the way that it should, it would be the wrong materials, the wrong reinforcements in the wrong places.

Roger Gugen

The new wetsuits were aimed at the top end of the market and designed to appeal to the serious windsurfer, water-skier and jet-skier. The technical demands of unusual waterproof fabrics, and the stresses and strains placed on the finished garment, make wetsuit design and manufacture particularly challenging. The advice of leading participants in these sports was obtained and the services of top designer Derek Ball were acquired.

The main form of promotion for wetsuits is through the specialist magazines. Other f rms of promotion include brochures and participation in trade shows. The image of Typhoon as wetsuit manufacturers has changed, but the safety element required is also included in promoting the product. Typhoon actively uses the credibility obtained in the survival/ protective clothing side of the business to market the quality and safety of their wetsuits.

In spite of the recession of the early 1990s, the company decided not to implement a price discounting policy, as it wished to pursue its image of quality products:

> *It would be easy to increase our volume of sales by giving the distributors our margin, but we are not interested in this. Gross profit, not turnover, is the real issue.*

A director

During 1991/2, part of the publicity budget was used to support a promotion within the specialist magazines, which included a coupon offering a sports bag at half-price in the appropriate retail outlets. The idea behind the promotion was, of course, to get people into these shops and the dealers were under an obligation to display the products advertised.

Virtually all of Typhoon's sportswear is sold through specialist retail outlets. In the UK, Typhoon has a sales force of three representatives and 70 dealers are designated as main wetsuit stockists.

MARKETING WETSUITS IN EUROPE AND THE WIDER WORLD

Typhoon does not view the EC as a single market for its products. The company exports to a range of countries, including Holland, Italy, Southern Ireland, and Spain, as well as Chile and the Middle East. Of the turnover of wetsuits, approximately 15 per cent is realized from exports.

In a number of countries, the costs of distribution and transportation make it difficult for Typhoon to compete with locally produced wetsuits. For example, Typhoon has not attempted to penetrate the German market. In Germany, most of the wetsuits are imported from the Far East, one factor being that the German watersports enthusiast prefers the mainly black rubber wetsuit, which is labour-intensive to produce. This type of wetsuit has rubber on the outside and rubber goods can enter Germany without duty being imposed, whereas the type of wetsuits produced by Typhoon are subject to duties.

The strategy to develop specialist suits for different sports has resulted in exporting success. Its decision to develop a new range each year, as well as to invest heavily in the production of new materials, has also contributed to this success. As with the UK market, the company is not concerned purely with increasing the volume of sales, so it has not greatly increased the distributors' margins.

There is some standardization of promotion across Europe. For example, the specialist sports magazines are targeted, and the general promotion of the brand name 'Typhoon' is directed to the upper end of the market, with an emphasis on the younger customer. The company also promotes its products on mainland Europe through trade shows. In general terms, Typhoon's pricing policy 'follows the customer': individual national circumstances have a major impact on pricing decisions.

The method of distribution is common across Europe. For example, in finding distributors the company uses the watersports network; 'watersports is a pretty small world.'– In Holland the distributor for the jet-ski suit is the distributor for Yamaha bikes, who clearly wishes to give a whole package to retail outlets.

In terms of product development, the main point of distinction is specialism by sports, but in terms of exporting to European countries and the rest of the world, Typhoon has to take account of some national requirements, especially in the area of colours and colour combinations.

MARKETING THE SURVIVAL/PROTECTIVE SUITS

In marketing the survival/protective range of drysuits, the users are targeted rather than the retail outlet. Typhoon has no real competition in this market in the UK, and in Europe and the wider world it is regarded as a market leader. The main strategy is to raise awareness of the product amongst appropriate organizations. The message that is being promoted is, 'Anyone working on water ought to be wearing a drysuit'. In partnership with another company, Typhoon is developing drysuits for use by the North Sea Oil Industry.

One of the real advantages of our suit is that we can adapt it to specific customer requirements. Customer specification is crucial so that he gets what he wants; to some extent, in this area pricing is a secondary issue.

Roger Gugen

In one respect, the completion of the internal European market is seen as providing additional opportunities. For example, under the legislation covering personal protective equipment and clothing, there are stringent controls on production and this prevents Far Eastern manufacturers who have a cheaper labour-base from exporting into the EC, as their factories would not be approved by the various authorities. In addition, the general emphasis given to health and safety across Europe is likely to increase the market potential for these products. But in the area of public contracting the company feels that non-tariff barriers are likely to remain: 'I can't see the French letting us in!'

THE FUTURE

The company sees major market development in the protective clothing side of the business, whereas expansion in the leisure/sports side is likely to be limited. The increased emphasis being given by the EC to health and safety, as well as the more general legislation on the environment, is seen by Typhoon as presenting a major marketing opportunity.

QUESTIONS/DISCUSSION TOPICS

1 Carry out a SWOT analysis of Typhoon International.

2 Should Typhoon expand its operations into Europe?

3 To what extent has Typhoon's marketing strategy taken into account of four Ps (product, price, promotion and place)?

4 How would you evaluate Typhoon's market selection?

THE MOUNTAIN BIKE: FROM REPACK TO GREENBACK

WOLODYMYR MAKSYMIW AND ALAN MARCHANT

ADVICE TO READERS

When it first went into commercial production in 1980, hardly anyone had heard of the mountain bike. Total sales that year consisted of 225 'home-made' machines, produced by a handful of experimental frame-builders in Northern California for fellow cycling enthusiasts. Although confident their designs had merit, none could have realized that the mountain bike would become the future of cycling.

Yet by 1991, commercial development of the mountain bike concept had resulted in the globalization of the bicycle market, with annual sales accounting for 80 per cent of the North American, Western European and developed Asian markets. This case should be used as a platform to explore how the idiosyncratic ideas of a small number of cycling enthusiasts in the mid-1970s came to transform national markets across the world. Readers are also encouraged to consider those issues that are likely to shape the future development of the global cycle industry.

CALIFORNIA DREAMING

Gary's home was a rundown one-room shack in a back-alley behind the town bar. Its thin, wooden walls were decorated with beat-up cycle frames and bike race posters. The coffee table was a sheet of ply supported by empty six-packs. Every few minutes, or so it seemed, a newcomer, covered in sweat and dust from some particularly hair-raising off-road ride, would pile into the tiny room – bike and all – and discuss how to fix some part on his clunker or improve its performance.

Kelly and Crane (1988, p. 9)

The quote from Kelly and Crane typifies the folklore of the early days of the mountain bike; the Gary in question being Gary Fisher, legendary frame-builder and one of the first modern mountain bikers, back in 1976.

People throughout the world have been riding off-road for as long as there have been bikes. Indeed, it could be argued that Kirkpatrick MacMillan, builder of the first bicycle in 1839,

The authors thank the following for their assistance with the background research for this case: Eddie Eccleston, Director and General Manager, British Eagle Cycles Co. Ltd; Roy Hatfield, Director, Schwinn (UK) Ltd; Greg Oxenham, Managing Director, Fusion Cycles; Mark Pemberton, Sales Director, Liyang (Europe) Industrial Ltd; John Wood, Warranty Manager, Muddy Fox (UK) Ltd, 1990–91.

who struggled along unsurfaced and potholed Scottish coaching roads, was the origin of the species. It was, however, the USA – home of the instant legend – which spawned the modern mountain bike in the 1970s, when North Californian enthusiasts were first to build off-road bikes specifically for 'hedonistic' pursuits. The invention of what became the mountain bike was not a deliberate act, but a striking example of the creative power of play. From the interaction and experimentation among a group of riders, racers and tinkerers, the bike that revolutionized an industry emerged.

It is generally accepted that mountain bikes originated around the Bay Area of San Francisco. Many of the mountain bike pioneers, or 'clunkers', had grown up in the psychedelic world of San Francisco's Haight-Ashbury in the 1960s. During the 1970s, increasingly disillusioned with alienating city life, many moved out across the Golden Gate Bridge to rural Marin County, in search of a more peaceful, laid-back life-style. Here the countryside, with its ample hills, numerous fire roads and trails, and idyllic climate, was made for off-road riding.

Hippies, 'clunkers' and alternative 'anything goes' life-styles pervade histories of the mountain bike, and it is worth pursuing this romantic imagery a little further, not least because of its role in taking what was semi-legal dirt-tracking into the commercial big-time.

The head badges on the early bikes sported the Hell's Angels' motto, 'Ride to Live, Live to Die'. And indeed, these off-road machines bore a closer resemblance to motorbikes without engines than conventional pedal cycles, with their cannibalized, Schwinn Excelsior frames 'used by the American paperboy bike, immortalized in many a Hollywood film' chunky balloon tyres, 'coaster' drum brakes and other heavy-duty parts. In many ways, these bikes epitomized the 1960s anti-materialist dream. As such, they present a paradoxical ancestry for today's profit-centred global industry, with its emphasis on mass-produced and readily accessible products – differentiated more by commercial brand name than by any significant difference in technical specification.

The frail, road-racing machines which domi-nated the contemporary US market were so unsuited to plummeting down mountain tracks that aspirant mountain bikers were forced to turn to the more sturdy machines from a bygone era. In stark contrast with today, the process of acquiring a mountain bike in the mid-1970s was not simply a case of walking into a shop and selecting one from a wide range of alternative products. It was more akin to a scavenging expedition, with each part having to be hunted down by first scouring the cellars and barns of friends and neighbours, then flea-markets, and then, as a last resort, the shelves of second-hand dealers.

The first item on any clunker's 'shopping list' was a frame salvaged from one of the *Beach-cruiser*, *Autocycle*, *Excelsior*, or *Spitfire* cycles of the Schwinn Bicycle Company of Chicago, ideally from the vintage produced between the early 1930s and the late 1940s. Despite being cumbersome and heavy, their rugged construction and inherent indestructibility meant they were ideally suited to the extreme conditions to which they were subjected by the riders of the Californian hill trails.

By 1976, Schwinns were no longer readily available so that many a prospective off-roader would have to travel far and wide to secure one. The search process involved is captured by Kelly's tale:

On a trip to a part of California about 200 miles from the Bay Area, I found a farmer who had a pile of rusting bikes behind his house. I bought five excellent frames and, more import-antly, acquired a pile of unbent forks. After I gloated about my fortune at home, several of my friends went back and cleaned the farmer out of everything else of any use, including a couple of frames I hadn't noticed.

Kelly and Crane (ibid., p. 29)

Having successfully acquired a frame, the aspirant mountain biker had still to explore many other unlikely locations for the rest of the required components:

I can remember finding a crate full of Morrow coaster brakes in a small town in Northern California – buying rare Schwinn cantilever brakes for a couple of dollars in Stockton – and the time in Denver I stumbled on literally dozens of Bendix coaster brake 2-speed hubs, complete with shifters and cables.

Kelly and Crane, (ibid. p. 30)

This pile of non-standard parts had then to be assembled, a task in itself calling for considerable dedication and expertise to create a mountain bike. It is not surprising that the finished article oft inspired the sardonic quip from proud owners: 'It don't work, but at least it's ugly.'

Although many Californian hill trails were used in the early days, the Cascades fire road on Mt Tamalpais, Marin County, soon established a reputation as the most notorious 'bike-breaker'. Better known as Repack Hill, it is a steep dirt track descending 1,300 feet in less than 2 miles. It has since assumed legendary status in mountain bike mythology, and was both a meeting-place and test site used by those now venerated as the high priests of the mountain bike world. The latter include: Gary Fisher, course record holder and first to put derailleur gears and drum brakes on Marin County's clunkers; Joe Breeze, holder of the second fastest time and pioneer frame designer and builder; Charlie Kelly author, journalist and unofficial historian of the sport; and Tom Ritchey, another of the original custom designer/builders. For these pioneers, the inspiration to improve their old bicycles turned into their life's work. Now 'middle-aged', many are immortalized via contracts from multinational cycle manufacturers for use of their names as branding devices on numerous bikes and their associated componentry.

The *Repack Downhill* was soon regarded as the ultimate, off-road event. Races were never scheduled, but spontaneously happened, 'when sun and moon assumed appropriate aspects'. After a fast descent, the fierce heat generated by the drum brakes of clunker machines would often cause the grease in their hub-bearings to turn to smoke. Shaving a second off rival descent times, rather than any thought of personal safety, demanded that contestants repack their wheel bearings before any subsequent descent – hence the name Repack.

The thrill of the event may be gleaned from the following account by an anonymous novice rider:

*You spend your last few seconds at the top of the hill asking questions about the course faster than anyone can answer, although answers are immaterial because you aren't listening . . . GO! . . . over the rise and into the downhill, standing on the pedals and stomping the highest gear . . . sliding into an eroded, off-camber turn you make a slight miscalculation. **Out of control**, you must make a rapid decision, off the edge or lay the bike down. You lay the bike down . . . **damn!** . . . torn shirt, bloody elbow. Since the arm still works, the shirt was old and the elbow was older, it's okay. Near the bottom of the course, out of the switchbacks in a cloud of dust and into the final straight. Speeding past the boulder that marks the finish, you skid to the flashiest possible stop, then throw down the bike and run to the time-keeper for your elapsed time.*

Adapted from Kelly and Crane
(ibid., pp. 21–25)

The pre-eminence of the Repack in mountain bike folklore remains unchallenged, yet no more than 200 people, mostly local Marin residents, ever took part. However, with its 'gonzo' riding style, absence of formality and obvious organization, it further reinforced the imagery of the self-indulgent and escapist life-style of the hippy movement.

It is hardly surprising that the inherently conservative, traditional, cycling fraternity perceived development of the mountain bike, and the value system associated with its riders, as a challenge to those premises fundamental to the essence of the 'modern' bike. In particular, the synonymity of lightness of construction with design quality and the assertion that, for legitimacy, cycling must be confined to classified roads.

FROM MARIN TO THE THE WORLD

SYMBIOSIS

Tom Ritchey was one of the first designers to produce frames for the commercial market but, being entirely hand-built, their price tag at the time (1979) of $1,300 restricted their purchase to an enthusiasts' élite. Mike Sinyard, founder of Specialized Bicycle Imports Inc. of San José, Silicon Valley, California, which had established itself in the mid-1960s as an importer of exotic Italian road-racing bikes and accessories, had formed contacts with Taiwanese engineering firms capable of producing low-cost cycle components. In 1980, Sinyard acquired a number of Ritchey's machines, which were to provide the design base for what became the world's first, mass-produced mountain bike. In 1981, the Specialized *Stumpjumper* was launched on the emergent US market and, priced at $750, 1,200 were sold with ease that year.

By being produced entirely in the Far East, first in Japan and then Taiwan, the *Stumpjumper* established the precedent for the global separation of the design from the production function, a formula which was adopted by all subsequent entrants with products targeted at the mass market.

Technological developments during the 1980s, particularly those relating to management information systems (MIS) have further encouraged the sub-contracting of operational tasks to foreign companies. As a direct consequence, the location-specific cost advantages possessed by the Far East are more fully exploitable by Western manufacturers, without the latter sacrificing the strategic advantages of centralizing the core functions, such as production scheduling, R&D, marketing and distribution in the home country.

TECHNOLOGY AND DIFFERENTIATION

By today's standards, the original *Stumpjumper* would warrant little more than a passing glance from any serious off-roader.

Even by the standards current in 1981, its frame geometry was considered inferior to that of custom machines available in the Bay Area. However, its inherent advantage to potential buyers was that no longer was mountain biking restricted to the few enthusiasts committed to paying high prices for a custom-built machine. Ownership was now as simple as any other high-street purchase and, apart from its chunky tyres, it looked remarkably similar to a traditional road bike. Frame construction was largely dependent on conventional technology, dominated by the standard diamond configuration.

In contrast, mountain bikes today are clearly identifiable, even to the lay person, as looking 'different'. Their unmistakable visual identity is largely due to the changes that have come about in frame construction techniques, permitting manufacturers an almost infinite degree of flexibility in frame design. Virtually all mass-produced bike frames, whether traditional or mountain, are built from steel. Whilst other more exotic materials for frame construction, such as oversized aluminium, titanium and carbon fibre, are gaining ground, they are mainly targeted at the higher end of the market. Steel is cheap, relatively easy to work with, readily available in a wide variety of forms, and has a proven record for strength and reliability. Until the advent of the mountain bike, however, the dominant method of construction involved lugged brazing.

The essence of this technology is that the ends of each steel tube are cut to length and then inserted into a lug, or metal outer sleeve, to form a snug butt joint with the next tube. The joints are then heated and the brazing medium, usually brass or silver solder, is introduced. As both brass and solder have a lower melting point than steel, when heated they turn to liquid and flow between the lug and the tubes. On cooling, a strong joint is then formed between the tubes.

Although perfectly adequate from a technical point of view, this method of frame construction suffers the major disadvantage of an inability to respond quickly to changes in consumer preferences and significant increases in required production volumes. Although lugs may be cast or stamped metal to pre-set frame angles, they will only fit specific diameters of steel tubing. Rather like the original Ford 'Model T' assembly lines, lugged brazing demanded long and steady production runs in order to achieve the necessary economies of scale.

A major breakthrough for the technology of mountain bike production came when manufacturers realized the enormous potential of TIG (Tungsten Inert Gas) welding. An arc of electricity is applied directly to steel tubes, which causes them to melt rapidly and fuse together. By liberating frame construction from the need for lugs, it facilitated an infinite variety of frame designs and configurations to be made available on a mass scale.

The introduction of flexible manufacturing systems (FMS), supported by computer-aided design and manufacturing technologies, further enhanced the freeing of production from any permanent geographic location. That unit costs are critical to the siting of production is reflected by the changing pattern of countries involved. Initially, Japan was dominant, but now Taiwan and, more recently, China are the major players. Indonesia, Malaysia and India are the most recent contract producers serving the global market.

As illustrated above, exotic styles were previously available only from custom-builders charging high prices for their individual designs. CAD/CAM and TIG technologies can generate significant benefits when used in isolation but, for their full potential to be realized, they must be fully integrated throughout the production process. The overall effect is then evident in terms of a concertina effect on the new product development process.

Mass producers soon realized that incorporating their use into frame design/production was an important way in which they could differentiate their products from those of their competitors. Furthermore, design changes could be introduced more frequently than was possible with lugged brazing. From the outset mountain bikes have had a visual identity which is distinct from that of traditional road bikes. By incorporating 'design' into consumer perceptions, there was an incentive for

manufacturers to launch a new model each year, thus rendering last year's version commercially obsolete. Mountain bikes could now be marketed, not just as a means of transport, but as a fashion accessory. In so doing, they have created their own independent sector, with its own broad range of market niches.

TAIWAN – A DEVELOPING FUSION

Prior to establishing links with Western cycle designers, most of today's Taiwanese cycle manufacturers had been involved in the production of, for example, heavy earth-moving-equipment or machinery related to the textile industry. Their adaptability and commitment to market-orientated development is illustrated by the pervasiveness of the claim in the cycle industry that, in many cases, within six months of having agreed contract terms with the West, the factories involved had switched entirely to producing cycles and related products. Although Taiwanese factories were capable of producing cycles of any type, it was the mountain bike which was responsible for the dramatic growth of their cycle industry.

The appropriately named Fusion Cycles, a UK-based organization, was formed in 1989 by Greg Oxenham, who had previously been a business partner of Gary Fisher. From the outset, Fusion has relied on combining its design skills and the production competencies of Eastern manufacturers. When interviewed in October 1992, Oxenham explained his confidence in the skills of, in particular, Taiwan:

> *Unlike most Western manufacturers, the Taiwanese were prepared to take the initiative to put the necessary investment and expertise into the industry. They replicate the best of Japanese work organization methods and benefit from significant labour, and other, cost advantages.*

By 1992 there were over 300 firms in Taiwan producing cycling-related products for overseas consumption. Although many are undoubtedly confined to the low price, low quality, end of the market, it is now recognized that the best

Exhibit 12.1
Manufacturers used by Western cycle companies

Manufacturer	Cycle company
Giant (Taiwan)	Specialized (USA)
Taioku (Taiwan)	Ridgeback (UK)
Fairly (Taiwan)	Kona (Canada)
Marvel (Taiwan)	Marin (USA)
Tai Huei (Taiwan)	Saracen (UK)
Ideal (Taiwan)	Trek[1] (USA), Fusion (UK)
Anlen (Japan)	Gary Fisher (USA)
Merida (Taiwan)	Trek[1] (USA)
Southern Cross (Taiwan)	not available
Various (Taiwan and Korea)	Muddy Fox[2] (UK)
CBC[3] (Shenphen, China)	Diamond Back (USA) now owned by CBC; Scott (USA); Schwinn (USA)[4]; Emmelle (UK).

Notes: 1 Limited to entry price models which account for one third of Trek's total sales.
2 Went into administrative receivership, March 1992. Purchased April 1992 for about £1 m by a consortium comprising Sitac (UK) and TI Cycles of India.
3 China Bicycle Company.
4 In October, 1992, filed for protection under Chapter 11 of the USA Bankruptcy Reform Act 1978.

Source: Authors' interviews with industry representatives, October, 1992.

Taiwanese quality equates to the best in the world. Taiwan won the ultimate seal of approval in 1992 when Joe Breeze announced that, despite having rejected the 'off-shore' option in the 1980s, he would be relying on their manufacturers in launching his traditional *Breezer* designs on the world market.

> *People think that, if it's from Taiwan, it's no good. . . . they said the same about Japan at one stage, but the problem is really with the decision makers in the bicycle industry. If you go to Taiwan and ask for the cheapest deal, the quality is cheap. Go and ask for the best they can offer and the quality is incredibly high.*
>
> Joe Breeze quoted in Clifford (Feb. 1992).

Exhibit 12.1 illustrates the extent of reliance upon Far Eastern manufacturers by some of the market leaders in the world mountain bike industry. It is now common for a single contract manufacturer to be making bikes for more than one company. As one bike importer commented when interviewed by the authors in March 1992:

> *Scott bikes on Monday, Tuesday its Kona, Specialized on Wednesday, Thursday . . . take your pick . . .*

TECHNOLOGY AND STANDARDIZATION

If the trend in mountain bike frame construction has been towards differentiation, then the other major components have become paradoxically more standardized. According to the 1992 edition of *Mountain Bike International: Buyer's Guide*, there were over 280 models available in Britain that year. Of these, only four did not have a groupset supplied by either of the two Japanese companies, Shimano or Suntour – a groupset is the set of moving parts which includes the hub, chainset, sprocket cluster, chain, brakes, gears, bottom bracket, pedals, gear levers and derailleurs.

In the August 1992 edition of *Cycling Plus*, a sharp contrast was drawn between a modern professional racing cycle and one typical of the 1960s. The modern bike was fitted throughout with a Shimano groupset, whereas the earlier example used components from no less than 13 manufacturers. Professional cyclists have always demanded the best components but, as late as the 1960s, these could only be obtained via a 'mix and match' approach. No average cyclist could then have had access to the detailed knowledge necessary to make such an effective choice.

Twenty-five years ago, Shimano was a little-known manufacturer, with products which rarely left the Far East; by the mid-1980s, it was world leader, supplying 80 per cent of all components used by both mountain and traditional road bikes. The components from the sixties cannot hold their own against modern-day ones and enormous technological improvements have taken place.

Today, even with a modicum of knowledge, it is possible for the average cyclist to tell at a glance the quality and price of a bike. Shimano developed an easy system of groupset identification, which demystified previous expert knowledge by making it accessible to the mass consumer. Today, even a professional's bikes are fitted with a groupset, suggesting that improvements in the marketing of components have been at least as great as changes in their technical performance.

TRADITION VERSUS INNOVATION

Formalized competitions have always played an important role in cycling. For example, the Liège-Bastogne-Liège Classic, the oldest in a long line of races on the European professional road-racing circuit, first took place in France in 1894. Not only does racing generate excitement and public interest, but it plays a central role for manufacturers in capitalizing on such activity as a platform for advertising their products.

The focus of European competition is endurance racing, typified by the Tour de France (established in 1903), its most famous event, which lasts for three weeks. Although such events have individual winners, it is the collective interests of the team to which each participant owes his allegiance and whose collective interests determine the conduct of riding strategy.

Such races place heavy reliance on riders' endurance. They need to acquire considerable experience in order to cope with the physical and psychological demands made on them in supporting the interests of their team. The competitive focus is the *peleton* where, in order to shelter from winds and conserve energy, riders ride in a large pack of anything up to 170 competitors. From such packs an eventual race winner emerges, but not without considerable knowledge of race tactics, a small army of mobile back-up mechanics and team strategists and, finally, the unselfish support of *domestiques*, whose sole purpose is to ensure that their team's 'star' is in the strongest possible position to make a credible challenge for the finishing line.

In contrast to this, the values of the New World permeate mountain bike racing. Races

are shorter, and although teams do take part, they are more for promotional reasons, as featured races are not conducive to team tactics. Moreover, the individualist spirit inspired by the early clunkers still pervades current races, and a rider must be able to keep his own bike running and be responsible for all repairs during a normal race. Indeed, it is current practice that, in large national events, the major bike and component manufacturers will service any registered competitor's bike during the meeting, thus allowing them to compete on comparable terms with riders of professional works teams.

Racing was an integral part of the early days of the mountain bike scene, with exotic races such as the Repack, the Pearl Pass Tour, the Punk Bike Enduro, and the Central Coast Clunker Classic. As has been mentioned previously in the account of the Repack, in keeping with the hippy theme, all these races were typified by a complete lack of formal rules and structure. However, as mountain biking gradually became an established, multi-million dollar world industry, these changes too were to be reflected in racing and competition, which expanded from an underground, outlaw event into a sanitized, athletic challenge.

Participation by amateurs in the same meetings as professional riders of international renown is the norm in mountain bike racing, but is very much the exception in traditional road-racing – a contrast which lends further testimony to the cultural divide that exists between the strongly demarcated European road-racing and the 'classlessness' of the American sport.

Mountain bike racing had, until recently, no limit on the type of equipment competitors may use, whereas European racing was constrained by rule books precisely defining the specification of the type of bike which could be used for racing, right down to designating black shorts and white socks as the only colours in which these particular garments might be worn. The inescapable fact is that the development, and subsequent success, of the mountain bike perhaps owed less to the Californian culture and more to the freedom afforded to innovators unfettered by the century-old prejudices of European race regulations and restrictions.

The mountain bike could not have been invented in Europe. It is, therefore, somewhat ironic that many of the recent innovations in European cycling were forced on its traditionalists by the American rider, Greg Lemond – three times winner of the Tour de France – who also runs his own mountain bike business in the USA. Although highly successful on the European circuit, because of his willingness to experiment with a vast array of new equipment, such as cycling sunglasses, clipless pedals, aerobars, helmets and suspension forks, he is considered unacceptably radical to the blinkered philosophy of the European *peloton*, often characterized as:

We'll ride what we're paid to ride unless we can find an excuse to ride what our fathers did.

AN ILLUSTRATIVE CASE

The transformation of the global cycle industry effected by the mountain bike is illustrated by recent trends in the UK market. For details of the UK market, see Appendices 1, 2A and 2B.

Exhibit 12.2 shows that since 1982 the UK cycle market has become increasingly reliant upon imports as its primary source of supply, thus confirming the *de facto* global nature of the industry. By 1991 only a handful of suppliers to the domestic market continued to manufacture

their product ranges in the UK. Although Raleigh, with a UK market share of 30 per cent by volume, is the most notable of these, it admits to importing all transmissions and most of the parts, excluding framesets, for its cycles.

The norm is for companies to import all parts, and operate domestic 'screwdriver' plants in which the parts are assembled to make a cycle. Alternatively, complete cycles are sourced from the Far East. Approximately one million cycles per annum continue to be manufactured or assembled in the UK, of which 20 per cent are exported, primarily to Ireland. The extent to which such cycles can be deemed to be British is questionable, given that their 'local content' comprises, almost exclusively, labour. There was, until recently, a strong financial incentive for UK producers to import ready-assembled bicycles, as they were not subject to the 8 per cent import duty imposed on components from the Far East.

The period since 1987 has witnessed a 68 per cent increase in imports by volume and a 130 per cent increase by value. This illustrates the fact that, although once seen as a cost-effective route to being price-competitive at the bottom end of the market, imports are increasingly being used to compete in the middle market and have now established a position as quality products featuring reliable, value-for-money, components.

Exhibit 12.3 overleaf demonstrates the recently established importance of Taiwan as a

Exhibit 12.2
Import and export trends 1982–1991

Year	Imports (000 units)	Exports (000 units)	Imports (as % of UK sales volume)
1982	581	238	31
1983	841	289	39
1984	837	359	41
1985	496	275	33
1986	589	174	38
1987	1,023	199	51
1988	1,454	205	63
1989	1,716	198	64
1990	2,262	270	98
1991	1,719	220	82

Source: Derived from estimates by Mintel, Euromonitor and HM Customs & Excise.

Exhibit 12.3
UK imports of bicycles by country of origin: 1986, 1987, 1991

	1986 % of total volume	value	1987 % of total volume	value	1991 % of total volume	value
Taiwan	23	15	36	34	38	41
Hong Kong	*	–	*	–	20	20
China	5	5	11	4	8	7
Italy	26	15	19	4	*	–
France	15	28	11	22	*	–
Germany	12	16	4	5	*	–
Others	19	21	19	31	34	32

Note: *figures not given separately

Source: HM Customs & Excise.

supplier to the UK market and confirms the movement of its products to the high value-added end of the market, at the expense of Italian, German and French manufacturers. Whilst the latter have retained their emphasis on production of traditional cycle products, Far Eastern producers have eagerly exploited the universal shift in consumer preferences in favour of All Terrain Bicycles (ATBs, or mountain bikes).

By 1991 Taiwan, Hong Kong and China together accounted for 66 per cent by volume and 68 per cent by value of all UK cycle imports, with Taiwan being responsible for 38 per cent and 41 per cent respectively. Although China's share of import volume has declined since 1987, in terms of import value its position has improved considerably. As supplier to the international market, China appears certain to become of increasing importance with, for example, the development of Shenzhen, the special economic zone bordering Hong Kong. During the past ten years, it has grown from a sleepy town of 100,000 people to a booming industrial and commercial city with a population in excess of two million.

The China Bicycle Company (CBC) exemplifies the great strides being made by China in terms of economic liberalization. The interests of Schwinn, the US cycle producer with a domestic status equivalent to that of Raleigh in the UK, are now enmeshed with those of CBC since it acquired a significant stake in the latter in 1990. This is but a natural progression from

Schwinn's decision in 1977 to transfer all its production capacity to the Far East, the initial stage of which was the sourcing of its cycles from Japan. In addition to the Schwinn shareholding, and those of Hong Kong entrepreneurs, the International Finance Corporation, the pro-private enterprise arm of the World Bank, has taken a 1.7 per cent stake in the company.

CBC is currently making 1.6 million cycles a year, none of which are traditional, 'sit-up-and-beg' Chinese models, but are almost exclusively mountain bikes and racing models for export throughout the world. The operation will soon move into a new factory which, with a projected capacity of 3.2 million units per annum, will be not only the world's largest cycle production plant, but also one of the most technologically advanced, utilizing computer-controlled robots to perform complex welding and assembly tasks.

MEANWHILE – BACK IN THE USA

By 1991 things had changed a little. At 7.5 million units per annum, mountain bike sales represented 68 per cent of all cycles sold in the USA. Since the late 1980s, the most dramatic growth in the domestic market has been in the sales of hybrid or cross-bikes, 1990 sales of which stood at 2.3 million units, compared with just over 1 million the previous year. Although inspired by the mountain bike, the hybrid is regarded by many as the likely next phase of market development. The hybrid concept combines a less bulky version of a mountain bike frame with the wheels and tyres of a touring cycle. It is not an off-road bike, but is intended to be light enough for touring and exploring byways with ease, whilst being strong enough to withstand the rigours of inner-city roads.

CALIFORNIA REVISITED

An alternative perspective on Marin County and its role in the mountain bike tale was evident when one of the authors of this case study visited California in August 1992. The reality of Marin is now somewhat at odds with the Marin of folklore, a contrast epitomized by Bosley *et al.* (1992, p. 415) in their guide to California. The entry for Marin County reads:

> *Across the Golden Gate Bridge lies Marin County, an unabashed introduction to Californian self-indulgence, an élitist pleasure zone of conspicuous luxury. Ranked as the wealthiest county in the USA, Marin has drawn a sizeable contingent of Northern California's wealthy young professionals to live in its swanky waterside towns, many of whom grew up during the flower power years of the 1960s, and lent the place its New Age feel and reputation. Locals get their shiitake mushroom pizzas delivered in Porsches and think nothing of spending a thousand dollars to see the Grateful Dead play at the Pyramids. [However] many of the cocaine-and-hot-tub devotees who seemed to populate the place in the 1970s have traded in their drug habits for mountain bikes.*

Although cycles remain very much in evidence on the streets of Marin, somewhat surprisingly, by far the greatest proportion appear to be traditional, lightweight, road-racing machines, albeit sporting state-of-the-art equipment, such as automatic rehydration systems, gas-powered seat adjusters, and computerized cardio-vascular monitors.

In contrast, before pushing off in search of cycling Utopia, cyclists in Los Angeles are best advised to put on their helmets and body armour because, 'there's a street war going on out there between bikers and motorists'.

Bibliography

Bosley, D., *et al.*, *California and West Coast USA: The Rough Guide,* (London, Harrap-Columbus, 1992).

Buyer's Guide, 1992, *Mountain Biker International,* 1992.

Clifford, T. 'Breezin'–Profile', *Mountain Biker International,* February, 1992.

Clifford, T., 'The Fisher King', *Mountain Biker International,* Midsummer 1992.

Department of Transport, *Transport Statistics GB 1991,* Tables 2.1, 7.4, (London, HMSO, September 1991).

Department of Employment, *Employment Gazette,* Vol. 97 No. 2, February 1989, Table 6.8, (London, HMSO, 1989).

Department of Employment, *Employment Gazette,* Vol. 100 No. 8, August 1992, Table 6.8, (London, HMSO, 1992).

Kelly, C. and Crane, N. *Richard's Mountain Bike Book* (London, Richard's Bicycle Books, 1988).

Kelly, C. 'The Year Clunk Revisited', *Mountain Biking UK,* Christmas Special, 1991, pp. 6–9.

OECD, *Globalization of Industrial Activities,* (Paris, Organization for Economic Co-operation and Development, 1992).

QUESTIONS/DISCUSSION TOPICS

1 By 1991, with world-wide sales of over 17 million units per annum, the mountain bike dominated the international cycle industry. Identify those factors which have contributed to the success of the product concept and assess their relative importance.

2 Examine the view that if the Californian 'clunkers' had not existed they would have been invented.

3 In a recent study, the OECD (Paris, 1992) identifies a range of company strategies used in the globalization of industrial activities. Examine which of the following have been most evident in the mountain bike industry:

   (a) international trade;
   (b) foreign direct investment;
   (c) international sub-contracting;
   (d) international licensing;
   (e) cross-border mergers and acquisitions;
   (f) international joint ventures;
   (g) international inter-firm agreements.

4 Undertake a survey of the bikes and related products available at cycle retailers in your local area.

   (a) How far do they illustrate the extent of globalization in the cycle industry?
   (b) What are the major differences apparent in cycle design and construction? Contrast their purpose from the perspectives of the consumer and the manufacturer/supplier.

5 Although mountain bikes are designed for extreme use over rough terrain, the vast majority of owners would never contemplate their use for other than urban commuting.

   (a) Discuss the view that this is hardly surprising because the mountain bike has more to do with 'conspicuous consumption', the fashion industry, the marketing of life-styles, than personal transport.
   (b) In the light of your discussion consider the future prospects for the mountain bike in international markets.

Appendix 1
Road traffic volume, GB: 1950–1990

	Total traffic (billion kms)	Percentage of total traffic by vehicle type:			
		Cars + Taxis	Motorcycles	Goods vehicles	Bus Pedal + Coach cycles
1950	73	49	7.5	36	838
1955	95	55	10.4	30	523
1960	125	60	8.8	27	411
1965	170	71	4.3	22	24
1970	205	77	2.0	18	22
1975	236	78	2.2	18	12
1980	278	79	2.9	16	12
1985	296	80	2.4	17	12
1990	413	81	1.5	16	11

Source: Adapted from Transport Statistics GB 1991, London, Department of Transport, HMSO, September 1991, Tables 2.1, 7.4.

Appendix 2A
UK bicycle market 1980–1991

	Sales in 000 units	Sales at current prices £million	Sales at 1980 prices £million	RPI all items 1980 = 100[1]
1980	1,563	130	130	100
1981	1,620	130	116	112
1982	1,850	160	132	122
1983	2,150	185	146	127
1984	2,050	180	135	133
1985	1,514	140	99	141
1986	1,569	135	92	146
1987	2,000	185	122	152
1988	2,300	230	144	160
1989	2,700	300	174	172
1990	2,300	290	154	189
1991	2,100	260	130	200

Note: 1 *Employment Gazette*, February 1989, Table 6.8, *Employment Gazette*, August 1992, Table 6.8.

Source: Derived from estimates by Bicycle Association of Great Britain/Mintel/Euromonitor.

Appendix 2B
UK bicycle market sectors by % volume

	1984	1986	1988	1990	1991
Sports/touring	22	32	31	16	19
Conventional	6	7	5	4	n/a
ATBs[1]:					
BMX[2]	40	25	21	19	n/a
Mountain	–	2	14	37	47
Other[3]	32	34	29	24	n/a
Total	100	100	100	100	100

Notes: 1 All terrain bicycles.
2 Bicycle motocross.
3 small wheel or 'shopper' cycles plus children's learner cycles.

Source: Derived from Euromonitor/Mintel/industry estimates.

INDEX